African Wildlife & Livelihoods

The Promise and Performance of Community Conservation

EDITED BY

David Hulme

Marshall Murphree

DAVID PHILIP
CAPE TOWN

WEAVER
HARARE

KACHERE
ZOMBA

E.A.E.P.
NAIROBI

FOUNTAIN PUBLISHERS
KAMPALA

HEINEMANN
PORTSMOUTH (N.H.)

JAMES CURREY
OXFORD

James Currey Ltd
73 Botley Road
Oxford
OX2 0BS

Heinemann
A division of Reed Elsevier Inc.
361 Hanover Street
Portsmouth NH 03801-3912

Kachere Press
PO Box 1037
Zomba, Malawi

Fountain Publishers
PO Box 488
Kampala, Uganda

E.A.E.P.
Kijabe Street
PO Box 45314
Nairobi, Kenya

Weaver Press
PO Box A1922
Avondale
Harare, Zimbabwe

David Philip Publishers (Pty) Ltd
208 Werdmuller Centre
Claremont 7708
Cape Town, South Africa

British Library Cataloguing in Publication Data
African wildlife & livelihoods: the promise and performance of community conservation
1. Wildlife conservation – Africa 2. Community 3. Natural resources, Communal – Africa
I. Hulme, D. II. Murphree, Marshall W.
639.9'096

ISBN 0-85255-413-3 (James Currey cloth)
ISBN 0-85255-414-1 (James Currey paper)

Library of Congress Cataloging-in-Publication Data

African wildlife & livelihoods: the promise and performance of community conservation/edited by David Hulme and Marshall Murphree.
    p.cm.
  Includes bibliographical references (p.).
  ISBN 0-325-07059-8 (paper: alk. paper) – ISBN 0-325-07060-1 (cloth: alk. paper)
  1. Wildlife conservation – Africa – Citizen participation 2. Wildlife conservation – Economic aspects – Africa
  I. Title: African wildlife and livelihoods. II. Hulme, David. III. Murphree, Marshall W.

QL84.6.A1 A34 2001
333.95'416'096–dc21

00-143913

ISBN 9970-02-247-4 (Fountain paper)

Typeset in 10½/11½ Bembo by Saxon Graphics Ltd, Derby
Printed and bound in Great Britain
by Woolnough, Irthlingborough

Contents

PART ONE
Setting the Scene

PART TWO
Conservation Policies & Institutions

Figures

Tables

Boxes

Chapter Appendices

Maps

Abbreviations

ARS	Ankole Ranching Scheme
AWF	African Wildlife Foundation
C4	Community Conservation Coordinating Committee (Tanzania)
CAMPFIRE	Communal Areas Management Programme for Indigenous Resources (Zimbabwe)
CASS	Centre for Applied Social Sciences (University of Zimbabwe)
CBC	community-based conservation
CBNRM	community-based natural resource management
CBTEs	community-based tourism enterprises
CC	community conservation
CCS	Community Conservation Service
CCSC	Community Conservation Service Centre (Tanzania)
CCUWAP	Community Conservation for Uganda Wildlife Authority Project
CCW	community conservation warden
CER	community extension ranger
CGGs	community game guards
CHA	Controlled Hunting Area (Uganda)
CIDA	Canadian International Development Agency
CM	collaborative management
COBRA	Conservation of Biodiverse Areas Project (Kenya)
CWM	community wildlife management
CWS	Community Wildlife Service (Kenya)
DEA	Directorate of Environmental Affairs (Namibia)
DFID	Department for International Development (United Kingdom)
DNFFB	National Directorate of Forestry and Wildlife (Mozambique)
DNPWLM	Department of National Parks and Wildlife Management (Zimbabwe)
DPAP	Provincial Directorate of Agriculture and Fisheries (Mozambique)
DRM	Directorate of Resource Management (Namibia)
DTC	development through conservation
EC	European Commission
EU	European Union
EWT	Endangered Wildlife Trust
FAO	Food and Agriculture Organization (UN)
GCA	Game Control Area (Tanzania)
GEF	Global Environmental Facility
ICDPs	Integrated Conservation and Development Projects
IDRC	International Development Research Centre (Canada)
IGCP	International Gorilla Conservation Programme (Uganda)
IIED	International Institute for Environment and Development
IRDNC	Integrated Rural Development and Nature Conservation (Namibia)
IUCN	International Union for the Conservation of Nature & Natural Resources

KAP	knowledge, attitudes and practices survey
KWS	Kenyan Wildlife Service
LMCCP	Lake Mburo Community Conservation Project (Uganda)
LMGR	Lake Mburo Game Reserve (Uganda)
LMNP	Lake Mburo National Park (Uganda)
MET	Ministry of Environment and Tourism (Namibia)
MGNP	Mgahinga Gorilla National Park (Uganda)
MICOA	Ministry for Environmental Co-ordination (Mozambique)
MNRT	Ministry of Natural Resources and Tourism
MoU	memorandum of understanding
NACOBTA	Namibian Community-based Tourism Association
NCAA	Ngorongoro Conservation Area Authority (Tanzania)
NGO	non-governmental organization
NP	national parks
NRA	National Resistance Army (Uganda)
NWT	Namibia Wildlife Trust
PA	protected areas
PAOPs	protected area outreach projects
PMAC	Park Management Advisory Committee (Uganda)
PPC	Park Parish Committee (Uganda)
PRMC	Parish Resource Management Committee (Uganda)
PROAGRI	Programme for Agriculture (Mozambique)
RDCs	rural district councils (Zimbabwe)
RRB	Ranch Restructuring Board (Uganda)
SCIP	Support for Community–initiated Projects
SIDA	Swedish International Development Agency
SPFFB	Provincial Forestry and Wildlife Service (Mozambique)
SWAPO	South West Africa People's Organization (Namibia)
TANAPA	Tanzanian National Parks
TFCAs	Transfrontier Conservation Areas
TNP	Tarangire National Park (Tanzania)
TPU	TANAPA planning unit
TWCM	Tanzanian Wildlife Conservation Monitoring
UN	United Nations
UNDP	United Nations Development Programme
UNESCO	United Nations Educational Science and Cultural Organization
UNP	Uganda National Parks
USAID	United States Agency for International Development
UWA	Uganda Wildlife Authority
VIDCO	Village Development Committee (Zimbabwe)
WADCO	Ward Development Committee (Zimbabwe)
WB	World Bank
WCAW	Wildlife Conservation Awareness Week (Tanzania)
WCED	World Commission on Environment and Development
WDF	Wildlife Development Fund (Kenya)
WEP	Wildlife Extension Project (Kenya)
WMA	wildlife management area (Tanzania)
WWF	World-wide Fund for Nature
ZANU-PF	Zimbabwe African National Union-Popular Front
ZSL	Zimbabwe Sun Limited

Contributors

William Adams is a Reader in Geography at the University of Cambridge. He works on conservation and rural development in Africa and the UK, and has been involved in research in Nigeria, Kenya, Tanzania and Uganda. He has written and edited a number of books on conservation, including *Future Nature: a vision for conservation* (Earthscan, London, 1996). His work on development and on Africa includes *Green Development: environment and sustainability in the Third World* (Routledge, London, 1990), *Wasting the Rain: rivers, people and planning in Africa* (Earthscan, London, 1992) and *Working the Sahel: Environment and society in Northern Nigeria* (with M. Mortimore, Routledge, London, 1999). Bill is a Trustee of the British Institute in Eastern Africa, and of Fauna and Flora International.

Simon Anstey is a senior research fellow at the WWF Southern African Regional Programme Office and is completing his PhD at the University of Zimbabwe. His academic background is in environmental science and conservation and he has worked for the IUCN in Mozambique and Angola and WWF-I in Liberia. He has particular interests in the influence of politics and history on the institutions involved in community-based natural resource management.

Edmund Barrow is Regional Coordinator for the IUCN's East Africa Forestry Programme. He originally trained as a zoologist at the University of Dublin and subsequently in Natural Resource Management (Antioch University). For many years he worked in Turkana as an extension worker and social forestry specialist. Before moving to IUCN he was Regional Community Conservation Officer for the African Wildlife Foundation in Nairobi (1992–7).

Patrick Bergin is a graduate of the University of Illinois at Urbana in the management of extension systems. From 1988 to 1989, he served as a Peace Corps Volunteer in Tanzania and in 1990 Bergin joined the African Wildlife Foundation (AWF) as a Project Officer assigned to Tanzania National Parks Community Conservation Service. After handing over this programme to his Tanzanian counterparts, he was awarded a PhD in Development from the University of East Anglia in the UK for his thesis 'The Institutionalization of Community Conservation in Tanzania National Parks'. Bergin currently serves as Vice President for Program for AWF.

Ivan Bond has been working with WWF, primarily in community-based conservation, for the last nine years. He has both a BSc and a DPhil from the University of Zimbabwe. As the resource economist for the WWF Support to CAMPFIRE Project he is responsible for the development of materials and implementation of training aimed at improving financial and project management by wildlife producer communities. He also collects and maintains economic data from CAMPFIRE and the wildlife sector in Zimbabwe.

Lucy Emerton has been working as a resource economist in Eastern and Southern Africa for the last 10 years. She has degrees in Anthropology and Development Economics from the Universities of London and East Anglia. Her work has focused on economic aspects of biodiversity conservation, at global, national and community levels, and on integrating resource economics into conservation and development organizations. Lucy Emerton currently coordinates the Nature and Economy Programme of the Eastern Africa Regional Office of IUCN, the World Conservation Union.

Helen Gichohi is Director of the African Conservation Centre (ACC) in Nairobi. This appointment followed several years as Director of the Kenya Programme for the Wildlife Conservation Society. She has a PhD in ecology and has spent a lot of time working at the community level in the Amboseli, Tsavo and Maasai Mara ecosystems. Her present work is focused on developing policies and institutions that can help communities to utilize and conserve wildlife resources.

David Hulme is Professor of Development Studies at the Institute for Development Policy and Management, University of Manchester. He has worked extensively on rural development and poverty-reduction strategies in South Asia, Africa and the Pacific. In recent years he has been researching on local environmental management in Africa with a particular focus on East Africa. His publications include *Governance, Administration and Development* (with M M Turner), *NGOs, States and Donors* (with M Edwards), *Finance Against Poverty* (with P Mosley) and *African Enclosures: The Social Dynamics of Wetlands in Drylands* (with P Woodhouse and H Bernstein).

Mark Infield has been working in wildlife conservation and protected area management in Africa since 1981. He studied Zoology at Durham University, and for an MSc at the University of Natal where he examined the potential for creating economic links between game reserves and local communities. He researched hunting in Korup National Park, Cameroon, for WWF. He is currently a Research Associate with the African Wildlife Foundation and studying for a PhD at the University of East Anglia. He is interested in the role that culture can play in the conceptualization and management of protected areas, and in the potential for building a constituency for conservation among rural communities based on cultural values.

Brian Jones is a consultant and researcher in community-based natural resource management (CBNRM), based in Namibia. He was born in London and is now a Namibian citizen. He has a BA degree from the University of the Witwatersrand in Johannesburg and began his career as a journalist in South Africa and Namibia. He moved into conservation in 1988 and was employed in the Namibian Ministry of Environment and Tourism. For six years he coordinated the Ministry's national CBNRM programme. He is now studying for an MPhil in social sciences at the University of Zimbabwe and works as a consultant.

Kadzo Kangwana studied zoology at the Universities of Oxford and Cambridge and completed a PhD on 'Elephants and the Maasai' in 1994. She then worked for the African Wildlife Foundation as Biodiversity Coordinator and was closely involved with AWF's community conservation work. At present she is based in the USA.

James Murombedzi is the Environment and Development Programme Officer for Southern Africa for the Ford Foundation. He was previously a Lecturer at the Centre for Applied Social Sciences, University of Zimbabwe, where he taught Political and Social Ecology. His research has focused on the micro-political dynamics of natural resources management in the communal tenure regimes of southern Africa. Dr Murombedzi has written extensively on the subjects of natural resource tenure and management and on the socio-political dynamics of the wildlife management programmes of the region. He has also consulted for various international organizations including the World Conservation Union (IUCN), the International Fund for Agricultural Development (IFAD), the Food and Agriculture Organization (FAO) and the Global Environment Facility (GEF).

Marshall Murphree was born in Zimbabwe and educated at universities in the USA and UK, holding a PhD in Social Anthropology from the University of London. From 1970 to 1996 he was Director of the Centre for Applied Social Sciences at the University of

Zimbabwe, a department with special responsibility for teaching and research in the social and institutional dimensions of natural resource management. He is the author of over 60 monographs and articles on rural development and natural resource management. Now Professor Emeritus, he is Chairman of the Sustainable Use Specialist group of IUCN.

Rafael Ole Mako comes from a remote village neighbouring the Serengeti and Maasai Mara. He trained at the Institute for Community Development in Arusha where he wrote a dissertation on pastoral economic viability in the Ngorongoro Conservation Area. He now works as a development project officer for the African Wildlife Foundation in Arusha.

Camila de Sousa was trained in forestry management in Australia. She is research officer at the Centre for Forestry Research in Manica, Mozambique. Her particular interests are in community forest management.

Russell Taylor holds a BSc (Agriculture) from the University of Natal and a DPhil from the University of Zimbabwe. He has worked in both the south-east lowveld and Zambezi valley regions of Zimbabwe over the past 25 years where he has been engaged in ecological research, park management, land-use planning and more recently, community-based natural resource management. For the past five years he has led WWF's Support to CAMPFIRE Project which is currently being developed into a regional training programme. He is the author of numerous scientific and conservation-related articles.

Preface

The origins of this book lie in a chance meeting between David Hulme and Kadzo Kangwana back in 1994. Out of this arose the idea of assessing the achievements of the community conservation initiatives and policies that were sweeping across Africa. Developing a full proposal demanded the skills and knowledge of other researchers and Ed Barrow, Marshall Murphree and Bill Adams soon joined in the enterprise. With the support of colleagues at the Institute for Development Policy and Management (IDPM) at the University of Manchester and the African Wildlife Foundation (AWF), especially Ros Aveling and Deborah Snelson, a successful bid for research funding was put together.

Reviewing the literature, exploring concepts and mounting research in six countries led to the progressive expansion of 'the team' to include Simon Anstey, Patrick Bergin, Ivan Bond, Lucy Emerton, Helen Gichohi, Mark Infield, Brian Jones, James Murombedzi, Rafael Ole Mako, Camila de Sousa and Russell Taylor. While we have had the privilege of editing this volume it must be recorded that it is genuinely the product of a team effort. Our group workshops in Nairobi (1996), Cockington Estate (1997) and Gatche Gatche (1998) led to patterns of individual and group learning from which it is impossible to identify who was the original source of an idea. These meetings were also great fun. Throughout the research, team members have given generously of their time to make comments on each other's working papers and chapters.

As the project evolved three main centres of research activity developed. In the UK David Hulme coordinated activities from the University of Manchester. He is deeply indebted to Bill Adams for the support he provided in terms of a continuous flow of ideas, advice, constructive criticism ('stop at Chapter 19') and good humour. All too rarely, because of the distance between Manchester and Cambridge, there was also beer! In East Africa Ed Barrow ably coordinated the project following Kadzo Kangwana's move to the USA. He did a great job initially based at the African Wildlife Foundation and later at IUCN (East Africa). From his base in Uganda Mark Infield provided important ideas about the case study methodology and launched the project's field research with studies in Uganda that would not have been feasible without his knowledge and energy. In Southern Africa Marshall Murphree orchestrated work in Zimbabwe, Namibia and Mozambique with the support of colleagues at the Centre for Applied Social Sciences (CASS) at the University of Zimbabwe. He arranged 'workshops to die for' in 1997 and 1998 and the hospitality provided by Betty-Jo and himself has left all the team with fond memories of Harare.

Many other people have provided intellectual and logistical support and assistance to the research. We mention some below but a lack of space and our fading memories mean that there are many who are not mentioned by name. To all of these we offer our heartfelt thanks.

In Mozambique, Namibia, Tanzania, Uganda and Zimbabwe large numbers of rural people kindly spared their time in interviews and group exercises. We are indebted to them for the information and insights provided, good humour and the kindness they showed to visiting researchers who often asked foolish questions. In the six countries researched in this book many conservation officials, public servants and NGO personnel also gave freely of their time and ideas. We are also grateful to our research assistants, interpreters and guides in all of these countries.

Several institutions provided support and, in particular, we record our thanks to the Economic and Social Research Council (ESRC) in the UK which financed the research (Grant No. Re: L32025311); IDPM at the University of Manchester; the African Wildlife Foundation in Nairobi and Washington, DC; CASS at the University of Zimbabwe; and the Department of Geography at the University of Cambridge.

The publication of this book and its dissemination in Africa have been supported by grants from the UK's Department for International Development (DFID) ESCOR funds and from the Ford Foundation in Southern Africa. The views and opinions expressed in this volume are those of the relevant authors and should not be attributed to any of the agencies that have provided support or with which the authors are associated.

The ESRC's Global Environmental Change Programme proved an ideal funding agency. The 'light but firm' oversight provided by Jim Skea, Allister Scott and Gary Grubb allowed us to redesign the research as contingencies arose but kept us focused on our goals. Collaborative links with IIED's 'Evaluating Eden' project, through Christo Fabricius and Dilys Roe, helped to ensure that our projects complemented each other. Special thanks must go to Kathy Homewood at University College London. We are only partly aware of the work that she has been doing as a referee and a reviewer of proposals, reports and manuscripts but we are grateful for her wise advice and warm encouragement.

The support from IDPM and the University of Manchester has been exceptional. Jayne Hindle initially took care of the project, until promotion stole her away! Cath Baker then took over and has prepared this manuscript and vast numbers of working papers as well as achieving world records for the numbers of e-mails she has dispatched to East and Southern Africa. She has borne with great good humour the task of supporting a pair of editors who are computer illiterate. Debra Whitehead assisted her in the preparation of the manuscript. Marion Moolna has kept her eye on the budgets and ensured that we all came in on time and within budget.

David Hulme   Marshall Murphree
Manchester   Harare
October 1999   October 1999

Dedication
For Georgina, Edd, Jaz and Saffi – and Samson, who taught us about African livelihoods and how to mend fishing nets (DH).

To my family and colleagues for their patience and support. Above all, thanks to the rural people of Zimbabwe who have opened their homes to me. Their wisdom has so often transcended the insights of abstract scholarship (MM).

PART ONE
Setting the Scene

1

Community Conservation in Africa
An Introduction

DAVID HULME & MARSHALL MURPHREE

'It is not fair. If their animals [the National Park] come on our land and do a lot of damage we get no compensation. If our cattle stray on to their land [the National Park] we are punished'. (A villager interviewed at Rwenjeru in Uganda in January 1997).

'It is both futile and an insult to the poor to tell them that they must remain in poverty to protect the environment' (World Commission on the Environment and Development 1987).

Conservation policies and agencies in Africa came under heavy fire in the 1980s. The charges against them were both empirical and conceptual. Evidence from many countries indicated that conservation goals were not being achieved. Increasing rates of illegal offtake on many mammals (most obviously elephant, rhinoceros and gorilla but also many less charismatic species) were interpreted as bringing many species to 'the edge of extinction'. At the same time the pushing forward of the agricultural and grazing frontiers into 'wild lands', ranging from savannas to moist tropical forest, was characterized as an irreversible loss of habitat.

Conceptually, a set of radical ideas of international provenance were introduced (and continue to be introduced) to the conservation agenda. There are three particular strands to these ideas and they are woven together in different ways by theorists, policy makers and managers of the African environment. The first is that conservation should involve the community rather than being purely state-centric. No longer should rural Africans be seen as degraders of the environment but as local heroes.[1] Secondly, the concept of 'sustainable development' has promoted the notion that the things to be conserved (species, habitats or biodiversity) should be viewed as exploitable natural resources that can be managed to achieve both developmental and conservation goals. Wildlife utilization, rather than wildlife preservation, might be best for conservation. Thirdly, and in keeping with the neo-liberal thinking that dominated the late twentieth century, are ideas that markets should play a greater role in shaping the structures of incentives for conservation. Following the dictum 'use it or lose it' these notions suggest that if species or habitats are to be conserved then they must not be isolated from the market: rather, they must be exposed to it as their uniqueness and scarcity lead to high valorization and thus promote conservation.

These new ideas, especially those related to community-oriented approaches, became so popular and so widely accepted during the 1990s that at times they appear to be almost a new orthodoxy, seeking to displace the conventional wisdom of state-enforced environmental protection (Hulme and Murphree 1999). While this conceptual shift has been welcomed by many individuals and agencies (e.g. African Wildlife Foundation, DFID, WWF, World Bank), coming from many different positions in terms of their values and interests, relatively little is known about the ways in which these ideas have been converted into policies and practices. Even less is known about what has been achieved by attempts to construct community conservation regimes in Africa.

Knowing more about the policy and institutional changes that have occurred and what impacts these have had is important for at least two main reasons. First, to ascertain whether community-oriented approaches are raising the likelihood of the conservation of Africa's unique environments, its extraordinarily high densities of large animals and its biodiversity. Second, to ascertain whether these new approaches are improving the livelihoods of rural Africans who have borne the costs of 'fortress conservation' for decades and who are often among the poorest people in the world.

In this book we bring together a set of studies that shed light on these important issues. Inevitably our coverage of different experiences and examples is only partial and we do not claim to cover all of the available materials or relevant programmes in an encyclopaedic fashion. In particular, our research has focused on East and Southern Africa with case studies drawn from Mozambique, Namibia, Tanzania, Uganda and Zimbabwe and also detailed work in Kenya (Map 1.1). In East Africa the focus has been on community conservation initiatives that centre on protected areas and are akin to 'park outreach' strategies (see Barrow and Murphree in Chapter 3 for an explanation of these terms). By contrast, in Southern Africa our focus has been much more on community-based conservation or community-based natural resource management on communally owned lands. This reflects the different emphases within these two regions on specific forms of community conservation. Our research has not been spread across an ecologically representative set of locations but has concentrated on areas where populations of 'larger' wild animals (and the ecosystems of which they are a part) are an important conservation or natural resource. As a consequence, the role of communities in managing larger, terrestrial animals (rather than forests, fisheries and reefs) is our prime focus. Despite this the case studies cover a wide variety of environments ranging from arid (Kunene in Namibia), semi-arid (Tarangire in Tanzania and Mahenye in Zimbabwe) and lacustrine (Lake Mburo in Uganda) to moist, montane areas (Chimanimani in Mozambique and Mgahinga in Uganda).

While the geographical and ecological foci have not been comprehensive, in other respects we have sought to adopt an holistic approach by examining social, political and institutional change, economics and incentive structures, ecological change, the role of intrinsic values and by considering the behaviours and activities of a wide range of stakeholders in the African environment. The latter range from local level stakeholders (villagers, pastoralists, government personnel, tourists), to intermediary stakeholders (businessmen, government departments, NGOs) and distant stakeholders (aid agencies, international NGOs, television viewers). The study has been truly multidisciplinary with a research team from backgrounds in anthropology, development studies, ecology, economics, forestry, geography, sociology and zoology and drawn

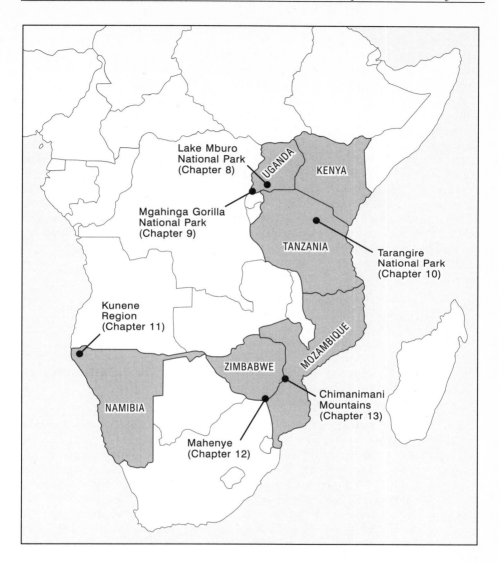

Map 1.1   The location of countries and case studies covered in this volume

from academia, the public sector and non-governmental organisations. The team includes practitioner-scholars and scholar-practitioners from Ireland, Kenya, Mozambique, Namibia, Tanzania, United Kingdom, USA and Zimbabwe. Wherever possible we have sought to use and build on the findings of 'local scholarship' which all too often is 'invisible' in international studies of Africa (Mkandawire 1998).

A variety of methods were used to gather information. These include interviews with key informants, participatory appraisals, surveys, data extraction from primary documents, secondary sources, aerial photographs and oral histories. In most cases these rapid appraisals have been backed up by the extensive personal experience of research team members at case study sites and countries. Wherever this has occurred efforts have been made to corroborate findings through partnering with an 'independent' researcher or review by an external referee. The detailed historical understanding of the institutions and policy processes associated with community conservation, which researchers brought to the study, has proved invaluable. For more detailed comments on methodology readers are referred to the individual chapters in this volume, the working papers listed in the references and Hulme (1997a).

Despite the limitations in our coverage of empirical experiences four ambitious objectives have been set for the volume.

(i) To describe what has been happening as the concept of community conservation has diffused through policies and practices in Africa.

(ii) To assess, as best we can, what changes have occurred in the processes and institutions surrounding conservation and natural resource management and what the results of these changes have been.

(iii) Through a comparative analysis to draw out the lessons that emerge and examine their implications for policy and practice.

(iv) To identify priority areas for future research and analysis.

We hope that our aspirations have not exceeded our capacity, but of that the reader must be the judge.

The origins and meaning of the terms 'community conservation' and 'community-based conservation' are discussed at length in the following chapters (Chapters 2 and 3) but a preliminary meaning for the term is needed in this introduction. By these terms we are referring to ideas, policies, practices and behaviours that seek to give those who live in rural environments greater involvement in managing the natural resources (soil, water, species, habitats, landscapes or biodiversity) that exist in the areas in which they reside (be that permanently or temporarily) and/or greater access to benefits derived from those resources. This meaning covers a wide range of possibilities. At one extreme are minimalist 'park outreach' initiatives that seek to give a national park's neighbours limited access to park benefits (e.g. that distribute a small share of gate-takings to passive communities). At the other extreme are community-based natural resource management initiatives that devolve tenure and responsibility for management of key resources to autonomous local institutions (e.g. that transfer ownership of large game to a legally autonomous local authority which fully manages the resource). In between these two poles there are many alternative positions.

Community conservation is not simply about technical choices or changes in laws or formal organizations. It is part of wider processes of social change and about attempts to redistribute social and political power. It is shaped by these wider social processes and, at the same time, contributes to those wider processes. In particular, while community approaches promise to 'empower' communities they may be seen as threatening those who will have reduced control over resources or flows of benefits. Throughout the book we seek to place our studies in this broader context and do not adopt a narrow environmental focus.

It must be noted that the commonly held notion that community-oriented approaches are replacing earlier conservation approaches is too simplistic. While community conservation indicates a shift of authority (and management and benefits) to local residents, they remain part of a regional, national and international framework in which a variety of organisations and institutions play a role. In particular, while community-oriented approaches have important implications for the state it is unlikely that they will lead to the cessation of state management of protected areas and/or species that are judged to be of national or international importance. Rather, community conservation is being integrated with law enforcement and other forms of conservation.

The reader should also be aware of the dynamic context within which community conservation operates. The idea of community conservation is evolving and is not fixed; the socio-economic contexts of the countries in which it is being introduced are rapidly changing as governments come and go, economic upturns and downturns occur and as the existence of the state or the legitimacy of its national boundaries are challenged; and the African environment is changing as short-term trends (e.g. droughts or floods) and longer-term processes (e.g. evolution and global climate change) re-shape ecologies. In addition, individuals, groups and organizations compete to manipulate both the meaning that is invested in the term and the nature of its practice so as to achieve their personal, group or organizational goals. Public statements about conservation often differ markedly from private behaviours.

The book is divided into seven parts. The first part (including this chapter) 'sets the scene' with Adams and Hulme (Chapter 2) tracing the evolution of the narrative of community conservation and examining the ways in which it has influenced policy and practice in Africa. In the following chapter (Barrow and Murphree) the practical forms and main components of community conservation in Africa are analysed. This provides a framework for understanding the case studies and identifies three main forms of community conservation: park outreach, collaborative management and community-based conservation.

The second part of the book reviews specific examples of the reforms that have occurred in public policy and institutions as more community-oriented approaches have been pursued. There are marked contrasts between Namibia and Zimbabwe (Chapter 4, Jones and Murphree) where policy has emphasized the commercial exploitation of wildlife on communal lands; East Africa (Chapter 5, Barrow, Gichohi and Infield) where policy has concentrated on park outreach and has only recently revived collaborative management and community-based wildlife utilization; and Mozambique (Chapter 6, Anstey), where a lengthy period of 'no policy' (during the civil war) has been followed by aid-financed policies of community conservation running parallel with genuinely community-based natural resource management and energetic, and sometimes rapacious, private sector activity. The final chapter in Part II (Bergin) explores the processes of organizational change that Tanzanian National

Parks (TANAPA) has undergone as it has absorbed and reworked the concept of community conservation.

Part III has an East African focus with detailed case studies of Lake Mburo National Park in Uganda (Chapter 8, Hulme and Infield), Mgahinga Gorilla National Park in Uganda (Chapter 9, Adams and Infield) and Tarangire National Park in Tanzania (Chapter 10, Kangwana and Ole Mako). These chapters examine community conservation as a component of park outreach strategy. They indicate that such initiatives can rapidly contribute to improved park–people relationships and can enhance the flow of benefits to local residents. However, such additional benefits in no way compensate for the 'loss' of exploitable natural resources to conservation. While all of these examples required significant policy changes they illustrate an incremental and non-radical approach towards community involvement in conservation that does not seek to devolve tenure over natural resources to local institutions.

By contrast, the papers in Part IV examine more devolutionary approaches in which communities gain significant control over important wildlife resources. Paradoxically, these radical approaches have allowed the protected areas in these countries to retain their protectionist regimes. Chapter 11 on the Kunene Conservancy in Namibia (Jones) explores the evolution of this initiative against the background of the move to national independence and the activity of an innovative NGO. Chapter 12 on Mahenye (Murphree) examines an area where Zimbabwe's much publicized CAMPFIRE programme has achieved excellent results.[2] It reveals, however, that favourable community–private sector relationships (as well as effective community–state relationships) may be needed if villagers are to capture a significant share of the benefits of 'value added' wildlife utilization in the form of international tourism and trophy hunting. The Mozambiquean case study (Chapter 13, Anstey and de Sousa) looks at indigenous community conservation and natural resource management in the Chimanimani Mountains. This provides an important reminder that many Africans have long practised 'community conservation' without state support or foreign aid. The intrinsic values that rural people hold for their environment are a cultural resource which is often ignored, or undermined, by external researchers and consultants whose personal values and academic training may lead them to believe that rural people see species and habitats purely in utilitarian terms.

Part V of the book provides economic insights into the new wave of conservation policies. Chapter 14 (Emerton) reviews the economics of community conservation and points out that while the idea of 'sharing' the benefits derived from protected areas and wildlife with local residents has strengthened benefit flows, the available evidence still indicates that rural Africans lose out in economic terms when protected areas are declared and/or wildlife is protected. Proponents of community conservation, particularly in its park outreach form, have been keen to publicize the additional benefits for communities that come from such reforms but steer clear of examining the direct and opportunity costs that conservation levies on local residents. The following two chapters examine CAMPFIRE which, to date, has had a favourable public perception in terms of its economic impacts. Bond (Chapter 15) examines whether the benefit flows from CAMPFIRE have created an incentive structure that will stimulate institutional change in natural resource management. His findings are quite negative as, in most areas, CAMPFIRE benefits are small in per capita terms. Murombedzi (Chapter 16) focuses on natural resource management, household accumulation strategies and local level conceptualizations of 'development' in the Masoka area. He concludes that CAMPFIRE has not led to wildlife being perceived as a resource to be sustainably managed. Villagers see 'development' as agriculture, roads, schools and higher population densities.

In Part VI we examine the ecological impacts of community conservation. Kangwana (Chapter 17) points out that the case that community approaches lead to greater conservation achievements (whether that means of species, habitats or biodiversity) is largely theoretical. There is little empirical evidence that 'proves' this case. The scientific assessment of the ecological impacts of community conservation is fraught with difficulties because of the many other factors that can influence ecological change and the long lags between intervention and outcome. Taylor (Chapter 18) argues that scientific approaches to environmental assessment (particularly with reference to measuring wildlife populations and setting offtake quotas) commonly have low reliability. On the basis of experience from Zimbabwe he argues that participatory strategies, which combine assessment with management and permit different stakeholders to provide their knowledge about populations trends, are likely to be the most effective way of sustainably managing wildlife. Accurate measurements of natural resources may be desirable in theory but, in practice, they are often infeasible and may undermine natural resource management regimes.

In the final chapter we compare the findings that emerge from the detailed studies and examine the implications for policy and practice. The opening section reviews 'who wins and who loses' through the intiatives that have been analysed. We then explore the achievements of community conservation. Reaching precise conclusions is difficult but the evidence indicates that the move to community conservation has only very partially achieved its conservation and developmental goals. The contextual constraints it faces – ineffective governments, weak markets, the slow pace of policy reform, the tensions generated by socio-economic change at the local level, donors looking for panaceas – are considerable and indicate that the speed at which goals will be achieved (if they can be) will be slow. Community conservation has created a much needed impetus for institutional change and development in natural resource management but such changes are slow, are conditioned by local contexts and their ultimate form cannot be clearly predicted.

From a policy perspective community-oriented approaches to conservation have been a belated step in the right direction and should be continued. However, changes will be needed in the way such initiatives are approached. They need longer time frames, should emphasize adaptive management rather than detailed blueprint planning, need to focus on the development of sets of institutions that are effectively linked and that can exercise checks and balances over each other (rather than just 'community-institutions') and must find ways of strengthening community–private business partnerships so that higher value forms of wildlife utilization can be developed and benefits shared more equitably with local residents. For generations, conservation policy in Africa has been socially illegitimate in the eyes of the continent's rural people. Community conservation has created opportunities for conservation to begin to develop a local constituency but the task of creating a conservation policy that is embedded in African society, rather than imposed from above, will be the work of generations.

Notes

[1] As Agrawal (1997: 8) expresses it 'communities are now the locus of conservationist imaginings'.

[2] Five of the chapters in this volume (Chapters 4, 12, 15, 16 and 18) examine different aspects of CAMPFIRE. This has been an important initiative because of the popular perception that it proves that conservation and development goals are compatible. Our work reveals that very different processes and outcomes are occurring at different CAMPFIRE sites. It also indicates that CAMPFIRE must be seen as 'work in progress': there is no final state for a community conservation programme.

2

Conservation & Community
Changing Narratives, Policies & Practices
in African Conservation

WILLIAM ADAMS & DAVID HULME

Introduction

The involvement of local people in conservation has become a major feature of conservation policy, both in Africa and more widely. However, while the principle of 'community conservation' has received widespread support, there has been little research either on the origins of the idea, or on the concepts and ideas it draws upon. In this paper we discuss these roots and also examine the factors that have favoured its international diffusion as a public policy.

Following Leach and Mearns (1996), Emery Roe's (1991 and 1995) notion of 'narratives and counter-narratives' is used to explore the significance of particular sets of ideas (discourses) within conservation and the ways they are contested and evolve. Conservation, like development planning, has to take place in the face of environmental, economic and political uncertainty. Policy makers and planners commonly make sets of simple and optimistic (and sometimes naive) assumptions that seek to provide plausible explanations of how to avoid uncertainty. These can be very useful in providing an apparently secure platform for policy so that action can be initiated (Hirschman 1968). Commonly, however, such narratives are operationalized into standard approaches with widespread application, leading to the 'blueprint' approaches to planning that have been so often condemned as ineffective (Korten 1980; Rondinelli 1983 and 1993).

African development narratives present stories about what will happen if events unfold as they describe. They seek to get their listeners to do something and they persist in the face of strong empirical evidence against their story lines (Roe 1991). Development narratives are established and rapidly entrenched by national leaders and aid donors, by elite interest groups that benefit from them (such as scientists, other researchers, and development professionals) (Chambers 1993); they become institutionalized as part of a 'received wisdom' (Leach and Mearns 1996); they are disseminated internationally by aid donors, nationally by media campaigns and accounts of 'success' (often associated with national symbols and political figures) and locally as community leaders learn what to say to access external resources. Thus development policy narratives become culturally, institutionally and politically embedded, their influence and their longevity related less to their actual economic, social or environmental achievements than to the interests of a complex web of politicians, policy makers, bureaucrats, donors, technical specialists and private sector operators whose needs they serve (Schaffer 1984; Hoben 1995). Narratives are replaced only by 'counter-narratives', that tell 'a better story' (Roe 1991, p.290). Point-by-point rebuttals are not stories, for they do not have a beginning, middle and end. Counter-narratives have to be as parsimonious, plausible and comprehensive as the original.

Roe's notion of narrative and counter-narrative fits changes that have taken place in the ideology of conservation. Ideas of the need to preserve wild species, exclude humans and minimize human influence (a narrative of 'fortress conservation') have been supplanted by a counter-narrative that we term 'community conservation', which has been adopted as a central element in global conservation discourse and policy (Hannah 1992; Lado 1992; United Nations 1992).

The Narrative of Fortress Conservation

Historically, conservation strategies have been dominated by attempts to reserve places for nature, and to separate humans and other species. Grove (1987) describes the emergence of ideas about environmental management in the British Empire from the mid-eighteenth century, in association with the interaction of imperial trade, a rising sensitivity to Romanticism and the growth of science. The central strategy that arose from this environmental concern was the creation of reserves, particularly for forests, for example in the West Indies in the eighteenth century, and in India and the South African Cape in the nineteenth century.

In Europe and North America, the establishment of formal conservation institutions began in the nineteenth century (Sheail 1976; Nash 1973). In the USA, the closing of the frontier of the West, and the natural marvels revealed by exploration, gave rise to the first National Parks. Similar government reservations of natural (or apparently natural) areas began to appear in the 1880s and 1890s in Canada, South Australia and New Zealand (Fitter and Scott 1978). Small nature reserves were established in the UK from the 1890s, and although it was the late 1940s before legislation empowered the government to establish nature reserves or national parks (Adams 1996a), the idea of conservation as something done on reserved land was common to both North America and Europe. A model, which has been called 'fortress conservation', the 'fences and fines approach' (Wells et al. 1992) or 'coercive conservation' (Peluso 1993), has dominated conservation thinking internationally, particularly the US idea of a national park as a pristine or wilderness area, and the British notion of a nature reserve that is managed intensively.

Fortress conservation involved the creation of protected areas, the exclusion of people as residents, the prevention of consumptive use and minimization of other forms of human impact. This narrative has been very influential in sub-Saharan Africa, and there is a long history of National Park creation, for example the Sabie Game Reserve (subsequently Kruger National Park) in Natal (1892), a game reserve enclosing the present Amboseli National Park in Kenya (1899), the Parc National Albert, now the Virunga National Park in Congo (1925) (Fitter and Scott 1978; Boardman 1981). The Society for the Preservation of the Wild Fauna of the Empire (the 'penitent butchers', Fitter and Scott 1978) was established in 1903 and promoted this protectionist agenda.

Conservation policy in Africa grew out of the imaginings of expatriate European men about 'the wild', a place where manhood could be proved, civilized virtues demonstrated by the manner in which animals were hunted and killed, and European rituals of hunting could be lived out (MacKenzie 1987 and 1989). The hunting of large mammals is inter-woven with the history of colonialism. Hunting could only properly be done using certain methods (shooting for example, certainly not trapping or spearing), under certain rules, and by Europeans. As colonial territories enacted laws restricting or banning hunting, Africans who hunted for the pot or for trade were reclassified, using a medieval European concept, as 'poachers'. Conservation legislation set aside areas of land, and certain quarry species, for European hunters. Most contemporary government conservation departments in sub-Saharan Africa have their origins in agencies established to defend hunting reserves and suppress 'poaching'.

Following the end of World War Two, increasingly formal regimes of conservation administration were established. Three arms of the public sector developed around the conservation agenda in most countries: the Game Department, the Forest Department and the National Parks Department (or Board). Colonial interest in hunting and poaching merged with a growing international consensus (based on UK and US models) about wildlife conservation and many controlled hunting areas and game reserves were reclassified as national parks. Many national parks were declared at this time, for example in East Africa, Nairobi National Park (1946), Tsavo (1948), and Serengeti and Murchinson Falls (1951) (Fitter and Scott 1978; Neumann 1997).

Conservation institutions were also developing rapidly in the post–World War Two years in the colonial metropole. In the UK, the government began to establish national nature reserves and national parks in the 1950s, and expertise was developed in the scientific management of protected areas, and the application of scientific principles to land management (Sheail 1976; Adams 1996b). These and other ideas about conservation also became part of a specific international discourse in the post-war period, particularly through the work of the International Union for the Conservation of Nature and Natural Resources (IUCN, originally established as the International Union for the Protection of Nature in 1934) and later through the World Wildlife Fund (WWF). This discourse was strongly rooted in the circuit of Paris (UNESCO), the Geneva region (IUCN), Washington (World Bank and US Government) and New York (UN). British scientists and conservationists (not least Thomas Huxley, first Director of UNESCO) were very influential in establishing the network within which this discourse developed.

Africa had a special place in the rise of global conservation concern because of its exceptional endowment of large and charismatic species, high densities of wildlife and rapidly increasing pace of development and landscape change. By 1960 Africa had become 'the central problem overshadowing all else' for IUCN (Boardman 1981, p.148). The IUCN and FAO launched the African Special Project in 1961. The 'Arusha Declaration on Conservation' came in the same year, stressing both a commitment to wildlife conservation and wider concerns about resource development. In 1963 a special conference on African conservation problems convened at Bukavu in the Belgian Congo. Africa was becoming independent, and political control was shifting as 'poachers' turned gamekeepers. The African Special Project was followed up by IUCN missions to 17 African countries (Fitter and Scott 1978) and, eventually (after considerable political haggling between the IUCN and FAO), a new African Convention on the Conservation of Nature and Natural Resources was adopted by the Organisation of African Unity in Addis Ababa in 1968 (Boardman 1981).

Not only was Africa the prime target for global conservation concern and action, it also provided potent conservation images that in their turn fed into the global discourse of extinction. African independence coincided with the growth of mass audiences for television in the industrialized countries and a series of popular books, such as *Serengeti Shall Not Die* (Grzimek 1960) and *SOS Rhino* (Guggisberg 1966) predicted the extinction of charismatic species. Africa was portrayed as Eden, humankind as its chief destroyer and conservation, through a protectionist strategy, its necessary regime of salvation (Graham 1973). Such images still retain their power, and remain a central feature of Western perceptions of Africa (Thornton and Currey 1991; Douglas-Hamilton and Douglas-Hamilton 1992; Gavron 1993). Western domination of the global media, the power of Western culture, and the increasingly easy communications between African cities and Europe and North America, mean that these images are fed back into Africa and, at least partly, internalized by Africa's elites and middle classes. International ideas about conservation are, in that sense, also now genuinely African.

While ideas about conservation were central to the establishment of Africa's protected areas, they were also in part, a by-product of the ideology of national development that dominated the late-colonial and independence periods. In this era of 'high modernism' (Scott 1998) development was seen as requiring the transformation of African agriculture and industrialization. Land was to be rationally appraised, and land use planned to yield maximum economic benefit. High and moderate quality lands would be ploughed up for arable farming while drier areas and poor soils would be dedicated to cattle ranching. As the planners drew lines on their maps, those with interests in conservation and wildlife – conservationists, white hunters, forestry and wildlife bureaucrats and miscellaneous romantics – argued and negotiated for their own spaces for wildlife: as Africa was mapped and carved up for development, controlled hunting areas, national parks, forest reserves and other lands were zoned for conservation. As in Europe and North America, the essence of conservation practice was the preservation of certain selected areas, their landscapes and species. People had little place in this vision of conservation.

Attacking the Fortress: The Rise of Community Conservation

The dominant narrative of fortress conservation no longer enjoys hegemony, either in Africa or globally. It has progressively been challenged by another discourse that stresses the need not to exclude local people, either physically from protected areas or politically from the conservation policy process, but to ensure their participation

(Western and Wright 1994a). This counter-narrative we label 'community conservation' (cf. IIED 1994). This term is used to describe a wide range of different kinds of projects and programmes (Barrow and Murphree, Chapter 3, this volume) but we define it here as 'those principles and practices that argue that conservation goals should be pursued by strategies that emphasize the role of local residents in decision-making about natural resources'. This includes community-based conservation, community wildlife management, collaborative management, community-based natural resource management, and integrated conservation and development programmes.

The idea that local communities can and do (and should be allowed to) manage wildlife is not new. Just as the formal conservation that was institutionalized in the late nineteenth century (through legislation, the creation of specific organizations, policies and activities) built on many pre-existing ideas and practices, so community conservation, which became institutionalized in the late twentieth century, built upon earlier experiences. Royal hunting reserves were established by the Shaka Zulu (contemporary Natal/Kwazulu), the Mwami of Rwanda and the King of Barotseland (Parker 1984). At Amboseli in Kenya, conflicts between Maasai and conservation agencies from the 1950s led to the development of an approach to its conservation that built in an element of concern for (and consultation with) local residents (Western 1982). However, the incorporation into global discourse of conservation policy that 'conservation will either contribute to solving the problems of the rural poor who live day to day with wild animals, or those animals will disappear' (Adams and McShane 1992: xix), is new.

Institutionally, the new community conservation counter-narrative was developed in the context of protected areas at successive World Congresses on National Parks and Protected Areas, particularly the Third in 1982 and Fourth in 1992 (McNeely and Miller 1984; McNeely 1993; Kemf 1993). It was a fundamental element in the concept of Biosphere Reserves developed in the 1970s by the Man and the Biosphere (*sic*) programme, and was recognized in the WWF's Wildlife and Human Needs Programme (launched in 1985). Within sub-Saharan Africa, the experience in Kenya perhaps demonstrates the development of the counter-narrative best. Experience at Amboseli National Park through the 1970s (Western 1982; Lindsay 1987) subsequently developed into the Wildlife Extension Project (WEP), which in turn led to the establishment of the African Wildlife Foundation's Tsavo Community Conservation Project (launched in 1988), the Kenyan Wildlife Service's Community Wildlife Programme and the USAID-funded COBRA project (Conservation of Biodiverse Areas), launched in 1991 (Barrow et al. 1995a; Barrow et al. 1998).

The community conservation counter-narrative has two distinct elements. The first is the imperative to allow people in and around protected areas, or others with property rights there (in land or living resources) or other claims on the land (e.g. spiritual claims) to participate in the management of conservation resources. (See Barrow and Murphree, Chapter 3, this volume, for a discussion of participation). Thus 'people and park' projects have been developed (Hannah 1992) such as the African Wildlife Foundation's 'Neighbours as Partners' programme and CARE's 'Development Through Conservation' project, begun in Uganda in 1988.

The second dimension of the community conservation counter-narrative has involved the linkage of conservation objectives to local development needs.

Examples include 'conservation-with-development projects' (Stocking and Perkin 1992) or 'integrated conservation and development projects' (Wells et al. 1992; Barrett and Arcese 1995). The economic impacts of conventional protected areas can be disastrously negative on local residents, particularly when the eviction of human communities is attempted or effected (e.g. Turnbull 1972; Schoepf 1984; Turton 1987; Brockington and Homewood 1996). The community conservation counter-narrative recognizes both the moral implications of imposing costs on local people in this way, and the pragmatic problem of the hostility of displaced or disadvantaged local people to conservation organizations practising a fortress conservation policy.

These two dimensions of community conservation, participation and a concern for economic welfare, create a space within which a great variety of different kinds of conservation interventions lie. At one extreme fall existing conservation projects (e.g. conventional protected areas) that belatedly make minor efforts to draw in local people (one might speak of them as conventional conservation projects 'retrofitted' with a participatory or community conservation approach). At the other extreme lie initiatives aimed specifically at the development of particular (often 'sustainable') uses of natural resources by local people who are given full tenure over those resources. These two polar forms of 'community conservation' draw on quite different meanings of the word conservation. The first is based on the idea that conservation has to do with concern for 'wild' species and their associations (ecosystems and habitats) and the conservation of 'nature' or 'wildlife'. Historically this has been the dominant meaning of conservation in sub-Saharan Africa. The second is based on the idea of conservation as the sustainable management of renewable resources, as origi-nally developed in the USA at the beginning of the twentieth century (most notably by the forester Gifford Pinchot): conservation as the 'gospel of efficiency' (Hays 1959; Norton 1991).

These differences in the meaning of conservation are fundamental to under-standing the breadth of policies and practices that community conservation encom-passes. Both stem from similar roots, in ideas about nature, and about the need to limit human use of nature. However, in the first case this is because of the intrinsic values of nature (i.e. 'conservation for its own sake'), whereas in the second case the limits are imposed for utilitarian reasons (because wise use demands careful husbanding of resources for greater future human benefit). The former meaning is basically biocentric (i.e. focused on the rights or needs of non-human species), whereas the latter is anthropocentric (i.e. focused on human rights, needs and benefits). There are, of course, significant overlaps between these categories, such as the possibility of economic non-use values and existence values (Swanson and Barbier 1992), and the concept of sustainable development which tries to combine both biocentric moral arguments about the need for conservation and anthro-pocentric arguments about optimal ways to sustain revenues from resource use (IUCN 1980).

Notwithstanding the complexities of these debates, the distinction between biocentric arguments and anthropocentric (and utilitarian) arguments is a useful analytical device for classifying conservation initiatives. A strict nature reserve involves little if any consumptive use of nature, and meets few if any utilitarian goals; however, it seeks to maximize gains to the existence-value of non-human species, i.e. the intrinsic value of nature. A project involving agreements about forest cutting or fishing seeks to achieve utilitarian goals (e.g. productivity, sustainability, equity), but may do little or nothing to preserve species that have little economic relevance. Choices about particular conservation activities inevitably involve a trade-off between utilitarian and non-utilitarian or intrinsic goals.

Community conservation projects not only differ in the way in which they relate to nature, but also in the degree to which they involve local people, and the way in which they do so. A critical problem is the definition of localness. Neumann (1997) rightly asks 'who are the local people?' and argues that many community conservation initiatives in Africa are happy to include 'traditional' peoples in their target groups but seek to exclude progressive farmers and immigrants. The terms on which local people are brought into 'community conservation' projects also vary from glorified public relations exercises (which try to make local people feel less antagonistic towards exclusion from a protected area by social investment and 'education') through to projects devised and run by local people alone (IIED 1994). A second axis can therefore be added to the biocentric/anthropocentric distinction to create a matrix, within which community conservation projects may be situated (Figure 2.1).

	Conservation for Use Values	Conservation for Non-use Values
LOW **Community Control**	CC to conserve resource (CBNRM overseen by government or fishing control area)	CC to protect wildlife (National Park Buffer Zone)
HIGH	CC to achieve development (e.g. CAMPFIRE)	CC to achieve conservation (e.g. sacred groves)

Figure 2.1 A typology for community conservation initiatives

The Success of Community Conservation

Why has the community conservation narrative been so successful? We identify five main reasons.

First, community conservation equates conservation with sustainable development, and hence captures the huge upwelling of policy commitment arising from the Brundtland Report (WCED 1987) and UN Conference on Environment and Development at Rio in 1992. Underlying this is the moral argument that conservation goals should contribute to and not conflict with basic human needs. This argument has led some commentators to argue that fortress conservation must be abandoned because of its adverse impacts on the living conditions of the rural poor. More generally, it is argued that conservation goals should be integrated with the development objective of meeting human need. Ideas about community conservation developed in tandem with ideas about the integration between preservationist goals and the consumptive and non-consumptive use of wildlife resources. The World

Conservation Strategy (IUCN 1980) sought to link conventional conservation concerns with those of development, using the notion of sustainable development, a concept later popularized by the Brundtland Report in 1987, and central to *Agenda 21* (UN 1992). From the perspective of sustainable development, the conservation of biodiversity and the challenge of meeting human needs must be integrated: community conservation provides a conceptual framework within which this could be made to happen in and around protected areas.

Second, community conservation draws on ideas about the 'community' and particularly about the need for local communities to be more involved in designing and implementing public policies than had been the case in the 'statist' era of the 1940s to the 1970s. Words like 'community' (and local, grassroots, tradition, participation) have a long history in development studies and are used widely but loosely; they carry complex associations, which gives them power, but at the same time makes them difficult to tie down. According to Shore (1993, p.98) 'community [is] one of the most vague and elusive concepts in social science'. These ideas became popular in the West from the late 1980s, for example in the 'communitarian' movement in the USA (Etzioni 1993). Their origins are complex lying partly in a response to the belief that state power was too great and too centralized, partly in a move to strengthen the legitimacy of public policies, and partly in response to the rise of the new social movements and demands for improved local democracy. Regulation over the behaviour of individuals, according to these ideas, is best performed by 'the community' rather than state officials.

This focus on 'community' tapped into long-established Western notions about social life in sub-Saharan Africa. These draw on ideas about the structure and organization of African society with origins in the sixteenth and seventeenth centuries that saw Africa as a kind of 'Eden', exotic alike in its fauna, flora and people; a 'Merrie Africa' of wild animals and pre-modern people located in discrete 'villages', classified into static 'tribal groups' and relating to each other through ties of kin and propinquity and experiencing low levels of economic differentiation. The idealistic and simplistic nature of such views is now being everywhere challenged by scholarship, but it retains power in general debates about Africa, on the part of Northern observers (from tour companies to conservationists), and in the minds of African bureaucrats and politicians.

The power of these idealistic notions of the existence of organic human communities in Africa reflects not only an outmoded understanding of anthropology and history, but also the continued currency of neo-populist ideas about development (Kitching 1982). Opposition to modernity (industrialization, urbanization, pollution, specialization) has been a potent theme within environmentalism and wildlife conservation in the North, for example in the UK and USA (Adams 1996b). 'Tradition' has been seen as an oppositional category to 'modernity', supporting the notion that conservation has a natural affinity with indigenous people and rural dwellers (Neumann 1997): those outside the urbanized existence common in industrialized countries. Both nature and 'traditional' lives and lifestyles can be seen to be threatened by 'modern' development and, since those lifestyles tend to be idealized and romanticized, it is easy to assume that conservation will be supported by a newly empowered and intrinsically pro-conservation 'indigenous community'. (Also see Barrow and Murphree, Chapter 3, this volume, for a discussion of how the concept of community is operationalized and of the problems that arise from this).

A third reason for the success of the community conservation narrative was that it developed at a time of significant shifts in the dominant discourses of development. During the 1970s 'top down', 'technocratic', 'blueprint' approaches to development came under increasing scrutiny as they failed to deliver the economic growth and social benefits that had been promised (Turner and Hulme 1997, pp. 132–50). An alternative agenda emerged arguing that development goals could only be achieved by 'bottom up planning', 'decentralization', 'process approaches', 'participation' and 'community organization' (e.g. Schumacher 1973; Korten 1980; Chambers 1983). By the early 1990s, aid donors and development planners had committed themselves in attempts to adopt participatory approaches. The link that had been forged between conservation and development gave conservationists a strong inducement to do the same. Indeed, it created an opportunity for conservationists (and particularly international and domestic NGOs) to tap into new sources of funds by making their activities fit 'development' aid budgets.

A fourth reason for the success of the community conservation narrative lies in the renewed interest in the 1980s in the market as a means of delivering development (Toye 1993). To achieve public policy goals (including conservation, development or 'sustainable development') economic incentives for all of the main actors must be set correctly, and this was best done by market mechanisms (Bromley 1994). Non-market actors, such as state agencies, tended to distort markets so that goals were not achieved. What was required to achieve conservation goals, therefore, was less regulation, the acceptance that all ecosystems and species are 'natural resources' and more entrepreneurial action by local communities, individual businessmen and private companies. This would permit the economic values of conservation resources to be unlocked – for leisure, tourism, trophy-hunting, meat, other products, theme parks, medicines – as they were traded in open (or relatively open) markets. The perverse incentives of the past would be corrected and the sustainable development of conservation resources would be achieved through their becoming part of the local and global economy, rather than trying to excise them from the economy. Conservation bureaucracies should promote small enterprise development, rather than set up fences and levy fines. Wildlife must 'pay its way'.

Community conservation fitted well with the 'New Policy Agenda' for foreign assistance (Robinson 1993) that had developed in Washington in the early 1990s. This was driven by beliefs focused around the twin poles of neo-classical economics and liberal democratic theory (Moore 1993). Community conservation appeared consonant with the former as it recognized the importance of economic incentives and markets, meant a reduced role for the state and created spaces for 'communities' (villagers, private individuals, companies, groups of companies) to be more involved in conservation. It supported the latter, as by helping communities to organize themselves to manage natural resources it added to the vibrancy of associational life and thus deepened the democratization process itself.

The final reason for the success of the community conservation narrative was biological. It was clear, from research in conservation biology and the genetics of small populations, that conservation goals can often not be achieved within the boundaries of protected areas, even if they are quite large. Viable populations of many of Africa's most prized mobile wildlife species cannot be sustained on small preservation 'islands' (i.e. national parks and buffer zones). Large dispersal areas are needed so that species can move from 'island' to 'island' to feed, to ensure healthy breeding stock and to respond to local extinctions and climatic change. Even if conservation 'fortresses' could be established, paid for and policed, they would not be enough. Conservation, therefore, needed to reach out of protected areas into the wider landscape, and that landscape was increasingly densely inhabited. The 'community' (i.e. the people whose land mobile species graze and cross) are key stakeholders in conservation and must be recognized as such, even if they are remote from protected areas, because of the mobility of wildlife and the complex linkages between all elements of the biotic environment.

The community conservation narrative has diffused particularly fast across Africa, and has become more solidly entrenched there than in many other regions. We believe the reasons for this lie in the level of aid-dependence of sub-Saharan Africa, the influence of multilateral and bilateral development agencies over domestic policies and the relative weakness of the state in Africa. Hoben has identified a set of conditions under which development narratives are likely to be strong (Table 2.1). These include countries with weak and/or authoritarian governments, where local research capacity is weak and countries are dependent on aid and expatriate 'experts'. These attributes are all exhibited strongly by the countries of sub-Saharan Africa. Narratives are also likely to be strong where donor experts and domestic constituents are strongly attached to them: this is certainly true of community conservation which has been formulated and disseminated at numerous international meetings, applied widely and rapidly in Africa by NGOs and international aid donors such as USAID, often developed and implemented by particular 'champions' (such as David Western in Kenya), and reported on positively in television programmes beamed around the world. (One author has seen programmes on Zimbabwe's CAMPFIRE project on television stations in Bangladesh, Kenya, Nepal and the UK.) In particular sub-Saharan Africa's dependence on foreign aid – and the expatriate consultants and experts this supports – has made it the world region in which exogenous ideas about 'what to do' hold the greatest influence. Conditions for the rapid transfer and acceptance of community conservation (at least at the policy level), in most sub-Saharan African countries have been strong over the last decade (Table 2.1).

Community Conservation as a Privileged Solution

Some issues and problems in development become entrenched in policy making (Hirschman 1963). These 'privileged problems' in turn tend to generate 'privileged solutions' (Moris 1987, p.99), 'material and organisational technologies which seem self-evidently suited for dealing with problem needs', and which are 'not thought to require testing and modification'. This concept of a 'privileged solution' is directly applicable to community conservation, because it has become so self-evidently the 'right' approach, on a range of grounds, that debate about its merits or demerits, about its costs and benefits, about the conditions under which it may prove effective and inef-fective, have only recently begun to surface. There is a large (and growing) descriptive literature on community conservation, but many studies are more or less optimistic descriptions of local level 'success', often early in a project's life, written by people

Table 2.1   Factors favouring strong narratives and their relevance to conservation in Africa

Factor*	Summary of the situation in Africa
1. Donor experts and domestic constituencies are attached to the narrative	1. Key donor countries (USA and UK) adopted a community conservation approach and this influenced their 'experts' overseas. Conferences (Airlie 1993, Sunningdale 1996, Istanbul 1997) financed by official donors and NGOs helped to transmit the idea of community conservation. Large numbers of leisure-time conservationists in such countries learned to support the new narrative
2. When there is political strategic or moral pressure on donors to act quickly	2. Media accounts of the imminent extinction of the gorilla, African elephant and rhino prompted donors to act rapidly. Where states emerged from civil wars (Ethiopia, Uganda, Mozambique, Angola) there was an urgent need to save 'the remnants' of the conservation estate. Crises narratives (Roe 1995) allow foreign 'techno-managerial elites' to shape policy and action on the African environment
3. When there has been little technical or socio-economic research locally	3. Despite the wealth of data on the zoology of charismatic species in Africa research on the ecology of Africa and on human–wildlife interaction remains in its infancy
4. When a recipient country relies heavily on expatriate experts for advice	4. Many African countries were more reliant on foreign advisers in the early 1990s than they were at independence. This relates to specific advice on conservation and broader advice about the policy and institutional frameworks that countries should adopt
5. When a recipient country relies heavily on foreign assistance	Sub-Saharan Africa is the most aid dependent region in the world. In 1990 foreign assistance, as a percentage of GNP, stood at 66% in Mozambique, 48% in Tanzania, 26% in Malawi, 18% in Uganda, 19% in Mali, 11% in Kenya, 14% in Zambia[†] (World Bank 1992, pp. 256–7). The setting up of the Global Environmental Fund (GEF) and specialist funds (e.g. USAID) post-Rio has led to a flush of external funding for conservation projects in Africa. The idea of 'sustainable development' has also meant that international conservation NGOs have gained influence (and control) over some development funds
6. When the recipient government is weak or authoritarian (or both)	1960–95 there have been frequent coups in African states. Elsewhere, authoritarian regimes have held power (e.g. Kenya, Zaire, Malawi). Such regimes have been weak in terms of their ability to meet the needs of their people

*From Hoben (1995)
[†]The country in Africa which has developed an indigenous model of community conservation, Zimbabwe, had an aid dependence (against GNP) of only 5% in 1990 (World Bank 1992, pp. 256–7)

involved in project development and perhaps without sufficient critical distance to provide a complete review (Western and Wright 1994a; Rihoy 1995; Barrow 1996a). A few case studies have been repeated and disseminated internationally to great effect. This phenomenon, which is also common to rural development, leads to what Chambers (1983) calls 'project bias', whereby successive evaluations of a region or programme look repeatedly at the same projects, and one another's reports, without properly questioning the nature of change on the ground. This leads to the narrowing of possible lessons that policy makers and researchers can learn, and constrains creativity and innovation.

The privileging of the community conservation narrative is problematic for conservation for several reasons. First, there is no guarantee that a participatory approach will necessarily be effective in delivering conservation goals. An emphasis on development can lead to a de-emphasis of conservation goals so they are no longer seriously addressed, as Oates (1995) argues in the case of the Okumu Forest Reserve in south-west Nigeria. For example, the direct contribution to conservation goals of development 'micro projects' in support of conservation in the Hadejia–Nguru Wetlands in Nigeria were slight (Adams and Thomas 1993). There may be a need to distinguish between the merits of development interventions of this kind as a contribution to local livelihoods, and their contribution to conservation. While at a rhetorical level it may be desirable to argue that conservation and development can go hand in hand through a joint programme, development expenditure for conservation purposes may not give results that are effective in conservation terms.

Second, a community conservation approach may not be cost-effective. Research on Integrated Conservation-Development Projects (ICDPs) suggests they perform poorly when considered against both developmental and conservation criteria (e.g. Stocking and Perkin 1992; Barrett and Arcese 1995). They may not achieve species or ecosystem conservation goals, for example because of technical uncertainties in setting a 'sustainable harvest', and may fail to break existing economic and cultural logics driving illegal and unsustainable harvests in critical areas. The positive impacts of ICDPs on local economies are typically transient and dependent on the maintenance of foreign aid flows. ICDPs are inherently complex, requiring high levels of skill from project staff, substantial funds and a realistic (i.e. long-term) time scale. Their chances of success depend on local perceptions of the project, which are vulnerable to any public failure in particular components (Stocking and Perkin 1992). Similarly, community-based natural resources management demands careful evaluation of the costs and benefits of project components at the level of the individual household, long-term commitments to funding and strong local participatory linkages (Gibson and Marks 1995). Effective community conservation requires a change in the organizational culture of conservation agencies (to see local residents as 'partners' not as poachers) and in the social norms of rural residents (to respond to wardens and rangers as 'partners' and not as corrupt policemen). Neither of these changes is likely to be achieved in a short-term project.

There is therefore nothing uniquely problematic about community conservation projects compared with their non-conservation development equivalents, attempting to do a great deal with limited funds at a sensible and localized scale. None the less, the complexity and persistence of these difficulties are easily under-estimated by conservation agencies that are relatively new to development work, and it is important to recognize that they are inherent in the practice of participatory local development. Participation, despite the rhetoric, is not a panacea.

Community projects are usually not cheap to implement, in terms of cost per participant or per unit area, or in terms of specific conservation outputs. They tend to have high administrative costs as they demand significant numbers of high-quality staff with locally specific knowledge, and can be frustratingly slow to bear fruit. They are therefore often not attractive to mainstream (and therefore high-budget) aid donors or governments who are interested in clearly visible and preferably rapid results. Not uncommonly project designers are compromised by donor pressures for results and at the planning stage set objectives for three or five year projects that they know will take 10 or 20 years to achieve. Rapidly implemented and broadly focused 'sustainable development' projects may have limited conservation benefits.

A third risk for conservation in the community conservation narrative relates to the instrumental way in which it is viewed. Participation is a process not a project input: thus, it may not be effective in delivering pre-selected conservation outcomes. The conservation goals that communities identify may well conflict with agency or national level goals. Moreover, participation is a process that often generates high local expectations. These may in turn trigger other processes, for example a debate about and affirmation of rights to resources, or the awakening of political consciousness. While the community conservation approach is conceived of as a way of placating local opinion, it may in fact inflame it as participants argue with the conservation agency (or with each other) about their rights, needs and aspirations. A community conservation strategy may be both morally right and politically necessary, but if implemented it may cause conservation goals to be challenged. This may be a valuable or even necessary process (if, for example, ideas from Europe or North America have been adopted that are inappropriate to a particular national situation), but it is likely to be a considerable institutional challenge for conservation bureau-cracies and environmental policy makers. Fortress conservation was an inherently authoritarian approach in which both means and end were clear and fixed. By contrast, community conservation is underpinned by much more democratic ideas which conceptually undermine the foundations of the fortress.

Conclusion: Policy Change in African Conservation

Contemporary frameworks for the analysis of change in the understanding of the environment and natural resource use in Africa highlight the cut and thrust of 'narrative' and 'counter-narrative' creation, the establishment of 'received wisdoms' and the need to cast them down (Roe 1995; Leach and Mearns 1996). If applied to conservation, one might conclude that the historically dominant narrative of 'fortress conservation' has been seriously challenged by the counter-narrative of 'community conservation'. One might further agree that at the present time the narrative of fortress conservation is being resurrected by a coalition of biologists and conservation bureaucrats (Kramer et al. 1997; Struhsaker 1997; *The Economist* 1999). However, while this narrative change may be observed at the level of academic and intellectual debate and at international conferences and meetings, it is erroneous to assume that such changes in discourse translate directly into changed policies and practices. Equally, it would be naive to assume that all of the elements of a narrative or received wisdom (e.g. fortress conservation) are 'wrong' and should disappear from policy and practice, while all the elements of a counter-narrative (e.g. community conservation) are 'right' and should be adopted.

In reality, the links between discourses, policies and practices are much more complex than the narrative/counter-narrative framework infers. Discourses contain many concepts from which policy makers can pick and mix to generate an enormous range of policy choices. Policy studies from around the world indicate that policy makers most commonly take an incrementalist approach to 'new' policy rather than totally rejecting earlier policies (Lindblom 1979; Schaffer 1984). The agencies and officials that implement policy have enormous discretion in the interpretation of policy so that the links between policy and action can take many different forms. National conservation agencies can and do shape national policy and practice of community conservation (e.g. in Tanzania, see Bergin, Chapter 7, this volume). Organizations rarely abandon their pre-existing ways of dealing with issues and stakeholders; these are continually evolving and past practice exerts considerable influence on future changes. This evolution is usually gradual, although crises may bring about more radical decisions (Grindle and Thomas 1991).

It may be beneficial that conservation policies and practices in African countries (as elsewhere) gradually evolve, rather than change dramatically as conservation narratives do. Lindblom (1979) has argued convincingly of the benefits of an incrementalist approach; Johnston and Clark (1982) made a strong case for 'adaptive learning' rather than dramatic policy changes; and Rondinelli (1983 and 1993) has argued for technical cooperation to focus on creating 'adaptive administration', rather than over-designed projects and policies that are based more on theory than practice. Uphoff (1992) argues that in a world that recognizes the diversity and complexity of humanity and the unpredictability of social, political and economic futures, there is a need for a less adversarial approach to knowledge-creation. He suggests that heightened levels of co-operation and trust among actors could allow for positive sum outcomes ('both-and' rather than 'either-or') to produce more effective policies.

We suggest that conservation in Africa does not simply need a new 'privileged solution': it requires a policy process that is more effective for meeting contemporary and future challenges. The achievement of the counter-narrative is not that it has proved that community conservation 'works': it is that it has created the space for a set of community conservation experiments that take many forms and are achieving very different results. These demand intensive monitoring and study so that the knowledge they create can be fed back into policy and action. The pressing contemporary issue is how to relate and mix strategies that incorporate elements of fortress conservation and community conservation, not to prove that one is always better than the other.

Our understanding of conservation policy in Africa must go beyond the 'Punch and Judy' style of analysis that recent scholarship has suggested. In an unpredictable world – complex, diverse and contingent – with goals that are constantly refined and redefined, the idea that the 'right policy' can be identified and then indefinitely pursued is an historic artefact. What is needed are broadly based 'enabling' policies that promote the creation and strengthening of networks of institutions and organizations that have the flexibility to deal with contingency and complexity. The question is not of whether state action or community action is better: both are essential, along with private sector support, and the challenge is how to develop effective mixes of state, community and private action in specific contexts.

At the 'grassroots' this is already the nature of day-to-day activity as wardens, villagers and business people interact to resolve local issues of conservation and development. Paradoxically, creating an enabling environment for conservation and development requires greater state capacities than did the 'fortress conservation' of the past. As the experience of TANAPA in Tanzania (Bergin, Chapter 7, this volume) and CAMPFIRE in Zimbabwe (Murphree 1997a) illustrate, working with communities and the private sector does not mean doing less, it means doing things differently and having to do more (meetings, negotiations, agreements and monitoring). Contradictory principles (law enforcement and community development) must be grappled with and turned into strategy. This has great implications for the staffing, training and financing of conservation bureaucracies and is not simply a matter of fostering a greater role for NGOs.

The economics of conservation in much of Africa (Swanson and Barbier 1992; Bromley 1994) also indicates a need for the 'community' beyond rural Africa to think about its role. Society in the West, with images of wild Africa transmitted to its television screens for hours every evening, will have to decide whether it is prepared to share the great costs of species and ecosystem conservation with the states and societies of Africa. Case studies in this volume (Chapters 8 and 10) reveal the value that communities close to African protected areas place on 'reciprocity' with the organizations that manage such areas. This concept can also be applied to the international conservation community. If this wider community reciprocates only in a token fashion then increasingly the meanings of conservation for local communities, and their local economic analyses, will determine the types of change that occur in the African environment.

3

Community Conservation
From Concept to Practice

EDMUND BARROW & MARSHALL MURPHREE

Introduction

The preceding chapter discussed the recent changes in conservation. These changes have been labelled 'community conservation' but this is a term that needs close scrutiny. 'Community' is a noun that has consistently defied precise definition while 'conservation' is often given meaning at odds with the cultural perspectives of the 'communities' that are expected to practise it. In spite of, or perhaps because of, this ambiguity the term has gained a prominent place in the international lexicon of environmental policy and practice embracing a broad spectrum of approaches and programmes.[1] These approaches exhibit differences of intent, emphasis and substance. The term covers a broad spectrum of management and benefit-sharing arrangements for the involvement in natural resource management of people who are not agents of the state but, by virtue of their location and activities, are critically placed to enhance or degrade the present and future status of natural resources. To bring structure and focus to the analysis of community conservation, this chapter examines some of the major definitional and conceptual perspectives involved and identifies key concepts which shape the policies, programmes and projects that fall within its ambit. While individual chapters in this book emphasize certain of these variables at the expense of others, cumulatively they provide the material for a synthesis based on this framework.

The Meaning of 'Community'

Community is one of the most vague and elusive concepts in social science and continues to defy precise definitions (Sjoberg 1964). The era of grand sociological theory in the nineteenth and early twentieth centuries gave prominence to the concept as central to schemes of societal evolution. Much of this theorizing had its roots in Tonnies' (1963) contrast between *Gemeinschaft* and *Gesellschaft*, or community and society. This distinction influenced the theories of Durkheim,

Weber and Marx who saw an inexorable evolutionary trend away from community. Subsequently, this theme was taken up by sociologists such as Wirth (1938), Parsons and Shils (1962) and anthropologists such as Redfield (1947) and Lerner (1962). The legacy of this debate greatly influenced development and conservation policies during the 1960s and 1970s. Communal systems of management and environmental control, whatever their past record might have been, were viewed as no longer adequate in the face of modernization, demographic growth and the penetration of market forces. Centralized management under state control was required, a strategy which found resonance with the aspirations of the newly independent governments of the day and the international bodies offering them aid and technical assistance. If 'communities' had a role in public action then this needed to be state-controlled, as in the community development policies practised across Africa and Asia in the 1960s (Hulme and Turner 1990). It was not until the 1980s that the community began to be taken seriously as a major actor in natural resource management as a flood of studies revealed the potential role of local collective action in irrigation (Coward 1979), rural development (Esman and Uphoff 1984), agriculture (Richards 1985), forestry and other fields. In the late 1980s the 'counter-narrative' of community conservation began to evolve (Adams and Hulme, Chapter 2, this volume). Driving this revived emphasis on community were the manifest incapacities of state bureaucracies to micromanage the environment, the dismal record of state and aid agency projects to protect biodiversity across the landscape, the dissonance between state and local incentives for conservation and new, systemic approaches to conservation biology which incorporated human activity. In the social sciences the counter-narrative has now become the locus for research as scholars 'alarmed by the loss of familiar forms of social organisation ...trace the loss to modernity, market forces, and state intrusions. The space vacated by a locus of longing that the future might provide is naturally filled in their writings by community' (Agrawal 1997: 6).

But what is this 'community'? In its study of community approaches to wildlife management, IIED (1994) points out that the concept can be approached in spatial, socio-cultural and economic terms. Spatially, communities can be viewed as 'groupings of people who physically live in the same place'. Socio-culturally, they can be considered as social groupings, who 'derive a unity from common history and cultural heritage, frequently based on kinship'. Economically they can be considered as 'groupings of people who share interests and control over particular resources'. Combining these constructs one can derive a model of community as an entity socially bound by a common cultural identity, living within a defined spatial boundary and having a common economic interest in the resources of this area. An example of this model is found in what IIED (1994: 5) calls 'the archetypal notion of the African village composed of founding lineages who have stewardship and control over a bounded set of resources within a territory, lineages who have married into the community, and more recent settlers, all of whom inter-marry, who speak the same language and who practise the same way of life'.

Such 'communities of place' can be identified where rural people are sedentary, primarily reliant on arable agriculture and where population mobility and migration are at low levels.

Problems arise, however, when we try to apply this ideal-type model everywhere, and in all cases, across contemporary rural Africa. The model is static, giving little hint of the heterogeneity, changing membership and composition of rural locales due to forced relocation, migration, rural/urban labour and resource flows, and changing agricultural practice. As a result 'communities' are far more internally differentiated and dynamic than the model implies. Their boundaries also change as development shifts land from one jurisdiction to another, and governments impose new units of local governance on rural areas. Analytically the model poses problems when its spatial dimension does not match socio-cultural or economic boundaries. This is illustrated at Masali Island off the Tanzanian coast where the resource management community, defined in terms of use, does not coincide with the community, as defined socio-culturally (Cooke and Hamid 1998). The model is not easily applied to semi-arid and arid areas where various forms of pastoralism prevail and where 'communities of place' interact with each other over a wide range seasonally and at times of environmental stress. These considerations make any attempt to provide an *a priori* polyvalent definition of community futile, except at a level so generalized as to be analytically sterile. As a consequence, in this book we take an actor-oriented and functional approach to the topic.

Firstly, we note the critical importance of the level of governance and civic organization which the concept addresses. This is the arena of social action requiring collaborative management of common pool natural resources by farmers, pastoralists, fisher folk and others, below those of the large-scale bureaucratic units which governments have created at sub-national levels. Institutionally this is a manifest gap in the structure of environmental governance in Africa today, and the arena in which community conservation, however conceived, operates.

Secondly, we see the nature of this action as being primarily inter-personal, guided by peer expectation and mutual reciprocities rather than by bureaucratic prescription. This characteristic has implications for institutional scale since any organization based primarily on personal interaction requires that members have the opportunity for at least occasional face-to-face contact. Such units will thus be restrained in their size and we can refer to them as small scale, bearing in mind that this refers to social and not necessarily spatial scale.

Thirdly, we ask the question: What is required by rural resource users to organize themselves for collective action for effective natural resource management? The answer to this question is likely to throw up a variety of profiles depending on content and context. While the detail is left for the analyses found in the following chapters, we suggest at this stage that any organizational vehicle for such collaboration is likely to require four characteristics: cohesion, demarcation, legitimacy and resilience.

Cohesion

This refers to a sense of common identity and interest which serves to bring people together for collaborative action, and leads them to collectively differentiate themselves from others. At its core this characteristic arises from subjective perceptions, although it is fed by instrumental considerations. Its sources commonly arise from a shared history and culture, although it may be a product of political and economic factors which force people to share a finite resource base. Whatever its history, cohesion is the social glue which persuades people, in spite of their differences, to act collectively to enhance mutual interest and represent it to others.

Demarcation

Cohesion sets social boundaries and determines membership. A parallel requirement is demarcation, which sets the boundaries of jurisdiction for the collective regime. This demarcation is commonly based on spatial criteria through the delineation of a fixed land area and the resources on it. It may, however, be drawn on the basis of socially sanctioned access to given resource categories, as in the case of pastoralism or some fisheries. Whatever the criteria used, the definition of jurisdiction limits and reinforces authority and responsibility for the collective grouping and is necessary for efficient organizational activity.

Legitimacy

Just as collective organization requires demarcation, it also requires legitimacy for its processes and leadership, which needs to relate to both power and authority. External authority can confer legitimacy but this on its own tends to be a necessary but not sufficient condition. More important is internal legitimacy arising from socio-cultural and socio-economic criteria. In many contexts these criteria are at odds with those which modern African states currently seek to impose on rural populations, and the persistence and adherence to them creates tension and conflict. An internal legitimacy endogenously derived but also sanctioned by the state is likely to produce a more robust base for organization.

Resilience

In the rapidly changing context of rural Africa the components of social organization are dynamic. The roots of social cohesion may change in their substance and combinations. Boundaries of jurisdiction and affiliation may shift. The sources of legitimacy may change. Effective organization must accommodate this change, evolving over time. Resilience, that is the organizational capacity to adapt in content and structure, is a key tool for the management of risk in uncertain environments and livelihood systems. This characteristic provides durability to organizations and creates scope for them to improve through processes of adaptive management.

The characteristics of social organization described above, located in small-scale, personalized arenas of interaction, provide the profile for what we take to be 'community' in this study. For the purposes of our topic 'community' is defined functionally as a principle manifest in social groupings with the actual or potential cohesion, incentive, demarcation, legitimacy and resilience to organize themselves for effective common pool natural resource management at levels below and beyond the reach of state bureaucratic management.

'Participation' and Community Conservation

The concept of 'participation' underpins the normative theory of community conservation (IIED 1994; Little 1994). It is part of a fundamental shift in development thinking (Chambers 1983 and 1993; Oakley 1991) that is now embraced in conservation approaches. However, the concept is very broad reflecting the differing interests people have in who participates, for what purposes and on what terms. For local residents these range from minimalist approaches, which merely entail receiving information, to empowering approaches that involve the creation of autonomous institutions operated by the 'community' (Table 3.1). In terms of the roles assigned to local people, the first two categories of Table 3.1 (passive and information giving) cannot be considered as falling under the rubric of community conservation since they do not involve local collective action. It is only in the last four categories in the table that collective activity is required and where the concept of 'community' has relevance. This serves as an analytic warning; not all projects and programmes that speak of 'participation' are communal in nature.

Table 3.1 How people can participate in development programmes

Participation typology	Roles assigned to local people
Passive	Told what is going to happen or already happened. Top-down, information belongs to external professionals
Information giving	Answer questions from extractive researchers. People not able to influence analysis or use
Consultative	Consulted. External agents listen to views. Usually externally defined problems and solutions. People not involved in decision making
Functional	Form groups to meet predetermined objectives. Usually done after major project decisions made, therefore initially dependent on outsiders but may become self-dependent, and enabling
Interactive	Joint analysis and actions. Use of local institutions. People have stake in maintaining or changing structures or practices
Self-mobilization or empowerment	Take decisions independent of external institutions. May challenge existing arrangements and structures

Sources: Adapted from Pimbert and Pretty (1994) and Oakley (1991)

For all of the case studies in this volume participation was viewed by planners and policymakers in an instrumental sense: as a means to achieve goals but not as a goal in its own right. While the nature of participation varied from case to case the most commonly found forms were consultative and functional.

Objectives and Community Conservation

The analysis in this volume highlights two key contextualizing variables which have significantly shaped the policies, programmes and projects that fall under the rubric of community conservation. One is tenure, which is taken up in the following section. The other is objective, a term which we use to cover other synonyms in general usage such as purpose, aim and goal. Here we use the term to denote the core motivational direction behind policy, planning and action. This core motivational direction is itself determined by a number of subjective values and instrumental goals (Murphree 1996).

The values and goals of specific community conservation initiatives reveal the meanings which their proponents assign to the term conservation. The weight that people give to these different forms of value correlates closely with their cultural and socio-economic location. For people in urban, industrial or post-industrial society wildlife has little direct economic significance (except for those employed in tourism or conservation) and emphasis is placed on its intrinsic or recreational worth. For rural peoples, for whom the presence of wildlife has important economic implications, wildlife valuations tend to be more instrumental, even where their cultures assign an intrinsic value to wildlife. Although there are important exceptions, the institutionalization of community conservation in Africa today is largely a product of initiatives by international conservation agencies (endorsed by state governments), shaped by conservation professionals and funded by international environmental grant sources. With its cultural and socio-economic location, it is not surprising that this provenance tends to reflect an emphasis on the intrinsic and aesthetic values of wildlife, to define conservation in terms of abstract concepts such as biodiversity and ecosystem maintenance, and to emphasize such goals as species preservation and the maintenance of micro-habitats for aesthetic and recreational use. In terms of the analysis of Adams and Hulme (Chapter 2) such a position is viewed as 'biocentric'.

Rural Africans are unlikely to hold the same values and goals, or to articulate conservation as a discrete set of concerns. Indeed their vernacular languages rarely have the abstract noun 'conservation' and translations usually involve the use of a phrase such as 'taking care of natural resources'. Their concerns are likely to be more instrumental and economic and this shapes their conservation ethic. Conservation is for them an investment for present and future value, the goal being the maintenance or enhancement of their livelihoods. They are unlikely to willingly collaborate in community conservation schemes if these initiatives do not achieve this goal.

These distinctions in objective critically shape the direction, content and processes of community conservation programmes. The provenance of most contemporary community conservation programmes tends to make them programmes of co-operation, seeking to co-opt the resources of local people for larger state and international conservation objectives. As noted above, there are exceptions, i.e. programmes which take as their starting point the potential value of wildlife and wild land for rural livelihoods and seek to create the conditions under which this potential can be realized on a sustainable basis. Examples of both approaches are found in the case studies of this volume. Neither approach should be judged on the basis of *a priori* preferences; evaluation must be grounded in an assessment of the fit between objective and specific content and context.

Tenure & Community Conservation

Tenure is the second key variable in determining the shape and performance of community conservation programmes. Here we use the term to cover the rights of secure, long-term access to land and other resources, their benefits, and the responsibilities related to these rights. A number of related terms dissect these rights, including ownership, property, proprietorship and entitlement.[2] Ownership is 'the placement with a person (or group of persons) of a certain group of rights to property:

the rights of possession, use and disposal of worth' (Harper 1974: 18). The term tenure has the same connotation, but includes a temporal dimension and relates to the period of this ownership.

These terms have several important dimensions.

a) Rights of tenure are rarely, if ever, absolute. Their strengths are determined by their time frames and the conditionalities attached to them. The fewer the conditionalities attached to them, the stronger their ownership will be. As Alchian says, the strength of ownership 'can be defined by the extent to which the owner's decision to use the resource actually determines its use' (Alchian 1987: 1031). The longer their sanctioned duration, the stronger their tenure will be.

b) These rights have a number of derivations. They can be conferred by the state, in a strong form as *de jure* rights or in weaker versions as *de facto* rights. They can arise from customary law derived from the norms and practices of long established non-state institutions and social groupings, or they can be the results of particular configurations of power in specific contexts of social interaction. The legitimacy of these derivations is dynamic and frequently contested. In the regions covered by this volume conflicts between statutory and customary law are endemic creating a dissonance in resource claims and usage (cf. Okoth-Owiro 1988).

c) Rights require regimes of authority ranging from small social units (such as a household or partnership) to the state. The scale of these regimes is usually influenced *inter alia* by the nature of the resource over which rights are exercised. Generally, resources are classified in a four-fold typology of state property, private property, common property and open-access resources. This typology, developed in Common Property Theory, is analytically useful but can be misleading when the resource and the regime are conflated. Open access resources do not constitute a regime; their defining characteristic is in fact the absence of a regime. Common property resources, defined as 'a class of resources for which exclusion is difficult and joint use involves subtractability' (Berkes 1989: 7), are not necessarily managed by a communal regime. They are often managed by a state regime; the management of the water of a large catchment area is a good example.

d) In most tenurial systems while rights confer authority they also confer responsibility. Authority and responsibility are functionally linked. When they are de-linked, and assigned to different institutional actors, then both are eroded. Authority without responsibility is likely to be dysfunctional or obstructive; responsibility without authority lacks the necessary instrumental and motivational components for its efficient exercise.

These definitional and conceptual issues relating to ownership and tenure are central to the analysis and assessment of the community conservation initiatives reviewed in this volume. The strength of ownership correlates closely with the strength of collective incentives to make the allocations of time, labour, land and resources necessary to make them work. Economic incentives rank high in this suite of incentives, particularly as rural people individually and collectively enter and evaluate larger markets in their production and livelihood activities. The strength of tenure, the duration of this ownership, is central to a community's conservation perspectives since it shapes the incentives to invest in the future. The degree of legitimacy accorded to the local resource rights regime will to a large extent determine whether the community can operate effectively as a negotiating entity and will also internally set the levels of incentive necessary to develop intra-communal institutional arrangements which are effective and resilient. Finally, the efficiency of such programmes will depend largely on the degree to which they link authority and responsibility.

Tenure, and its sub-sets of component elements, is thus a key variable in determining the performance of community conservation initiatives. Unfortunately for such initiatives in Eastern and Southern Africa, they exist in an arena where tenure conditions are not generally propitious. As inhabitants of what is technically state land, the residents of most communal lands in Africa do not have strong property rights. Their tenure is uncertain and their decisions on the use of resources subject to a plethora of conditionalities. As in colonial times, communal lands continue to be in various degrees the fiefdoms of state bureaucracies, political elites and their private sector partners. The persistence of this condition into the modern post-colonial state is an indication that the devolution of strong property rights to the peoples of communal land is a fundamental allocative and political issue and that power structures at the political and economic centre are unlikely to surrender their present position easily (Murphree 1995). This is the larger context in which community conservation initiatives exist and to a large extent their performance will be determined by the degree to which they are able to reconcile the conflicts created by property regimes that emphasize the responsibilities of communities but devolve few rights to them.

A Typology of Community Conservation Initiatives

In policy and practice three major types of community conservation approach can be identified.

a) *Protected area outreach*, which seeks to enhance the biological integrity of national parks and reserves by working to educate and benefit local communities and enhance the role of protected areas in local plans. In East Africa this has been the predominant approach (see Chapters 5 and 7–10). It is also used in other regions, as at Kruger National Park in South Africa (Venter and Breen 1996).

b) *Collaborative management*, which seeks to create agreements between local communities or groups of resource users and conservation authorities for negotiated access to natural resources which are usually under some form of statutory authority. In Uganda some components of the UWA's community conservation programme take this form through the negotiation of resource sharing agreements (see Chapters 5, 8 and 9).[3]

c) *Community-based conservation*, which has the sustainable management of natural resources through the devolution of control over these resources to the community as its chief objective. This has been the predominant approach in Southern Africa as illustrated by the cases in this volume (Chapters 4, 11–13, 15 and 16) from Zimbabwe, Namibia and Mozambique.[4]

As with most typologies, this categorization is a simplification, and many programmes attempt to incorporate elements of more than one of these approaches. These categories do, however, focus analysis, and using the two key variables of objectives and tenure, Table 3.2 summarizes some of the main characteristics of these three approaches to community conservation.

Table 3.2 Approaches to community conservation and some key characteristics

	Protected area outreach	Collaborative management	Community-based conservation
Objectives	Conservation of ecosystems, biodiversity and species	Conservation with some rural livelihood benefit	Sustainable rural livelihoods
Ownership/tenure status	State owned land and resources (e.g. national parks, forest and game reserves)	State-owned land with mechanisms for collaborative management of certain resources with the community. Complex tenure and ownership arrangements	Local resource users own land and resources either *de jure* or *de facto*. State may have some control of last resort
Management characteristics	State determines all decisions about resource management	Agreement between state and user groups about managing some resource(s) which are state owned. Management arrangements critical	Conservation as an element of land use. An emphasis on developing the rural economy
Focus in East and Southern Africa	Common in East Africa, with a little in Southern Africa	East Africa, with some in Southern Africa	Predominant in Southern Africa, but increasing in East Africa

Protected area outreach

Africa has an extensive protected area (PA) system (Groombridge 1992; IUCN 1992). The most important shortcomings in the functioning of this system are not geographical or ecological but social and institutional. Protected areas in Africa were usually established without the participation or consent of local people and many times involved their forced removal (West and Brechin 1991; Adams and McShane 1992). PAs were not established with any clear linkages to local land use plans or the local economy. Protected area outreach is a recent and pragmatic attempt to achieve long-term conservation goals, while redressing some of the injustices of the past. Over the last decade it has been institutionalized in some conservation authorities recognizing the importance of resource users who border protected areas.

When protected areas were declared, governments replaced pre-existing tenure with state ownership. This exclusive ownership led to no community or resource user involvement or benefit flows except through 'theft'. Protected area outreach attempts to introduce the idea of broadening the tenure arrangement, by permitting some level of rights for local communities, converted into benefits, while the state retains 'legal' ownership of the protected area. Protected area outreach seeks to:

- identify the problems that people who live close to PAs experience, and solve them in a mutually beneficial manner;
- create benefit flows for local people to improve their livelihoods using the protected area as a basis; and
- resolve PA–people conflicts in a mutually agreeable manner.

Tanzania National Parks (TANAPA) is an example of a state agency with a strong protected area outreach programme. Its Community Conservation Service is well integrated within TANAPA, and has agreed policies and procedures both at head-quarters and in the individual national parks, and agreed mechanisms for benefit sharing (see Bergin, Chapter 7, this volume). Protected area outreach has been the predominant approach to community conservation in East Africa, partly in recognition of the importance of the East African system of protected areas, and the growing recognition of the costs this imposes on local communities.

Conservation objectives are the key management priority for protected area outreach, with rural livelihoods being secondary. Dialogue, conflict resolution, and forms of benefit-sharing arrangements which do not include use of protected area natural resources, are the major components of outreach. Benefits to protected area 'neighbours' may contribute to poverty alleviation through the provision of improved services. An important additional consideration of protected area outreach approaches is their potential for reducing the costs of PA law enforcement, so that protected area outreach costs may be offset by savings.

Collaborative management[5]

Borrini-Feyerbend (1996: 12) states that '"collaborative management" describes situations in which "some" or all of the relevant stakeholders in a protected area are involved in a substantial way in management activities'. Collaborative management is a negotiated arrangement whereby a group of resource users and a conservation authority agree to jointly manage a resource or an area that has conservation value. The collaborative arrangement may also be between a private sector interest and a community or a conservation authority. The resource(s) or conservation area are usually governed by national policy and legal instruments, and are not legally owned by local resource users. Collaborative management seeks to:

- identify resources that are important for local people but occur in state-controlled lands;
- negotiate formal agreements, with agreed rights and responsibilities for all involved stakeholders to use the resources or a conservation area sustainably; and
- establish local responsibility for the management of such resources so as to achieve conservation as well as livelihood objectives.

Collaborative management differs from protected area outreach in permitting local people access to and use of state-controlled conservation resources. This represents a shift in the balance of recognized rights. While collaborative management arrangements may cover a variety of types of resource use, conservation objectives remain the driving force. Management focuses on conserving, through sustainable use, a resource or a habitat. Where the benefits derived from resource use are an important contribution to local livelihoods the collaborative management agreement is likely to be stronger than when benefits are few or unimportant for local resource users.

Community-based conservation

This category covers programmes which have the sustainable use of wildlife and wild land by rural people, under communal tenure conditions, as their objective. The emphasis is not on park/people relations but on the incorporation of floral and faunal resources into the livelihood and development strategies of communities.

Three particular emphases are found in this approach. Firstly, there is a focus on economic incentives, the assumption being that rural people will not sustainably manage wildlife or wild land unless these are perceived to yield greater returns than other forms of land use such as crop growing and cattle rearing. A second emphasis is on the devolution of authority and responsibility to communities, the assumption being that this creates an incentive framework favouring sustainable utilization. The third emphasis is on the development of communal institutions and structures for the management of these entitlements in a manner which allows communities to effectively control use, distribute benefits to their membership and efficiently exploit opportunities in the natural resources market.

Community-based conservation thus seeks to:

- create an enabling legal and policy context for local people to manage their own resources sustainably;
- encourage the development of wildlife offtake, safari-hunting and tourism in communal lands;
- establish institutions for the effective local management of natural resources; and
- ensure that benefits accrue on a sustainable and equitable basis.

The community-based conservation approach has been particularly pursued in Southern Africa (see Jones and Murphree, Chapter 4, this volume for a detailed discussion) but is now being experimented with in other parts of the continent.

The three types of community conservation described above are not mutually exclusive in the context of a suite of national conservation policies. We emphasize this since there is a tendency in debates on environmental management to see these types as representing intrinsically opposed and competing approaches to conservation. This is not necessarily the case, particularly if it is accepted that national conservation policies must encompass multiple objectives, from the maintenance of state-protected habitats and species to the efficient and sustainable use of natural resources for human livelihoods. Multiple objectives require multiple approaches and it is the match between objective, context and approach which forms one of the principal evaluative criteria in the analyses of this volume.

Organizational Evolution and the Process of Implementation

Contemporary critiques of community conservation initiatives note that they are often informed by a naive view of communities as organic, homogeneous entities with few problems in self-regulation. They can thus be 'attempts to link static, undifferentiated "communities" with "the environment", which have characterised so many past analyses informing community-based sustainable development' (Leach et al. 1997: 12). Agrawal points out that this vision of community 'disregards the multiple interests harboured within communities', neglects 'the fact that different actors within communities have differential access to resources and channels of influence' and ignores both intra-communal and community/external political processes (Agrawal 1997: viii).

These critiques have substance, particularly when one reviews the project proposals and consultancy reports of agencies involved in community conservation projects. They are less convincing when applied to the publications of scholar practitioners with experience in the facilitation of community conservation and who are well aware of these issues.[6] Nevertheless, the main thrust of these critiques is valid: effective community conservation involves collective action, effectively organized. This organization must incorporate the first three characteristics required for collective action which we have already mentioned – cohesion (of identity and interest), demarcation and legitimacy – and enhance them to produce a fourth characteristic, resilience. This organization must be able to arbitrate between and reconcile internal differences. It must have the capacity to create and generate rules which have collective support and be able to enforce them; to monitor the state of communal resources and experiment in the modes of their use; to negotiate effectively with external bureaucratic, political and entrepreneurial agents; to create consensus on the use of communal revenues and handle finances to the satisfaction of its internal constituency and external monitors. It also needs to provide for a throughput of leadership as generational change occurs. And it must do all this in a manner that controls transaction costs and retains legitimacy!

To this point we have written of 'organization' generically, as a single entity.[7] In reality a community will have several organizations, formal or informal, which impact on community conservation. Nevertheless the imperative remains for there to be a coalescent structure of organization which is the overall arbiter of community stance and action.

The organizations involved in community conservation show mixed provenance, with some endogenous and some exogenous to communities.[8] Exogenously derived organizations may be imposed by government or fostered by aid agencies. Their strength frequently correlates with the financial or bureaucratic resources which lie behind them. But unless they find a synergy with endogenous organizational imperatives their resilience is questionable. These imperatives arise from a different source of legitimacy and are shaped *inter alia* by the social capital[9] and social energy[10] found within the community. Thus the profile of organizational imperatives is highly contextualized, highly variable and highly dynamic, defying any *a priori* reductionist definition. Ultimately the effectiveness of organization in community conservation is determined by the will and capacities of communities themselves and cannot be imported from outside. External agents can assist, but this assistance must largely be in creating conducive environments for the evolution of community organization, the provision of training in specific skills and 'light touch' facilitation of a non-directive kind which elaborates on alternatives and their consequences.

These observations on the complexity and dynamics of community organization bring us to a second operational variable, which is process in implementation. Projects and programmes are the principal contexts which bring together local and international incentives for conservation. However, implementation has tended to fall into two approaches. One is reductionist, bureaucratic and directive operating through the project cycle; the other incrementalist, personalized and consensual operating through adaptation and indeterminate time frames. This 'blueprint or process' debate has been analysed in a number of publications[11] and there is a growing consensus among analysts and practitioners that community conservation initiatives require a process approach in implementation.

However, the modalities of the donor agencies which fund community conservation projects and programmes in Africa remain largely wedded to blueprint approaches. This has negative consequences. Community conservation initiatives are locked into time frames too short for the organizational evolution required. When positive results are not immediately apparent the temptation is to throw more funding into the project, under the fallacy that money can substitute for time. As the inevitable increase in dependency diminishes the incentives for community self-direction and self-sufficiency, the structural utopianism implicit in blueprint approaches is disillusioned and the conclusion is reached that the project has failed. It probably has, but for implementational rather than intrinsic reasons.

Evaluation of community conservation initiatives should therefore examine their potential to escape from this dissonance between external expectations and the process required for the necessary and on-going evolution of organizations for community conservation. In some cases, particularly those which fall in the community-based conservation category, this may require a complete delinking of any direct donor inputs and the community enterprise. The case studies of Namibia (Chapter 11) and Zimbabwe (Chapter 12) presented in this volume are instructive in this respect. In other cases where the resource endowments of communities are more meagre a re-adjustment of donor expectations and time frames may be necessary. In the case of initiatives which fall into the protected area outreach category, international and state agencies should accept long-term responsibilities for fiscal and other inputs, not on the basis of dependency but on the basis of negotiated exchanges between the community and state or international interests for mutual benefit.

A Concluding Comment

One central lesson arises from this review of issues involved in understanding and operationalizing community conservation initiatives. This is of the importance of context. While all community conservation initiatives have one common element: collective organization and action by social aggregates at small social scale in the interests of conservation, beyond this they vary widely in objective, characteristics and in the tenure conditions under which they operate. They vary in their assignments of authority and responsibility, in the resources they address, in the organizational characteristics they exhibit and the mode through which they are implemented. The case studies in this volume illustrate the range of these variables. Comparison between them can yield useful insights, but more analytically important is the issue of whether content, context, implementation and objectives effectively fit together. It is in this match that the promise of community conservation lies, and it is its presence or absence that most often determines the performance of community conservation initiatives.

Notes

[1]For example Integrated Conservation and Development Projects (ICDPs), Community-based Conservation (CBC), Community-based Natural Resource Management (CBNRM), Community Wildlife Management (CWM), Collaborative (or Co-) Management (CM), and Protected Area Outreach Projects (PAOPs).

[2]Leach et al. lay emphasis in their analysis on 'environmental entitlements', which they define as 'alternative sets of benefits derived from environmental goods and services over which people have legitimate effective command and which are instrumental in achieving well-being.' They link these 'entitlements' to 'endowments' which they define as 'the rights and resources that people have. For example, land, labour, skills and so on.' (Leach et al. 1997: 8–9) The inclusion of endowments in the analysis of community conservation is important since the level of resource richness in a given community clearly affects the resource/demand ratios involved. Bond (Chapter 15) highlights the importance of this ratio for community conservation.

[3]Forestry departments across Africa appear, however, to be taking the lead in collaborative management (Wily 1995; Wily and Othmar 1995; Fotso 1996; Ibo and Leonard 1996).

[4]The ADMADE programme in Zambia also falls into this category.

[5]Also referred to as co-management, participatory management, joint management, shared-management, multi-stakeholder management or round table management.

[6]The invisibility of this body of publications by scholar practitioners involved in community conservation is an important issue, worthy of analysis in itself. A vast grey literature describing and analysing intra-communal heterogeneity and conflict exists in the form of reports, occasional papers and theses in libraries of universities and archives of agencies in Africa, largely ignored by international scholars. In part this is due to the audiences that much of the literature addresses: fellow practitioners, national policy makers, bureaucrats and community leaders rather than an international academic audience. Its idiom is thus frequently different and its content often focuses on what Mkandawire refers to as local minutiae (Mkandawire 1998: 110). In part this is due to the limited circulation of this literature, constrained by inadequate publication facilities. For a more extended discussion, see Mkandawire (1998).

[7]The text has, in fact, used the term both as a verb and a noun. We have also used the term to cover aspects which are usually analysed under the term 'institution'. Institutions are complexes of norms and behaviours that persist over time by serving collectively valued purposes (Uphoff 1986). Organizations structure these institutions in specific arenas through assigned roles, and may operate on a formal or informal basis. Most community conservation thinking places emphasis on organizational capacity and efficiency, but the effectiveness of organizational structures is largely dependent on their correspondence with the institutional requirements to which they are responsive. For further discussion, see Leach et al. (1997: 11–12).

[8]See, for example, Barrow (1996a), Metcalfe (1994), Jones (1997), and Barrow et al. (1998), for a listing of some such organizations.

[9]On the concept of social capital, see Coleman (1990), Brown and Ashman (1996) and Putnam (1993).

[10]Murphree (Chapter 12) introduces this concept in his analysis of the Mahenye case study.

[11]See, for example, Chambers (1983), Chambers et al. (1989) and Bond and Hulme (1999).

PART TWO
Conservation Policies & Institutions

4

The Evolution of Policy on Community Conservation in Namibia & Zimbabwe

BRIAN JONES & MARSHALL MURPHREE

Introduction

The histories of community conservation in Namibia and Zimbabwe provide an instructive comparative case study on the origins and development of community conservation policy over time.[1] In their similarities both histories represent a 'polar type' in the spectrum of policies examined in this book, emphasizing extensive devolution through strong local proprietorship and conceptualized primarily in terms of rural development rather than conservation objectives. They are a 'community-based conservation' approach (see Barrow and Murphree, Chapter 3, this volume). In their differences the two histories show that this 'polar type' can mask significant policy divergence in important dimensions, providing a warning that the aggregations of typology may obscure specifics that are operationally determinative.

This reference to operational specifics underlines an analytic stance which informs this chapter. We see policy as dynamic, in constant and evolving interaction with implementation. Operational specifics continually feed back into policy, which in turn responds to implementation experience. This insight has been implicit in conservation and wildlife policy evolution in Namibia and Zimbabwe, often expressed as 'adaptive management'. At any point in time policy represents the attempt to reconcile diverse interests; the experience of implementation constantly changes the nature of this arena of conflicting interest. Our analysis of the two histories thus gives attention to issues of resource competition and the processes of policy formulation.

Particular attention is given to certain key issues. We examine the degree and context of devolution in rights, authority and responsibility implied by policy. We look at the reach of this devolution and the level to which policy suggests it should extend. Put another way, we ask the questions, 'devolution to whom?' and 'what is the primary unit of proprietorship?' We examine the incentives for participation built into policy.

Finally, we look at the degree to which international perspectives and interests have influenced national policy through donor involvement in implementation.

Land, Ecology and Politico-economic Background

Namibia and Zimbabwe share a number of common characteristics. Zimbabwe is classified as mainly semi-arid, while Namibia is semi-arid to arid and both are prone to regular droughts. Zimbabwe is predominantly broad-leaved woodland savanna, while Namibia is predominantly thorn savanna with dwarf shrub savanna in the south. The frequency of drought conditions leads to considerable uncertainty for rural people in both countries who have devised a number of risk aversion strategies, often based on diversification or transhumance. Both countries have relatively recently emerged from long periods of white rule, Zimbabwe in 1980 and Namibia in 1990. Politics in both countries are still dominated by racial issues. Government agendas still focus on removing past discrimination and on the indigenization of the civil service and the business sector. There is also a tendency to use the racial legacy to legitimize the concentration of political and economic power in the hands of the new post-independence elite. These ecological and politico-ideological contexts have influenced the evolution of policy in Namibia and Zimbabwe aimed at enabling the development of collective resource management regimes. The struggle over land between existing landholders, whether white commercial farmers or black peasants, and the landless, whether the rural poor or aspiring new black elite, is crucial to understanding the politics of natural resource management in much of southern Africa.

Namibia

Namibia has a total land area of approximately 825 000 km^2 and a population estimated at 1.6 million, with an annual growth rate of 3 per cent. It is the driest country south of the Sahara, with average rainfall varying from above 600 mm in the north-east to less than 25 mm in the Namibia desert to the west. Rainfall is highly erratic both temporally and spatially. Drought is a regular occurrence.[2] The shortage of water is the main limiting factor on Namibia's economy, which is almost entirely reliant on natural resources. Two-thirds of the population live in rural areas and are directly dependent upon the soil and living natural resources for their livelihoods.

Land distribution in Namibia has been skewed by the country's colonial history. Under German rule from 1888 to 1917, white settlers appropriated much of the central part of the country, and began the process of developing 'reserves' for black tribal groups. The South African administration, which replaced the German colonial government, continued this process and consolidated the reserves into a system of black homelands based on apartheid policy. In many instances the land allocated to black tribal groups was among the least suitable for crop growing and livestock rearing, constituting large parts of the arid north-west and of the Kalahari sandveld in the north-east.

Commercial farmland is held under freehold title, while the state owns communal land. Residents of communal land have usufruct rights over the land and its resources, such as grazing. Under the South African colonial administration land allocation was the function of government officials. In practice, traditional leaders believed that communal land was owned by the chief or the king, and have always allocated land in terms of customary law (Corbett and Daniels 1996). However this *de facto* allocation of land by traditional leaders has been eroded by post-independence government policy. The erosion of the powers and status of traditional leaders has combined with other factors to create an open access situation on much communal land. Without secure and exclusive group tenure over communal land, many residents are unable to guard their land against appropriation by wealthy individuals and settlers from other areas.

The SWAPO Government, which came to power in democratic elections in 1990, and which gained a two-thirds parliamentary majority in 1994, has publicly committed itself to multi-party democracy, a mixed economy and to decentralization of decision-making. A decentralization policy sets out government functions which should be shifted to the regional councils created after independence. There is no administrative unit below the regional council except for municipalities. The regional councils currently have little power, no authority to raise revenue and virtually no officials of their own. Within the ruling party and within the higher echelons of the civil service there are competing ideological tendencies representing on the one hand democracy and decentralization and, on the other, command and control through centralization.

Zimbabwe

Although receiving on average higher rainfall than Namibia, much of Zimbabwe is classified as semi-arid. Rainfall has a considerable correlation with altitude and the 'lowveld' of the south-west and south-east is the driest region, suitable only for extensive livestock production. The most viable arable land lies in an arc from the centre to the eastern borders on the 'highveld'.[3]

During the British colonial period white settlers appropriated much of the best agricultural land removing resident people to 'native reserves', now known as communal land. In 1931 nearly 60 per cent of land was under white commercial freehold ownership with black farmers being confined to just over 20 per cent. Subsequent shifts in land allocation have led to a reduction in the area of commercial freehold land, which stood at 37 per cent in 1996. In late 1996 the Zimbabwean government announced plans to reduce this area further. With an annual population growth of just over 3 per cent per annum, pressure on viable arable land is growing and migration to lower rainfall areas has increased, putting ecological and social systems in these regions under stress.

As in Namibia, communal land users in Zimbabwe enjoy only usufruct rights to the natural resources on the land, and neither individually nor as groups have ownership over the land or its resources. The post-independence government has perpetuated the tenure situation of the colonial period with some modifications. Rural district councils (RDCs) may under certain circumstances lease land and exploit natural resources on behalf of communal residents. Below the district is an administrative sub-unit called the Ward, run by a Ward Development Committee (WADCO), and below that is the Village, with its own Development Committee (VIDCO). The delineation of WADCOs and VIDCOs does not necessarily follow traditional boundaries, while between and within rural districts there is considerable variation of human population density and natural resource availability. The administrative system introduced by the post-independence government has further marginalized the role of traditional leaders in land allocation and resource management.

Wildlife and Conservation Policy

There are important parallels in the development of wildlife and conservation policy in Namibia and Zimbabwe. In both countries prior to colonial rule, wildlife was managed in a number of direct and indirect ways. Game products were used for a wide variety of purposes including the provision of meat and clothing and for trade. But use was not indiscriminate. Chiefs and headmen had authority over the use of certain species and reserved areas of land as their own hunting domains. Religious and cultural taboos also limited the use of game animals, and the modes of hunting technology limited the success rate. During the colonial period, the state appropriated formal control over all wildlife, and passed legislation providing hunting rights to white settlers and visiting sport hunters. Blacks were alienated from wildlife as a resource by laws which removed control from traditional leaders and made what had been customary use of wildlife illegal. Even on white farms, the wildlife belonged to the state and commercial farmers tended to see wildlife as competing with their livestock and crop farming. On both communal and freehold land conversion of wild habitat to farmland and illegal use led to declines in wildlife numbers. Parallel to the centralization of control over wildlife, the state also created 'game reserves', often in the process removing black people from their land.

In the 1960s a radical shift in wildlife policy, away from a protectionist philosophy to one of conservation through sustainable use, occurred in both countries. The shift was away from state control to individual proprietorship for white commercial farmers, who could now benefit financially from the wildlife on their farms. Proprietorship and benefit were seen as key incentives for sustainable management. During the 1980s and 1990s both countries sought ways of extending proprietorship to farmers on communal lands, based on the legislation originally designed to benefit white commercial farmers.

Interestingly, the focus on the devolution of rights to use wildlife on private and communal lands has meant that other approaches to community conservation – particularly park outreach and the collaborative management of resources in protected areas (see Barrow and Murphree, Chapter 3, this volume) – have received little attention. The management of the extensive national park systems in both countries focuses on law enforcement and the types of initiative experimented with in East Africa, such as park revenue-sharing and resource-sharing (see Barrow et al., in Chapter 5, this volume), have not been as important in Namibia and Zimbabwe. In consequence the focus in this chapter is on communal lands and not PAs.

Namibia

Rights over wildlife were conferred on white commercial farmers in 1968 and consolidated in the Nature Conservation Ordinance (1975), which is still Namibia's primary legislation for protected areas and the conservation and utilization of wildlife. The Ordinance gave conditional ownership over certain of the more common species of game and limited use rights over other species through a permit system. Ownership and use rights were conditional upon a farmer owning land of an appropriate size and enclosed by game-proof fencing. Commercial farmers were thus able to hunt game for their own use, buy and sell game, cull for the commercial sale of meat and entertain foreign trophy hunters on their farms. None of these rights were extended to people in communal areas, who only had access to game through a state managed annual hunting season or permits for traditional feasts. Trophy hunting could take place on communal land, but the income went entirely to the state.

The changes in legislation had important results. Namibia now has about 75 per cent of its wildlife outside protected areas, and much of this on commercial farms. A multi-million pound industry has developed on commercial farms based on both consumptive and non-consumptive use of wildlife.

Driven by the need to remove discrimination and a belief that what worked on commercial land could work on communal land, the post-independence government developed a new conservation approach for communal land set out in the Policy on Wildlife Management, Utilization and Tourism in Communal Areas (MET 1995). Two of the important objectives of the policy were to enable rural communities to gain the same rights of use and benefit from wildlife as commercial farmers, and to gain rights over tourism concessions. These rights would be conferred on a community that formed a collective management institution called a 'conservancy'. This needed to be legally constituted, have clearly defined boundaries, a defined membership, a committee representative of the membership and a plan for the equitable distribution of benefits to members. The Nature Conservation Amendment Act of 1996 put this policy into effect, enabling the Minister of Environment and Tourism to declare communal area conservancies once he or she was satisfied that they met the conditions contained in the Act.

Zimbabwe

The 1975 Parks and Wild Life Act in Zimbabwe formalized the policy shift towards sustainable utilization by aiming 'to confer privileges on owners or occupiers of alienated land as custodians of wildlife, fish and plants' (Government of Zimbabwe 1975). The Act designates these 'owners or occupiers of alienated land' as 'appropriate authorities' over wildlife. Although this does not go so far as the Namibian legislation in conferring 'ownership' of certain species, the Zimbabwean Act still effectively makes farms and ranches proprietorial units for wildlife management. The Act allows for the exemption of specially protected species and for government to impose restriction orders in cases of abuse. As in Namibia, since the inception of the new approach, wildlife populations have increased on farms and ranches, their ecological health has improved and the wildlife industry makes a significant contribution to the Zimbabwean economy.[4]

Zimbabwean independence in 1980 gave government the opportunity to remove past discrimination and extend similar rights to communal farmers. A simple amendment to the Parks and Wild Life Act of 1975, enacted in 1982, allowed the Minister of Environment to appoint a rural district council 'to be the Appropriate Authority for such area of Communal Land as may be specified'. In 1989 the Zimbabwean Government published its Policy for Wildlife, which consolidated into official policy the thinking which had developed concerning wildlife use and incentives for sustainable management. Apart from commitments to protected areas and preservation of endangered species, the policy also contained the following statement: 'Outside the Parks and Wild Life Estate, government views wildlife as a resource capable of complementing domestic livestock and will favour neither one above the other in the development of the country. It will rather allow economic processes to determine the outcome of competition' (Government of Zimbabwe 1989: 7). As Murphree (1997a: 5) points out: 'This is a bold and radical statement, placing wildlife outside of parks in the realm of economics and land use rather than in the realm of conservation *per se*.'

The Conceptual Roots of Policy

Community conservation policy in Namibia and Zimbabwe rests on four conceptual foundations. None of these is unique to the two countries concerned, and all have their origins in earlier periods of policy discourse. However, their combination in policy and programme has led to the reputation of policy radicalism which the two countries hold.

Economic instrumentalism

The first of these roots is an approach to wildlife conservation based on sustainable use. Early policies based on intrinsic and recreational incentives for wildlife conservation were associated with the rapid conversion of wildlife habitat to agriculture and the elimination of wildlife to make way for livestock. It was concluded that the future of wildlife could only be ensured in a policy context where wildlife could be made an economically competitive form of land use. The assumption behind this was that most critical decisions regarding the allocation of land, resources and management investments are based primarily on economics, at both state and landholder levels. Policy should therefore seek to confer high economic values on wildlife and wild land.[5] It should also seek to provide a supportive investment climate through enduring entitlements which motivate the sustainable utilization of wildlife.[6]

There are corollaries to such economic instrumentalism. Firstly, it implies that in contexts where wildlife cannot be made economically competitive, its displacement by other forms of land use must be accepted. Secondly, it moves wildlife conservation objectives much closer to rural development objectives in a mosaic which accommodates both. This is made explicit, for instance, in Zimbabwe's policy statement on CAMPFIRE, where the ultimate objective of the programme is stated to be 'the realisation of an agrarian system able to optimise land-use patterns and maximise group and individual investment and effort' (Martin 1986: 19).

Devolutionism

A pragmatic understanding on the part of government wildlife professionals has influenced this component of policy in Namibia and Zimbabwe. Both countries share the colonial legacy of a highly centralized state system. Equally they have shared the experience, in both colonial and post-colonial phases, of governments with resources inadequate to meet the responsibilities of this status. In the wildlife sector, this has been manifestly clear with state agencies being hard pressed to manage the national parks, let alone carry out enforcement and extension functions. Legislation notwithstanding, land occupiers were in fact the *de facto* determinants of wildlife status and were generally in an oppositional relationship with government wildlife agencies. At the same time, by virtue of their in-place location and experience, these same people constituted a vast untapped potential for wildlife management. Devolution[7] of authority over and responsibility for wildlife resources outside the national parks to land owners and occupiers was thus an imperative which, coupled with long-term economic incentives, would result in improved habitat and species status. Societal interest in the preservation of endangered species and collaboration between landholders in the use of free-ranging species would be maintained by the oversight of the state wildlife authorities.

Collective proprietorship

The devolutionism and economic instrumentalism of Namibian and Zimbabwean thinking on wildlife policy resulted, as mentioned above, in the enactment in the 1960s and 1970s of legislation conferring strong proprietorial rights over wildlife to the owners of private land in the commercial agricultural sector. The initial success of this policy shift must be noted. The influence of this 'successful model' on further policy evolution has been profound. In both countries there were compelling reasons to transfer this successful model to communal areas. These constituted large proportions of total land surface and often held significant populations of wildlife. After independence, there were political imperatives for the extension of the policy beyond the commercial, and largely white, commercial farming sector.

However, the transfer of the model from private lands to communal lands posed important legal and institutional issues. Firstly, the proprietorship units analogous to farms and ranches in communal lands were communities of collective interest.[8] How could these communities be defined, and could they develop effective institutions of collective management? The answer to this question was met through the concept of a communal property regime, i.e. a regime in which a defined group collectively manages and exploits a common property resource within a defined jurisdiction.[9] To be effective such a regime requires strong internal legitimacy. Ideally its membership and jurisdiction should be self-defined. To be effective such a regime also requires external legitimacy. This raised a second important issue. How could tenurially strong units of collective proprietorship be created under conditions of state tenure in communal lands? The answer was, in part, to embark on a strategic process leading to legislative change. It was, however, iterative in its approach to process. This leads to the fourth conceptual foundation of community conservation policy in Namibia and Zimbabwe, discussed below.

Process as policy

Process can be regarded as the sequence of actions necessary to determine and implement policy. Process in this sense has certainly been a component of community conservation in Namibia and Zimbabwe. Policy development in the two countries has, however, gone beyond this to assign epistemological status to process. Process is seen as an integral component of policy, both as a source of its refinement and as an objective in its own right. Picking up on concerns expressed in debates within conservation biology and the social sciences about uncertainty, chaos, contingency and the predictive limitations of ecological and social science,[10] this perspective seeks to deal with these issues through a self-testing and self-evaluating policy process operating by negative feedback in relation to clearly defined objectives (Bell 1987: 3). From this perspective, policies are themselves experiments (Lee 1993: 9) and the development of resilient systems capable of adaptation becomes a major objective of policy.

In Namibia and Zimbabwe, this perspective has generally been termed 'adaptive management' although in practice it has also been 'adaptive policy'. Its incorporation into policy has injected an innovative dynamic into community conservation in the two countries. It has also set the stage for potential conflict with the conventional blueprint approaches of international development and conservation agencies. Finally, it has provided, in its stochastic stance towards change, the basis for implementation compromises. Some of the most important of these compromises are indicated in the sections on implementational history which follow.

Implementation and Outcomes: Zimbabwe

Strategic compromises

Drawing on these conceptual roots, Zimbabwe's community conservation policy was first presented in the Department of National Parks and Wild Life Management (DNPWLM) document *Communal Areas Management Programme for Indigenous Resources (CAMPFIRE)*. The revised version of this document (Martin 1986) was a highly detailed 'landmark' statement of objectives, structures and implementational requirements. While the 1982 amendment of the 1975 Parks and Wild Life Act permitted devolution of authority over wildlife to rural district councils (RDCs) the DNPWLM document proposed further devolution to communal proprietorial units within the RDCs. It suggested the formation by communities of 'Natural Resource Co-operatives with territorial rights over defined tracts of land called Communal Resource Areas within the Communal Lands' (ibid. p.17). These co-operatives would be formed under the provisions of the Co-operative Societies Act, giving their membership stronger tenurial rights than those provided under the Communal Lands Act. On the identification of communities, the document proposed a strategy of self-definition through dialogue and negotiation (ibid. pp. 33–5).

However, having gained ministerial endorsement, DNPWLM in 1986 had little means of putting the programme in place. A 'CAMPFIRE Agency' located in DNPWLM had been projected (ibid. pp. 30–31) but the cash-strapped department had no funds for this. DNPWLM thus turned to the agencies that had participated in the conceptual development of the programme for assistance in its initiation. Among these were the Centre for Applied Social Sciences (CASS) at the University of Zimbabwe, which had been assigned a socio-economic research and evaluation role (ibid. pp. 104–10); the WWF Multispecies Animal Production System Project in Zimbabwe; and the Zimbabwe Trust, a rural development NGO. This brought together a coalition of partners with different objectives. DNPWLM and WWF had conservation as their primary objective. The Zimbabwe Trust had a mission to promote rural economic and institutional development while CASS had a mandate for the application of social science research in the fields of rural development and governance. What was important was that these different formal objectives were complementary, and compatible both programmatically and conceptually. It is also worth noting that this coalition between DNPWLM and local Zimbabwean agencies meant that at inception CAMPFIRE was free from international donor influence. While its design drew on international ecological and social science scholarship, its origins were Zimbabwean.

Over the period 1986 to 1988 DNPWLM and its partner agencies engaged in proto-CAMPFIRE discussions with district councils and communities. In part this was to identify locations for the inception of the programme using two main criteria: a) voluntary interest in participation by communities and district councils; and b) the presence of wildlife populations capable of producing sustainable and economically significant revenues. Regarding the first of these criteria, the exercise involved extensive debates and meetings over many months. Given the colonial history of wildlife policy, the idea of the programme met with a great deal of scepticism. In some cases the idea was rejected categorically at communal meetings; in others it was side-lined by polite prevarication. However in certain communities the programme gained provisional acceptance after much debate.

The second criterion clearly reflects the weight given to economic incentives by the programme. Of the natural resources putatively addressed by CAMPFIRE, it was wildlife which could produce high returns with little capital investment in a short time frame through safari hunting. It followed that the 'test cases' should be selected in areas with high wildlife densities. In the event, the combination of these criteria produced an initial focus on communal lands in the Zambezi Valley and the south-east Lowveld.

During the 1986 to 1988 period DNPWLM and its CAMPFIRE partners were also involved in adjusting the programme proposals to the views of political and bureaucratic gatekeepers and the demands of institutional and administrative detail. For programme acceptance at this stage compromise was needed. These compromises reflect the 'pragmatic tactics' that have been a component of CAMPFIRE's evolution. Three compromises merit particular mention.

Natural resource co-operatives
This approach to creating tenurially strong communal regimes was quietly shelved. It became apparent that RDCs would not support such a development, seeing it (rightly) as a step which would remove areas of communal land from their authority and reduce their income. As recently established local authorities struggling to demonstrate their financial viability in the face of central government budgetary cutbacks, RDCs were not interested in any *de jure* devolution of what was, actually or potentially, their greatest source of revenue. The compromise was that RDCs would undertake a *de facto* devolution of wildlife management and revenue.

This rejection of a *de jure* tenure status for wildlife production units in communal lands created what is the major current weakness of the CAMPFIRE programme. It created pervasive uncertainties for producers regarding the security of any of their investments in wildlife management. It undermined one of CAMPFIRE's fundamental conceptual roots, as it meant communal land residents had fewer access rights to wildlife than commercial farmers. Finally, by placing devolution at the discretion of councils, it led to wide variations in the programme's operation and performance.

Defining the community
The definition and delineation of the natural resource co-operative was, in the programme document, to be a process of facilitation, negotiation and self-definition.

Once again, this notion was quietly shelved. Three main reasons were involved. Firstly, the process would be a massive and drawn-out exercise, for which neither time nor resources were available. Secondly, with the scrapping of the natural resources co-operative approach the legal imperative for delineation had disappeared. Thirdly and most importantly, the Ministry of Local Government and the RDCs were committed to the sub-district structures of WADCOs and VIDCOs which had been identified after Independence. They did not support the recognition of a different, socio-ecologically derived, set of boundaries and local organizations.

The result was again a compromise. CAMPFIRE would operate within the existing sub-district structures, and the localized unit of management and production would be the ward represented by the WADCO. RDCs would delegate to wards such aspects of proprietorship as their commitments to the programme implied. This was the easy way out; ready-made structures were on the ground and both councils and the Ministry of Local Government were comfortable with the approach. It carried with it the possibility of authority and responsibility for wildlife management being de-linked (see Barrow and Murphree, Chapter 3, this volume for a discussion of this problem).

Revenue distribution

Having won general acceptance for the programme through the above compromises, DNPWLM wished to ensure that revenues generated by producer communities would return to them. Wards bore the costs of production and they should receive associated benefits. As the legal proprietors of wildlife resources, it was the RDCs which entered into the lease arrangements which marketed wildlife and received the cheques from safari hunting concessionaires. They could not be allowed to appropriate such revenues for council purposes without compromising the incentives shaping producer behaviour. RDCs countered that they also met some of the costs of production such as the provision of infrastructure, administration and district-level wildlife management.

In this situation DNPWLM fell back on a tactic of conditionality. 'Guidelines' for implementation and revenue distribution would be attached to the conferment of Appropriate Authority status to RDCs. If these were not followed, the Appropriate Authority status would be withdrawn. The guidelines for revenue distribution specified that the RDCs could keep 15 per cent of revenue as a levy (or tax), up to 35 per cent for district wildlife management costs, and would distribute not less than 50 per cent of gross revenue to producer communities. The guidelines also specified that it was the wards that should decide on the use of this revenue.

With the three accommodations described above the programme gained the support of all the major stakeholders and CAMPFIRE was formally initiated in October 1988 when two RDCs – Guruve and Nyaminyami – were gazetted as appropriate authorities.[11] In the process of CAMPFIRE's transition, from concept to acceptance and initiation, DNPWLM had conceded on two fundamental points, the legal status and the self-definition of the communal units for management and production. It was forced to fall back on conditionality and intent as the instruments to produce its intended institutional profile. In so doing it produced a programme with inherent defects. At the same time it created the opportunity for an approach which, for all its defects, had the potential for evolution to a close approximation of its conceptual ideal. Whether the pragmatism of these negotiated compromises was appropriate is a matter for debate. While it can be argued that they introduced flaws which will ultimately be fatal for the programme, it can also be argued that without them CAMPFIRE would still be only 'on the drawing board'.

Outcomes: a qualified success

With the conferment of appropriate authority status to the Nyaminyami and Guruve Districts came their right to receive 1988 hunting revenues. The deposit of these monies into the two RDC accounts had a dramatic effect in other areas. The historically underdeveloped but wildlife rich districts on the periphery of the country lined up for inclusion in the programme. By the end of 1989 seven additional districts had received appropriate authority status. In the national press and in public circles CAMPFIRE was hailed as a leap forward in rural development and the programme received the ultimate approbation when the 1990 election manifesto of the ZANU-PF ruling party claimed that CAMPFIRE had been a party innovation!

By the end of 1991 12 districts were in the programme and collectively grossed US$1.1million in revenue for that year. By 1995 there were 25 districts in the programme and revenues had continued to move upwards.[12] A national CAMPFIRE Association was formed, with the objective of promoting the wildlife interests of RDCs at the political centre and also serving as an association of producer communities. The Association has played an important role in making communal land wildlife producers an important political constituency of government, a dimension often neglected in community conservation programmes in other countries. It has been less successful in its role as a producer association, since its formal membership remains the RDCs, not the producer wards.

Since its inception CAMPFIRE has attracted large amounts of donor funding, particularly from USAID. Some of this funding has been directed to DNPWLM, but much of it has gone to the non-governmental organizations supporting the programme. More recently a large proportion of donor funding has been channelled through the CAMPFIRE Association to CAMPFIRE RDCs and communities for the enhancement of institutional capacities and natural resource microproject development. This has been a mixed blessing. Donor funding has assisted in the rapid expansion of the programme, enabled the NGOs to expand their capacities and has contributed to a vastly enlarged training and extension programme in RDCs. At the same time these large amounts of donor funds have had a tendency in certain circles to erode CAMPFIRE's vision of self-directed and self-sufficient development, and in a few districts and wards it is probably true to say that CAMPFIRE is as much about leveraging donor funds as it is about sustainable wildlife management and production. Donors have been sensitive to the national proprietorship of the programme and Zimbabwean agencies have carefully guarded this status. In the on-going relationship between the programme and donors, however, the issue of adjusting the expectations of donors' bureaucratic cultures to the adaptive dynamism of the programme remains a challenge.

CAMPFIRE's performance from 1989 to 1995 can be considered a success, if the criteria used are geographical spread, RDC acceptance and participation, public and political endorsement, revenue generation and the devolution of the control of this revenue to RDCs. To judge it a success in terms of the realization of its central conceptual objectives – the creation of economic incentives to make wildlife a competitive form of land use where this made ecological and economic sense, and to create strong communal proprietorial natural resource regimes – is more problematic since the record shows a mix of results (also see Chapters 15 and 16, this volume). The reasons for this are now explored.

Constraints

Of the factors which have constrained success, seven of the most important are discussed here.

a) *Devolution through persuasion and conditionality rather than statute.* The delegation of proprietorship to RDCs, on the basis of intent and guidelines for further delegation to producer communities, gave them wide discretion. The threat of the withdrawal of appropriate authority status in cases of non-conformity was relatively hollow, as RDCs soon realized. As a result some RDCs have appropriated the bulk of the revenues generated by their producer communities, made promises which they have not kept, marginalized participation in wildlife planning and management by communities, and created hypertrophic district-level wildlife management structures which serve the interests of RDC bureaucracies. In such instances the 'decentralization' of CAMPFIRE has become 'recentralization' to a district-level elite (Murombedzi 1992). The result has been hostility to the CAMPFIRE programme, mistrust of the councils concerned and increasing intolerance of wildlife.

b) *Imposition of pre-existing administrative units.* The CAMPFIRE concept rests on the self-definition and voluntary participation of local-level natural resource management entities. This was compromised by the designation of council wards as the communal production units. In some instances, where the socio-ecological topography[13] was suitable, this compromise worked. In many instances, however, ward boundaries do not match producer groups. Wards are often internally differentiated socially and ecologically and lack the cohesion to motivate consensual entry into the programme (Dzingirai 1994; Moore 1996). This has been the case particularly in wards with histories of recent in-migration. Councils, on the other hand, have had strong economic motivations to expand wildlife land and in several instances have imposed their district versions of the programme, relocating settlement to make way for contiguous wildlife areas.[14]

c) *The differential contexts of economic incentive.* The programme assumes that high wildlife values, combined with collective interests, can create the incentives for individual or household participation. However, the programme has not fully addressed intra-communal differentiation or the difference between household and communal economic strategies. A community may, for instance, reach the conclusion that buffalo provide greater collective economic value for the use of their range than cattle and have a collective incentive to move into wildlife production. This value is, however, realized through collective receipts and finds its way back to households through the filter of communal decision-making. At the household level, the farmer, while recognizing the higher value of buffalo in comparison with cattle, may nevertheless wish to opt for cattle since cattle are individually owned and the disposal of worth is at his or her sole discretion. Murombedzi (1994 and Chapter 16, this volume) has suggested that under smallholder agricultural conditions prevailing in communal lands cattle are a main form of household accumulation and that unless CAMPFIRE revenues at household levels are at levels sufficient to off-set the perceived loss of the accumulative potential of livestock, the programme is likely to encounter opposition at these levels.

d) *Resource to demand ratios.* This is an issue closely related to (c). CAMPFIRE benefits in cash and kind at household levels are highest where human population densities are low and wildlife resources high. Within the programme districts these ratios differ widely. In 1993 all wards in the programme earning above Z$200,000 had population densities of less than 20 persons per square kilometre (see Bond, Chapter 15, this volume). This could lead to the conclusion that the programme can truly be successful only in certain favourable demand/resource ratio contexts, especially if it continues to be based primarily on economic incentive.

e) *Devolution of revenue appropriation.* The devolution of revenue appropriation from state to councils and from councils to producer communities (at various levels, see (a) above) is demonstrable in the programme's history. Whether this has meant a devolution of resource value in real terms has been questioned. At the national level the government has forgone direct revenues from safari hunting but has maintained the base for a rapidly expanding tourism industry which is taxed, suggesting a win/win arrangement for both the state and district councils. At the council level the programme has provided revenues from a commodity which previously had little financial value to councils, leading Hill (1996: 116) to make the perceptive comment that CAMPFIRE 'not only is a wildlife program; it is also very much a rural taxation program'. At the locality level there remains the possibility that real appropriation of value can be siphoned away, if government uses the development of local infrastructure through wildlife revenues as an excuse to avoid its commitments to provide these through central funding.

f) *The politics of resource appropriation.* The high and escalating values of the wildlife resource have had the effect of intensifying political conflict over the appropriation of these values at community, district and national levels. Within communities and districts the programme has brought into sharper focus competing interests drawn on class, gender[15] and ethnic lines. At the national level the economic performance of the industry has attracted the attention of the political elite and their private sector allies, who seek to gain a higher share of its earnings through patronage, shrewd negotiation or bureaucratic re-centralization. CAMPFIRE, which from its conceptualization had profound political implications, has through its relative success now become a high-profile arena of political manoeuvring with outcomes which will remain dynamic and dependent on the strength of its constituency.

g) *Vertical compartmentalization in legislation and agency responsibility.* Legislatively CAMPFIRE has been based largely on the Parks and Wild Life Act, as amended. Other resources, notably forestry and water resources, fall under different legislation and are served by other government agencies. Beyond this a number of other government ministries have jurisdictional responsibilities relevant to the programme, including the Ministry of Agriculture. This vertical compartmentalization of resource jurisdictions is one of the reasons why CAMPFIRE, in concept and name a holistic programme encompassing all natural resources, has in practice been a programme focused on wildlife, fisheries and tourism. Devolution as conceptualized in CAMPFIRE requires a much wider legislative base than the Parks and Wild Life Act. Strategically, the programme needs to shift its government linkages to a broader spectrum of ministries. The CAMPFIRE Association is aware of this, and is attempting to form alliances with farmer associations and closer communication with the Forestry Commission and the Ministries of Agriculture and Lands.

The seven issues discussed above are among the primary factors constraining the performance of the programme. They are CAMPFIRE's clay feet, arising from conceptual gaps, implementational compromise and, paradoxically, its elements of success. They have been outlined in a form which masks the fact that the programme has made progress in dealing with some of them. Particularly in regard to the first two it should be noted that revenue retention by councils has progressively dropped and that imposition in implementation is diminishing (Madzudzo 1997). These issues nevertheless must remain high on CAMPFIRE's agenda if its goals are to be fully realized.

Implementation and Outcomes: Namibia

Developing policy

In drafting a policy for devolving rights over wildlife and tourism to rural communities, the Ministry of Environment and Tourism (MET) had to solve the problem of transferring proprietorship over wildlife (often a mobile resource) and tourism (a 'resource' linked to land use and land rights) to groups of individuals who do not own the land and whose traditional management systems and leadership structures have been largely undermined. The policy had to find ways of defining *who* should be given proprietorship and how far these rights should extend spatially. It had to ensure that the existing or emerging elite would not capture the process at community level and appropriate the benefits that were expected to accrue. It also had to ensure that while devolving proprietorship to the local level, the State retained a regulatory role so that if the new system was abused, the rights could be withdrawn. Five major influences shaped policy.

1. The pioneering work carried out by the Namibian NGO, Integrated Rural Development and Nature Conservation (IRDNC), in the north-west of the country. IRDNC helped local communities establish a network of community game guards and established a pilot project to bring tourism revenue to a local community as an incentive for conservation of local wildlife. IRDNC's work yielded important lessons about the need to combine responsibility and control over a resource with financial benefit, and to link this to local conservation ethics as incentives for conservation. Local leaders and other community members were concerned at the decline in wildlife in the early 1980s and agreed to take on some responsibility for conserving wildlife before there was any prospect of economic benefits. Emphasis has since shifted towards economic benefit and

legally sanctioned proprietorship over wildlife to reinforce the existing conservation ethic and sense of ownership and responsibility (Jones, Chapter 11, this volume). Other lessons were that benefits need to go directly to the community and the importance of bottom-up approaches which involve the whole community and not just traditional leaders.[16]

2. Theory about the design and implementation of common property resource management regimes (Ostrom 1990; Berkes 1989) helped answer some of the questions of how to devolve proprietorship to a group of individuals over a common resource on land owned by the State.

3. The experiences of neighbouring countries, particularly Zimbabwe and its CAMPFIRE programme, provided models to follow and to avoid. Of particular importance was the CAMPFIRE experience of the mismatch between the unit of authority (rural district councils) and the unit of responsibility (producer communities). CAMPFIRE personnel also advised the MET to avoid a division of revenue between government and community, as this would represent an inequitable tax on wildlife as a land use.

4. Socio-ecological surveys carried out by the MET in a number of rural areas (Brown 1991; Brown and Jones 1994; Rodwell et al. 1995) provided policy drafters with a picture of the problems faced by rural communities with wildlife and conservation. It became clear that rights of proprietorship and benefit would solve or mitigate a number of these problems. However, these surveys and other work have concentrated on large mammals (particularly those that attract tourists and hunters) and it has recently become clear that policy has neglected indigenous knowledge about and use of floral and smaller faunal resources (Sullivan 1999). This has meant that the roles played by women as users and managers of natural resources have been obscured and may have consolidated male control over both resources and management institutions (Sullivan 2000).

5. The policy drafters also drew upon an existing MET policy on commercial area conservancies. This promoted the collaboration of individual freehold ranch owners in managing wildlife collectively across their farms. The policy envisaged extending the approach to communal farmers, but did not address the fact that while individual freehold ranchers already had rights over wildlife, these were still denied to communal farmers. Policy drafters overcame this problem by making the formation of a conservancy the mechanism by which communal area residents could gain rights over wildlife.

The above influences gave rise to an approach which makes provision for the collective management of wildlife and tourism by a group of individuals who form a common property resource management institution, the conservancy. The policy deals with the question of *who* should receive proprietorship, by leaving communities to define themselves. It expects that individuals with access to the same land and other natural resources, with perhaps a shared culture and a commitment to work together on wildlife and tourism management will combine to form the conservancy.[17] The incentives for them to combine are gaining control over a resource they were alienated from; deriving direct benefits from the resource; and increased risk spreading against drought. The rights and the benefits go directly to the defined group of individuals who make up the conservancy, which has defined boundaries.

The rights are devolved directly from central government to a local community and benefits are not handed out by a government or other agency, but are earned by the community and accrue directly to them.

This approach involved a number of conscious decisions, and in some cases compromises, each with its own set of implications.

Communities define themselves

The decision to ask communities to define themselves, while meeting an important requirement of institutional design for communal property resource management, contains inherent risks that existing land and resource disputes between communities could indefinitely delay conservancy formation. It is tempting and easier to demarcate 'communities' using arbitrary administrative boundaries. Border disputes have delayed the registration of several conservancies. Design principles for common property resource management institutions (Ostrom 1990; Murphree 1991) point to the need for relatively small groups of individuals in order to ensure ease of decision-making, transparency and accountability. Asking communities to define themselves carries the risk that a relatively large group of people will form a conservancy and then face a number of practical organizational problems.

Resource tenure not land tenure

Secure tenure for communities or individuals over land is an important foundation for sustainable resource management, whether wildlife, grazing or forest resources. MET was only able to grant proprietorship over wildlife and tourism, not over the land itself. Yet once a conservancy was established as a common property institution for wildlife and tourism management, what was to stop individuals or groups of people from moving on to the conservancy's land and establishing incompatible uses? Indeed what was to stop government from establishing a 'development' project on the conservancy's land contrary to the conservancy's own land use planning? One view within the ministry was that nothing should be attempted until the government had produced a new land policy.[18] The prevailing view was that it was better to put something in place, which the land policy would then have to accommodate, and which might even shape the land policy. This contained the risk that the land policy would contain features that would undermine the conservancy approach.

Ignoring emerging regional councils

The policy does not assign a role for Namibia's regional councils who are looking for revenue-generating opportunities and to establish their power and patronage in the regions. Some policy makers feared that the regional councils would try to capture the conservancy process and that the CAMPFIRE experience of extractive councils would be replicated. This omission of a major political stakeholder, although rectified to some extent in legislation, had significant implications for the implementation phase discussed later.

Policy and projects in parallel

A key strategic decision was to develop the enabling policy and legal environment at the same time as establishing projects with local communities. These local-level activities focused on giving back to communities some measure of responsibility over wildlife through community game guard networks and involving communities in decision-making where possible, and enabling communities to gain income from tourism on their land within existing legislation. The aim was threefold: to develop a sense of responsibility for wildlife before substantial benefits accrued; to demonstrate to communities that benefits from wildlife were in fact possible; and to develop a constituency of local people who would support the proposed policy changes.

In forging ahead with these proposals proponents of a community-based approach were conscious that the need for institutional reform within MET was being ignored. For the first five years after independence the Ministry remained largely unchanged in its staff composition, particularly at senior levels. The majority of MET personnel were still steeped in conservation as preservation and ideologies which emphasized law enforcement as the primary mode of conservation. They viewed rural Africans as largely incapable of managing resources sustainably and believed in 'top-down' planning methods. The community-based programme was being driven by a small policy and planning directorate within MET and not by the powerful parks and wildlife directorate. The reformers took a decision not to pursue the institutional-ization of community-based conservation within MET but to concentrate on policy and legislative change, in the belief that once conservancies began emerging change within MET would be inevitable.

One result of this was that communities received conflicting messages from reformers and traditionalists. More importantly, the decision meant that when policy began to change there were significant conceptual differences about the goals of the approach within the ministry. The policy and planning directorate viewed propri-etorship and benefits as incentives for sustainable management while the parks and wildlife directorate viewed benefits as an end in themselves. This had important consequences for the development of the legislation which gave effect to the new policy.

Donor involvement

During the phase of local-level project development the planners sought donor funding for project implementation. In the early stages donor influence was fairly benign. The main donor at the time was WWF (both US and International) and it allowed in-country personnel to act as project managers with occasional supervisory visits from WWF staff from Washington or Gland. Later, as the Namibian activities began to take on a more programmatic approach, funding was secured from United States Agency for International Development (USAID) as there was a significant overlap of interests and agendas between MET and USAID (see USAID 1995). However, over time, it became clear that MET and USAID had different approaches and these became sources of conflict. Institutionally USAID had an interventionist approach to project management and wanted rapid results. At one stage USAID wanted to withdraw funds from a particular community and use them more 'strategi-cally' where there was more chance of success. This was resisted by project imple-menters and the community concerned went on to become the first in Namibia to have a communal conservancy registered. Clearly, the time frames and criteria for the estimation of possible success for the donor and the Namibian agencies were quite different. The process model of the Namibian agencies was subsequently justified by the outcomes achieved.

From policy to legislation

Once policy had been passed by Cabinet in March 1995, the next step was to give effect to the policy through legislation. As the parks and wildlife directorate within MET would administer the legislation it had to be involved in drafting a legislative amendment. This was when the disadvantages of the MET's policy and planning directorate forging ahead without institutionalizing community-based conservation became apparent. During discussions it became clear that the goal of the parks and wildlife directorate was to enable all people in communal areas, and not simply 'producer communities', to benefit from wildlife utilization. Representatives of this directorate insisted that legislation make provision for a second institution, a Wildlife Council, which would enable those people not incorporated within a conservancy to gain benefits. A Wildlife Council (GRN 1996a and b) would comprise a mix of central government staff and local representatives and would be advised by the minister on how to spend its revenues. A MET internal policy document on Wildlife Councils envisages that income will be used for general rural development projects.

Such an institution clearly does not combine proprietorship with management, cost and benefit. If operationalized it will manifest many of the problems inherent within CAMPFIRE, i.e. that revenue derived from a 'producer' community which suffers the costs of living with wildlife may not reach that community. There is no special reward for a community investing in conserving the resource if the benefits are widely spread across a region. The Wildlife Council at a regional level holds authority, but those at the local level are expected to manage the resource.

Reluctantly, and in order to move ahead with the legislation, the policy and planning directorate compromised and Wildlife Councils were included in the amendment. They effectively replaced the regional natural resource management committees that had been proposed in the new policy, as mechanisms for regional coordination between MET, conservancies, NGOs and others involved in community-based conservation (MET 1995).

From legislation to implementation

The legislation providing for conservancies was gazetted in June 1997 and by January 1998, the Minister of Environment and Tourism had approved one conservancy and another was awaiting his signature. Given the approach of working with local communities and changing the enabling policy and legal environment at the same time, conservancies might have been expected to emerge more rapidly and in greater numbers. Some of the delay can be ascribed to the demands placed upon communities by the legislation to hold meetings and register all members. But delays have also been caused because of the strategic decisions and compromises described above.

1. *Communities define themselves.* In Kunene Region three emerging conservancies are disputing 'ownership' of parcels of land which have been allocated according to a Headman's Ward system. Some residents of these areas wish to be included in the conservancy being established by the neighbouring ward, and insist that they fall under the jurisdiction of the neighbouring headman. The MET response has been to inform these communities that it is willing to register these conservancies without the disputed areas pending adjudication by the Regional Council and Traditional Authority.

2. *Resource tenure, not land tenure.* The lack of clearly defined group rights over land has prevented emerging conservancies in the Omusati and Caprivi Regions from asserting their claims to decide on land use within the proto-conservancies. Other people have laid claim to parts of the conservancy and in one case intervention by the President and the Deputy Minister of Environment and Tourism was necessary to resolve the issue.

3. *Ignoring regional councils.* In the Kunene and Caprivi Regions, governors and regional councillors were unwilling to endorse conservancies, as required by legislation, because they believed they should have a greater say in the approval process. A meeting between MET officials and all 14 governors has helped to develop a more positive attitude.

4. *Policy and projects in parallel.* In Kunene Region MET local staff, in alliance with the traditional leadership, pushed to install a Wildlife Council while a number of conservancies were emerging. The traditional leadership was reported to want to use the Wildlife Council to control where conservancies are established and who should be members. Pressure from communities wanting to form conservancies led to a reduction in efforts to form a Wildlife Council and one has yet to be established.

The costs of not institutionalizing the idea of community conservation within MET at an earlier stage are now becoming apparent. Nationwide, MET staff require further training in conservancy extension and need to view working with communities as part of their day-to-day work. While there are attempts to do this, progress remains slow, with the result that many communities are not yet receiving the support that they require from the Ministry.

In spite of these constraints, the conservancy programme in Namibia has made headway. By December 1998, four conservancies had been gazetted. Their establishment provides an incentive for conservancy applications by other communities, particularly those which border them. Within these gazetted conservancies, their new status will set the stage for a phase of intra-communal institutional development, with its attendant processes of conflict, compromise and innovation.

Concluding Observations

As noted earlier in this chapter, the greatest single common antecedent and determinant in the policy evolution of community conservation in Namibia and Zimbabwe was their shared experience of successfully devolving authority and responsibility for wildlife to white commercial farmers on private lands during the 1950s and 1960s. This has set community conservation policy in the two countries apart from that of many other countries discussed in this volume in two important dimensions. Firstly, it is a policy directed at wildlife management, use and conservation on land outside state managed conservation areas and has never had the preoccupation with parks/people relationships which characterizes community conservation policy elsewhere. Secondly, the achievements of landowners with strong tenure and access rights has led policy to emphasize the replication of these rights for resource users in communal lands under state control. This has placed Namibian and Zimbabwean community conservation policy at the devolutionist extremity of the typology discussed by Barrow and Murphree (Chapter 3).

The means of producing these rights, under communal tenure conditions, is conceptually identical in both countries. This was a communal common property regime of defined membership and jurisdiction legitimated internally by self-definition and societally by legal recognition. Where the two policies have diverged has been the strategy to achieve this goal. In Zimbabwe, with a clearly delineated system of sub-district structures of local government in place, the strategy has been to accept pre-existing ward level units as the equivalent of communities of proprietorship and to confer legal proprietorial status only to the level of their rural district council superstructure. While this strategic compromise had the advantage of gaining the rapid acceptance of the bureaucratic and political elite and short-circuiting protracted negotiations on the delineation of communal proprietorial regimes, it compromised the principle of full devolution to self-defined units of management and production. In Namibia, with sub-units of local government not yet statuted, the strategy has been to follow concept more closely, legislate for the provision of strong access rights to conservancies and allow for their delineation through communal negotiation and determination. This has required longer time frames for implementation but has resulted in a closer approximation to the model used on private land.

Both strategies have their risks. The Zimbabwean strategic compromise carries the risk of devolution stalling at the RDC level, unfulfilled aspirations and ultimate policy failure. Murombedzi (Chapter 16) explores this scenario. Namibian strategy, in legislating resource rights in advance of legislation on land tenure, carries with it the risk that other sectoral interests will ultimately undermine a pre-emptive sectoral initiative. Both sets of risk have, however, been calculated risks. Policy in both countries has aimed at putting in place a process of increasing values for wildlife and escalating communal assertiveness in claiming this value. It has set an agenda for devolved, communal wildlife management. This process has been in conflict with powerful bureaucratic and sectional interests, leading to oscillation in government policy stances over time.[19] It has, however, achieved momentum by seizing opportunities at times when the general political ethos in each country was emphasizing civil governance and local self-sufficiency. The future of this process will be determined by the direction that this national political ethos takes in both countries and the way that it is articulated. For the present, however, it is worth noting that community conservation policy in Namibia and Zimbabwe, with its emphasis on *policy-as-process*, has shown the potential to be an influence on the direction that this ethos takes.

Notes

[1] In writing this chapter the authors have drawn on materials published elsewhere, i.e. Jones (1997) and Murphree (1997a).

[2] For further detail see Brown (1996), Dewdney (1996), MET (1994a) and MET (1994b).

[3] For more detailed discussion see Murphree and Cumming (1993).

[4] See Cumming (1990) and Child (1988).

[5] Policy itself cannot confer high economic value directly, but it can create enabling conditions for this. This includes the removal of subsidies or taxation structures which favour livestock or crop production, restrictions on the use and marketing of wildlife which do not apply to livestock and the encouragement of a wildlife and tourism industry with the required infrastructure.

[6]By 'investment climate' we refer to a central component of conservation, the willingness to accept current costs (either direct or opportunity costs) for future benefit. For a discussion of 'enduring entitlements', i.e. tenure, see Chapter 3 in this volume.

[7]We distinguish between deconcentration and devolution. Deconcentration is a structural dispersal of state control to sub-units of the state in a bureaucratic hierarchy. Devolution involves the surrender of elements of authority and responsibility to units with non-state constituencies.

[8]On the specification of these 'communities of collective interest', see Barrow and Murphree (Chapter 3).

[9]These can be 'communities of place' or 'communities of use'. See Barrow and Murphree (Chapter 3) for further discussion. See also McLain and Jones (1997).

[10]See Ludwig et al. (1993), Holling (1993), Holling and Meffe (1996) and Lele and Norgaard (1996).

[11]This highly condensed history does not mention the proto-CAMPFIRE experience of Mahenye Ward in the Chipinge District. For more detail on this case, see Murphree (Chapter 12).

[12]While increases in CAMPFIRE revenues have been dramatic over time when calculated in Zimbabwe dollars they are less so when calculated in US dollars due to the falling exchange rate of the Zimbabwean dollar. For a detailed analysis, see Bond (Chapter 15).

[13]For a discussion of social topography see Murphree (1996) and Turner (1996).

[14]For further description and discussion, see Madzudzo (1997) and Alexander and McGregor (1996). Patel (1998) cites such instances as revealing that CAMPFIRE compromises human rights.

[15]For a case study of the gender impact of CAMPFIRE see Nabane (1997).

[16]For further detail on IRDNC see Durbin et al. (1997), IRDNC (1996), IRDNC (1997), Nott et al. (1993) and Odendaal (1995).

[17]On tourism in communal contexts see Ashley and Barnes (1996), MET (1995) and NACOBTA (1995).

[18]A 'White Paper' on land policy has been produced, but is still under discussion (GRN 1997).

[19]In Namibia, parliamentary debates continue to provoke discussion over conservancy policy, especially in contexts where it is seen as enhancing or diminishing the interests of a particular political constituency. In Zimbabwe a change of the minister and permanent secretary in the Ministry of Environment and Tourism in the second half of 1995 introduced a new regime of government direction which was more centrist in its stances. While the new regime did not challenge CAMPFIRE *per se*, it introduced regulations and procedures which further restricted the range of effective control exercised over wildlife by Appropriate Authorities, both RDCs and private landowners. The Ministry also aligned itself with the Ministry of Local Government, which favoured the appropriation of CAMPFIRE revenues for council determined budgets rather than their return to wildlife producing communities. At the beginning of 1998 the pendulum had swung back to a more devolutionist approach by government. A new minister and permanent secretary in a reconstituted ministry (now the Ministry of Mines, Environment and Tourism) took a market-oriented stance that the wildlife and tourism industry should be encouraged through the removal of any unnecessary bureaucratic restrictions which increased transaction costs. It also stated its intention to push for further legislative reform to devolve authority over wildlife to sub-district levels. In a speech delivered on 26 February 1998 the new minister (Simon Khaya Moyo) suggested that this thrust was in line with government's 'decentralization programme through which communities will assume greater control over their own development'. Observing that 'Over the years communities have attained the capacity to run financially viable ventures, to count game, to market their products, to prioritize their needs and to make rational decisions,' he stated that government felt that 'communities should be trusted to deal with such challenges without being micromanaged by the DNPWLM'. As a result government was 'considering further devolution of Appropriate Authority below the RDC level to villages and wards. This will be beneficial to RDCs, central government and the communities. We envision a situation where communities eventually have the legislative backup when they decide to go into business transactions and to negotiate deals on their own without needing an overlord in the form of an RDC, which should ideally concentrate on being a regulatory body' (Moyo 1998).

5

The Evolution of Community Conservation Policy & Practice in East Africa

EDMUND BARROW, HELEN GICHOHI & MARK INFIELD

Introduction

Community-based approaches to conservation in East Africa (Kenya, Tanzania and Uganda) have evolved through complex interactions between factors operating at many levels. Historical events, before and since independence, have influenced systems of natural resource use and the development of conservation policies and institutions. Characteristics held in common have also had a bearing on community-based approaches, leading to a focus on protected areas. This contrasts with Southern Africa, where the emphasis has been on the management of wildlife resources on private and communal lands. In recent years, differences in circumstance and experience between countries has influenced both the development and implementation of community conservation, creating a range of policies and programmes.

Tanzania is the largest of the three countries (945,090 km²), but has the lowest human population densities (33.6 per km²). About half of the country is semi-arid land. Although three-quarters of Kenya's 580,370 km² of land is classified as arid or semi-arid, it has a higher population density (49.7 per km²). Uganda, the smallest of the countries at 236,580 km², has both the highest population density (106.7 per km²), and the highest proportion of land with agricultural potential (75 per cent). Only 2 per cent of Kenya is forested, while the figures for Tanzania and Uganda are 36.8 per cent and 27 per cent respectively. There are a total of 36 National Parks and Game Reserves in Kenya occupying 43,673 km² (7.5 per cent of the surface area); 32 National Parks and Game Reserves in Tanzania occupying 151,496 km² (16 per cent of surface area); and 26 National Parks and Game Reserves in Uganda occupying 20,650 km² (8.7 per cent of surface area) (FAO 1988; IUCN 1990; Harcourt and Collins 1992; World Conservation Monitoring Centre 1992; World Conservation Union 1996).

It is not possible to present a detailed account of the biological resources of the region, or of its historical and current circumstances.[1] A range of climatic and geographical characteristics give rise to habitats ranging from coral reefs to miombo woodlands, and from montane forests to deserts. This diversity is challenged by the need to provide livelihoods for a population growing at 3.5 per cent per annum. Land is cleared, forests cut down, and the frontiers of cultivation pushed into drier lands to meet this demand at a high cost for the environment and biodiversity. It is in this nexus of competing demands, and the need to secure livelihoods, conserve biodiversity, and maintain functioning ecosystems, that community conservation seeks to play a significant role.

The low agricultural potential and, in historical times, low human population densities over much of the region have been central to the development of conservation in East Africa. Occupied largely by pastoralists, the lands which contained the bulk of the region's large mammal populations were not generally settled under colonial rule, and remained under customary management and tenure regimes until recently. By contrast, the settler communities in Southern Africa alienated extensive areas of wildlife-rich terrain and converted it into private farms and cattle ranches, establishing a tradition of rangeland management and private ownership. These differing histories of settlement have had a great influence on the evolution of conservation policies in the two regions.[2]

Since gaining independence during the early 1960s, each country has pursued different development strategies, though agriculture remains important to all three. Kenya has diversified into tourism and light industry. Tanzania has also developed an important tourism industry, which includes safari hunting, though agriculture continues to be the most important economic activity. Uganda, which fell from relative prosperity in the mid-1960s to a state of social and economic collapse by 1985, remains dependent on agriculture, and has little tourism. All three countries are characterized by large and often inefficient bureaucracies, stagnant or declining per capita incomes and corruption. All have undertaken structural adjustment programmes to reduce government expenditure and all have adopted decentralization and privatization policies.

A large number of state agencies and local-level institutions manage the East African environment. This complexity calls for conservation that is sensitive and responsive, and for effective policy coordination. However, coordination has been weak as environmental issues are handled by several vertically structured government bodies which have resisted horizontal integration. The lack of policy coordination has led to confused actions in which different departments may pursue conflicting goals (Southgate and Hulme 2000). Both conservation and development have suffered because of this.

While extensive areas in East Africa are legally conserved, their gazetting and subsequent management failed to consider the needs and interests of the disenfranchized local resource users that were displaced. Such policies alienated rural people,[3] destroyed local responsibility for the environment and placed it in the hands of distant national governments. Most community conservation initiatives have been based around such protected areas, the majority of which were savanna. Less attention was given to forest reserves and wetland and marine systems though the gradual emergence of collaborative management arrangements has recently started to change this (Scott 1996a; Hinchley and Turyomurugyendo 1998; Nurse and Kabamba 1998). Tanzania is presently the only East African country which permits hunting. This is carried out by national and international hunting companies in areas controlled by the Wildlife Division. Few benefits accrue back to the local communities who live in such areas, with a few notable exceptions.[4]

Ownership, control of, and access to land and resources is becoming the single most contentious political issue in East Africa. Currently, each country has processes in place for the reform of tenure and land-use policies. In Tanzania and Uganda the process is advanced, with draft tenure reform statutes before the parliaments. It appears that conservation agencies have had little involvement in these processes, particularly with regard to recognizing 'conservation' as a valid form of land use. Issues concerning tenure are similar and include the role of the state in land ownership; the future of customary forms of land ownership; the extent to which land regulation should be democratized; and the extent to which a market in land should be encouraged (Wily 1997).

This chapter reviews the development of community conservation in East Africa, and examines factors influencing the evolution of policy, and the effects of circumstances, opportunities and constraints on its implementation. It is derived from a detailed study of community conservation in East Africa to which those seeking a fuller account are referred (Barrow et al. 1998).

The Development of Community Conservation Policy in East Africa

The development of policy and legislation for community conservation in East Africa has been rapid since the late 1980s. Though visionary, early efforts to develop policies and structures for community conservation in the late 1970s lacked continuity and institutional commitment (Barrow et al. 1995c). The wave of protected area outreach projects initiated by NGOs in the 1980s responded to the growing recognition that law enforcement approaches to conservation were not only failing, but were increasingly difficult to justify in moral terms and may be questionable in international human rights terms. The primary interest of international environmental NGOs such as AWF, IUCN and WWF (all of which have worked extensively in the region) was the conservation of nature, particularly in protected areas. Community conservation programmes around Amboseli and Tsavo National Parks in Kenya, Serengeti, Tarangire and Arusha National Parks in Tanzania, and Lake Mburo in Uganda are all good examples of the kind of early projects implemented by NGOs (Berger 1988; Barrow et al. 1995a and b). Usually such projects were funded by bilateral and multilateral donor agencies, often from development budgets, and were intended to support conservation authorities. Little interest was shown in conservation on private or customary lands, and the focus remained on the management of wildlife in protected areas.

International trends toward decentralization and strengthening the role of communities in natural resource management placed pressure on governments to adopt community approaches to the protection and management of biodiversity (see Adams and Hulme, Chapter 2, this volume). Declining government budgets and structural adjustment induced retrenchment of government staff and led conservation organizations to understand that the management of protected areas would be increasingly difficult without community support. Partnerships between conservation authorities and NGOs provided an initial basis for this 're-tooling' of agencies founded on preservationist and law-enforcement approaches. Though the development of community conservation policy has tended to be uncoordinated and, in many cases, has been driven by donor funding, a rich variety of approaches has emerged, often in response to specific situations on the ground. However, policies in Kenya and Uganda show several similarities reflecting the influence of donor involvement. In Tanzania, the process has been somewhat different, with TANAPA adopting a more strategic approach to the idea.

While agencies have been important, key individuals have influenced policies, directions and paces of community conservation, and often their role is overlooked in analyses (Murphree 1993). Conservation in East Africa has attracted an array of dynamic and charismatic players such as Richard Leakey and David Western. Individuals have been critical to the success or failure of activities, the degree of influence that experiments have on national practices, and on shaping the thinking of senior management within conservation authorities. Chance factors have also been important. Where the 'right person' has been in the right position, at the right time, rapid progress has been possible.[5] The risks taken by some individuals, such as the Directors of KWS and TANAPA between 1989 and 1992, to support an untried and initially unpopular approach to conservation have also been instrumental.

However, such initiative is often set against conservation and environmental policies and legislation which are generally inadequate and often date back to colonial times. This, combined with weak government capacity, has contributed to both environmental degradation and poverty. Customary forms of natural resource tenure and management have been undermined through state centralization based on the belief that local management was ineffective. While quick to take rights and respon-sibilities away from rural people, governments have been slow at reversing the process. In recent times governments have begun to both adopt and implement more decentralized approaches to natural resource management and these have led to the initial experiments from which community-based approaches have evolved.

Kenya: Innovation and early lessons

One of Africa's first 'formal' initiatives in community conservation took place in the Amboseli ecosystem in the early 1970s (Western and Thresher 1973; Western 1982; Berger 1988; Berger 1993). The lessons learnt were important, and although impact was localized and short lived, they established the idea of community conservation in Kenya and have influenced events in Tanzania. The legislative picture has remained confused; Sessional Paper No. 3 (Kenya, Republic of 1975) was based on the prin-ciple of wildlife paying its way outside parks, but this was not articulated in the 1977 Wildlife Act (Kenya, Republic of 1976).

The early experience at Amboseli was used to inform the Kenya Wildlife Service's (KWS) Community Wildlife Programme (KWS 1990b), as well as the overall 'Policy Framework and Development Programme' from 1991 to 1996 (KWS 1990a), after KWS was established in 1989. By this time a number of protected area outreach initia-tives were under way (Berger 1993; African Wildlife Foundation 1994; Western and Wright 1994b), and lessons from other countries were becoming available. These examples of field-based practice were used extensively by KWS. NGOs implementing community conservation projects also took part in the process of policy development.

KWS's Community Wildlife Service (CWS) was created in 1991. It has since evolved into the Partnership Department with a focus on enabling local people to benefit from wildlife; minimizing conflicts between conservation interests and local populations; educating people about Kenya's wildlife; promoting better land use outside of protected areas; and increasing co-operation with other sectors. For the first time in Kenya, policy provided a comprehensive analysis of the role of local people around protected areas and wildlife management outside protected areas (Kenya, Republic of 1989; KWS 1990b). Combined with the results of two studies on wildlife utilization, and a review of land use and land legislation, this has created the framework for a revised Wildlife Act.

The re-appointment of Richard Leakey as head of KWS in 1998 seemed likely to reverse the pro-community policies that were being espoused. He announced new policies to ensure that national parks had 'hard edges' and *The Economist* (12 June 1999, p.121) reported that 'Kenya's national parks are declaring independence from the rest of the country...they will be surrounded by fences and defended by border guards'. However, he resigned in late 1999 and a less militaristic emphasis in policy seems likely.

Tanzania: Building on a socialist past

Tanzania differs from Kenya and Uganda in having a large number of state agencies involved in conservation. While Tanzania National Parks (TANAPA) manages the country's national parks, the Wildlife Division is the central body responsible for the country's overall policy relating to wildlife (Boshe 1996). In addition to the national parks, Tanzania has 23 game reserves which, while not allowing permanent habitation and cultivation, provide for sport hunting and some local consumptive use of resources. There is a network of forest reserves which provides for similar management objectives with an emphasis on forest products and water catchment, while the Ngorongoro Crater has its own specialist management agency.

Tanzania would appear to be ideally placed for the development of community approaches. The creation of Ujamaa villages, though problematic in many respects, resulted in defined community groups with rights to specified territories, many rich with wildlife resources. Legal process allows these villages to become corporate bodies and manage their wildlife resources (Tanzania, Government of 1975). The promotion of African Socialism following independence (Nyerere 1973) should have provided an institutional framework for community-based wildlife management. Community conservation remains, however, relatively underdeveloped, despite the economic opportunity provided by commercial safari hunting.[6] In 1961, the Ngorongoro Conservation Area was excised from Serengeti National Park as an early experiment to promote and balance both conservation and the needs of the pastoralist community (Thompson 1997). The Wildlife Division initiated the Selous Conservation Programme (Baldus 1991; Krishke et al. 1995), which combined assistance for the management of the core area of the Selous Game Reserve with support for community-based conservation in villages around the reserve, following a model similar to Zimbabwe and Zambia (Mwenya 1990; Murphree 1995). However, this has not led to the adoption of this model beyond these areas.

The Planning and Wildlife Assessment and Management Project in 1994 helped the Wildlife Department draft a policy for community-based conservation. Finally adopted in 1998, this policy supports both tourist and resident hunting and includes provisions for wildlife ranching. Most importantly, it provides for the establishment of Wildlife Management Areas (WMAs) as a means 'to promote the conservation of wildlife and its habitats outside conservation areas ... and ensure that the local communities obtain tangible benefits from wildlife conservation' (Tanzania, United Republic of 1998). Communities which demonstrate a capacity to manage wildlife can be granted rights to WMA resources and can benefit directly from them. A Community Based Conservation Unit has been created to support this, and apply the lessons learned in the several pilot WMAs which have been operating since 1996[7] (Baldus 1991; Leader-Williams et al. 1995; Hartley 1997). Though progress has been slow, the recent adoption of a facilitatory policy may speed things up. In addition the Wildlife Division shares 25 per cent of certain revenues with District Councils, but these funds rarely benefit the rural people directly affected by the wildlife.

Progress in protected area outreach policy has been much more rapid (see Bergin, Chapter 7, this volume). It demonstrates a much stronger institutional approach based around the development of national and park level strategic plans for community conservation (Tanzania National Parks 1994). The implementation of these plans is supervised by a national level TANAPA committee. Most importantly, the community conservation programme is supported by TANAPA policy, has an operational budget allocated to it, and is not dependent on donor funds. Unlike many pilot community conservation programmes which have stayed 'pilot', the Community Conservation Service has grown into a national programme operating in all 12 of Tanzania's parks.

The Ngorongoro Conservation Area experiment in multiple land use seeks to allow Maasai pastoralists to co-exist with, and benefit from wildlife (Parkipuny 1989; Homewood and Rodgers 1991; Berger 1993). Though it represents one of the earliest and most innovative initiatives in community conservation in Africa, performance has been mixed (Perkin and Mshanga 1992), and has not led to similar initiatives elsewhere. The Ngorongoro Conservation Area Authority has been criticized for the low degree of community involvement in management, and for the limited range and level of benefits accruing to the Maasai (Lane 1996; Taylor and Johannson 1996). Despite criticism (Lane 1996; Taylor and Johannson 1996), the recently published General Management Plan (Ngorongoro Conservation Area Authority 1995) was a more participatory process than any preceding it (Bensted-Smith and Leaver 1996) and it provides a possible means for developing greater Maasai participation in the future. Of more concern than the plan itself is the Authority's ability to implement its provisions. While a major reorganization of the community development department has occurred, the commitment of the Authority to a more community-based approach remains to be seen.

Uganda: Developing policy in an institutional vacuum

Protected area management policy recognized 'communities' in the 1950s and the Game Department was created to protect communities from wildlife. Uganda's early legislation even provided for 'local game committees' to advise the government on game conservation and hunting, giving community leaders a role in the management of wildlife and protected areas (Kamugisha 1993). At the same time, 50 per cent of revenues earned from entry fees to national parks was allocated to local government

(Willock 1964). Despite these measures the strict separation of conservation areas from local communities was as marked in Uganda as elsewhere. The clearing of areas of human settlement was a common response to the threat of sleeping sickness in the country and, after clearance, several areas were gazetted as protected areas.[8]

More recently, the development of community conservation has been strongly influenced by NGOs and donor agencies. Since the late 1980s, international NGOs including AWF, CARE, IUCN and WWF, have implemented community conservation projects in and around national parks (see for example Pomeroy 1991; Uganda National Parks 1994; Barrow 1995; Wild and Mutebi 1996; Hinchley and Turyomurugyendo 1998). Their focus on national parks reflected the need to rebuild Uganda's protected area system, which had been severely damaged by encroachment and the collapse of infrastructure during the civil war. Rural development and land-use issues were of secondary concern to many of the NGOs and donors.

The initial success of some of these initiatives (see Hulme and Infield, Chapter 8, this volume) encouraged the development of new wildlife policy and legislation. The context of re-building Uganda's protected area system and the capacity of staff to manage it created many opportunities for NGOs and donors to influence policy. The merger of Uganda National Parks (UNP) with the Game Department into the Uganda Wildlife Authority (UWA) required the development of new policy and legislation. The European Commission provided technical and financial support for this process, and policy influence was sometimes very direct.[9] Both the Wildlife Policy of 1995 and the Uganda Wildlife Statute of 1996 highlight community issues and include provisions for protected area outreach and community-based conservation (Uganda, Government of 1995; Uganda, Government of 1996). However, the progressive nature of the policy and legislation is not necessarily a reflection of the thinking of UWA staff. 'Fines and fences' views of park management continue to dominate, and poor relations with local communities still persist. Expenditure and staffing for law enforcement are much greater than for community programmes.[10] The decline of a four-person community conservation department at UWA headquarters to a single officer under the recent restructuring is indicative of UWA's low prioritization of community conservation, despite a policy to the contrary.

When Kenya announced the sharing of park revenues with local communities in 1991, demand for a similar arrangement in Uganda was strong. Despite the reluctance of UNP, who were justifiably concerned that their limited funds were already over-stretched, the idea of revenue sharing with communities resonated with policies of decentralization. The Director of Uganda National Parks, tacitly bowing to this pressure, publicly announced intentions to share 'up to 20 per cent of revenues' of national parks in 1991. By 1994, a formal policy had been developed (Uganda National Parks 1994), which was implemented by 1995. This policy became law when the requirement to share 20 per cent of park entry fees with local government to benefit local communities was included in the Wildlife Statute of 1996 (Uganda Government of 1996).

International aid agencies remain concerned about the weak capacity of UWA and in 1999 an expatriate Director, financed by the World Bank, was appointed. His brief was to clear out bad personnel (in terms of both incompetence and corruption) and install operational systems in UWA so that it could meet its mandate and become self-financing.

Uganda differs from Kenya and Tanzania in allowing consumptive use of resources within national parks (see Hulme and Infield, Chapter 8, this volume). The high population densities around many parks and the lack of natural resources outside perhaps made this inevitable. The new legislation which allows such resource use through a 'back-door clause' rather than as a requirement, is supported by internal UWA policy. Though international NGOs played a role, it was historical events which provided the need for this. In 1990, it was proposed that Mgahinga and Bwindi Forest Reserves be re-gazetted as national parks (see Adams and Infield, Chapter 9, this volume). During consultations local communities made it clear that support would only be given if resource use within these areas was permitted to continue. UNP agreed, and a policy allowing up to 20 per cent of the area of a national park to be used for sustainable resource harvesting was adopted.

The Implementation of Community Conservation Programmes

The previous section discussed the evolution of policy and legislation for community conservation. This section examines the development of programmes and their implementation. A variety of initiatives have emerged focusing mainly on park outreach and, occasionally, collaborative management (see Barrow and Murphree, Chapter 3, for the definitions of these terms). Community-based conservation activities are now evolving in East Africa, but not as fast as in Southern Africa. Several factors underpin this difference. The preservationist lobby, which tends to support central control, has been strong in East Africa, as the region is a hearth for international conservation interest. The governments of East Africa have been centralist and, despite policy rhetoric, have been reluctant to delegate power. Perhaps most important of all, however, was the region's lack of an organized group of private landowners demanding the right to use wildlife consumptively. In Southern Africa this was the key historical element from which community-based conservation later emerged (Jones and Murphree, Chapter 4, this volume).

Protected area outreach programmes were more acceptable, as they did not fundamentally challenge the nature of the relationship between the people and government with regard to conservation. These provide a linking mechanism between state conservation area management 'inside' the PA and community management 'outside'. Domestic and foreign pressures have grown on conservation authorities to embrace this more enabling approach. Commonly they involve a three-way 'partnership' between a conservation authority, an international NGO and an aid agency.

The growing recognition in East Africa that conservation may require the creation of tangible benefits for local people has recently been pushing ideas about community conservation beyond the limitations of protected area outreach. The negotiated arrangements for access to certain resources within protected areas in Uganda, the development of conservancies in Kenya, and the provisions for the establishment of Wildlife Management Areas in Tanzania and Uganda all point to a less conservative approach. However, a general reluctance to implement community-based approaches can be discerned among conservation authority staff. This reflects a continued concern over the loss of power equated with loss of control over national parks and/or large mammals. By practising community conservation as an optional activity and using language such as 'limited trials', 'at the discretion of the Director' and 'pilot programme', conservation authorities are able to avoid a whole-hearted commitment to the principles, while claiming that they are implementing the approach. Whether this will remain the case or not remains to be seen. The present context of enabling legislation, and reductions in government budgets and staff, seem likely to make such approaches a necessity, and not merely an option, in the future.

Kenya: Building community conservation on tourism

Kenya's community conservation programme has a strong protected area outreach focus that seeks to increase local support for conservation and bring tangible benefits to communities through wildlife tourism. The growing popular resistance to national parks and wildlife in general, despite the national economic importance of wildlife tourism, means that government has increasingly recognized the need to mobilize public support.

Since 1991, KWS has offered a 25 per cent share of revenues from gate fees to the communities neighbouring national parks. The initial plan was that revenue would be shared in relation to the ecological value of dispersal areas owned by communities, combined with the degree of damage inflicted on communities by wildlife (Bensted-Smith 1992). This linked land use outside protected areas to conservation efforts within them. It soon became clear that KWS could not handle the administrative demands of implementing such a complex scheme. The revenue-sharing programme evolved into the Wildlife for Development Fund (WDF) in 1993, as a mechanism to share benefits and encourage conservation–related enterprise projects (KWS 1994). The WDF provides support to community projects, but emphasizes wildlife-related enterprises rather than social infrastructure projects which are not directly related to conservation or wildlife . In this way the fund helps local people to get involved in Kenya's wildlife industry. This approach has enabled some communities to set up conservation-related enterprises but there is a problem when such businesses fail.

KWS is now mounting programmes to influence land use outside parks. With large areas of land of low agricultural potential but considerable wildlife value, this makes economic sense. Community-based conservation programmes have recently begun to develop opportunities for wildlife culling, commercial bird hunting and tourism on communal lands. The country's first communally managed conservancy was established in 1997 at Kimana in Southern Kajiado. It is seeking to tap into the large numbers of tourists that visit the Amboseli area. However, the managerial demands on such enterprises are high and it is on privately owned lands, such as those adjoining the Aberdare National Park, that wildlife tourism is developing most rapidly.

Tanzania: The institutionalisation of protected area outreach

TANAPA has developed a powerful protected area outreach programme based firmly around the inviolable nature of protected areas (TANAPA 1994c).

Community wardens and their assistants are engaged primarily in a set of activities to reduce overt conflict, to demonstrate that the parks and their staff can be good neighbours and to assist communities living around parks. It has not, however, re-examined the management of protected areas in any fundamental way, or tried to significantly change the relationship between park authorities and local communities. In effect, the TANAPA Community Conservation Service (CCS) gives conservation a more human face. The CCS shows the highest level of local budgetary and personnel commitment of the three East African countries. Initially established in 1990 with donor funds of about US$100,000 per year, the CCS was sufficiently respected by 1992 to argue successfully for operational budgets in all national parks. The number of community wardens steadily increased, and at least one community officer is now based at each park (see Bergin, Chapter 7, for a detailed account of the development of CCS).

The principles behind community conservation are beginning to influence other agencies. The Forestry Department is exploring collaborative forest management and agreements have been signed with villages for the management of a number of forest areas (Wily 1995; Wily and Othmar 1995).[11] Likewise the Wildlife Division is making progress with the implementation of community-based wildlife management in WMAs. The slow speed of progress may be partly attributed to the complexity of institutional structures in Tanzania and a history of institutional rivalry and animosity (Wildlife Sector Review Task Force 1995). Where responsibility is divided, government bodies resist giving up authority, and long-running pilot projects under the Wildlife Division have been slow to expand. This may also be attributable to the high cost of donor-supported projects in both human and financial resource terms and the complacency of the authorities, happy to continue with showcase examples of community-based conservation rather than a comprehensive programme. Many observers also hint that such changes threaten the incomes that many officials make from bribes, poaching and other illegal activities.

Uganda: action driven programme development

Community conservation programmes in Uganda have focused almost entirely on protected area outreach. When stability returned to the country in 1986 both government and international interest focused on protected areas because there were few large mammals or obvious conservation interests outside protected areas; and because the protected areas themselves were in a vulnerable position after years of neglect. While the protected area outreach programme is quite highly developed, Uganda has lagged behind in the development of a wildlife industry based on tourism or consumptive use of resources, and much of its institutional arrangements for community-based conservation exist only on paper.

The early development of Uganda's community conservation programme must be largely attributed to NGOs. Government played a facilitatory role, tending to observe rather than be directly involved. CARE and WWF became involved in Bwindi Forest Reserve in 1988, prior to its re-gazetting as a national park (Wild and Mutebi 1996). The Development Through Conservation Project followed an integrated conservation and development project model, and promoted rural development and improved agriculture in communities around the forest, and substitutes for forest products (Wells et al. 1992). In 1991, AWF began work in Lake Mburo National Park to help park staff to adopt a community approach to park management and to determine whether this could help make the park viable (Turyaho and Infield 1996; Hulme and Infield, Chapter 8, this volume).

Within a few years almost all of the national parks had the support of an international NGO.[12] The park authorities, however, tended to be left on the sidelines of such initiatives. Implementation mechanisms were usually separate from park management and positive community responses were associated with the projects and NGOs rather than with the management of the parks. In effect, the projects bypassed the Uganda National Parks. The Lake Mburo Community Conservation Project avoided this by implementing directly through park management structures, and building the capacity of park staff in community conservation. Local communities had little awareness of the 'project', and relate the benefits and the improved interactions with park staff as emanating directly from park management (Namara and Infield 1998, p.87). Several other projects have since increased direct support to park management through the provision of technical advisers, support for participatory park planning processes, and funding of community conservation programmes.

Most parks and reserves in Uganda earn too little income to cover their recurrent costs. Though its tourist industry in the 1960s had been one of the most developed in Africa, with over 150,000 arrivals a year, figures during the early 1990s barely reached 5000. Thus, despite a revenue-sharing policy, there were few opportunities for communities to benefit directly from national parks, except for the lucrative gorilla tourism around Bwindi and Mgahinga (Uganda National Parks 1994; Adams and Infield, Chapter 9, this volume). This, combined with NGO interests, has encouraged a focus on community resource access programmes, or collaborative management of protected areas. The poverty of many communities bordering parks, their dependence on forest resources, and the weakness of government's capacity to enforce exclusionary laws supported such an approach. UWA established a Collaborative Management Task Force to examine the viability of implementing this approach in Uganda's national parks (Ministry of Tourism 1996). Between 1996 and 1998 collaborative management agreements have been signed with communities around Mt Elgon, Lake Mburo and Rwenzori Mountains National Parks (Turyaho and Infield 1996; Scott 1996a; Hoefsloot 1997; Hinchley and Turyomurugyendo 1998).

Project staff and enthusiastic wardens pioneered several Memoranda of Understanding (MoU) with community groups allowing controlled access to resources including medicinal plants, fibres for handicrafts, bamboo shoots, fish and water (Chapters 8 and 9, this volume; Scott 1994b; Scott 1996a; Hinchley and Turyomurugyendo 1998). Though the process of MoU negotiation was largely controlled by the park authorities, and may be removed if policies change, they represent a departure from conventional protected area management with wardens having to negotiate with, rather than 'tell', communities. An analysis of the value of contributions made to communities would almost certainly reveal that they are insignificant in economic terms. They are locally important, however, as access to specific resources often has social and cultural significance[13] and can have a significant impact on the perceptions of local residents (Hulme and Infield, Chapter 8, this volume). Potentially, they are also important as stepping stones towards more fundamental changes in protected area management.

Community Conservation and Donor Support

Though community conservation has been promoted as a way to reduce government expenditure on conservation, it is not clear that this can be achieved in the short term. Community conservation programmes, certainly as developed under donor-funded projects, are expensive,[14] and do not result in immediate returns (see Chapters 8 and 14). The tendency among bureaucrats to adopt low-risk strategies and avoid innovation has meant that the development of community conservation programmes has been largely dependent on donor funds. If external project support reduces then community conservation will have to compete for limited funds with other, perhaps better understood and more favoured practices such as law enforcement. External funding will continue to be required to support community conservation in East Africa for many years to come and to promote innovation. Advisers with knowledge and experience from inside and outside the region, and without the constraints of working within often stifling government bureaucracies, are able to act rapidly and promote experimentation and innovation. Though some projects may have been over-zealous in their promotion of community conservation, focusing on 'project outputs' rather than the needs of local and national stakeholders, they have helped drive the pro-community agenda forward.

Conservation authority commitment to community conservation has often remained weak, and there is a real threat that this will continue to be the case. To date only TANAPA has established an internal budget for its community conservation programme. In Kenya and Uganda community conservation remains heavily donor dependent. There is a real need to develop more representative structures at the local level that will create a domestic constituency that provides political support for a community-based approach.[15]

In Uganda, a proliferation of donor-supported initiatives, resulting from the lack of a clear UWA agenda and policy for community conservation, led to a potentially unmanageable set of activities on the ground. UWA was perhaps too open to outside influences and may be accused of accepting donor funds uncritically. As a result many community conservation activities were implemented in the absence of policies or even legal provisions, and the approaches taken were often inconsistent. This had the advantage of allowing, even encouraging, innovation, but the disadvantage that UWA was left with a confused picture of what was happening on the ground (see Box 5.1). In Tanzania, though a range of NGOs and donors were involved, there was strong coordination by the TANAPA Community Conservation Coordinating Committee. Individual donors were not allowed to operate independently, and all funds for community development projects were administered by TANAPA. An important result has been the strong sense of ownership of the community programme within TANAPA. However, a less positive result has been the relatively conservative approach to community conservation, which has allowed protectionist thinking to go largely unchallenged. In Kenya, community conservation was initiated through a number of pilot areas, and has since become a national programme. The entire programme benefited from donor funding and was centrally coordinated. The range of experience created by projects has informed and influenced evolving policy and practice, providing a rich set of examples based on field level conditions.

Box 5.1   Effects of uncoordinated community conservation activities in Uganda

Advantages:
- Experimentation with community dialogue mechanisms
- Evolution of varying institutional arrangements for working with local communities
- Development of community conservation practices yielding a range of practical experience
- Wide range of training opportunities using different approaches
- Variety of benefit-sharing arrangements established and tested over time
- Impetus given to community conservation that might have been lacking at the time
- State institutions had to 'catch up' with developments
- Field-led experience informed development of supporting policy and legislation
- High profile for community conservation

Disadvantages:
- Focus at protected area levels left headquarters capacity undeveloped
- Lessons learned not shared systematically between different projects
- Lack of a coordinated process to inform national policies
- Case-specific procedures evolved leading to a lack of institutional uniformity of approach
- Donor and NGO focus on 'the project' rather than a process of evolution of a national programme
- Government able to vacillate over its commitment, labelling them as 'donor-driven' when appropriate
- No significant funding commitment required from government
- Protected area level activities and operated outside of formal policies
- Individual protected area managers able to compromise consistency of implementation

---

Conclusion

Since the beginning of the 1990s conservation authorities in the East African region have moved to foster the involvement of local communities in conservation, create mechanisms for dialogue and establish structures allowing for the participation of a wide range of stakeholders. Community conservation has been recognized and adopted as an important tool for protected area management and has created benefit flows to communities affected by conservation, increasing their support for, or reducing their resistance to conservation. Less developed, but increasingly the focus of attention in Kenya and Tanzania, is the role of community-based conservation on private and communal land as a mechanism for promoting rural development and achieving conservation goals. Collaborative management of protected areas has made some progress in Uganda and Tanzania.

This state of affairs represents a considerable achievement given the reluctance of the conservation authorities to reform, and the fact that they faced and continue to face fundamental problems in terms of finances, staff capacities, leadership and organizational structures. While it reflects the global shift that has occurred in conservation ideas and policies the changes have also been stimulated by aid donors. Using both carrots (more project funds) and sticks (threats to withdraw support) donors have encouraged experimentation with community-oriented approaches. This has led to a number of creative experiments and the development of new models. On the downside, it may have led to a dependence on donors and, at least in Kenya and Uganda, for conservation authorities to see community conservation as an additional rather than a core activity.

The stage is now set for community conservation to become a central aspect of both conservation and development but the extent to which this opportunity will be taken is unclear. Protected area outreach is contributing to the management of nearly all protected areas in the region. Its efficacy has been demonstrated in terms of making conservation management more effective as well as by the creation of a limited flow of social and economic benefits for communities. As the future of protected areas is enhanced by community conservation, the region is experimenting with community-based conservation outside protected areas. All three countries now have policies and legislation to allow this and the work carried out on the development of community institutions has helped to establish a positive climate. Whether the pace of change is fast enough to cater for raised community aspirations and political expectations remains to be seen.

Conservation must find a distinctive niche in rural economies and societies and contribute financially and socially to rural lives if it is to be incorporated into the land-use decisions of the future. Community conservation has reduced levels of conflict and opposition and is beginning to establish a local constituency for conservation. However, fundamental conflicts of interest exist between the short-term needs of poor rural communities and the interests and obligations of governments. These are not going to disappear. Protected areas need the determined support of governments and the international community but protected areas must create a local constituency for conservation by increasing the level and range of benefits to the extent possible within conservation objectives. Outside protected areas, wildlife is likely to persist only if its conservation adds value to land uses, or can be demonstrated to provide the most remunerative land use on its own. This is currently not the case in most of the region, though the potential for tourism and safari hunting in the arid and semi-arid parts of the region is high.

Community management of natural resources presupposes the commitment of communities to sustainable use. Genuine commitment of management authorities to share responsibility and control is also required. When these two conditions are met, governments and the international community can feel confident that promoting collaborative management of protected areas and the establishment of community-based conservation initiatives on community lands will strengthen the conservation of nature and biodiversity. As these conditions do not fully exist in much of East Africa, it is perhaps not surprising that wildlife authorities have gravitated towards the protected area outreach end of the community conservation continuum. Until it is clear that communities and conservation authorities are ready and able to take up their responsibilities, and put in place management regimes that are based on long-term intentions, community conservation will remain an uneasy though productive compromise between the demands of communities for resources and power, the reservations and intrinsic conservatism of governments and conservation authorities, and the result-orientated interventions of donors and NGOs.

Notes

[1]Readers are referred to (Pratt and Gwynne 1977; Groombridge 1992; IUCN 1992; World Conservation Monitoring Centre 1992) for general or contemporary texts on the region.

[2]See Jones and Murphree (Chapter 4, this volume) for an analysis of the development of community conservation policy in Zimbabwe and Namibia. It is interesting to note that private landowners have provided the stimulus for the recent development of conservancies in East Africa as has been the case in Southern Africa.

[3]The forced relocation of people has continued through to contemporary times and creates a negative image for conservation across the region. See Brockington and Homewood (1996) for an example.

[4]For example the Cullman Wildlife Project, and the Selous Conservation Project are efforts to foster an improved conservation ethic through sharing hunting benefits with local residents.

[5]The examples of the community conservation coordinators of UWA and TANAPA during the mid-1990s are instructive.

[6]For example projects around Selous Game Reserve, Ruaha National Park and the Cullman Award Scheme.

[7]For example, in Lunda-Mkwambi near Ruaha NP, a WMA was created and the community was allowed to auction off their wildlife quota for significant earnings.

[8]The creation of Queen Elizabeth National Park in 1952 presents a good example, as the park was gazetted after the area had been cleared of people. Despite the threat of sleeping sickness, and against the orders of the colonial government, many people returned to the area to continue fishing on Lakes Edward and George inside the park. To this day, these villages are seen as a management problem for the park (Olivier 1990), and periodic efforts have been made to remove or relocate villages (Infield 1989).The expulsion of the Ek people from their hunting grounds with the creation of the Kidepo Valley National Park 1962 is also well documented (Turnbull 1972).

[9]USAID, for example, directly commissioned a study into the means of increasing community participation in protected area management (Ogwang and DeGeorge 1992). Funding for UNP was made contingent on their accepting and implementing the report.

[10]The recent restructuring of UWA suggests the relative importance of community conservation within the organization. Out of a total of 1113 staff, only 46 (4%) are specified as community conservation staff, compared to 765 (69%) who are indicated as security staff or are undesignated junior staff (Uganda National Parks Restructuring Committee 1997) .

[11]Examples include Mgori, Singida and in Tanga region (Wily 1995; Wily and Othmar 1995; Nurse and Kabamba 1998)

[12]CARE's Development Through Conservation project focused initial activities on improving rural livelihoods, and reducing demand for protected area resources. A similar emphasis was adopted by IUCN programmes supporting Mount Elgon, Kibale and Semliki National Parks, and WWF's support to Rwenzori Mountain National Park.

[13]Provision of access to bamboo shoots in Mount Elgon National Park to the local Bagisu people, for whom the bamboo plays a critical role in their ritual as well as their diet, is an example as 'there is no substitute' for the ritual functions of bamboo (Scott 1994a and b). The negotiation of access to water through Lake Mburo National Park for the livestock of certain communities living around the park has been of critical economic importance to these people, as is the general understanding that the park forms the water resource of last resort during severe drought. Provision of access to valued plant resources in Bwindi Impenetrable National Park for use in both handicrafts and medicine has helped to support and strengthen traditional institutions as well as stimulating the development of new ones.

[14]Struhsaker (1997: 334) cites the example of 'an EEC expatriate adviser on vehicle and road maintenance to the Uganda National Parks was paid US$144,000 per year while the Ugandan Director of Parks earned between US$150 and US$200 per year'.

[15]Including, for example, formal district development structures; forums and associations in Kenya, Park Management Advisory Committees in Uganda though this function has now become the responsibility of the District Environment Committees; and Wildlife Management Areas in Tanzania and Uganda.

6

Necessarily Vague
The Political Economy of Community
Conservation in Mozambique

SIMON ANSTEY

'The truth is that we understand fully what we do not want. But as to what we do want and how
to get it our ideas are necessarily vague'. President Samora Machel speaking at Mozambique
independence in 1975 (quoted in Middleton 1994, p.33).

Introduction

In 1992 Mozambique government policy emphasized the state management of
protected areas and forest resources and specified as a key goal the 'elimination of
poaching'. By 1998, the dominant phrase in programmes and policies was the 'participation of local communities in wildlife and forestry management'. In the space of
just over five years (at least in rhetoric), the 'poacher' had become a 'participant' and
the state was presenting itself as a partner rather than a prosecutor (DNFFB 1997).

This chapter explores how this change happened. An overview is presented of the
evolution of approaches and programmes for the involvement of local communities
in the management and conservation of natural resources in Mozambique from the
early 1990s to 1998. Rather than a formal assessment, such as a case study of a
particular initiative or an analysis of policy and legislation, the paper takes an
historical approach to try to understand why there has been such a radical shift in
public pronouncements about the involvement of communities in conservation. As
such it explores the dynamics of conservation narratives and counter-narratives (see
Adams and Hulme, Chapter 2, this volume). It is inevitably a personal view, at a
particular moment in time, of an ongoing process. It tries to pull out some of the
often obscure features of politics, history and personal motivations which influence
why and how things happen. The main questions looked at in this chapter are:

- Why has there been such a radical change in perceptions, policy and practice
  about the involvement of communities in conservation over the past few years?
- Who have been the actors involved in this shift and what have been their motivations?
- What have been the practical results of this shift?

Mozambique Background

Mozambique is one of the larger countries in Southern Africa covering some 800,000 km² with a population estimated at 16 million, of which 70 per cent live in rural areas. The country is emerging from both the destructive effects of two decades of war, which started shortly after the transition from colonial rule by Portugal, and the effects of centrally planned economic and political strategies. Peace was achieved in the internal conflict in 1992 and multi-party elections were held in 1994. The economic policies now in place focus on free market approaches.

The costs of the conflicts of the past decades have been high. Large segments of the population were internally (3 million) or externally (1.7 million) displaced as refugees, much of the basic infrastructure of the country was damaged or destroyed, and at US$80 in 1995 per capita income was the lowest in the world (Vines 1996). The vast majority of Mozambicans live below the poverty line and literacy rates are estimated at 35 per cent. Approximately 70 per cent of the national budget is sourced from donors or multilateral funding facilities (Abrahamson 1997).

The broad history of Mozambique also has considerable relevance to the evolution of community conservation. While Portuguese involvement in the country stretches back almost 500 years the colonial process was very different from that of other Southern African states (see Newitt 1995; Abrahamson and Nilsson 1995). For most of this period Mozambique served as a supply of cheap resources such as ivory, slaves and cotton with little Portuguese investment in development or administration. From the 1890s until the 1940s the majority of the central and northern areas of the country were rented off to private companies and, as Vines (1996) notes, 'only between 1941 when the last of the company charters lapsed and 1974 was Mozambique governed by a single administration with a single economy'. Much of the economy and administration was focused in the coastal area and in the southern urban centre of Maputo, where it still remains. With the independence of Mozambique in 1975, after a decade of war, the new socialist orientated Frelimo government attempted a major transformation of the economy, society and political structure of the country (Hanlon 1996; Abrahamson 1997) in a rapid process which was frequently rooted more in theory than the realities of the country (Newitt 1995). In particular the focus on grand projects such as collectives and huge state farms in a society characterized by subsistence farmers with very limited administrative capacity or formal skills (illiteracy rates at independence were 98 per cent) was problematic (Abrahamson 1997).

The result was 'an over centralised economy which displayed all the worst features of Portuguese bureaucracy and eastern European central planning' (Vines 1996). This was further compounded by destabilization from Rhodesia and South Africa, with internal conflict lasting up to 1992 further weakening administrative structures and increasing dependence on foreign aid and technical assistance. Since this time a second transformation has been underway, in many ways as extreme as those of the 1970s. This has included a structural adjustment programme, multi-party democracy, decentralization, local level empowerment, a major land reform and the embracing of free market capitalism. This has placed a heavy load on an already weak administrative system and while powerfully promoted by the IMF, World Bank and other donors, the stress on the economic and social fabric of Mozambique has been considerable.

Some features of this stress have been the rise in corruption and the increasingly unequal ownership of wealth and control of property, as noted under similar conditions in Vietnam, where 'the new economic elite is emerging largely out of the party itself for whom market theory is only a facade to justify their sustained confiscation of wealth' (Kolko 1997).

The key point is that the colonial heritage, the revolutionary heritage and the current transformation have not provided Mozambique with a strong state or administration at either the central or the local levels. The paradox of community conservation is that elsewhere in Africa a strong state has proved to be a critical prerequisite for the decentralization and devolution required to empower local community institutions to manage and benefit from natural resources. The threads of this history run throughout much of the rest of this chapter.

Environmental context

Mozambique has a rich and varied land and marine environment. Forest cover is estimated at 600,000 km² and only around 7 per cent of the country is currently cultivated. The coastline with wetland and coral systems is the third longest in Africa covering 2700 km. About half the country could be described as wilderness as it supports populations of less than 15 people/km² (compared with the mean of over 100 people/km² in Malawi). Protected areas for wildlife, forest or marine resources cover 87,000 km² or around 11 per cent of the country and include national parks, forest and wildlife reserves, and controlled hunting areas or *coutadas* (Map 6.1).

The past 30 years of conflict resulted in the depopulation of rural areas and the negative impacts of conflict on the environment in general have been relatively low. An exception has been around urban areas, in the coastal zone, and on megafauna whose densities have been greatly reduced as a result of hunting for food or products (ivory and rhino horn) during the conflict. Apart from the slaughter of the megafauna, the other main environmental problems have been the over-harvesting of marine fisheries and the impacts of large dams. Since the cessation of hostilities and the opening up of transport routes and infrastructure, the new threats have been the uncontrolled exploitation of hardwood timber and other high-value natural resources. However, Mozambique has considerable potential for community-based natural resource management to be one of the major forms of land use, given the large uncultivated areas with a range of natural resources and the low human population densities.

Policies, Legislation and Institutions

The period from the early 1990s to the present has seen a great deal of change in government policy and the enactment of much new legislation in the decentralization of political and economic power, reform in land and resource tenure and environment and natural resource laws. Many of these changes, while not necessarily directed at community conservation specifically, have created an 'enabling environment' for it. The key reforms (based on da Cunha 1998; DNFFB 1998; Negrao 1998) are listed below:

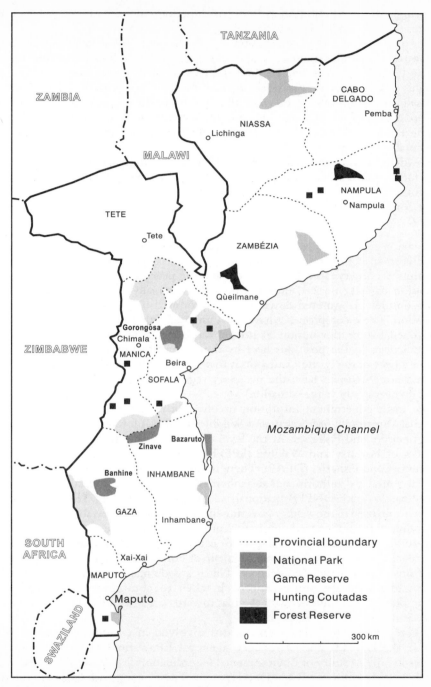

Map 6.1 State protected areas in Mozambique

- Changes to the constitution in 1990 which permitted multi-party democracy and promoted policies of decentralization.
- The Local Government Policy and acts of the mid-1990s which, in principle, transferred considerable powers to democratically elected local structures.
- The Land Policy of 1995 and the Land Law of 1997 which guaranteed tenurial rights to local communities over land and resources, a process for leasehold titling based on oral history, access to conflict resolution mechanisms, rights to participate in natural resource management (the state remained the owner of all land).
- The Framework Environment Law of 1997 which provided the base environmental legislation.
- The draft Forestry and Wildlife Act of 1998 which emphasized the role and rights of local communities in the planning and management and benefits from natural resources. These were even more powerfully identified in the policy and strategies for forestry and wildlife management developed in 1996 and 1997 (DNFFB 1997).

However, a central feature of all these developments has been their lack of capacity to deliver an 'enabling environment', i.e. the legal mechanisms promoting community conservation. In almost all cases the process of moving from policy to legislation has taken years, during which the originally dynamic intentions have been considerably watered down and compromised when drawing up or passing legislation. These compromises have been imposed either by the new elite, who are threatened by the devolution of power and management to lower levels or by contradictions in the positions held by donors and technical agencies. The most serious aspect of the current situation is that while the relevant laws may have been enacted none of them have the necessary regulations approved to put them into effect (a 'necessarily vague' situation).

The main government institution involved in community conservation is the National Directorate of Forestry and Wildlife (DNFFB) located within the Ministry of Agriculture and Fisheries. At the level of the provinces there are the Provincial Services of Forestry and Wildlife (SPFFB) within the Provincial Directorate of Agriculture and Fisheries (DPAP). There is thus a semi-federal structure with inherently decentralized authority but also inherently complex administration, as SPFFB is subordinate to both DNFFB (national) and DPAP (provincial). This dual subordination is mirrored in most other government agencies and, in the absence of effective communication, leads to administrative problems such as the granting of multiple concessions for the same physical space or natural resource. The mandate of DNFFB includes the conservation and management of both forestry and wildlife resources and protection of marine biodiversity. This is a wide mandate which is reflected in the broader natural resource approach taken to community conservation in Mozambique. This contrasts with the bias towards large mammals typical in the rest of the Southern African region.

Other government-related institutions involved in community conservation include the DNFFB-related research agency CEF, various faculties within the University, the Ministry of Environmental Coordination (MICOA) and increasingly the National Institute for Rural Development. These, along with local and international NGOs and donors, provide a contrast to the situation elsewhere in the region as there is no overall national programme for community conservation (such as CAMPFIRE or LIFE) but a series of individual initiatives with a great variety of methods and objectives (Appendix 6.1).

Community Conservation: Projects and Programmes

Between the early 1990s and the late 1990s there was a major shift in the types of conservation programmes, their numbers and the levels of funding. This mirrored the changing dynamics of the country in the post-war period and the changing policies and legislation outlined in the previous section. The following discussion looks at how the projects and programmes during this period developed. It does so through a division into three historical phases.

1992–4 The transition years

This period was one of dramatic political change, with the end of 15 years of internal conflict between Frelimo and Renamo and the holding of the first democratic elections in late 1994. It was also a period of economic change with the opening up of the natural resources of Mozambique to the private sector because of the improved security and the change in government economic policy from centralized state management to a free market approach. While this change had been initiated in the late 1980s it was not until the cessation of the war that the 'market' was open and the result was a scramble, largely by external investors, to secure options in the country. There was little in the way of a regulatory framework to oversee these investments as the capacity of state institutions was weak and most were still orientated towards a command economy. Many at senior levels in the state structures regarded these developments in a positive light because their institutions received benefits from this opening up to new investment (after years of stagnation or dependency on unreliable donor aid). Individuals within these institutions could also parley their professional skills for consultancy fees or their influence in decision-making and facilitation of investment for joint venture partnerships. Some left the state sector entirely but most remained in technical positions, thereby creating a confusing situation between their official regulatory functions and their private involvement in business initiatives.

The donor community was also often in a contradictory position. The pressures to make a 'success' out of the transition to peace, democracy and free market capitalism in Mozambique after the failures in Angola and Cambodia were intense in this period and Mozambique was a critical case in the promotion of the new post-Cold War narrative (Hanlon 1996). The primary concern was securing key political and economic transformations and the evidence of the inequalities resulting from them was frequently set aside as part of 'growing pains' which would resolve themselves with time or through donor-supported macro level policy solutions, such as the promotion of a policy for decentralization and policies for tenure reform.

The NGOs and international technical agencies (such as the UN agencies) were in a transitional phase from being the implementing agencies for emergency food relief or the provision of basic health or education services to being more orientated to development assistance in a collaborative process with government and donors. In many cases NGOs were perceived as an intermediary between donors and government agencies (Hanlon 1996). However, they were now required to compete for attention and roles with the private sector which was becoming increasingly important.

In the section responsible for Forestry and Wildlife (DNFFB) the transition between 1992 and 1994 was especially dynamic. The mainstay of DNFFB for the previous decade had been support from FAO/UNDP with a particular focus on conventional forest production (largely plantation forestry) and by the late 1980s and early 1990s urban fuelwood and biomass energy programmes. The majority of senior staff in DNFFB were trained as conventional foresters, having graduated from local and foreign universities in the late 1970s. Their practical field experience had been limited because of the conflict. The foreign technical advisers were also largely trained in conventional forestry management and mainly concerned with managing finance from UN agencies (which, apart from staff salaries paid by government, was the only funding for DNFFB). The wildlife department within DNFFB was a 'Cinderella' section staffed at the senior level by three newly graduated veterinary scientists with no field experience. The perceived importance of wildlife management in DNFFB at that time can be gathered from the semantics used for wildlife as a 'non-wood forest product'. The sudden opening up of Mozambique in 1992 led to a flood of investment proposals, concessions for hardwood timber exploitation and hunting areas which the institution was technically and administratively unable to manage. At that time donor and technical assistance inputs were very low as aid programmes focused on peace and stability and had little interest in natural resource or environment management. The dynamism of the private sector was attractive to many in DNFFB after the hiatus of the war and years of donor dependency. Considerable freedom was given to investors in forestry and wildlife enterprises to plan and implement initiatives (DNFFB had little capacity in any case to define offtake quotas, monitor or enforce regulations) and this brought in income through taxes and 'facilitation' fees (i.e. bribes).

In the theatre of conservation and natural resource management the primary actors in 1992–3 were private sector investors and speculators in timber and wildlife hunting. State capacity was limited, donors and NGOs were in the background and local communities were somewhere off stage. This contrasted strongly with the post-conflict 'transition' years of Zimbabwe or Namibia where NGOs, academics, the private sector and some state institutions all emphasized the transfer of natural resource management to local communities (see Jones and Murphree, Chapter 4, this volume).

However, there was also in this period the beginning of support for ideas of involving local communities in conservation in Mozambique and a broadening of initiatives and donors away from the conventional approaches. By 1992 the World Bank was starting to explore options with DNFFB for the development of natural resource management programmes linked with neighbouring countries to be funded by the Global Environment Facility. While the original proposal for what would later be called the 'Transfrontier Conservation Areas' (TFCAs) programme was biased towards protected areas, the associated consultancy reports, involving specialists from Southern and Eastern Africa, stressed the participation of the rural communities living in the areas to be conserved. While the TFCA remained at proposal preparation stage up to 1994, the increasing involvement of DNFFB staff in its development and the potentially large scale of its funding encouraged a greater interest in options involving local communities.

Another initiative which created interest in community conservation was a marine protected areas project on the Bazaruto Archipelago, which was a collaboration between DNFFB and the Endangered Wildlife Trust (EWT) and later WWF. Although focused on the development of a protected area, it also included the recruitment of law enforcement staff from local communities and proposals that private sector tourist lodges should make voluntary financial contributions to a fund for local communities and a fund for turtle protection by local people.

A further NGO actor was IUCN, the World Conservation Union, which from the beginning of its work in Mozambique in 1993 emphasized community conservation approaches as this was the focus of its regional programme. By mid-1993 funds had been sourced to second a Zimbabwean wildlife officer with experience of the CAMPFIRE programme to provide technical advice to the wildlife section of DNFFB and arrange for Mozambicans to visit CAMPFIRE areas in Zimbabwe. In addition, funds were provided by the European Union for the development of emergency proposals for the rehabilitation of Gorongosa National Park in central Mozambique. This proposal, which emphasized the participation of the local residents in the management and development of activities, plus the preparation of a long-term integrated natural resource management plan was funded by the European Union in late 1994. The injection of US$1 million in this process and over US$500,000 in the Bazaruto project by the EU in 1994 had an influence both on the field implementation of conservation by DNFFB (albeit with NGO intermediaries) and in the promotion (within at least the wildlife sector) of community conservation approaches.

The final initiative was perhaps the most significant. In early 1993 two wildlife officers, newly graduated from Mweka Wildlife College in Tanzania, were sent by DNFFB to a safari hunting concession in Tete Province. They found a situation of considerable conflict between the safari operator and the local community. As both the officers and the local community had been exposed to community conservation approaches (the officers while students and the communities as refugees in neighbouring Zimbabwe and Zambia: CAMPFIRE and ADMADE) they designed a proposal for resolving the conflict through the inclusion of local people in the management of the resources and benefits from them. By late 1993 this initiative had captured the enthusiasm of the Ford Foundation representative and during 1994 it secured two-year pilot funding from the Ford Foundation.

So, by the end of 1994 there had been a remarkable shift towards community conservation in Mozambique. From being non-existent in 1992 it had grown in terms of the actors involved (government agencies and individual staff, conservation NGOs with a regional background, specific donors) and initiatives planned or initiated. This was happening not because of changes in policy or legislation but for the reasons listed below:

- Key staff in government agencies were observing some of the limitations of state–private sector natural resource management when the state had weak regulatory, monitoring and enforcement capacity and conflict with local people was increasing. They were seeking alternatives.

- Some specific NGOs, donors and individuals within these institutions were promoting non-conventional approaches to natural resource management based on regional experiences.
- Signing up to the 'narrative' of community conservation (Adams and Hulme, Chapter 2, this volume) was a means of increasing access to aid funds and technical assistance at a time when conventional sources of support for forest and wildlife sector management (and DNFFB) were declining.

1995–6 The bubbling up years

During the period 1995–6 the main advances in community conservation were at the provincial and local levels which were frequently remote from the direction of DNFFB at central level. Ironically, DNFFB was facing problems of institutional survival and its headquarters was trying to capture some of the aid funding going directly to field initiatives and provincial programmes. It was also facing increasing competition with the emergence of a Ministry for Environmental Coordination (MICOA) in late 1994 which was successful at fund-raising. The institutional complexities of central government were increased as donors struggled for dominance of the environment sector – to be the Lead Donor Agency. Following the multi-party elections in late 1994, foreign aid became increasingly available for development (rather than the peace process or emergency relief) and a number of donors had funds earmarked for the environment. The main actors were the World Bank, the Dutch and the Scandinavian donor group. The Bank was increasingly linked to DNFFB for the implementation of its environmental activities, the Dutch pledged US$20 million to MICOA and the Scandinavians focused on specific institution-building initiatives within MICOA.

Of particular relevance for the evolution of community conservation was the emphasis of a number of donors on policies for land tenure reform and decentralization. While in principle a state-driven process, these policies developed in a situation in which strong and sometimes contradictory positions were held by those who were paying for the process (the donors) and their technical advisers (NGOs, UN agencies and consultants), whose influence was considerable. While both the new land tenure policy (published in 1995) and the policy for decentralized local government were progressive in terms of opening up options for greater community level management and benefit rights, these were generally delayed or watered down when passed through the legislature. There remained a powerful group within the ruling Frelimo party resistant to the delegation of power and control over economic assets and development plans. This was partly ideological and partly due to the success of the party, and its members, in securing a dominant role in the economy. This contrasted with the Renamo opposition, which was virtually broke and whose electoral constituency was rural (Abrahamson 1997).

Thus the factors shaping environment and conservation policy at this time involved many stakeholders and a complex mix of ideology, influence, access, power and funds. Agendas ranged from promoting particular policy positions or ideological approaches, securing the most aid possible, acquiring benefits in terms of personal careers or private income and institutional survival. All of this activity occurred almost entirely within the capital city of Maputo. Paradoxically, it was at local and provincial levels, far from Maputo, that breakthroughs in approaches to conservation were occurring. These relatively small initiatives increasingly focused on community conservation and their experience eventually had influence at the central level. This 'bubbling up' of community approaches from field initiatives was an increasingly powerful force on the national agenda from 1995 onwards. Two initiatives can serve to illustrate this, one being focused on protected areas and the other on community involvement in natural resource management.

Tchuma Tchato community conservation initiative

The Tchuma Tchato initiative (see also Wilson 1997; Anstey and Chonguica 1997) grew from the work of two young DNFFB staff who sought to find a solution to the conflicts between a safari operator and the local people in the Bawa area of Tete through a process of community participation in decisions about wildlife use and the distribution of benefits. Between 1993 and 1995, with minimal funds and support, a member of DNFFB (Luis Namanha) negotiated with the local population for their involvement in the initiative, for the setting up of informal 'community councils' elected democratically and for councils to control illegal hunting and manage any economic revenue earned. In the absence of laws or mechanisms there was no apparent way for the community to earn revenue from the safari hunting. This was solved through an unusual bureaucratic 'trick' by one of the central DNFFB staff who trebled the trophy fees for the hunting in that specific area by obtaining the signatures of three government ministers to do so. By 1995 almost all illegal hunting had ceased and in 1996 the community earned US$15,000 from trophy fees. More importantly, they recovered a sense of local control over their future, reflected in the name they gave to the initiative of *Tchuma Tchato* (Our Wealth).

Protected areas: Gorongosa National Park rehabilitation

This project was primarily a protected area rehabilitation scheme. But, from its initiation the implementing officer (Baldeu Chande) stressed the practical involvement of the people from surrounding communities. Traditional ceremonies were held at the start of the project showing respect to the original owners of the area (the traditional chiefs), with the field staff selected from candidates presented by the traditional leadership, and a gentle approach to those who had settled within the Park (in terms of negotiated and voluntary resettlement). Law enforcement, in terms of illegal activities, was also largely mediated through the traditional leadership rather than the formal courts. During a famine period local people were permitted to enter the park in rotation to harvest fish. Formally this was an illegal activity which Chande had no authority to permit, but together with the other initiatives this convinced the population to genuinely participate in the park management. The results of these activities were a remarkably rapid stabilization of what had been a highly militarized and over-exploited area. They derived from Chande's own initiative and not a formally designed programme.

The key finding from the above two examples (and others) is that innovation took place not as a result of central policy or legislation, but on the initiative of field level Mozambicans who independently sought solutions to local problems which actively involved the local population in developing practical solutions to conservation problems.

This period was also characterized by the start of larger programmes (see Appendix 6.1), a growth in studies on traditional use of natural resources and an expansion in the amount of donor funding and interest in community conservation. Additionally, there was an increase in the development of large-scale private sector wildlife-based projects (Blanchard Enterprises in Maputo Province and Niassa Reserve project in northern Mozambique) which stressed their intentions to involve communities in the planning and management of schemes and as shareholders in the companies to be formed for the areas. This was in contrast to the private sector concessions in forestry and wildlife of the previous period when communities had been ignored.

1997 onwards: The convergence years

If the 1995–6 period was characterized by the bubbling up of a community conservation approach from the local level, the period since then has been increasingly dominated by the mainstreaming of the narrative of 'local community participation in natural resource management' by the private sector, the government, a range of local and international NGOs and donors. While the previous period was characterized by small-scale adaptive management experiments by a few committed staff in remote areas, with minimal funding, the current phase is increasingly being developed through central government, is large-scale, addresses macro-level factors (such as national legislation and regulations for resource tenure and community-level institutions), and is being promoted via a number of large-scale, donor-funded programmes.

Three programmes now dominate the national process. The GEF Transfrontier Conservation Areas programme funded through the World Bank and implemented under DNFFB (US$7 million); the Dutch funded Community Forestry and Wildlife Programme of DNFFB and FAO (US$9 million); and PROAGRI, an integrated five-year multi-donor programme due to start implementation in 1999. The latter emphasizes community participation in most of its elements, and is costed out at over US$40 million.

A key feature of these programmes is that they are all primarily focused on capacity building within the DNFFB central government agency and the related provincial sections of SPFFB. They provide support for training, research and national legal and policy change. In all cases the funding for pilot projects and capacity building of local communities is at a far lower level of funding and technical support. The rationale is apparently that the building of capacity at the government core will ensure the implementation of decentralization at progressively lower levels over the longer term. It is clear that there has been a general reversal in the trend of targeting funds and projects to the provincial level.

However, support continues for a range of other, smaller projects operating at the provincial or local level which are experimenting with mechanisms for community-based natural resource management within the current legal constraints. A variety of partnerships including government agencies, local NGOs and associations and even communities themselves and their traditional leaders are active (see Appendix 6.1). As in the earlier period, it will probably be these local initiatives that will generate the experiences from which central government, the ruling elite and donor agencies will design their programmes.

Conclusions

This chapter has explored the experience of community conservation in Mozambique and particularly stresses the great change that has occurred in the last five years. A remaining question is the extent to which the two critical variables that provide the incentive for community involvement in conservation, benefits and control over resources, have changed.

A rough estimate is that over these five years the economic benefits to communities have been relatively small, probably not exceeding US$50,000 in terms of cash dividends paid out to community level structures (assuming *Tchuma Tchato* project is the main dividend producer). In terms of increased control over management and decision-making by local institutions in formal community conservation programmes, the scale and degree is limited to specific initiatives in specific areas. Certainly in comparison to informal, traditional and frequently illegal use of wildlife, the gains of this formal process have so far been very limited at the level of household income. For example, recent estimates of the trade in wildlife meat (Serodio 1998) in Maputo Province alone, during only a six-month period, indicate that this trade provides US$800,000 to local communities. Crude extrapolations to the national level would suggest an annual value of around US$10 million for the illegal bushmeat trade. Estimates of the annual value of informal fuelwood harvested in Mozambique by local communities in 1997 were US$240 million (quoted in DNFFB 1998). Given this context it is clear that the incentives of additional benefits and control through formal community conservation programmes have little significance at regional and national scales.

The chapter has also illustrated the frequent existence of the 'necessarily vague' in the evolution of community conservation in Mozambique. This includes the structural basis of policies and legislation (existing on paper but not in practice), the organization of the main government agency (in terms of dual subordination), the great diversity of initiatives, methods used and funds available, the range of implementing agencies, NGOs and donors (without a coordinating body), and the dominance of rhetoric over action. However, while this may be very different from the experiences and processes elsewhere in Southern Africa (see particularly Jones and Murphree, Chapter 4, this volume), and while it may provide a large gap within which the elite is able to retain its personal control of the benefits from natural resources, it also provides considerable space for experimentation with different approaches to community conservation. It is essentially a Mozambican way and while it may take longer to secure the benefits and control at the level of local communities, which is its goal, it may well prove more robust than the processes driven by the rapid 'master-stroke' of legislating an enabling environment and aid-financed big projects.

In conclusion, returning to the quotation from the speech by the late President Samora Machel on the challenges facing Mozambique at independence and the reality of 'necessarily vague' ideas to solve them, his corollary was that the country was facing a process not a single solution.

> … as to what we want our ideas are necessarily vague. They are born out of practice, corrected by practice. We undoubtedly will run into setbacks. But it is from these setbacks that we will learn.

The same reality faces community conservation in its continued evolution in Mozambique. It cannot be divorced either from the influences of the past or the massive political, social and economic transformations of the present and there are no single or simple legal master-strokes or technical solutions. But community conservation has made some progress based on practice and learning from setbacks. It is only six years since the radical change in policy and four years since practice commenced. These are still early days.

Appendix 6.1 Summary of programmes and projects in community conservation in Mozambique 1992 to 1998

Programme details	Start–end date
Tchuma Tchato Programme, Tete. Community-based natural resource management pilot programme based in Tete Province and implemented by provincial forestry and wildlife agency (SPFFB). Approximately US$700,000 since 1994. Funded by Ford Foundation.	1994–ongoing
Emergency Rehabilitation of Gorongosa National Park and Management Plan for Natural Resources of Northern Sofala. Implemented by IUCN in partnership with provincial (SPFFB) and central government agencies (DNFFB). Components relating to community conservation approx. US$300,000. Funded by European Union	1995–7
Transfrontier Conservation Areas Programme. Focus on rehabilitation of protected areas in southern Mozambique with integrated community conservation. Implemented by DNFFB in partnership with other government agencies and NGOs. Project development approx. US$1 million (1993–6); implementation funding US$8 million from GEF	1997–2000
Support to Community Management of Forestry and Wildlife. A programme focused on both institutional capacity building in central government agencies and university research to support community conservation and two pilot projects in Nampula and Maputo Provinces. Implemented by DNFFB and funded by Dutch/FAO with budget of approx. US$9 million	1997–2007
Community Management of Forestry (Licuati area). A programme studying and undertaking some pilot implementation based on traditional knowledge of forest management. Implemented by a partnership between the University and DNFFB. Funded by World Bank approx. US$1 million	1997–8
Community Management of Forestry (Tanga area). A similar programme to above in same zone. Implemented by the Forest Research Centre (CEF) of DNFFB with funding from Ford Foundation. Approx. US$30,000	1996–ongoing
Conservation Programme for Bazaruto Archipelago. A marine protected area and communities project. Implemented by DNFFB with support from WWF and EWT (2 regional NGOs). Funded by European Union with other smaller donations. Approx. US$600,000.	1989–98
Management of Forestry and Wildlife Resources (GERFFA). A project focused on Gorongosa protected area (and surrounding communities) management and social and timber forestry, Sofala and Manica in central Mozambique. Loan from African Development Bank of approx. US$13 million	1996–2000
Moribane Forest Reserve. Research programme studying the involvement of local communities in forest resource management. Implemented by CEF and funded by Ford Foundation. Approx. funding US$200,000	1995–ongoing

Appendix 6.1 *continued*

Programme details	Start–end date
Chimanimani Community Conservation Programme. Involving the community of this area in central Mozambique in the planning of new conservation areas, provincial level capacity building of government agencies and development of community conservation initiatives. Implemented by SPFFB and funded by Ford Foundation. Approx. funding US$350,000	1996–ongoing
Marine Biodiversity Conservation. Involving communities in management and planning for conservation of coastal resources. In final planning process. Implemented by MICOA and DNFFB with funds from GEF, approx. US$5 million.	1997–ongoing
Zambezi Delta Wetlands Conservation and Community Management Programme. A component of the programme is concerned with local community management and conservation of wetland resources in central Mozambique. Implemented by IUCN in partnership with provincial agencies and NGOs. Funded by CIDA, approx. US$1 million	1997–2000
Gorongosa Mountain Programme. Focused on supporting community institutions to manage sustainably the forest resources of Gorongosa Mountain. Implemented by Food for Hungry International and funded by USAID, US$600,000.	1997–2000
Local Management of Coastal Resources Xai Xai. Programme addressing the involvement of local communities in coastal resources management. Implemented by local NGO (GTA) and funded by European Union, approx. US$300,000.	1997–8
Niassa Reserve Programme. A consortium between the state and private sector for the management of Niassa Reserve and surrounding areas (total of 39,000 km²) involving the local communities. Implemented by the consortium largely with funds from private donor. Funds for community component approx. US$500,000 over next five years.	1997–ongoing
Programme for Agriculture: Forestry and Wildlife Component. Joint donor programme for support to relevant government sector emphasizing community involvement. Overall funding US$40 million.	1998–2003
Niassa Support Programme. Focused on the evolution of community conservation pilot projects in partnership with SPFFB, local NGOs and Associations, provincial resource planning and support to Niassa Reserve community sector. Implemented by IUCN and funded by Ford Foundation and Dutch government, approximately US$200,000	1998–9
Matatuine Community Conservation Programme. Programme for participatory management of local communities in private sector developments in the area (Blanchard Enterprises). Implemented by Helvetas (international NGO) in partnership with local agencies. Funding from IDRC approx. US$350,000.	1998–2000

7

Accommodating New Narratives in a Conservation Bureaucracy
TANAPA & Community Conservation

PATRICK BERGIN

Introduction

A review of the literature on community conservation suggests that the main protagonists of community approaches are community activists, NGOs, development workers and even human rights advocates. An impression is given that the community conservation counter-narrative (Adams and Hulme, Chapter 2, this volume) has been formulated, if not in direct opposition to conventional conservation agencies (such as National Parks Departments), then at least in a way that reduced their importance while more innovative institutions took centre stage. Even CAMPFIRE, which began in Zimbabwe's Department of National Parks and Wildlife Management, ultimately got most of its support from outside (Metcalfe 1992).

However, adopting this view as a generalization of institutional roles in community-conservation approaches would be incomplete, as the present chapter will demonstrate. Tanzania National Parks (TANAPA) is a parastatal organization charged with the management of the country's twelve designated national parks.[1] After initial pilot work in the 1980s, TANAPA undertook the systematic development of a park outreach capacity from 1991 to 1995 (Bergin 1995b). The steps which TANAPA took to build a community conservation capacity, as well as some of the effects of this programme within the organization, are discussed in this chapter. Organizational reform may be catalysed from within or without, but change from within an organization may be more embedded and longer lasting than that resulting from external pressure.

In its broadest sense, community conservation is about a re-alignment of relationships between people as individuals, groups and organizations. With rising populations and increasing conservation management costs, the balance sheet for conservation initiatives during the 1980s largely reflected a losing scenario. Community conservation seeks to renegotiate the terms of the contract between different stakeholder groups so that win–win situations can be achieved. Although the 'inherent rightness' of such an approach may seem obvious at the policy level or in academic fora, it is much more difficult for local community members and park staff to overcome years of antipathy and organizational habits of mind in order to collaborate with each other.

The means by which each side in the park–people conflict maintained its own sense of rightness was the myth of the 'inherent wrongness' of the other side. For park staff, and especially rangers, a local person inside the park boundary was dehumanized. This was no longer a person but rather a *poacher*, and with poachers a different set of rules applied. According to this thinking, poachers (those who break park rules) are not *bona fide* members of society and do not need to be treated as citizens. They can therefore be dealt with in ways different from those normally used to solve conflicts in society. Likewise communities have gone to great lengths to maintain elaborate myths about park staff. According to this thinking, park staff are not truly human. They lack natural affection for humans and prefer the company of four-legged beasts. They do not value human life as being higher than and more important than that of wild animals (Newmark et al. 1993). So much time in the bush away from village life has probably affected their minds. Do not try to reason with park staff. They are not normal Tanzanians trying to do a job but traitors to humanity.

It is into this context that community conservation was introduced in Tanzania National Parks. In its initial stages, the community conservation (CC) programme was focused on the ethical imperative for improving the relationship between park staff and people by restoring a human face to the park management, and by bringing park staff into contact with the village community as citizens rather than potential criminals.

The Introduction of Community Conservation in Tanzania National Parks

From the time of its founding until the late 1980s, TANAPA had no institutional capacity for collaboration with the communities surrounding its parks. This situation has now changed dramatically. By 1995, TANAPA had created a special cadre to work with communities, had community activities operating in all twelve parks, a community small projects support fund and had written community activities into its policy and planning documents. This section looks at how this change came about and identifies the three main conceptual phases that led to the development of the Community Conservation Service (CCS).

Pilot phase

In 1985, a workshop for the Serengeti Regional Conservation Strategy called for the establishment of 'extension and education' activities with local communities (IUCN 1986). Although earlier 'education' programmes had existed, a distinction can be noted as the rhetoric changed from 'if only communities understood the value of wildlife' to 'we need to solve problems together and make the value of wildlife tangible'. In 1987, TANAPA and the African Wildlife Foundation (AWF) embarked on a pilot programme in the north-east of Serengeti. Under this programme, a Community Conservation Warden (CCW), who was from the Maasai villages near to the park, was assigned to spend half of his working time conducting community visits and working with local people to try to prevent large-scale land alienation near the park.

Much of the thinking behind this work was based on the Wildlife Extension Project (WEP) in Kenyan Maasailand (see Berger 1989). During this phase, the creation of lines of communication with villagers was emphasized rather than incentives or economic benefits. However, a new park ranger post was established and funded by AWF to demonstrate that it was possible to improve both the park's infrastructure and to address local communities' priority need, for more security against cattle rustlers, at the same time.

Expansion phase

A workshop co-sponsored by TANAPA and AWF in 1989 reviewed the Serengeti experience and held it up as a model for possible wider use. The report of this workshop suggests, however, that TANAPA was not yet committed to the reciprocity required for an on-going dialogue with communities:

> … it was emphasized that up to now there has been no response from TANAPA authorities to the [CCW's] reports and the requests of the villagers. For community relations work to be sustained, communications must be two way, and the communities must feel that they are being listened to. If this does not happen, enthusiasm will be lost and cynicism may develop. The result may in fact be a worsening of relations with the park (TANAPA/AWF 1989)

Senior officials in TANAPA appear to have listened to such concerns, and by 1991 TANAPA had expanded the CCS programme to Tarangire and Arusha National Parks, followed by Lake Manyara in 1992. A small CCS support unit was set up in the national headquarters to coordinate and backstop these field activities. In a move towards independence from the initial AWF funding, TANAPA established an operations budget line to allow CCWs to travel and visit communities, and an initial fund for Support for Community Initiated Projects (SCIP), a small grants mechanism for communities living adjacent to parks.

However, the most significant move in the long-term institutionalization of the CC programme within TANAPA was the creation of a steering committee for CC activities across all parks in 1991. The coordinating committee was established with three basic functions: developing an appropriate community approach for TANAPA; ensuring a rational and consistent approach to community issues throughout the park system; and coordinating donor input to the CC programme. The committee met quarterly and played a strategic role in shaping the form, policies and activities of the department (Bergin 1995b). Membership of the Community Conservation Coordinating Committee (C4) combined key internal units in TANAPA whose support was necessary for the success of the programme (planning, public relations, finance) as well as donors and NGOs helping to fund and implement programmes in the field. This weaving together of the warp and weft of internal and external collaborators strengthened the moral and material support for the programme.

In contrast to the less-structured extension work of the earlier phase, the C4 was used as the forum for the development and adoption of a number of specific tools and protocols to be used for CC work in all national parks (Table 7.1). The mechanisms

Table 7.1 Tools and protocols developed by the Community Conservation Coordinating Committee to guide community conservation work throughout TANAPA

- CCW job description
- village profile form
- district profile form
- community survey methodology
- small project selection guidelines
- SCIP application form
- training protocol
- NGO policy guidelines
- community fund modalities
- technical assistance partnerships
- publicity and public relations materials

developed by the members of the C4 from different parks had the advantage of using a consistent approach and providing comparable data while ensuring the flexibility needed to adapt the tools to the different conditions existing in different parks.

In early 1992, a proposal was presented to the C4 to create a written plan for the development and expansion of the programme. In July of that year, the CCS held a national level strategic planning workshop facilitated by Price Waterhouse. This created a form of private sector imperative, which demanded that the CCS be successful in attracting supporters and resources to its work. The workshop included TANAPA headquarters staff, members of the C4, and representatives from parks in the southern and western zones not yet formally included in the programme. It produced a plan for further institutional strengthening of the CCS (through funding, training and additional staff) as well as for strategic actions (lobbying, networking with district development programmes, working with different donors). The plan also provided TANAPA with a document for politicians and donors to demonstrate that the organization had thought systematically about where it was going with its community programme (TANAPA 1992).

The benefit sharing with communities aspect of the CCS programme also began to take shape during this phase. The SCIP fund (Support for Community Initiated Projects) was established to help support small projects such as schools, dispensaries and shallow wells in villages bordering parks. The SCIP fund never claimed to be able to provide compensation for crop damage or to substitute for the opportunity costs of parks. Rather, it was based on the idea of reciprocity. The park management was asking local people to assist with certain activities that would help meet the park's (conservation) objectives. It was only to be expected that the community would welcome the park's assistance in meeting their objectives, which were usually in the area of social services provision. A small and relatively unstructured fund was initially established to enable TANAPA to respond in kind to worthy requests. Decisions on the use of this fund were taken by the TANAPA Board of Trustees itself.

The consolidation phase

The third phase of the institutionalization of CC in TANAPA was marked by the decision to make CC 'the way we do business' across the organization. This is a rare achievement as CC initiatives have been criticized (Feldmann 1994; Wright 1993) for not moving beyond the pilot phase or for becoming showcase exceptions, rather than the rule. Many countries have one or two project areas that are used to show 'development tourists' that villagers are involved in wildlife conservation. As a result of the workshop process, TANAPA systematically planned for the expansion of CCS activities and extension of the programme to all twelve parks. TANAPA developed its first-ever set of national policies for park management around the issue of CC. These policies included a section on 'Extension and Benefit Sharing' drafted by the C4. This section affirms that CC activities are an official part of the management strategy for all national parks.

Each year as classes graduated from the College of African Wildlife Management (Mweka) new CCWs were recruited until all twelve parks had designated CCWs. As the programme grew, zonal meetings were held in the south and west of the country to bring CCWs and other park staff, who could not all attend the C4, into a consultative process about the programme. Finally, the SCIP fund was enlarged and established as a separate account with its own procedures and accountant. In order to make the fund more responsive to the requests and seasonal needs of local communities, the allocation of SCIP funds was devolved from the Board of Trustees to a committee in each park. A short checklist of 'SCIP guidelines' was developed for these committees to ensure that projects have been properly planned, benefit the whole community and will not have serious negative impacts. The number of communities benefiting from the SCIP fund has risen from a few to the majority of villages bordering parks.

Understanding Organizational Change in TANAPA

This section[2] looks at organizational change in TANAPA using a classic organizational analysis approach. It will consider, in turn, the organizational environment, and then changes in organizational structure, processes and culture.

The organizational environment

The role of international agencies

The ideas of community conservation have many roots including the application of thinking about democracy, participation and economic incentives to issues of conservation (see Adams and Hulme, Chapter 2, this volume). For its part, TANAPA was aware of, and amenable to, the wider processes of change in Tanzania and elsewhere. TANAPA's most active partner in the establishment of the CCS was AWF. As part of the AWF programme, the CCS benefited from a full-time technical adviser and from linkages to community programmes in Kenya and Uganda (Barrow et al., Chapter 5, this volume). TANAPA staff participated in many fora such as the IUCN World Congress on Parks and Protected Areas in which ideas from other conservation authorities were shared, and in which the TANAPA CCS model was also presented and feedback acquired.

In the 1990s, virtually all new aid-financed projects for TANAPA were required to have a 'community component' and the existence of the CCS made it easier to treat such conditionalities as opportunities. The C4 committee provided a structure through which foreign agencies could contribute to and help shape TANAPA's programme. Through this forum technical advisers from AWF, World Wildlife Fund, DFID and Frankfurt Zoological Society all made inputs to the design of various tools and activities, and also made resources and training available to the agency. TANAPA CCS staff used the existence of outside staff, resources and ideas to promote the growth and acceptance of the CCS internally. In turn, it would appear that TANAPA has been well 'rewarded' for this programme through funding and recognition from development and conservation agencies.

The national environment

Three particular national factors influenced CCS. These were competition among conservation agencies, the political legacy of Ujamaa and the recent liberalization of the economy and politics. Unlike most African countries, community conservation in Tanzania has emerged in a wildlife sector that contains a number of national level management agencies that compete in many ways (Chapter 5). In addition to TANAPA, the Division of Wildlife in the Ministry of Natural Resources and Tourism manages the country's game reserves as well as wildlife outside protected areas. The Ngorongoro Conservation Area Authority (NCAA) is charged with the management of the multiple land use Ngorongoro Crater. Each of these institutions struggled over this period to promote community-oriented approaches within the context of its institutional mandate: the Wildlife Division focusing on consumptive use and hunting, the NCAA on its resident population, and TANAPA on neighbours to parks (Wildlife Division 1994). This situation led to some controversy about the nature of 'real' community conservation and competition between programmes. At the same time it exemplifies the diverse arrangements possible in different contexts. In fact, it seems that each agency interpreted the idea of community conservation in a way most suited to its specific context, and then applied it with varying degrees of commitment and success.

Another feature of the national level environment for the evolution of community conservation in TANAPA was the political climate and legacy of the country. Julius Nyerere's name has been associated with the Arusha Declaration, much quoted by conservationists for its clarion call to conserve wildlife, and also with the Arusha Declaration and the attendant policies of villagization, socialism and party organization at all levels (Nyerere 1973). The CCS needed to take a form that accommodated the diverse and sometimes contradictory messages coming from a socialist, single party government, moving to multi-partyism and economic liberalization. The ways in which this political legacy helped shape the CCS could be a study in itself, but a few examples can illustrate the significance. The high level of local organization in villages and wards gave the CCS a ready-made local institutional network with which to work. The promulgation of Swahili as a national language ensured that CCWs could communicate readily wherever they were posted. The overlap between central government (represented by the District Commissioner) and local government (represented by the District Executive Director of the District Council) gave TANAPA recourse to intervention whenever it felt that national interests were being unduly compromised by parochial concerns.

The emergence of the CCS coincided with the opening of the economy, the introduction of political pluralism and the growth of the NGO sector. According to

Cooksey (1994), literature on rural development in Tanzania in the post-liberalization period does not reflect any consensus as to who have been the winners and the losers in the flux of the period. However, most writers agree that social services for rural people have declined during this period, both in absolute terms and in relation to growing populations and expectations. The growth of poverty has been greater in rural than in urban areas and the agricultural sector has been particularly slow to show benefits. Thus, 'the low functional efficiency of the state bureaucracy...despite a decade of liberalisation ...further inhibits economic growth and helps perpetuate widespread poverty' (Cooksey 1992, p.62). The CCS, along with other new actors, such as the private sector and indigenous NGOs, seems to have found a role in assisting with the provision of social services in rural areas at a time when government provision was in decline.

Park–people relationships

Local environments influenced the development of the CCS significantly, but these are complex, differ with each park, and cannot be readily generalized. A few key points can be identified. A history of conflict certainly exists between local communities and national parks. In a 1994 survey two school teachers from a village near Arusha National Park gave reasons why they felt the park should be abolished (Table 7.2). The rhetoric of community-based approaches frequently begins with references to righting the wrongs of those who were originally evicted from national parks. While this is certainly true in a number of cases (Serengeti and Arusha) many conflicts in Tanzania are not between parks and previous inhabitants but rather between parks and recent arrivals to the area. TANAPA is more often in league with the 'indigenous' community in trying to plan for and mitigate the impacts of newcomers as in Tarangire, Katavi, Ruaha and Manyara national parks.

The lack of communication and the tension between local people and park staff is a common theme from different parks (Newmark et al. 1993). The issue of ranger harassment has also been a common and persistent issue. However, in the Tanzanian context this conflict seems not to be as insoluble as in some other places. Indeed when the CCS programme was being introduced in villages for the first time, a common reaction was that 'we villagers have always been ready for dialogue, we have just been

Table 7.2   Local residents' opinions on Arusha National Park

Reasons to Abolish Arusha National Park
'It should be abolished because of the huge annoyance of wildlife and because the park has failed to establish any sort of barrier, and also does not pay compensation for destroyed crops'
'Because of the destruction by animals of people's crops and bothering people when they are collecting firewood'

Reasons for Supporting the Park's Existence
'The park has many resources which can be used to promote development'
'It should not be abolished because it helps to teach students different kinds of animals, and people are helped a great deal by the forest'
'Because we get many of our needs from the park: money from portering, rain for the crops of the farmers, and foreign exchange for the nation'
'If it is abolished it is we poor ones (wanyonge) who will not get money to support our lives'

Source: Responses to the author during a survey.

waiting for TANAPA to come around'. A large part of the attitude of local communities to TANAPA seems to be that of TANAPA as a government institution with 'means'. Government institutions at all levels in Tanzania are usually grossly under-resourced, and this is particularly true in rural areas. Although TANAPA would also argue that its resources are insufficient, its access to significant tourism revenues as well as donor assistance is reflected in the fact that it has running vehicles, that its staff are better paid than most civil servants, and that new infrastructure is being developed. As a result of this unusual situation, many rural people view the park as a potential source of help or resources (Table 7.2) for their community (Bergin 1995b).

Changes in organizational structure

The organizational environment discussed above provides a context for the external conditions that influenced change in TANAPA. Internal factors and manifestations of change are discussed below.

Opportunities for change in a parastatal organization
The growth of the CCS in TANAPA has been heavily influenced by the pre-existing characteristics of the organization. Fortunately, as a parastatal organization, TANAPA has a degree of flexibility not found in line departments of the civil service, and this has aided creativity and reduced constraints. For example, the Director General of TANAPA was able to provisionally establish the post of Community Conservation Coordinator and later seek ratification from his Board. Creating an equivalent post in the government Division of Wildlife would require permission from the Civil Service Commission in the President's Office, a time-consuming process with a high probability of rejection. Also, as a parastatal, TANAPA was able to maintain and budget for its own revenues. Thus when TANAPA determined that it was in its best interests to provide some resources for community work, it was able to effect this change within six months. Again, a similar decision in government would require negotiation with the Treasury and could require years. Perhaps the most important factor was senior management's belief that TANAPA had both the right and responsibility to experiment with new approaches that could result in more effective implementation of the organization's mandate.

Changes in the structure of TANAPA management
Park management in Tanzania through the 1970s and 80s consisted of five major functions: anti-poaching, ecological monitoring, tourism, works and administration. With the creation of the post of Community Conservation Warden in each park, and the Community Conservation Coordinator at headquarters level, came the implicit admission that it is impossible to manage a national park without someone whose function it is to interact with surrounding communities. The establishment of the CCS created a sixth major function of park management and led to a revision of TANAPA's official organogram.

Deployment of human resources and capability
Another characteristic of TANAPA's organizational structure has been the overall uniformity in the training and qualifications of its senior staff. The key qualification of

the majority of TANAPA park management staff is a two-year diploma from the College of African Wildlife Management at Mweka. Degrees and training beyond this level were not actively encouraged, and those pursuing such training on their own initiative frequently found themselves sidelined out of management and into ecologist postings. As a result, there has been relatively little technical specialization within senior management. There is also less opportunity for the interplay of differing technical opinions than if staff came from a broader set of educational backgrounds. In this context, and despite government freezes in hiring, the CCS has been able to gradually argue for more staff with a CC specialization. For example, Tarangire NP had around 50 rangers pursuing law enforcement and only one CCW. While no one was arguing for exact balance, it did seem that the work of the CCS merited a ratio of perhaps 3 CC staff to 47 law enforcement rangers and this change was negotiated. Another indication of change is recent internal debates about the function of the deputy in charge of each park. Traditionally, the warden in charge of anti-poaching has automatically held the post of deputy and has usually acted when the warden was away. However, in recent wardens' meetings it has been agreed that a warden should be free to hand over the park to his most capable assistant, who may be in charge of CC, tourism or some other section. Finally, with regard to training and specialization, in the past few years five CCS staff have completed MSc degrees with a specialized focus in community work. This increase in training, greater breadth of experience and focus on CC as a career specialization augur well for the leadership of the CCS and TANAPA in the future.

Finance
The allocation of finance is often viewed as a prime indicator of an organization's priorities. A review of TANAPA budgets in the early 1980s shows a small amount for education activities and rewards for those who report poachers. With the establishment of the CCS, these votes were replaced first by a CCS operations vote which ensured that the CCWs were visiting communities and also that community members could visit the parks. Following this the SCIP fund was established to help fund small community projects. The SCIP fund currently amounts to about 7.5 per cent of each park's operations budget. Community members place great emphasis on the knowledge that TANAPA is actually putting its institutional hand into its pocket and pulling out something substantial from its own revenues. Tanzanians are used to a donor culture, but it is highly unusual for a Tanzanian parastatal to voluntarily spend over US$350,000 of its revenue in a year on assisting community projects.

Legal character of TANAPA and CCS
Tanzania is one of relatively few countries in which the IUCN category of 'National Park' has been strictly followed. Its parks do not allow for any permanent human habitation or any consumptive use of park resources. TANAPA's principal legislation, originally written in 1959 for the Serengeti, has never undergone a major revision, although one was in process in 1998 (FAO 1997). At a recent meeting of SADC countries on community conservation, it was noted that the policy and legislative basis has varied greatly between countries (Africa Resources Trust 1998). In Zimbabwe, laws originally written to help white landowners were later used and interpreted to the benefit of communal areas. In Namibia, it is generally agreed that a sound legislative

and policy context is now in place while examples on the ground are still developing (see Chapter 4, this volume). In other countries, great innovation has taken place under experimental permits from the Director of Wildlife; policy and legislation have caught up later. Tanzania has tended to follow the latter model with policy and legislation following, rather than preceding, new developments on the ground. TANAPA has formalized the participation of communities in its management guidelines and in its new draft legislation. The new sectoral policy for the Wildlife sector recognizes park outreach work as part of park management. In the most recent developments, the possibility has been discussed of playing a direct role in promoting and supporting Wildlife Management Areas (WMAs) on lands adjacent to parks.

Changes in processes and systems

Park planning
Concurrent with the establishment of the CCS, a new TANAPA Planning Unit (TPU) was set up for several national parks. The TPU has designed and implemented a participatory process for involving different stakeholders and different technical disciplines in the production of park management plans. The existence of the CCS has led to a fundamental change in the planning process that recognizes neighbours as key stakeholders. The TPU and the CCS collaborated at Lake Manyara Park in setting up a process for local input into the plan. The strategy had three major steps: a head-of-household survey to identify key issues for individuals and families, a series of community leaders' workshops in different localities to make leaders aware of the process and to identify and prioritize issues and, finally, limited representation in the actual planning workshops themselves. Due to delays in completing the plan, continuity was lost and it seems unlikely that the community members would view it as a single process in which they participated from beginning to end. However, an experienced CCW has recently been transferred to the TPU to build on and refine this methodology of local participation in park planning. Full integration of participation with orthodox approaches will take time, but these initiatives reveal a fundamental change in TANAPA's approach to planning.

New park areas
After a period of years in which the total area of lands protected by national park status in Tanzania did not change, several new areas were proposed for gazetting or annexation to existing national parks. These included part of the Udzungwa Mountains Forest Reserve, now a national park; the Marang Forest, to be annexed to Lake Manyara NP; and an expansion of the area of Katavi NP. While the process for acquiring these areas differed in each case, it was clear that community level issues had to be addressed at a level of priority that had not been considered during earlier periods of park gazetting. In the case of the Marang Forest extension, a Community Conservation Assistant (CCA) was posted to the area months in advance of the proposed consultation process in order to open up a means of communication. Later a series of consultative meetings were held at the village, ward, district and regional levels before submitting the proposed extension to central government.

Wildlife Conservation Awareness Week (WCAW)

In years past, many would have described TANAPA as an inward looking, if not introverted organization. In recent years this has clearly changed. The most visible sign of this change is the week long campaign held each year since 1995 in which TANAPA summarizes the results of its year's activities, especially those of the CCS, and disseminates them to the public, the press and politicians, along with an annual 'theme message'. During WCAW the Minister and members of the Board of Trustees visit villages around a designated park and open SCIP assisted projects. Seminars are held in which local leaders can debate conservation approaches with Ministry officials. Articles with statistics on TANAPA's accomplishments are fed to the newspapers, radio and television.

Changes in organizational culture

A former Director General of Tanzania National Parks was well known for frequently reminding his staff that a national park is a 'paramilitary institution'. In outward appearances this is certainly true. National park rangers wear green uniforms, carry arms and hold military ranks such as sergeant and corporal. Subordinates greet their superiors with a salute and the title *afandi* (sir or officer). Military discipline is very much valued during dangerous and sensitive operations such as combating heavily armed poachers, fighting wildfires and conducting rescue operations. TANAPA Board of Trustee meetings have traditionally included a military parade of park rangers before the Board Chairman. However, there is evidence that changes in the structures and processes used by TANAPA have also resulted in changes in the 'corporate culture' with regard to community conservation. Charting such changes is difficult, given the intangibility of culture, but there are visible signs at both the individual staff member and organizational levels.

Cultural compatibility of CC and TANAPA

Self-preservation is a strong behavioural determinant in both individuals and organizations. TANAPA has developed a version of the community conservation counter-narrative that is ideologically and culturally compatible with its vision and continued existence. There are many models and interpretations of community based approaches along the 'participation continuum' (see IIED 1994 and Barrow and Murphree, Chapter 3, this volume). While some of these interpretations have a distinctly anti-park and anti-state management theme, TANAPA cast the community conservation message in a form that was friendly not only to communities but also to itself. The CCS programme is referred to in Swahili as *Ujirani Mwema*, or 'Good Neighbourliness'. The philosophy of 'Good Neighbourliness' is not that parks are evil, colonial relics that should be turned back over to local communities, but rather that parks should have a good and mutually beneficial relationship with surrounding people and land owners. This ideological message made it possible for parks to 'be nice' to local communities while maintaining and indeed strengthening the status of parks. If TANAPA had not been proactive, other versions of the community conservation counter-narrative, such as collaborative management, might have been proposed, and would have been much less likely to find acceptance within the organization.

The politically correct park warden

As the CCS programme has grown in size and importance, one of the factors which influences the way a park warden is perceived by his/her peers, and evaluated by his/her superiors, is the performance of the CCS programme in his/her park. It was stated above that Board of Trustees meetings usually include a military parade by the rangers. In more recent years, members of the Board (the meetings are usually rotated among parks) have taken to spending an extra day to visit SCIP projects and communities near parks. While the functioning of the entire meeting reflects on the warden's managerial abilities, nothing speaks louder to the trustees than well-completed SCIP projects and contented villagers near the park. While it is appreciated by all that the relations between a given park and TANAPA are the result of many years and many factors (some parks being much more difficult than others) yet success in solving or mitigating such issues is becoming part of what it means to be a successful warden. Rather than building reputations as people to be feared, park wardens are now expected to enhance TANAPA's acceptability both locally and nationally. For example, Katavi NP in the south of the country has taken to hosting meetings of the local district councils each year as a way of keeping local leaders abreast of developments within the park, and emphasizing the park as a national institution which is nevertheless part of the local scene (pers. comm., Kyambile).

The corporate image

The CCS programme has now also become part of the corporate image which TANAPA projects. In place of the view that TANAPA staff are inhuman and care more for beasts than for humans, a recent TANAPA calendar shows wildlife on one side and a SCIP shallow well project on the other. This is a cultural revolution in some ways. Even at international trade shows, TANAPA staff have found that tourists and operators want to know about how wildlife tourism is being used to promote human well-being (pers. comm., Melamari). In radio shows, publications and newspaper articles, TANAPA now promotes the activities of the CCS as part of its image as an organization that cares and contributes to local society.

These changes in TANAPA's organizational culture should not be taken as reflecting a completely uniform view across the organization. A recent evaluation of the TANAPA CCS by independent consultants expressed some shock at discovering that there are still many people in TANAPA who have negative views towards communities (Kipuri and Ole Nangoro 1996). Change in a large and complex bureaucracy does not happen uniformly and does not happen overnight. Many may view CC as the political necessity of the day, but not one that they would choose if given the option. Nevertheless, the record shows a shift in the overall norms of the organization that is larger than the ingrained views of some individuals.

Institutional Change and CC: Some Analytical Conclusions from the TANAPA Experience

Internal and external actors and CC at TANAPA

Contemporary ideas about narrative and counter-narrative in environmental policy in Africa may exaggerate the role of outside ideas or change agents. Where a new idea meets an existing organization, complex interactions result rather than a one-way process of transfer. The sections above have discussed concrete ways in which TANAPA's adoption of the community conservation narrative has resulted in organizational change. However, it would be equally true to say that the narrative has been adapted by TANAPA, and that the CCS has become a reflection of TANAPA's most prominent organizational characteristics.

The role of individuals

Studies of organizational change indicate that for a new idea to take root in an organization, it often requires a champion (Blunt and Jones 1992). Murphree (1994b) has also discussed the role of individuals in prompting successful community-based programmes. The CCS has had only two national coordinators over eight years, which in itself suggests continuity, especially in the Tanzanian public sector where mobility is high. Both of these coordinators have championed the CCS within the organization. The first coordinator was largely responsible for the emergence of the CCS as a permanent part of the management structure, rather than being viewed as a temporary project. Under his tenacious pursuit, the budget lines for CC were created without which the programme would have been a temporary phenomenon.[3] The second coordinator has been largely responsible for taking CC issues to the top of the organization's agenda for board meetings, policy and planning. Both have worked successfully to overcome the earlier situation in which conversations between CCWs and communities at the field level were not followed up at TANAPA headquarters.

Individuals have also played an essential, if less obvious, role at the field level. For example, in Tarangire a successful CCW from another ethnic group single-handedly destroyed the myth that in order to be successful in community work in Maasailand, you must yourself be a Maasai. This has had important implications for policy in the recognition that CCWs and CCAs can operate outside of their home areas.

Developing, rather than buying, capacity

In setting up a community conservation programme there are many possible models. For example, different models were followed in Tanzania and Kenya with different implications for the organizational sustainability of the service (Barrow et al., Chapter 5, this volume). In Kenya, the Community Wildlife Service (CWS) was established by using largely 'imported labour' from community development and agricultural extension backgrounds. The coordinator of the programme was hired through an open recruitment process from a non-wildlife background. As a result, the CWS was often viewed as not a genuine part of the mainstream organization, and much of the expertise that was artificially brought into the organization has subsequently moved out.

In TANAPA, a decision was made that in order to be a Community Conservation Warden, one must first be a warden. This meant that all CCWs were Mweka-trained wardens, like those in other departments. It meant that they were qualified to take on other duties when colleagues were away from work, to serve as deputy and eventually to rise to a warden-in-charge. The TANAPA CCS gambled with CCWs initially less trained in community work so as to ensure the mainstream acceptability of the CCS as part of park management. Perhaps as a result, retention rates have been high. Only two professional CC staff have left the CCS and even these are still within TANAPA.

Making people's jobs easier, not harder

With any proposed innovation in a workplace, whether organizational or techno-logical, one of the factors in its acceptance is whether the workers perceive that it will make their jobs easier or more difficult. The available evidence indicates that on balance most TANAPA staff, including rangers, felt that the CCS made their jobs less stressful, made it less likely that they would be shot at or injured, and made it more likely that they would benefit from favours from the community, such as access to farming land. The social benefits of villagers being friendly rather than antagonistic to rangers should not be underestimated. Although a few rangers feel that the CCS is 'colluding with poachers', evidence from Arusha National Park shows that 83 per cent (*n*=38) felt their work had become easier since the introduction of the CCS programme (see Table 7.3 for more detail).

Table 7.3 Ways in which CCS has made work easier for park rangers

'First of all by visiting the community, then by having meetings with them now and again, and finally by putting a barrier along the boundary so that wildlife would not be able to destroy their crops'.
'The people have understood the meaning of the park and poaching has been reduced in some places'.
'There was poaching but [at that time] the village leaders were protecting the poachers when they went to hunt at night'.
'CCS has helped because the long process of educating each other about the importance of national parks has been seen, and the result is that even poachers to a certain extent have become fewer, not like it was in the past'.
'In many places which are frequently attacked by wildlife the villagers give a great deal of assistance to rangers, and when there is a fire in the park the villagers are in the front lines putting it out'.

Source: Bergin (1995a).

Sharing the credit

A final analytical theme deals with credit and 'benefit'. One contemporary theory of natural resource management is that where an individual or community has sufficient incentive to act in a certain way, they will. Organizations, conservation bureaucracies and donors also need incentives. Donors and NGOs need to claim credit for successful programmes that they sponsor, but it seems possible that they may some-times claim such a large share of the credit that little incentive remains for the local partner to feel and look successful. As a result, the local partner may disengage, and when the donors move on to something more exciting, there is little local ownership of the programme. As described above, TANAPA's CCS, like many other CC initia-tives, has been started with support from outside organizations. In the case of TANAPA, however, it is clear that TANAPA has taken ownership of the programme, and receives most of the credit. In doing so, TANAPA has ensured that it has sufficient organizational interest to make the CCS work. This seems to have operated in favour of the sustainability of the CCS programme.

Conclusions: Lessons for Policy and Practice

There are many lessons that can be drawn from the experience of organizational change in TANAPA as community conservation was introduced and developed. Three particular lessons have particular significance.

Expectations management

Economic analyses of the benefits and incentives provided under CC programmes suggest that there is an absolute threshold at which a benefit becomes sufficient to motivate a certain behaviour (Swanson and Barbier 1992). At any given moment this may be true; however, over time the theory of 'relative deprivation' explains that a person will be contented with a salary, a house or item of clothing, not because of an absolute standard, but in relation to what he thinks he 'deserves' and sees other having (Hutton 1973). The same is true for benefits received from parks and wildlife. An example of this principle came from Mahale Mountains NP on the shores of Lake Tanganyika where a community's attitude towards the park was transformed when the local schools inspector was given a bicycle. Although the benefit was small and did not impact on the wider community, a local leader reported that 'it was just so unexpected, coming as it did from the park, a place from which we had never expected to receive anything but trouble'. Of course this change in attitude may not have been permanent but this is just the point: benefit sharing and generation must be seen as a process over time which should become more rather than less attractive as expectations continue to rise. The perceived value of the benefit is equal to the difference between what is expected and what is actually received.

Community conservation and programmes and advocates who stress demonstrating 'significant' economic benefits from the beginning, and who continuously raise expectations about the sorts of benefits which parks or wildlife can generate, will eventually see a levelling off or even a worsening of villagers' attitudes towards the resource. CC programmes may experience a 'honeymoon' period of improved attitudes from local people when a benefit-sharing scheme is initiated. Indeed, a common model of CC programmes is one in which a donor picking up many of the administrative costs artificially boosts the economic returns from wildlife at the beginning. This is a recipe for disappointment and alienation when the true costs of the wildlife management enter the community balance sheet and net benefits stagnate or decline.

The TANAPA experience suggests a reversal in this approach to quick benefits. The CCS started by emphasizing communication and extension, not benefits. The SCIP programme started small and gradually expanded. As the SCIP programme nears the threshold of what can be sustainably drawn from park revenues without damaging park operations, communities are now being encouraged and assisted to start generating their own revenues on their own lands with assistance from the park. Like any 'real' business enterprise, the returns will reflect the investment in land, time and effort that the community makes. This will necessarily start small and gradually build up to a level where further investment or effort would not bring significantly better results (diminishing returns) and the community will have discovered its own 'benefits' threshold.

Community conservation and law enforcement

One of the most persistent myths of community conservation is that it is either unreconcilable with law enforcement, or obviates the need for law enforcement. Although writers such as Wells et al. (1992) have pointed out that a community approach in no way assures that all threats to park resources will disappear, yet many people seem to assume that a community focus means that there will be no more need for paramilitary anti-poaching operations.

However, community conservation is a democratic process which requires a context of basic law and order to function. For example, a 1996 study of the potential for initiating CC around Game Reserves in western Tanzania found that although many local people were receptive to such a programme, armed gangs of former Rwandan soldiers were conducting banditry and poaching in the area and destabilizing the security necessary for a viable community-based programme. Local people suggested that until the government could secure the area properly, they would have no incentive to worry about the long-term state of natural resources in the area (Bergin and Lyamuya 1996).

At Arusha NP, the park authorities and village governments agreed to try to handle more law enforcement between themselves, without depending on the police. Leaders in the village agreed to use traditional and village institutions to take more responsibility for controlling community members who were known to be poaching. In exchange, the park agreed that when people were caught for minor violations, they would be brought to the village office first to try to find some local way of dealing with the problem. Persons apprehended in the park for major violations would continue to be taken to the police, as the law requires, and the park staff and the village concerned would in addition take up the incident in future extension meetings. Where a few individuals in a community are chronic violators of the law, the village government is usually happy to see them taken before the law as they represent a threat to the security and reputation of the village (Bergin 1995b).

TANAPA staff see no contradiction between good law enforcement and CC work. Indeed, rather than diminishing its law enforcement capability, the anti-poaching capacity of TANAPA was increased over the period in which the CCS was being developed. CCWs reporting to the C4 repeatedly suggested that they saw no problem with wardens in charge of zonal ranger posts conducting both anti-poaching and CC activities. Both are two sides of the same proposition, with CC providing incentives for conservation-friendly behaviour and law enforcement providing disincentives for illegal activity. They are the right and left hands of one management strategy if used effectively. TANAPA is slowly taking steps to try to ensure that the balance between anti-poaching and CC is optimal, and that the two complement rather than contradict one another. A draft training model has been prepared to sensitize all rangers to CC issues. In recent years the *relative* importance of TANAPA's anti-poaching capacity may have diminished as CC, planning, tourism management and financial management have all grown in relative importance, but law enforcement remains an essential management function.

Learning from this experience, it appears that taking an either/or approach to law enforcement and CC is unwise and unnecessary. Putting all of conservation's eggs in one basket would be poor management when, for example, the insecurity discussed above is still a reality in many parts of Africa.

Combining CC with planning and management regimes

Tanzania's complex system of categories of protected areas, each under its own management regime, provides flexibility in choosing different prescriptive combinations of preservation and use. However, the different protected area laws can be confusing to local communities and are rarely applied in an ideal way. The TANAPA Planning Unit (TANAPA 1994b) could develop a more rational zoning of different resource areas as part of a participatory planning process such as that promoted. Most national parks in Tanzania are partially surrounded by game reserve, forest reserve or game controlled area. Participatory planning in a regional context could provide designs and combinations of protected areas which would serve both conservation and development objectives better.

The simultaneous emergence of the CCS and the TANAPA Planning Unit served to emphasize the fact that community conservation is not a cure for poorly planned and rationalized conservation, nor for management regimes ill-suited to the resource and context. Conservation planning in any country should be participatory and can provide for a range of conservation management regimes running from communal to private to national. Community conservation is not in itself a management regime but rather a commitment to 'do the right thing' for the stakeholders at each level.

Epilogue

As of this writing in late 1998, a snapshot of the TANAPA CCS provides some further clues about its institutionalization and future. Some of the core activities of the unit appear to have slid backwards, while other aspects have shown amazing resilience. Over the past 18 months, meetings of the C4 have been erratic, the disbursement of SCIP funds has been frequently delayed and there has been little evidence of training or new initiatives to improve the department's capacity and to take the programme forward. On the other hand, the basic structure of the department and the recognition of CC as one of the most important aspects of park management appears as strong as ever. It may be that after an initial period of euphoria and investment, the CCS is settling down into one more park management function that must compete for resources and management attention.

However, there also seems to be the sense that, having made the initial breakthroughs in communication and gestures of goodwill between parks and their neighbours, there is a cost-benefit threshold in simply doing more of the same. Instead, the frontier has moved to the question of how to make community lands themselves as economically and ecologically productive as possible without relying directly on park resources.

Tanzania adopted a new wildlife policy in March 1998 that calls for the establishment of 'Wildlife Management Areas (WMAs)' for communities who wish to manage wildlife on their lands. However, the role that the TANAPA CCS will play in supporting WMAs is not yet clear.

Notes

[1] Tanzania's wildlife sector is institutionally complex, with TANAPA being a separate agency from others including the Wildlife Division of the Ministry of Natural Resources and Tourism and the Ngorongoro Conservation Area Authority (see Barrow et al., Chapter 5, this volume). Thus this discussion of TANAPA's programme should not be seen as representative of the state of community conservation as a whole in Tanzania.

[2] David Hulme provided advice on the structuring of this section.

[3] The creation of a new budget line in a public sector institution is a difficult feat which requires major political negotiating and lobbying, particularly in the climate of pressure for smaller government bodies pared down to core functions only. This modification of the format of the budget and accounts required the highest and most conservative sections of the organization to concede that extension and benefit sharing were now essential and permanent aspects of the organization's functions, requiring regular allocations of resources, along with more conventional activities such as anti-poaching patrols.

8

Community Conservation, Reciprocity
& Park–People Relationships
Lake Mburo National Park, Uganda

DAVID HULME & MARK INFIELD

Introduction

This paper describes the community conservation (CC) programme at Lake Mburo National Park (LMNP) and assesses its achievements in terms of tangible benefits and influences on park–people relationships.[1] Despite its relative success community conservation at LMNP is found to be institutionally fragile and remains dependent on donor support. It has not been able to tackle the fundamental resource conflict in the region: the desire of local people to convert the park for cultivation and cattle grazing.

Conservation in Uganda

Contemporary conservation policies and practices in Uganda have their roots in the country's colonial history (Kamugisha 1993). This legacy has created a protectionist orientation that conceptualizes resource users (particularly farmers, cattle-keepers and hunters) as a 'problem' and seeks to achieve conservation goals by excluding them from resources identified as having conservation value. Arising from this paradigm is the patchwork of national parks, wildlife reserves and forest reserves, comprising some 8 per cent of the land area (Green 1995: 2) in and around which state conservation agencies concentrate. Although significant institutional changes have been made recently (Government of Uganda 1996; Uganda Wildlife Authority 1997), policies and practices established in the earlier part of the twentieth century retain a powerful influence over state conservation initiatives.

Over the last decade, however, conservation policy has shifted away from an almost exclusive focus on government interests, to adopt a more society-based perspective. Though many of the ideas underlying these changes were introduced by international bodies, the development of grass-roots democratic structures (the local councils) and the decentralization of political and administrative authority were also important (Barrow and Infield 1997).

In 1991, Lake Mburo National Park (LMNP) became the first park in Uganda to employ designated community conservation (CC) wardens and rangers. CC staff were subsequently employed in 19 of the 21 national parks and wildlife reserves (UWA establishment records, January 1997). Park Management Advisory Committees (PMACs), comprising members from communities bordering national parks, were established as a formal channel for park–community interactions. The Wildlife Statute of 1996[2] strongly emphasized community participation and development, and a Community Conservation Coordinator was appointed at headquarters. Since January 1995, a policy of 'revenue sharing' with communities, now formalized in the Wildlife Statute, has been in operation, alongside a policy of community resource access where appropriate.

Despite these changes the Uganda Wildlife Authority retains a culture that is both strongly paramilitary and primarily protectionist (Kazoora and Victurine 1997: 13). The community conservation approach has only recently begun to find partial acceptance with rangers and wardens, the majority of whom remain ambivalent towards the new policies. As one senior UWA official put it, 'community conservation is like a bitter pill being pushed down our throat'. In the field, community conservation has tended to be treated as peripheral to mainstream protected area management, an 'add on', rather than something that has profound implications for the law enforcement work that remains central to Ugandan conservation practice. UWA staff may recognize that local residents are neighbours, and understand the importance of working with local councils, but they continue to see communities as opponents rather than partners.

Lake Mburo National Park: Context and History[3]

Lake Mburo National Park covers an area of 260 km² of open and wooded savanna and wetlands in south central Uganda (Map 8.1). It was gazetted to protect the area's rich fauna and flora, including Uganda's only population of impala (*Aepyceros melampus*). That most other intralacustrine habitats of this nature had already been modified was important in the decision to create the national park, as was the area's potential value for tourism and recreation.

Prior to the turn of the century substantial parts of the Mburo area, controlled by the *Mugabe*, the King of the Banyankole people, were reserved for the royal herds. Periodic access was allowed to semi-nomadic Bahima pastoralists, who pursued an opportunistic grazing strategy. Small numbers of client Beiru cultivators and Bakooki hunters and fishermen had settled in the area. In the 1890s, devastating bovine pleuropneumonia, rinderpest and smallpox epidemics dramatically reduced human and cattle numbers, and though populations of the area's large mammal wildlife were also decimated, these recovered rapidly. Hunting was limited as the Bahima did not traditionally eat game.

In the 1930s the King and members of the royal clan became concerned at the increasing use of the area for hunting. Discussions with the colonial authorities led to

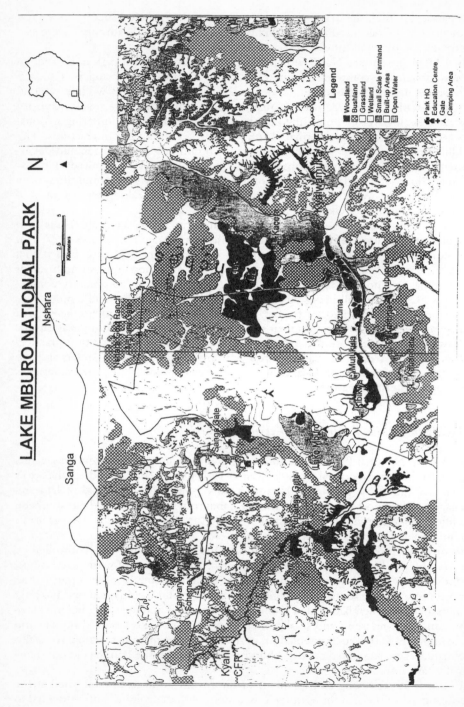

Map 8.1 Lake Mburo National Park, Uganda

the declaration of a 650 km² controlled hunting area (CHA) which regulated hunting, thus shoring up the King's declining authority. In the 1940s depopulation occurred as bush encroachment encouraged tsetse fly into the area causing sleeping sickness and *nagana* epidemics. Game numbers continued to expand, however, and the area became popular with visiting hunters, so a Game Department Camp was established.

As the colonial era drew to a close a flurry of state initiatives to promote development were initiated. A tsetse fly eradication campaign was begun which involved the clearance of bush and the shooting out of wild animals. By eradicating the tsetse fly, opening up the savanna and dramatically reducing game numbers, ideal conditions for both pastoralists and cultivators were created and migration into the area dramatically increased. In 1962, however, 650 km² of land to the north and east of Lake Mburo was alienated to form the Ankole Ranching Scheme (ARS), replacing subsistence pastoralism with commercial ranching. In 1964 Lake Mburo CHA was upgraded to a Game Reserve (LMGR). Permits were issued to 241 families judged to be 'resident', allowing them to remain and cultivate around their homesteads. They were soon joined by pastoralists displaced by the ARS, and by cultivators moving from overcrowded areas in western Uganda. Despite the area's legal status, the human population steadily increased, often with the connivance of Game Department officers. Many local residents reported during interviews that the 'bush' in LMGR was cleared during this period.

During the turbulent years of Idi Amin and civil war (1971–86) the management of LMGR was weakened by lack of operational funds, increasing corruption, and inconsistency in government policy and practice. People moved in and out as conflicts and economic opportunities ebbed and flowed. In the mid-1970s, 210 km² were excised from the reserve to form private ranches and the government Nshaara Dairy Cross Breeding Ranch. By the time of Obote's return to power in 1980 the Game Reserve contained approximately 4500 huts (suggesting a population of between 18,000 and 25,000) and 45,000 cattle (Eltringham and Malpas 1992: 5). Considerable areas in the west were under cultivation, and fishing and farming communities existed by most lakes. In 1983, the Obote regime re-gazetted the Game Reserve as a national park, ignoring all earlier de-gazetting.[4] National Park status made all residence illegal and the 241 households with permits, along with non-permit holding 'squatters', were evicted. During fieldwork many respondents described the evictions. Huts were set on fire and cattle and goats chased into the bush or stolen. People were physically attacked and there were unconfirmed reports of killings.

In 1985, Museveni's National Resistance Army (NRA) gained control over the Mburo area as it pushed forward to depose Obote. The NRA regarded the evictions from the park as an injustice and people were directed to 'return to their land'. Park staff were attacked and driven off, infrastructure was looted and destroyed, and many families moved in. Though some were families evicted in 1983, others were encouraged to occupy the park as a strategy to destroy the park's conservation value. Hunters were invited to help eliminate the wildlife. Respondents stated during interviews that it was believed that, if the game could be killed off, government would let the land be used for farming and grazing and abandon the idea of conservation.

The new government responded to this situation with great speed, especially considering the scale of the national political and economic problems it faced. The

Lake Mburo Taskforce was established and President Museveni himself is said to have taken a personal interest in the future of the park. Following the report of the Taskforce, some 60 per cent of the park was degazetted.[5] Uganda National Parks were left with the task of managing the downsized park, an almost impossible task at the time. The new boundary was not marked and remained contentious; the local population despised the park and continued to pursue its total occupation and de-gazetting; and government officials shied away from supporting the park authorities. Between 350 and 400 'landless' pastoralist households were given permission to remain in the park until provided with land. The legal status of these and the 200 farming and 100 fishing households remained unclear.[6] They viewed themselves as resident, however, and began to develop schools, churches and trading centres. Efforts by park staff to limit this, stop hunting, discourage the clearance of new lands for agriculture, and prevent the in-migration of new people led to tension. Respondents reported that at meetings between park staff and community members, both 'sides' regularly turned up with firearms.

During the 1990s the conservation status of the park has improved substantially. Government provided the promised resettlement land enabling resident households to leave the Park. By 1996 there were no permanent residents, allowing the park to be managed in accordance with the Management Plan: 'to preserve and develop the values of LMNP by conserving biodiversity, maintaining ecological processes, promoting the sustainable use of its resources, and safeguarding Uganda's aesthetic and cultural needs for present and future generations' (Muhweezi 1994).

Visitor numbers have increased significantly (Table 8.1), providing income for park management, improving staff morale and demonstrating the park's potential to local authorities. Income has remained low, however, and the financial viability of the park, with an annual budget of approximately US$60,000, remains doubtful. However, the financial and technical support provided by donor-funded projects has helped to develop infrastructure, train staff and pay staff bonuses.

Table 8.1 Visitor numbers at Lake Mburo National Park, Uganda 1986–96

Year	Total number of visitors*
1986	194
1987	1,375
1988	3,054
1989	2,217
1990	1,213
1991	1,543
1992	2,501
1993	3,687
1994	3,962
1995	5,137
1996	8,365

*This includes all visitors, both fee-paying and no charge.
Source: LMNP records.

Communities and Stakeholders at LMNP

The implementation of a community conservation approach at LMNP required that the park's 'community' be defined. This was not merely a technical task as it also has important political dimensions. The vagueness of the term 'community' (see Barrow and Murphree, Chapter 3, this volume) means it can be applied at a variety of levels: from a very local level (people who live in or around LMNP) to a global level (the global conservation community). Different actors will support different definitions of 'community' in order to achieve their particular objectives. Nine groups of primary stakeholders were identified (including resource users, government and non-government conservation agencies, and investors in the tourism industry), and five secondary stakeholder groups.[7]

Conceptually, 'community' might be specified through social identity, resource use, ecology, biology or territory.[8] Each of these has strengths and weaknesses. The limited resources available for CC operations led to the park 'community' being defined as 'those local people directly affected by LMNP or whose activities directly impacted on the park'. This was interpreted, in operational terms, as a territorial definition, and was subsequently adopted by the Park Management Advisory Committee (PMAC) which defined membership of the park's community as 'The people or a group of individuals, regardless of age, sex, ethnicity, creed or otherwise who are the true residents[9] within the parishes sharing a common boundary with the National Park' (LMNP records). Currently, the park 'community' is operationally defined as residents of the 13 parishes bordering the park[10] with an estimated population in excess of 80,000.[11] It has the disadvantage, however, of including within the park's community some people who have little or no interaction with or interest in LMNP, while excluding others who might have a substantial impact on the park.

Only a brief description of LMNP's 'community' can be provided here (for detailed descriptions see Marquardt et al. 1994; Namara et al. 1998). It is highly heterogeneous in ethnic, cultural, economic and social terms. The majority of the population are Banyankole with 43 per cent Beiru cultivators and approximately 30 per cent Bahima pastoralists[12] (Table 8.2). While a broad association remains between ethnic groups and economic activities, the boundaries between groups are increasingly fuzzy (Namara et al. 1998). Respondents to a survey indicated that household economies are based on a dynamic, portfolio strategy which, within a single year, might include cultivation of crops for subsistence and sale, animal husbandry, milk sales, charcoal burning, trading, paid labour, hunting and fishing. While 'pure' Bahima pastoralists were encountered in fieldwork, with government encouragement and support many families now also cultivate (ibid.).

Three important points should be noted about the park 'community'. First, like many in rural Africa, it is 'on the move' with very high rates of in-migration and some out-migration.[13] There is an active land market around the park enabling people to buy rights to be part of the 'community'. Second, standards of living in the community vary enormously. Some members own extensive areas of land, large houses, businesses and vehicles, while others are landless, live in temporary huts and are unsure of their next day's dinner. Third, not all stakeholders who have an interest in the park are included in the park 'community' as currently defined. Some geographically remote stakeholders have more influence over or

Table 8.2 Ethnic composition of the parishes adjoining LMNP, Uganda

	1991 Census (%)	LMNP socio-economic survey (%)
Banyankole, Beiru cultivators	45	43
Banyankole, Bahima pastoralists	23	29
Baganda	14	11*
Bakiga	8	9
Banyarwanda	7	8
Other	3	–

*Includes 'other' groups.
Source: Marquardt et al. (1994).

interest in conservation policies and practice than the park's immediate neighbours (e.g. Members of Parliament, local council members, businessmen, dispersal area residents).

This study confirmed the findings of Marquardt et al. (1994), that households close to the park boundary tend to be poorer than those some distance away. This reflects the relative unattractiveness of the park boundary, which is poorly provided with social infrastructure and badly affected by problem animals. Households on the boundary also tend to be the most recent in-migrants, and have not yet accumulated assets and resources (ibid.).

Community Conservation at LMNP

The introduction of a community conservation approach at LMNP was first mooted in 1987. Visiting international conservation workers feared the park would disappear in all but name without external support. They suggested, however, that park–people relationships appeared so negative and support for the park so weak that a conventional law-enforcement approach would fail without the development of a strong community approach in parallel. As UNP had minimal experience with non-militaristic conservation approaches, international technical and financial assistance was sought and in 1990 UNP, the African Wildlife Foundation (AWF) and the Swedish International Development Agency (SIDA) agreed to initiate the Lake Mburo Community Conservation Project (LMCCP) to develop CC capacity within the park and implement a CC programme in neighbouring communities. In February 1991 an expatriate Technical Adviser was appointed and in September, UNP's first Community Conservation Warden position was filled. Three Community Extension Ranger (CER) positions were then established, forming the Park's Community Conservation Unit (CCU).

Initially, the CCU focused on improving relationships with the park's neighbours and other stakeholders (including district and local government officials). Large numbers of visits to the communities were undertaken to begin the process of establishing a dialogue and breaking down perceptions of park staff as enemies. Reducing the aggressive behaviour of the park's Law Enforcement Rangers was also important. LMCCP intervened in the growing tension between park management and the park's resident 'squatters', striving to demonstrate that a negotiated settlement would be more effective than forced eviction. In particular, the project helped to develop relations with locally important politicians and administrators and initiated research to help understand and define the park's neighbours (Marquardt et al. 1994). As park–people relationships stabilized, the CCU moved on to initiatives designed to demonstrate that LMNP could contribute tangible economic benefits to its neighbours. Project funds were used to assist small-scale community development projects, generally the construction of social infrastucture such as primary schools or clinics. Later, in response to requests from community groups, enterprises such as bakeries, bee-keeping and handicraft production were supported. Emphasis was laid on encouraging villagers to look for ways of deriving income from park visitors.[14]

In 1993 the CCU began work to involve community institutions in conservation (Metcalfe and Kamugisha-Ruhombe 1993). Early work with the Uganda Wildlife Clubs to create clubs in schools was switched to focus on the establishment and development of a Park Management Advisory Committee (PMAC) and Parish Resource Management Committees (PRMCs).[15] As these began to function the issue of community access to the park's natural resources was frequently raised. Park management responded by examining mechanisms for sustainable use, and subsequently negotiated agreements for community access to lake and swamp fisheries, papyrus, medicinal plants and water (see below).

The Community Conservation for Uganda Wildlife Authority Project (CCUWAP), funded by USAID, was initiated in 1995. Designed to build on LMCCP's work, and expand it to a national level, it suggests that the CC approach taken at LMNP was perceived by UWA, AWF and USAID, as successful.

Community Conservation at LMNP: What Was Achieved?

One of the greatest difficulties associated with community-oriented programmes is determining their performance (Wells et al. 1992). The CC programme at LMNP was premised, in part, on the assumption that park objectives could only be achieved in the long term, if neighbouring communities received tangible economic benefits from the park. It was believed that the creation of benefits, by altering the balance of costs and benefits, would encourage communities to make their natural resource use practices and behaviours more compatible with conservation[16] (AWF 1990). At LMNP in 1991, creating economic benefits was clearly going to be difficult: the park attracted few visitors and earned little revenue, so tourist-dependent businesses were unlikely to succeed; UNP had no policy on revenue sharing; and consumptive use of park resources was illegal. The CC programme was designed to support the park by providing benefits to communities and strengthening structures through which both benefits and information could flow. While the six-year operational period of CC at LMNP makes it difficult to assess the impact of CC on the natural resource base of the park,[17] the ultimate objective of the programme, it is a reasonable time scale for judging the initial effects on local residents and institutions.

Economic benefits and costs to communities

Table 8.3 summarizes the benefits that accrue to the park 'community' directly from the park and contrasts these with the costs experienced. The institutional mechanisms through which these benefits are mediated, and the implications for the communities and the park are discussed in more detail below. Benefits are divided into direct cash contributions to communities, and the contributions made to the economy by the park's natural resources.

Cash benefits

Community conservation at LMNP envisaged that benefit flows could be increased by creating jobs and involving local residents in an expanding tourist industry. Although visitor numbers have increased (Table 8.1), they remain small and contribute little to the local economy. Support for village campsites and bandas, a cultural centre and handicraft production achieved little in economic terms, while other initiatives, such as the training of community members as guides, have been blocked by park management fearing competition. The 50 or so jobs at LMNP are held largely by people from outside the park 'community' despite the introduction of a local hiring policy. The two tourist concessions awarded in 1993 to Kampala-based companies employ only about 10 people and bring few other benefits. Early signs of a recovering national tourist industry have failed to consolidate, and tourism is not expected to grow significantly in coming years (Kazoora and Victurine 1997).

To overcome these problems LMCCP channelled aid funds directly to communities. A range of small-scale community projects (SCIPs), both social infrastructure and revenue generating in nature, were supported (Table 8.4). Initially, projects were identified and implemented by the CCU working directly with community groups. From 1995, however, to help strengthen community institutions and support UNP's revenue-sharing policy, SCIP funds were used to supplement LMNP's revenue-sharing programme. Projects were then selected and implemented by PMAC.[18] Under both regimes, the CCU provided substantial support to the process of project development, selection and implementation.

To ensure that the community funds achieved conservation results, UNP established criteria for community proposals, and PMAC was encouraged to select projects by scoring proposals in relation to these criteria. PMAC's key concerns in project selection, however, have tended to be political rather than technical in nature, requiring that all parishes receive a 'fair share' of the funds. Projects are thus sequenced across parishes, each getting equal access to revenue-sharing funds over time. Most went to primary school building projects (Table 8.4), the earlier focus on revenue-generating projects having fallen away entirely.

PMAC's approach to project selection contrasts strongly with that planned by UNP and reveals the types of negotiation and compromise that a CC approach to PA management requires. To its credit, LMNP management deferred to PMAC preferences and agendas and accepted a project portfolio which had limited direct relevance to park or project objectives.

Overall the projects funded produced a wide range of results (Table 8.4). While both income-generating and social infrastructure projects achieved successes (e.g. the Rwabarata Bee Farm and Rwentango sub-dispensary), and failures (e.g. Kakagati Bee

Table 8.3 The economic benefits and costs of LMNP for its 'community'

Activity	Benefits*	Costs	Role of Community Conservation Unit
Fishing	Offtake valued at USh 51 million in 1994 and USh 102 million in 1995/96, a major part of which accrues to the community. Also illegal fish offtake in swamps and other lakes		Has attempted to strengthen the fisheries co-operative without success. Negotiating for extension of legal fishing into swamps and other lakes
Wild animals	Substantial commercial and subsistence poaching, valued at USh 115 to 230 million per annum in 1996. A good share of this accrues to the community	Very high costs reported by farmers because of bush pig and baboon raids. Sweet potato, cassava and peanuts cannot be grown in some areas. A part of this problem, but not all, is LMNP induced Occasional loss of life and insecurity because of buffalo and hippo attacks	Has attempted to ensure that responses to problem animals and raids are dealt with more rapidly and sympathetically, but few tangible changes. Has promoted *bwara* fences, but none adopted to date
Water	2200 cattle permitted to water at River Ruizi for 3 dry seasons. 580 cattle permitted to water at Kizimbi swamp for one dry season		Negotiated through CCU, and very much appreciated by cattle-keepers
Grazing	Illicit grazing in the park	Fines, beatings and 'harassment' if caught in the park	Has initiated research on role of grazing for habitat management
Vegetation	Production of mats valued at USh 7.8 million in 1994. Provision of planting materials for medicinal plants		Research commissioned into use of vegetative products by community. Propagation of medicinal plants outside of LMNP unsuccessful to date
Tourism	Revenue-sharing has funded community projects valued at USh 8.5 million (1995) and USh 4.4 million (1996). In future 20 per cent of gate royalties for community projects		CCU has been central to the promotion of revenue sharing at LMNP and throughout Uganda. Other project activities have expanded the number of visitors

Table 8.3 *continued*

Activity	Benefits	Costs	Role of Community Conservation Unit
Attracting aid funds	CCU activity attracted SCIP funds for local communities 1991–4 and matching grants with revenue share 1995–7 Aid-associated activity (a small number of jobs and local purchases) has fed into local economy Donors provided several million USh to meet the costs of compensation for 'squatters' resettled out of LMNP		CCU directly responsible for attracting aid funds
Amenity value	Increasing number of community members (645 in 1996) and students (2029 in 1996) visit the park. Around 2 per cent of the defined 'community' visit the park each year.		CCU has encouraged local resident visitors and worked with the Park's Education Unit to increase student visits

Sources: See text

*In March 1998 US$1 = 1150 Ugandan Shillings

Table 8.4 Projects financed by the Support for Community Initiated Projects (SCIP) fund and their achievements

Project	Main activities	Size of SCIP committee	Active SCIP committee members (%)	Status
Rwentango Dispensary	Rebuilding sub-dispensary	9	100	Successful
Birunduma School	Rebuilding primary school	7	100	Successful
Sanga School	Roofing primary school	5	20	Unsuccessful
Kyarugaju Aid Post	Rebuilding sub-dispensary	5	0	Doubtful
Rwenikinju School	Rebuilding primary school	7	0	Doubtful
Kamuli Traditional Healer	Building facilities for a traditional healer	7	29	Successful (still operating)
Kakagatu Tree Nursery	Raising tree seedlings	35	100	Unsuccessful
Kakagatu Bee Farm	Honey production	n/k	n/k	Unsuccessful
Rwabarata Bee Farm	Honey production	28	100	Successful
Joyce's Tree Nursery	Raising tree seedlings	1	100	Successful
Rwabarata Women's Group	Tree nursery, bakery and handicrafts	28	4	Unsuccessful
Rwakukuku Women's Group	Handicrafts	n/k	n/k	Unsuccessful
Paulo's Live Fence	Bwara fence to stop wild animals	2	100	Successful
Godiano's Live Fence	Bwara fence to stop wild animals	1	0	Unsuccessful
Valley tank digging	Well and tank digging	n/k	n/k	Successful
Sanga Road	Maintenance of road	n/k	n/k	Successful

Source: SCIP file at LMNP and reports from CCU. For a recent review see Kazoora and Victurine (1997: 10–12)

Farm and Kyarugaju sub-dispensary), it is clear that social infrastructure projects were generally viewed as more successful than income-generating projects. Social infrastructure projects were relatively simple to design and implement, and tended to have wider community support.

Community projects have contributed little to local enterprise development or income generation, and have thus made minimal contributions to the livelihoods of the park's 80,000 neighbours. They have been, however, of sufficient value to suggest to communities that being a member of the park community has tangible benefits. During fieldwork the most commonly cited positive interaction with the park was 'improving schools'. Other research has also indicated the importance of these contributions (Ratter 1997; Namara et al. 1998). In economic terms, the community projects have been insignificant, but at the subjective level of community relations, they have been effective in demonstrating that the relationship with LMNP does not have to be exclusively negative and confrontational. Though the sums involved are small (see Table 8.5), they are considerably larger than those that could normally be expected from government sources.

Table 8.5   Projects supported by revenue sharing at LMNP 1995 and 1996

Year	Parish	Project	Financial support* (millions of Ugandan shillings)†
1996	Rwamaranda	Primary school	3.0
1996	Akaku	Primary school	3.0
1996	Rwambira	Primary school	6.0
1996	Rushsa	Primary school	5.0
1995	Rwenjeru	Primary school	4.4
1995	Nyakahita	Primary school	4.4

Source: Interview with Peter Karoho, Chair of LMNP Park Management Advisory Committee (22/1/97).
*Financial support to community projects was on a cost sharing basis. Communities contributed between 30 and 50 per cent of the project costs.
†In March 1998 US$1 = 1150 Ugandan shillings.

Resource access benefits
Until the early 1990s Uganda's national parks were managed in accordance with IUCN's categories of protected areas, precluding consumptive use of natural resources. Changes in UNP policy resulting from the inclusion of former forest reserves within the UNP estate (Barrow and Infield 1997) allowed LMNP management to negotiate community access to certain park resources. At the time of this research, formal or informal agreements had been reached on access to lake and swamp fisheries, collection of propagules for medicinal plant cultivation, access to water for cattle, collection of firewood for fish-smoking and papyrus harvesting.

Fisheries
The Mburo wetlands have been fished for decades. Though most of the lakes outside the park have been over-fished, Lake Mburo remains productive (Busulwa 1992). In 1995/96 318 tonnes of fish with an estimated valued of USh 102 million was landed

(Barrow and Infield 1997). Monthly catch data collected by the Fisheries Assistant for 1994, however, indicate a much lower figure (Table 8.6). The actual economic contribution of the fishery to the park community is difficult to assess. Though some of the 50 fishermen and many *barias*[19] are local residents, a significant proportion of the value of the fishery leaves the community and at least 25 per cent of the catch value went to park staff in the mid-1990s (ibid.).[20]

CCU involvement with the fishing industry has been considerable. Re-location of the 'fish landing'[21] to a new site closer to the park boundary was negotiated in mid-1997, and initial reports suggest that the move was successful and that the fishing community is happy with the new site. Efforts were made to re-establish a defunct fishing and marketing co-operative society, with a view to strengthening local involvement in and control of the fishery. Representatives of the park community argued for a 10 per cent share of the value of the catch for community development projects, rather than more control of the fishery. These funds will be administered by PMAC, almost doubling their funding.[22] Park management influence over the fishery, and their interest in creating local benefits for the park community, has thus both established sustainable use of the fishery and increased direct economic benefits.

For several years there have been informal agreements to allow spearing of catfish during seasonal flooding of the grassy valleys, and in 1998 the park reached formal agreement with the Kakobo community to allow basket fishing for mud fish in the swamps to the south of the park. No data exist on the economic value of these resources.

Table 8.6 Fish catches, fish mat production* and boat numbers at LMNP, 1994†

Month	Value of fish landed at Rwonyo (USh)	Value of fish mats produced (USh)	Number of boats fishing
December (1993)	1,762,160	364,800	55
January	3,356,600	554,400	60
February	3,585,496	646,485	56
March	3,860,872	392,160	50
April	3,007,750	899,460	55
May	3,434,350	1,002,060	55
June	2,614,370	968,500	55
July	3,842,220	922,500	47
August	4,796,927	876,000	47
September	3,177,630	528,500	63
October	5,225,920	332,400	66
November	4,361,652	270,550	66
Total	43,025,946	7,757,815	56 (average)

*Fish mats are small, dried fish (*Haplochromis* spp.) woven into 'mats' using strips of papyrus.
†Most recent year for which data are available.

Source: Fisheries Files, LMNP.

Vegetation

Only three consumptive uses of plants by the park community are authorized:

- collection of dead wood for fish smoking;
- periodic collection of medicinal plant propagules and seed;[23] and

- cutting of papyrus reeds for the production of 'fish mats'. Access to papyrus for other purposes has been researched and recommended (Guard 1993) but there has been no demand to date.

The use of pasture (see below), timber and poles, firewood and medicinal plants is not allowed. The park community thus suffers the lost opportunity cost to a significant resource.

Pasture

A priority activity for LMNP management has been the exclusion of cattle from the park. Most rangers see pastoralists as 'enemies', alongside poachers. The 9160 cattle[24] grazing in LMNP in January 1991 (Kasoma and Kamugisha 1993) were reduced to around 1000 when 'squatters' were resettled by the Ranch Restructuring Board (interviews with wardens). The remaining cattle are on privately owned land within the park whose titleholders rent grazing to pastoralists.[25]

The legislation banning cattle from grazing in the park is enforced by Law Enforcement Ranger patrols. Cattle found grazing in the park (by accident or by intent) are seized and owners are required to pay a fine, generally USh 50,000, to recover their cattle. The fines are negotiable, however, and PMAC, PRMC members or LCs can sometimes intervene and bargain down the fine. At other times rangers take a bribe. The ban on grazing thus imposes two costs on the park community: the opportunity cost of lost access to pasture within the park; and the cost of the fines and bribes paid (plus the time and energy spent negotiating them and retrieving cattle). Even so, park management and local authorities reported that pastoralist families continue to move to the edge of the park and 'push' their cattle into the park. It is reported to be cheaper to pay the park fines than pay the commercial rate for renting grazing (pers. comm. Kasisi). Namara found that illegal access to grazing was perceived as a benefit, quoting a respondent as saying: 'The park can be of great help, especially in the dry seasons. Aren't we better off than people living far away from the park?' (Namara et al. 1998: 60–61).

Ironically, the policy of cattle exclusion may be hindering conservation of the biodiversity and touristic values of LMNP (see Kangwana 1998). Acacia scrub encroachment (mainly *Acacia hockii*) is reducing open grassland habitats critical for many species, and making the park less attractive to visitors. Wardens and rangers are aware that the lack of grazing and trampling by large herbivores, including cattle, may be contributing to the problem, but most were adamant that 'keeping cattle out' must remain a park priority.[26]

Water

For centuries, Lake Mburo, the wetlands surrounding it, and the River Ruizi have been important dry season water sources. By denying access to these, LMNP causes considerable difficulties to pastoralists, and during severe droughts park management has been periodically required by government to establish water access 'corridors'[27] through the park for cattle. Concerns over their long-term management meant, however, that they were not incorporated into the LMNP Management Plan (Bataamba 1994). More recently, the CCU undertook negotiations with two communities, which had no alternative dry season water sources, to establish a 'corridor' to the River Ruizi across the park. An MoU was signed with the PRMC permitting 47 specified cattle keepers to water their herds (2233 animals in all) in the park. The MoU was for a period of three dry seasons, during which period the communities were to develop permanent water sources outside the park.

Reports on the achievements of this arrangement differ markedly. Community members reported favourably on the 'corridor' and on the park's assistance in solving their problem and CC staff reported that it had both greatly assisted the cattle herders and helped improve relationships with a community that had previously resented the park. Other park staff, however, believed that the agreement had been abused by the community members who had '...used it as an excuse to graze cattle in the park...cheated by taking their relatives' cattle along the corridor...and done other illegal activities'. It is apparent that this MoU was perceived by park management as a temporary arrangement agreed in order to overcome a short-term crisis, not as a mutually negotiated, mutually beneficial use of resources that supported conservation and development goals.[28] Senior management took a very contractual approach to the agreement, arguing that it should not be renewed on completion as the communities had failed to develop alternative water supplies. The problem that cattle herders would then face was felt to be '...nothing to do with the park'.

Wildlife

Though hunting is illegal, wildlife is an important resource for some community members and both subsistence and commerical use occurs (Namara et al. 1998).[29] Poaching, particularly of impala, takes place in the park and on surrounding ranches, and arrests and seizure of meat are common. Local residents described to the researchers how they poach and several respondents, including park rangers, reported that Local Defence Committee members use their guns for poaching. The involvement of staff of the former Game Department in organized poaching is well known and openly discussed, and personnel from military barracks at Mbarara have, at least in the past, engaged in poaching. Although Kazoora and Victurine (1997) report a widespread belief that poaching has reduced, this is unproven. Namara et al. (1998) report that local communities see poaching as a way of reducing damage caused by wildlife, while local authorities and LCs do not accept any responsibility for preventing it.

Only crude computations of the economic value of poaching can be made because of the limited data available. Fraser Stewart (1992) estimated an annual offtake of impala of around 600 per annum which, at a value of US$45 per carcass (pers. comm., Mark Infield), would give an annual value of around US$27,000. A sustainable offtake of 11 per cent per annum (easily achieved in impala) on a population of 18,000 impala (Olivier 1992) with a carcass value of US$50 to 70 for meat and other products (pers. comm., Brian Heath), would yield between US$100,000 and 140,000 per annum. Given that other species are also poached, including zebra and buffalo, the present value of poaching could reach US$200,000 per annum.

The community conservation programme has had limited effect on wildlife utilization. UWA is not able to negotiate with communities on hunting because it remains illegal. CC activity has reduced 'extermination' or 'revenge' hunting and increased 'tip offs', but these are insignificant impacts given the scale of poaching. The new legislation provides opportunities for wildlife utilization to become a key focus for community conservation in the future, and UWA will be able to negotiate use rights for wildlife on private land with communities.

Three conclusions can be drawn from this section. Firstly, the financial benefits accruing from LMNP are very small in per capita terms, of the order of USh 2650 per capita (US$2.30) per annum, and are probably more than offset by the costs of crop raiding and loss of livestock to wild animals. Secondly, though the CC programme has helped to increase the level of benefits and marginally reduce costs, it has not managed to significantly alter the balance of costs and benefits. Thirdly, the costs and benefits continue to be unevenly distributed, both between and within communities. For example, people living north of the park incur high costs through crop raiding and fines for illegal grazing, while communities living to the south incur few direct costs, but have received at least average levels of benefit from the park. Old people and widows reported that they cannot protect their crops from wild animals at night, so they suffer higher levels of crop damage than younger, more active farmers.

Community institutions and participation in park management

Prior to the adoption of the CC programme at LMNP, no formal structures for park–people communication existed. People with complaints or grievances could approach the Warden-in-Charge directly or through the LC system. Following pressure from donors to increase the level of community participation,[30] Park Management Advisory Committees (PMACs) were established. It is clear, however, that the PMAC was developed to meet UNP's perceived needs, and was not derived from the demands of park neighbours.[31] At LMNP, management, guided by perspectives gained from participatory processes used in the preparation of the park management plan (Muhweezi 1994), ignored UNP Headquarter's suggested structure, restricted voting membership to parish level representatives, and arranged for the election of PMAC representatives from the 13 parishes bordering the park. The decision to structure PMAC at parish level follows from the definition of the park 'community' as neighbouring parishes (see above) and logistical considerations. Working at village level (LC1) would be difficult as there are over 100 around the park, while working at sub-county (LC3) level would increase the park 'community' to more than 250,000 people. Operating at parish level has enabled PMAC to avoid being co-opted by local politicians, but has meant that its institutional ties are weak, and must liaise with a tier of local government which has minimal resources or responsibilities.

PMAC contributions to park management have been limited and sporadic. Interviews and records show that it is highly dependent on the resources of the park. Thus, despite its wide terms of reference, which include representing community interests, advising park management, channelling information to and from communities, and raising awareness on natural resource issues, PMAC has tended to pursue park identified priorities. PMAC has thus focused almost exclusively on revenue-sharing while resource sharing and other important management issues have been largely ignored. This was perhaps inevitable as the costs of PMAC meetings (roughly USh 300,000 including allowances for members) are met by the park (with donor support). Meetings are thus called by park management and tend to address their interests and concerns, while PMAC members seem loath to 'rock the boat'. PMAC minutes reveal that many members are unsure of their role. Most seem more closely aligned with park and government perspectives and positions than with community interests, while some members see themselves as 'auxiliary rangers'.

The intrinsic weakness of PMAC, the tendency of its members to become co-opted to the park position, and the attitudes and perceptions of park staff have meant that efforts to strengthen PMAC have achieved little. UWA is happy with a PMAC that is strong on implementation of park policy, but weak in negotiating on community interests. Recent initiatives to change UWA policy suggest a reconstituted PMAC with direct links to local government. At present, as senior staff at LMNP observed, PMAC is an institution 'without roots'.

Community attitudes and park–people relationships

Assessing changes in the relationships between LMNP and the people who live on its borders is difficult. Different communities have very different relationships with the park and, even within communities, relationships and attitudes vary between individuals. Older people, for example, tend to have more negative opinions of the park than younger people, while landless people tend to be more negative than land owners (Marquardt et al. 1994: 106). Furthermore, the nature of attitudes and relationships expressed by respondents seemed to vary markedly depending on recent events. Support for the construction of a primary school, for example, causes an immediate upturn in community support for LMNP, while a single aggressive raid on a village by Law Enforcement Rangers can sour relations for several years. The animosity caused, for example, by the widespread corruption surrounding the system of fining illegal grazing (Namara et al. 1998) is apparent (see Box 8.1) and again emphasizes community perceptions of demonstrable lack of reciprocity in park–community relations.

Despite these problems a number of trends in park–people relations can be identified. Field research for this study confirmed earlier work showing that animosity towards the park, its staff and its wildlife, has reduced dramatically over the 1991 to 1997 period (cf. Metcalfe and Kamugisha-Ruhombe 1993; Kazoora and Victurine 1997: 11). Rangers contrasted the present situation, being greeted by local residents and offered drinks, with that of earlier periods when travel to Sanga was difficult because of stonings and attacks. Wardens and rangers argued that 'tip offs' about poachers provided by communities demonstrate the changed relationship. In the late 1980s and early 1990s such assistance would have been inconceivable.[32] These improvements do not mean, however, that relations are always friendly, but confrontation is now relatively rare.

Box 8.1   Cattle and pasture at LMNP: an incident at Nombe

During a focus group meeting, participants complained about being harassed and beaten up by rangers. When asked to provide details of a specific incident a young man reported that he had been grazing 30 cattle in LMNP some weeks earlier as he could not find good pasture in Nombe. He had two young children herding the cattle. Rangers spotted the cattle and took them to Park headquarters. When he went to fetch the cattle he was 'beaten up and put in jail' at the park, and only released when he agreed to pay a USh 100,000 fine. Group members stated that he was bruised and cut on his return from the park. He raised the money from friends, paid the fine, took the cattle back to Nombe and sold one off to repay debts to friends. The young man made it clear that he would take any opportunity to 'pay back' the park, its staff and its animals because of this incident. Group members regarded this attitude as normal.

A key issue underpinning community attitudes was whether relations were seen as 'fair'or not. Where people perceived the park as behaving unfairly, relations were fractious. The nature of community use of park resources, the physical proximity to the park influencing both problems caused by wild animals and negative interactions with law enforcement rangers, and the history of interactions with park staff, both positive and negative, all influenced whether relations were perceived as reciprocal. Two specific cases illustrate this.

In one village, people complained that wild animals[33] caused extensive damage to their crops and made it impossible to grow maize, sweet potatoes and cassava. For this they received no compensation. When their cattle graze in the park, however, they are seized, and the owners are heavily fined and 'harassed' by rangers. Villagers were emphatic: 'It is not fair. If their animals [the park's] come on our land and do a lot of damage we get no compensation. If our cattle stray on to their land we are punished.' In this village the support from the park for the construction of a primary school had gone badly wrong. Money was embezzled and recriminations were made on both sides.

In contrast, the people of another village reported good relations with LMNP, suggesting indeed that the park was generous. A swamp separates this village from the park, reducing negative interactions. The villagers accept that the animals raiding their crops are not from LMNP and their cattle cannot accidentally enter the park. The community is pleased with the Primary School that LMNP assisted them to renovate, and they are negotiating for official access to park swamps to catch mudfish. When villagers do fish illegally in the park they are rarely 'harassed' as rangers do not often visit the area.

Marquardt et al. (1994: 104) found that cultivating households had a markedly more positive attitude to the park than mixed farmers and cattle keepers. Namara et al. found a similar result (1998: 51). Location is also important; households located close to the park express more negative attitudes than do more distant ones (Marquardt et al. 1994). During fieldwork people in parishes to the north of LMNP seemed to perceive the park and its staff as treating them unfairly. The relatively high population densities pushed them to farm and graze cattle directly on the park boundary, leading to more frequent negative interactions with wildlife or park staff. To the south, the existence of a natural physical barrier reduced negative park–people interactions, leading to more favourable perceptions.

The degree to which the changes in relations with the community can be attributed to the CC progamme and how much to other reasons (e.g. changes in LMNP staff, reductions in animal numbers, the improved local economy, etc.) is difficult to determine. Namara et al. present data suggesting that the CC programme has had significant effects on community attitudes towards the park (1998: 46). This study found that CCU activities have shifted the balance of park–people interactions sufficiently to enable community members to view them as more reciprocal. Revenue-sharing and resource-sharing initiatives have contributed tangible benefits to communities. Education programmes for school children have been appreciated by parents. Persuading park management to negotiate the voluntary resettlement of 'squatters', rather than opting for eviction, prevented the creation of another group of park neighbours with a 'historical' reason for viewing LMNP as 'bad' (Marquardt et al. 1994: 102). The destruction of dangerous animals (buffaloes and hippos) outside the park has reduced some of the costs imposed on local residents by LMNP, and the

CCU's live fencing[34] programme may do more. In addition, the participatory approach adopted by the CCU, involving discussions, negotiations and attempts to find opportunities for agreement, has begun to shift park–people communications away from always 'telling' towards 'listening'. The evidence points to CC having made a significant contribution to improvements in park–people relations. '...[C]ommunities enjoy the good neighbour policy and prefer dialogue to force' (Kazoora and Victurine 1997: 19).

Effects of the CC programme on park management and UWA

The CC programme at LMNP has produced considerable benefits for the park as an institution. The improvement in park–people relations discussed above clearly constitutes a benefit to both parties. The park has also benefited financially from the CC programme, with increased funding for routine operations and development. Although donors in the early 1990s would have been unlikely to finance a 'protection only' initiative in Uganda, the CC programme provided a framework for donors to provide parallel funding directly for general management purposes (e.g. development of park and tourist infrastructure, preparation of Park Management Plan). In addition, leakages from the CC programme (e.g. vehicle operations, field allowances) provided additional funds for general management. The activities generated by the CC programme also 'snowballed', attracting donor funding to areas around the park.[35] Adopting a CC approach as a means of gaining additional resources may not have been a conscious strategy of UWA, but this has undoubtedly resulted.

Though the LMNP experiment in CC has led to the establishment of a CCU with two wardens and three rangers, the unit will have to overcome substantial challenges if it is to become an effective part of the park's management structure. It will need to reduce costs (Kazoora and Victurine 1997), and strengthen claims on park funds when donor funds are withdrawn. The CCU will need to clarify its role and methods so that other sections at LMNP can understand what CC is. Critically, the CCU must develop a strategy for the CC programme to become an integral component of park management, not simply an 'add on' as at present. Its success in this will be measured by its ability to attract a recurrent budget, increase staffing levels, influence the implementation of 'law enforcement' and, more generally, help create policies and practices on employment, road maintenance and sharing revenues and resources which benefit communities.

While a wide set of factors persuaded policy makers and UWA senior managers that approaches to conservation had to modify historical relations and interactions with rural communities, there is evidence that the LMNP experience helped push CC on to the policy agenda at the national level. The establishment of the Community Conservation Department at UWA headquarters in 1997 resulted from LMCCP and is supported by CCUWA. Many UWA staff have been introduced to community conservation by working at or visiting LMNP or have been briefed on the work of the CCU. Donors and international NGOs have kept a close eye on LMNP to identify 'lessons' for other projects in Uganda. The contribution of the CCU to improved park–people relationships at LMNP was seen as practical proof that 'community conservation works', and aided the rapid diffusion of CC through UWA.

However, the CC approach developed at LMNP has left a legacy that must be dealt with if CC is to be institutionalized within UWA. The CC programme at LMNP has high operational costs. It depends on four-wheel-drive vehicles, staff travel allowances and incentives, and park-based wardens and rangers. Such a model was probably inevitable given donor involvement and the pressing need to achieve significant results in the first two to three years. It is clear, however, that the capacity of UWA to service such costs is low. Having demonstrated that CC can be effective in Uganda, the next task is to find means by which it can produce similar results at lower cost (Kazoora and Victurine 1997). The ultimate challenge for CC will be whether UWA funds it as a core activity when donors withdraw, or whether it is treated as a donor-financed 'luxury' that can be abandoned when the aid flows stop.

Conclusions

The conclusions drawn from the community conservation experience at LMNP depend on the perspective that is taken, the timescale that is employed and the level of analysis. Community conservation at LMNP represents a passive and consultative participation approach to what Barrow and Murphree (Chapter 3, this volume) classify as 'protected area outreach'. It has informed and consulted neighbours, helped establish channels for communication, broken down long-established antipathies and produced a limited flow of tangible benefits. It has not, however, sought to empower the park 'community' to manage the park by taking the more radical 'collaborative management' approach (Chapter 3). This would probably have been difficult if not impossible to implement in 1991, when communities were distrustful of the park staff, were vulnerable to manipulation and exploitation by their leaderships, had few technical management skills and when UNP was unwilling to relinquish power over the parks. The CC approach has, however, enriched the structure of incentives for conservation which now comprises 'carrots' as well as 'sticks'. The protectionist 'fines and fences' approach has not been replaced at LMNP, but supplemented with community conservation, as is the case in most protected areas in Africa and else-where. Indeed, for the CC approach to have yielded results at LMNP, the law enforcement platform needed to strengthen, as by 1991 the 'community' had gained effective control over the park and it was, from a conservation perspective, being rapidly degraded. At LMNP, a small investment in 'reciprocity' through the CC programme produced high returns in improved relations as government control over the park was re-establishing.

At the park management level, community conservation has been an effective additional supplement to existing strategies. It has aided the achievement of short- and medium-term targets, although at the cost of dependence on donor funding (this may be a norm for protected areas in Africa). However, even after seven years, CC remains a fragile transplant, heavily dependent on aid finance and reliant on a small number of key personnel. When LMCCP ended in August 1994, despite a promise of future funding, there was 'no project' for a 10-month period. During this period, CC activities were largely suspended and the CCU ceased to exist as a unit. The knowledge that there would be a second phase, however, may have helped the CC approach to persist, and park management continued to provide support for CC initiatives during this period, including the negotiation of the cattle 'corridor', one of the most interesting of the CCU's achievements. The CCU had clearly not been fully integrated into the park's management structure, despite the apparent change in the park's management approach. Real committment to CC among park staff remains weak, or at best patchy (Kazoora and Victurine 1997; Namara et al. 1998). At present, the CC programme brings sufficient benefit to the park staff to elicit some support. In the absence of donor finance for CC, this may well change, and the hard won progress in park–people relationships achieved by the CCU could be rapidly undone by a return to a heavy-handed law enforcement approach.

From a conservation perspective (key species, biodiversity, habitat, park integrity) there is evidence that CC has helped to reduce the likelihood of rapid biological degradation in the park and has been effective in retaining the potential for conservation in the future (Kangwana 1998). This has been achieved by significantly contributing to improved park–people relationships, increasing support for the park among community leaders at local and district levels, strengthening the flow of visible benefits accruing to neighbours from the park and reducing levels of local resident behaviours that are detrimental to park integrity.

At the community level, CC remains weak, demonstrating the difficulties of building support for conservation in communities largely interested in development, where conservation is defined in terms of meeting production or development needs (i.e. conservation of soil, water, grass), and wildlife viewed as worthless. The CC programme has made small but potentially significant contributions to community cohesion and has reduced levels of tension between state officials and local people. However, the institutional framework for negotiating conservation objectives and natural resource use between government agencies and communities remains in its infancy. Power clearly continues to reside in the park management and co-opted local elites.

Economically, CC has increased the flow of tangible benefits to the community and marginally reduced some of the costs imposed on it. Compared, however, with the value of cultivation[36] and grazing potentials denied, these benefits are minute. The costs to the local community of not developing this area of high agricultural potential are monumental compared with the benefits created by the CC programme. The broader social and economic context will therefore continue to present a threat to LMNP. In-migration to Mbarara District means that its population is growing faster than the national average of 2.8 per cent per annum (UNDP 1994). The agricultural frontier is being rapidly pushed forward to meet the opportunities created by the growing dairy industry and for cash crop production. Community conservation has thus failed to reverse the economic fundamentals of conservation at LMNP and the park remains a significant drain on the national and local economy.[37]

The main beneficiaries of community conservation at LMNP, it could be argued, are international and Ugandan conservationists, the Ugandan conservation bureaucracy, donor agencies and foreign tourists. The CC programme, by improving the conservation status of the park, is supporting a well-disguised form of 'quiet violence' that provides benefits to a small national elite, and tens of millions of 'couch potato' conservationists worried about African wildlife, while making tens of thousands of rural Ugandans poorer. Park staff describe the park as being 'for the people of Uganda', both present and future. The priorities of local communities, however, are on economic developments which would require land uses that are incompatible with national park status. Expecting to create a situation in which local residents describe the park as '…our park' may be unreasonable given the unavoidable costs to local communities of conservation. By creating a rhetoric of 'partnership' in an asymmetric conflict (Mitchell 1991) in which the interests of the parties may be ultimately irreconcilable,[38] CC may have unrealistically raised expectations of the degree to which UWA is prepared or able to negotiate on conservation objectives. Namara et al. (1998) found that the CC programme has increased community demands, especially for access to resources, while UWA's policy and conservation mandate continue to prevent these demands being met. National legislation makes it clear that the Park belongs to the state, not to 'the people', and certainly not to the Park community. It is important for CC to 'work out just how much local participation is consistent with the projects' objectives, and to be honest about the answer' (Wells 1995: 29).

The fundamental question of who bears the costs of conservation thus remains unresolved. The CC programme at LMNP has created a refinement of traditional protected area management strategies which leaves the relative power of the state and communities largely unchanged. If UWA continues down the path of 'participation', however, which may be inevitable in a decentralized adminstration, the long-term outcome is unclear. If the logical conclusion of CC is that communities are empowered to define conservation values for themselves, without reference to national or international values, conservation, at LMNP at least, will be fundamentally different. Production values, including opportunities for tourism, and culturally relevant landscapes, rather than biodiversity, will determine its form. Perhaps the ultimate achievement of community conservation at LMNP, from a conservation perspective, will be the way in which it contributes towards changing the ideas that local communities hold about conservation.

Notes

[1] The original research for this paper was conducted in January 1997. For details of the methodology and researchers see Hulme (1997b) and Kangwana (Chapter 17, this volume). Subsequent data have been acquired from the 1997 socio-economic survey, key informant interviews and documentation by Mark Infield.

[2] The Uganda Wildlife Statute of 1996 established the Uganda Wildlife Authority (UWA) which took over the responsibilities of Uganda National Parks (UNP) and the Game Department following a restructuring exercise in 1996. The Statute includes the requirement that 20 per cent of park entry fees are shared with local communities. This revenue sharing policy has only been partially implemented in many parks.

[3] The information in this section has been gathered from Bataamba (1994), Kamugisha and Stahl (1993), Marquardt et al. (1994), Namara et al. (1998), Snelson and Wilson (1994) and field research.

[4] Although conversion from a game reserve to a national park had long been discussed, the decision was made as much for political reasons, to damage the interests of the Banyankole people because of their believed support for the anti-Obote resistance movement, as for conservation reasons.

[5] The degazetting and allocation of land to individuals was far from transparent. There is evidence of politically powerful individuals and groups competing in complex 'land grabbing' contests at this time alongside the more legitimate claims of families who had been evicted.

[6] While some, having entered the area after 1983, were viewed by government as having exploited the period of chaos to 'grab' land, others were former residents who had returned, and were thus viewed as legitimate and entitled to compensation.

[7]Stakeholders are persons, groups or organizations with interests in a specific organization, project, programme or policy. Primary stakeholders are those who directly benefit or suffer from the specific organization, project, programme or policy. Secondary stakeholders are those who indirectly benefit or suffer from the specific organization, project, programme or policy.

[8]The resource-user model would define all those who use resources within LMNP as the 'community'. The ecological model would define the ecosystem within which LMNP is located, perhaps on the basis of a watershed, and the population that lives within that area would be the 'community'. A biological model would focus on a key species or set of species (e.g. impala) and identify the community as all who live within LMNP and the dispersal area of the key species. Finally, a territorial model would define the community in terms of proximity to LMNP. The criteria that could be used for 'territory' are many, but the commonest is to adopt existing administrative boundaries.

[9]'True residents' is not defined in the document. The CCW indicated that it refers to any legal resident, probably any Ugandan citizen, confirmed at the village level by the LC I Committee.

[10]By late 1997 the original 13 parishes became 15 as two parishes were subdivided. The PMAC did not feel able to exclude the two new parishes from the park community. While this changed the number of parishes, and meant that two parishes included in the 'community' actually had no direct boundary with the park, the geographical area covered remained identical.

[11]The 1991 Housing and Population Census recorded the population of the 13 parishes as 71,240 (Government of Uganda 1992). If one assumes that two-thirds of the 6 per cent of the 1991 population that was of Rwandan origin has returned to Rwanda (with its offspring) and that the remaining population has grown at the national average of 2.8 per cent per annum, then the population of the 13 parishes would reach 80,715 in 1997. This is a crude estimate, however, as the population around LMNP is very mobile with substantial in-migration occurring but also some out-migration.

[12]The Banyankole are divided into two ethnic groups or classes based on their primary economic activity; historically, Bahima are pastoralists while Beiru are cultivators.

[13]In 1991/92, almost 10 per cent of the park 'community' was found to have been resident for less than one year, while only half had been resident for more than ten years (Marquardt et al. 1994). This very high rate of in-migration seems to have reduced in more recent years (Namara et al. 1998).

[14]Another component of the project began to upgrade park visitor facilities and improve its marketing.

[15]PMAC was created as part of a national level initiative taken by UNP to increase community participation and interest in the management of the national parks. PRMCs were developed to enable PMAC to be representative and to reach down to the 'grass roots' level.

[16]It should also be added that CC was seen as a means of influencing LMNP management to modify its approach to relations with the local community.

[17]See Kangwana (Chapter 17, this volume) for a discussion of the monitoring of impact on conservation values of CC or other protected area support programmes.

[18]In 1995 UNP introduced a revenue-sharing policy which set aside 12 per cent of total park revenues for community projects, subsequently amended by national legislation to 20 per cent of park gate fees. UNP policy specified that Park Management Advisory Committees would be the primary conduit for revenue-sharing funds, responsible for selecting projects to be supported, allocating funds and overseeing implementation.

[19]Generally, the word 'fisherman' refers to the licence holder and owner of the canoe and nets, while *baria* refers to the worker who actually does the fishing.

[20]LMNP staff operated 18 of the 50 canoes working on Lake Mburo. Since 1997, however, park staff have ceased to be involved in the fishing industry; only 36 canoes now operate, reducing fishing effort significantly.

[21]Park management does not recognize fishing community rights to the land and therefore refers to a 'fish landing' rather than a 'fishing village'. The Lake Mburo Task Force agreed that the lake should be fished but that no village should be formed. The park management therefore charged 'camping fees' at the old site and rents out the rooms at the new site.

[22]The first payment of USh 360,000, representing one month's 'tax', was made to PMAC in April 1998.

[23]While the majority of medicinal plants are found outside the park, a small number can only be found inside (Scott 1993). The CCU has provided technical assistance for the cultivation of these materials outside the park.

[24]Other observers believe that this figure is an underestimate and that in 1991 some 20,000 cattle were 'resident' in LMNP while up to another 60,000 were moved in temporarily because of a severe drought (pers. comm., Mark Infield).

[25]Three freehold land titles covering approximately 13km² were issued in the 1930s prior to the establishment of the Game Reserve. In 1997, the Government paid USh 168 million in compensation for the compulsory purchase of this land. There are thus currently no cattle legally resident in the park.

[26]Bush encroachment is a complex and little understood phenomenon. At LMNP, key variables include rainfall, patterns and intensity of grazing and browsing, the frequency and form of bush fires, cessation of bush cutting by people, and the extinction of elephant and black rhino.

[27]In addition to the water access corridor, park management also granted permission for cattle keepers in Rwabarata parish to cross the park in mid-1996 to avoid a foot and mouth disease area.

[28]Subsequent to fieldwork the cattle corridor agreement was extended. PMAC and the project have agreed that Akaku and Rwamuranda parishes should receive US$10,000 from the project's Community Development Funds for dam construction to solve this problem. The local community have failed, however, to contribute the agreed US$5000 (in cash or kind), as a large World Bank-funded dam has recently been built.

[29]All wildlife utilization (i.e. hunting) in Uganda is prohibited under a Presidential ban issued in 1978. The recent 1996 Wildlife Statute provides for hunting through the granting of use rights, but this has not yet been implemented and the ban remains in place.

[30]UNP was under strong pressure from USAID which had made community participation in park management a condition for future funding. A USAID-commissioned report had recommended that Park Management Committees (PMCs) with community representatives would be the appropriate vehicle for community participation (Ogwang and De George 1992). In the process of adopting and adapting these recommendations UNP determined that community participation would be 'advisory' and not executive.

[31]Community groups drawn together to contribute towards the development of the Park Management Plan expressed the need for a body or committee to improve communications between the park and the community, but no initiative was taken to determine a suitable structure.

[32]Although 'tip-offs' do occur, this is by no means the norm. Namara et al. (1998) found that most respondents found no reason to assist the park to combat poaching and often supported poachers as a means of reducing damage to their crops by wild animals.

[33]The most commonly cited pests were bush pigs and baboons. It must be noted that while the park is a sanctuary for these species they also live outside the park and are not necessarily 'park animals'. However, the popular perception is that these vermin 'belong' to the government and thus that the government (i.e. the park) is responsible for them.

[34]The CCU has been working on the promotion of live fencing with *Ceaselpina decipetela* which has been shown to create an effective barrier against bush pigs, baboons and buffaloes, though problems of maintenance and competition for water remain unresolved to date.

[35]Intensive efforts by project staff eventually led to the establishment of the GTZ-funded Integrated Pastoralist Development Project on ranches to the north and east of the park.

[36]Mason (1995) estimated that agricultural production forgone at LMNP as a result of National Park status is in the order of a minimum value of US$42.7 million per annum but may be as high as US$103.9 million per annum. Clearly, however, much of this would not directly benefit the park community.

[37]LMNP may represent an unusual position for African parks, having relatively high-level agricultural potential and relatively low tourist potential compared with more typical arid and semi-arid environments. However, the economics of many, perhaps most, protected areas in Africa, in production terms, is weak (cf. Howard 1995; Norton–Griffiths 1995; Mason 1995).

[38]Mitchell (1991) suggests that resource conflicts tend to be asymmetrical in that one or both groups in the conflict are not concerned with the position and interests of the other, and therefore avoid negotiation and attempt coercion. Conflicts concerning PAs clearly tend to be asymmetric (Carpenter and Kennedy 1985) and LMNP is no exception. Park management is constrained by the law and by its mandate for biodiversity conservation, while the park community tends to discount these in its demands for access to resources.

9

Park Outreach & Gorilla Conservation
Mgahinga Gorilla National Park, Uganda

WILLIAM ADAMS & MARK INFIELD

Introduction

The notion of re-building conservation strategies to give the needs and wishes of rural people a high priority has become almost universal in sub-Saharan Africa since the late 1980s (Adams and Hulme, Chapter 2, this volume). While this 'community conservation' approach has been widely applied in and around savanna protected areas (e.g. Lindsay 1987; Western and Wright 1994a; Kangwana and Ole Mako, Chapter 10, this volume), such approaches have a particular attraction in evergreen forest environments. Here conservation resources exist in areas of high population density and hence there is competition for land between the priorities of wildlife conservation (and now the formal international commitments of African governments under the Convention on Biological Diversity) and the needs of local people.

Rates of loss of African moist forests have been very rapid, because of both logging and clearance for agriculture (Grainger 1993 and 1996; Ite 1997). This situation has been confirmed for Uganda (Struhsaker 1997). Forest environments are therefore among those where conservation action has been most urgently promoted in Africa. Conventional protected area strategies ('fences and fines') have been used in the past to tackle the problem of forest loss. However, these are increasingly problematic both in narrow pragmatic terms (because illegal penetration of the protected forest for meat, timber or farmland is very difficult to stop) and politically and morally (because those challenging the ecological integrity of the protected area are mostly genuinely below the poverty line and in great human need of land, food and a sustainable livelihood). The notion of community conservation (Adams and Hulme, Chapter 2, this volume) and particularly 'integrated conservation-development projects' (ICDPs) has provided a possible escape from the *impasse* of conflicting conservation and development demands for forest land (Ite 1996; Noss 1997). Afromontane forest is of particular importance for conservation because of its biological diversity and high level of endemicity, but it is also often a prime agricultural resource.

This chapter describes a community conservation programme designed to promote the integrity of a residual patch of montane evergreen forest in Uganda, now designated the Mgahinga Gorilla National Park (hereafter 'Mgahinga'). This was created in 1991. It covers 3400 ha, and is contiguous with the larger Parc National des Virunga in the Democratic Republic of Congo and Parc National des Volcans in Rwanda (Butynski and Kalina 1993; Wild and Mutebi 1996). The chapter draws on interviews held with park staff, local government and non-governmental organizations, local informants, and a programme of eight group meetings (using adapted PRA-type techniques) with mixed gender, all-women and minority groups in parishes adjoining and adjacent to the Park boundary (Adams and Infield 1998).

The community conservation programme at Mgahinga falls at the protected area outreach end of the continuum of community conservation activity described by Barrow and Murphree (Chapter 3, this volume). Park outreach can involve a range of different activities, a number of which have been attempted at Mgahinga (Table 9.1).

Mgahinga Gorilla National Park

The residual forests of Mgahinga form part of the once continuous cover of the Albertine Rift Afromontane Region Forests across what is now south-west Uganda, the western parts of Rwanda and Burundi and eastern Zaire. In recent centuries, clearance of these forests for agriculture has been extensive (Hamilton 1984; Butynski and Kalina 1993). Twentieth-century deforestation has been rapid, and Mgahinga now represents one of a small number of remaining fragments of forest. It is believed it was a faunal refuge during the late Pleistocene arid phase. Its species diversity is thought to be high, although recording is incomplete. There are 276 plant species and 39 recorded mammals, although over 89 may occur (Uganda National Parks 1996). These include eleven primates, most notably the mountain gorilla (*Gorilla gorilla beringei*) and the golden monkey (*Cercopithecus mitis* sp.). Werikhe (1991) found eight groups of gorillas, totalling 42 animals, which cross the international border from adjacent parks.

The park consists of the Ugandan slopes of three inactive volcanoes (Muhavura, Gahinga and Sabinyo) along the Rwandan border. The vegetation follows broadly

Table 9.1 Typology of community conservation and park outreach activities

Conservation education
Public relations/explain strategic goals of conservation
Grants for community projects
To meet specific development or welfare problems
To allow communities to benefit economically from park
Dealing with on-site costs of having a park as neighbour
Promotion of sustainable and productive management of land outside park (both for welfare and to
    benefit the Park)
Revenue sharing (visitor revenue dividend; linking grants to revenue)
Local access for extractive use of park resources
Adjusting park management to favour neighbours
Giving neighbours a say in how the park is managed★

Note: ★ This is transitional to 'collaborative management', 'co-management' or 'joint management' (see Barrow and Murphree, Chapter 3, this volume).

altitudinal zones, with an alpine zone (with giant *Senecio* and lobelia) above a subalpine or ericaceous belt (moorland and tree heather forest) at the top of the mountains, with montane forest (*Hagenia–Hypericum*) and extensive bamboo forest (*Arundinaria alpina*) below it. Below the bamboo zone, extensive evergreen forest occurred, but this has been largely cleared for agriculture (Uganda National Parks 1996). Below the Park boundary, the slopes are intensively cultivated and densely settled by Bufumbira people. There are also a few Batwa people (Kingdon 1990).

The Need for a Community Conservation Programme

The need for a CC programme at Mgahinga stems from the poverty and demand for land in the surrounding communities. The forests of the Park represent the last enclave of an agricultural frontier that has advanced rapidly during the twentieth century in Kigezi (Carswell 1997). Population densities in the parishes bordering the Park (hereafter 'park–neighbour parishes') are 300 to 499 people per km^2, and the population growth rate of Kisoro District in 1991 was estimated to be 3.5 per cent. Women outnumber men in park–neighbour parishes, reflecting male out-migration to find work in Kisoro town, other rural destinations and Kampala.

Information from group meetings in the field (Adams and Infield 1998) suggests that the agricultural frontier closed in the park–neighbour parishes before the Second World War. Settlement was said to have begun in Gitendere in the 1870s, with scattered homesteads by 1900. Rukonge Parish was said to be extensively cultivated by the end of the 1930s. At this time the government recommended people with too little land to emigrate to other districts. In 1941–5, the County Chief requested more land for agriculture because of this emigration.

Agriculture is the dominant source of income in all parishes surveyed. In those parishes on the Park boundary ('inner parishes') it was followed in importance by livestock, paid employment and trading/marketing. In their neighbours' parishes ('outer parishes') lack of grazing land means that livestock keeping was less important. Meetings with groups of women showed distinctive views of livelihood options. Agriculture was still seen to be the most important, although less dominantly so. A wider range of activities were important, including craftwork and participation in credit and savings co-operatives.

Agriculture around Mgahinga is diverse and intensive. Beans, sorghum, maize, Irish potatoes and sweet potatoes are the main crops on lower ground, with Irish potatoes and wheat up nearer the Park boundary. Bananas are grown, and are expanding, particularly at lower altitude. Rain falls in every month, but particularly in the periods April–May and October–January. Crops are grown on large mounds, and crop residues are incorporated to act as compost. Crops are rotated, and several crops are grown a year. In Kigezi, indigenous soil conservation practices were relatively well-developed by the early twentieth century (Carswell 1997). Despite continuing careful husbandry, local crop yields are said to be falling: estimates of Parish Chairmen suggested that yields had fallen by a quarter over 20 years. None the less, data from the District Agriculture Office at Kisoro suggest yields are still good compared with other regions of Uganda.

The main constraints to agriculture identified in ranking exercises in parish meetings were lack of land, followed by tools, seed, knowledge and capital (together ranked second), then labour, manure, availability of markets and technical support (ranked third). These were followed in order by lack of fertilizer, stores (bamboo stores being virtually unobtainable following the end of the bamboo harvest in the forest) and insecticide.

Land scarcity and poverty are also key constraints on other forms of resource use. All villages lack grazing areas (mostly, but not solely, because of loss of access to grazing in the Park), and people are too poor to buy stock. Other problems were the cost of veterinary drugs and access to water in the dry season. Paid employment is limited by lack of job opportunities, contacts, and the cost of transport to urban areas. Local labouring work is limited and poorly paid because of the poverty of potential employers. For the Batwa in particular, field labour for local farmers is a major source of subsistence (particularly work by women for women farmers). Trading (chiefly in agricultural produce) was limited by lack of capital and poor access to larger markets. Women's brewing of beer is constrained by lack of water in the dry season. Craft work requires raw materials that are harder to get now that access to the Park is prevented. Men need bamboo for making baskets and granaries, and this can now only be obtained by those few people with farm bamboo clumps, or from Echuya Forest Reserve (some 50 km away). Similarly women now cannot obtain grasses to make mats from swamps in the Park, and have to buy them from Kisoro.

The forests of Mgahinga are not only significant to local people because they cover the only areas of uncleared potential farmland in south-west Uganda, but also because some were farmed in the recent past. The present boundaries of Mgahingha Gorilla National Park are aligned on previous Forest Reserve and Game Reserve boundaries. The history of boundary changes is complex (Map 9.1). A Game Sanctuary was gazetted in 1930 (3370 ha), and a Forest Reserve was superimposed (with the same boundaries) in 1939. There was thus dual authority in the reserved area. In 1951 the Forest Reserve was reduced in size to 2330 ha specifically to meet growing demand by the local people for more land for cultivation (Werikhe 1991: 5). Settlement of this area followed, and was not opposed by the Game Department. In 1964 the Game Sanctuary was re-gazetted as a Game Reserve, but in this case its boundary was extended to 4750 ha, including land already cultivated and settled (Werikhe 1991). However this new boundary was not demarcated on the ground, and residents were not informed or evicted (Uganda National Parks 1996).

The 1954 Forest Act, and the 1967 working plan for the Forest Reserve, allowed consumptive use of resources within the Reserve for domestic use. Such use included harvesting of non-planted trees (for timber, bark, charcoal, fruits, seeds), and harvesting of honey, grass, litter, soil, stone and gravel (Werikhe 1991). There were also 80 licences to cut 900 bamboo stems. In theory, residence, hunting, fires, agriculture and livestock grazing were illegal under the Game (Preservation and Control) Act 1964. However, in practice these activities were not strictly controlled at Mgahinga. Communication and collaboration between the Game and Forest Departments were very limited, and conservation efforts were slight until the 1980s, when a German NGO funded an expatriate warden who began to tighten control of human activities within the Park.

When the Uganda National Resistance Council proclaimed the Mgahinga Gorilla National Park in May 1991, all human use of resources within the Park became

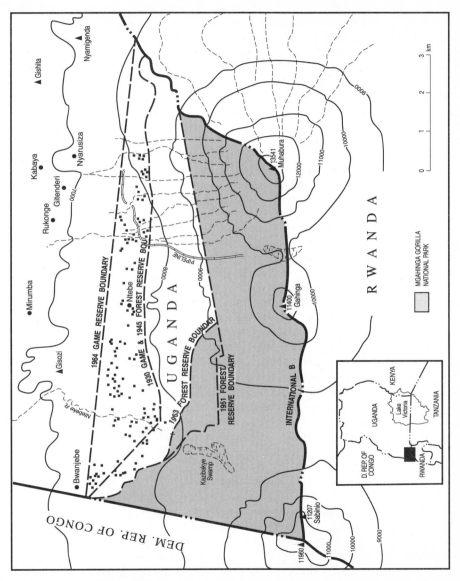

Map 9.1 Mgahinga Gorilla National Park, Uganda

illegal. However, at that time the forests were extensively used by local people for the collection of bamboo bean poles, timber and firewood, the collection of water in the dry season (from swamps high on the Rwanda border) and grazing. The park was traversed by more than 12 heavily used paths to Rwanda (Werikhe n.d. and 1991). Animal snares were found in 63 per cent of the Park, and honey barrels in 30 per cent (Werikhe 1991). More seriously, from the point of view of gorilla conservation, 1773 people in 272 households were living in the new park, and 680 more were farming there (Werikhe n.d.). In total 4020 non-resident people from six parishes and Kisoro and Kabale towns were partially dependent on park land, and there were 113 houses, two bars, four stores and a church (Werikhe n.d.). This settlement was not new: three households had lived in the area before it became a Gorilla Sanctuary, 26 per cent had been given land by the Forest Department between 1920 and 1979, and 71 per cent claimed to have inherited land, presumably from pre-existing residents. Over half the residents in the Park had been born there.

A Memorandum of Agreement was signed in June 1992, under which all farmers and residents agreed to leave the Park, while in return Uganda National Parks agreed to pay 'compensation', seek donor support to improve agricultural self-reliance, construct a road, and build an air strip.[1] The park was duly cleared of people and all resource use (and access) was stopped. Average compensation was US$27 per person, ranging from US$1200 to US$6 (Cunningham et al. 1993). Compensation was paid for physical structures and permanent crops and trees, but not for land.

At Mgahinga, the new National Park faced a major challenge of legitimacy. A widespread local perception was (and indeed still is) that those living or farming in the Park had acquired land there properly and had a right to it. Legally, once the land had been declared a Game Reserve, *all* those resident became 'encroachers', regardless of how long they had resided there and the basis for their land claim. They were 'untitled' land holders, and traditional tenure was not recognized under the law. Local people argued (and argue still) that the compensation was inadequate, especially in that it was insufficient to allow replacement land to be acquired (Adams and Infield 1998). These problems of legitimacy are exacerbated by poverty, itself associated with the creation of the Park, which has cut local people off from resources, especially land, that they were previously able to use, or that they might have expected to be able to use. At Mgahinga, 'community conservation' is the chief strategy developed to tackle the challenges of poverty and the Park's legitimacy.

The Challenge for Community Conservation

Parish meetings overwhelmingly identified the most important former resource of the Park as 'food' (*ubuhinzi*), i.e. agricultural produce (Table 9.2). In the inner parishes, this was followed by bamboo, grazing and water, and in the outer parishes by homes, water, bamboo and firewood. In Soko Parish, for example, all participants in the meeting had lost land and suffered from lack of water and firewood. Half had suffered from lost grazing and access through the mountains to Rwanda. One man had collected bamboo, medicinal plants and meat. Women's groups saw water (obtained from swamps within the Park), bamboo, grazing and firewood as the most significant following 'food'.

Table 9.2 Importance of different forest resources at Mgahinga

	Inner parish (%)	Outer parish (%)	Women's groups (%)
Food	57	72	44
Grazing	12	0	13
Water	10	9	18
Bamboo	13	4	10
Firewood	3	4	9
Thatching	1	0	0
Beekeeping	3	0	0
Med. plants	0	0	0
Homes	0	10	0
Stones	0	0	0
Meat	1	2	0
Grass for mats	0	0	0
Paths through the mountains	0	0	0

Source: Field research.

Substitutes are not readily available for forest resources. Bamboo is now bought from Echuya Forest or Kisoro, or elephant grass is used as a substitute. Firewood is obtained from planted eucalyptus (where there is suitable land), or sorghum stalks, or by purchasing charcoal in Kisoro. Medicinal plants are now unavailable. Grass for mats is available only from Kisoro Market. Food must be stored in sleeping huts, but this is a poor substitute for bamboo grain stores.

The Batwa people face particular problems. They relied almost exclusively on forest land and resources for subsistence, and as the agricultural frontier rose up the mountain, they drew these resources from the area within what became the Park. The most important products of the forest were meat (hunted for food and also sold), wild honey and firewood. They also held and cultivated land, and worked for non-Batwa neighbours in return for food. In addition they cut, used and sold bamboo poles and spear grass for thatching and made string, mats and other products from forest plants for sale. Some kept livestock (sheep, goats and chickens).

Parish meetings were asked to identify the impacts of the creation of the Park (Table 9.3). In the inner parishes, the largest impacts were seen to be eviction for the land (28 per cent) and the inadequacy of compensation (26 per cent), the resulting poverty (16 per cent) and hunger (14 per cent). Thus for example in Gisozi, 5 people out of the 20 present claimed to have had houses within the Park, while 12 had held land. In most parishes it was claimed that compensation was insufficient. Outer parish meetings and women's groups reported similar responses. The Batwa people suffered the greatest losses following closure of the Park to resource use, losing their homes in the forest, and access to land for cultivation, meat, firewood, honey, bamboo, string and grass for mat-making. Their biggest problem, as for their Bufumbira neighbours, became shortage of land; they had nowhere to build and nowhere to plant crops.

Table 9.3 Problems of the Mgahinga Gorilla National Park

	Inner parishes (%)	Outer parishes (%)	Women's groups (%)
Poverty	16	0	10
Crop raiding	4	3	0
Eviction/famine/hunger	14	67	32
Compensation	26	20	15
Harassment by Rangers	1	0	0
Interahamwe*	5	13	0
No resources	0	7	
Eviction from land	28		0
Eviction from homes	6		0
Emigration (and death)	0	2	0
Loss of grazing area	0	0	7
Shortage of land	0	0	34
No firewood	0	0	3
No water	0	7	0

Source: Field research.

Notes: * *Interahamwe*, deriving from the troubles in Rwanda, refers to armed bandits or fighters of various kinds. Some argued that *Interahamwe* were being blamed for more ordinary thieving.

The Community Conservation Programme

The Uganda Wildlife Authority (UWA) has an office in Kisoro, staffed by a Chief Warden, and Wardens for Community Conservation, Enforcement and Tourism. The Community Conservation Warden directs three Community Rangers, one allocated to each parish immediately adjoining the Park boundary. These Rangers are recruited from the boundary parishes. They do various kinds of work, mobilizing people with and for the CARE programme (CARE is an international NGO), and offering improving lectures and exhortations of many kinds. They are also responsible for organizing access for local people to the Park to collect bamboo rhizomes; the placement of beehives; and they have been involved personally in the development of the Amajambere Iwacu Community Campground in Gisozi Parish, and hence in the capture of tourist revenue by local people.

UWA has established a Park Management Advisory Committee (PMAC), to bring together various governmental, non-governmental and local interests. The Mgahinga PMAC has seven members, two from each parish and the Senior Warden. Other interested parties (including all development NGOs, researchers and local government officials) are ex officio members. The cost of PMAC meetings is considerable (500,000 USh per meeting, to cover accommodation, transport and other expenses). This expenditure is not covered by revenue-sharing funds, but from the Park's own budget. Each park-neighbour parish also has a Park Parish Committee (PPC), whose Chair is a member of the PMAC, to oversee revenue-sharing projects.

The chief channel of communications between the Park and local communities is through the Community Conservation Rangers. In interviews they suggested that the benefits of revenue sharing (i.e. the construction of school buildings) were beginning to be reflected in the attitudes of local people. They hold regular meetings with people in the three park-neighbour parishes, to mobilize them (chiefly to work on the schools), to inform them about aspects of the Park's environment or activities, and to listen to their problems. They report problems back and the Warden, if necessary, takes them on to the PMAC. The Rangers also discuss any locality-specific problems with the Parish Chairmen.

Community Conservation Action

Education and public relations

The work of the Community Conservation Rangers includes responsibility for general conservation education, and for interpreting the plans and actions of the Park to local people. A succession of planners and consultants have also worked in park-neighbour parishes, in particular connected with multiple use initiatives (e.g. Cunningham 1996). The CARE 'Development through Conservation' (DTC) project has also worked closely with local communities, undertaking 'participatory needs assessment' exercises.

Funding community projects

The major source of funds for community-initiated projects at Mgahinga has been the Mgahinga Bwindi Impenetrable Forest Conservation Trust (MBIFCT). This is an independent trust set up with capital (US$4 million) from the Global Environmental Facility now invested offshore. The Trust's aim is to accumulate sufficient capital to provide long-term (and perhaps perpetual) funds for community projects around the two parks. Sixty per cent of MBIFCT funds supports local projects, 20 per cent supports the work of the two Parks' administrations (e.g. paying for a photocopier and rangers' clothing at Mgahinga) and 20 per cent supports research (through the Institute for Tropical Forest Conservation). The Trust works in both inner and outer parishes around the borders of Mgahinga. To date the Trust has five ongoing projects at Mgahinga, which it runs through local committees. The Trust has a permanent technical staff based in Kabale, its operations funded by USAID (1995–7) and the Dutch Government (1997–2002).

On-site costs of having the park as a neighbour

Crop raiding was identified as a problem for farmers adjacent to the Park boundary at an early stage, particularly as buffalo numbers rose when they re-colonized the abandoned farmland in the Park. In response, CARE funded a locally made lava-block wall constructed along the northern two-thirds of the Park boundary (approximately 9 km) which both demarcates the Park boundary, and stops buffalo raiding.

Infrastructural investment

Several donors have made significant investments in the infrastructure of park-neighbour parishes, notably the European Development Fund and CARE. Water supply problems have consistently been rated as important in CARE's participatory

needs assessment work with communities, and water is seen as having a real conservation potential both by providing a tangible benefit to justify creation of the Park,
and by obviating the need for people to penetrate the Park in the depths of the dry
season in (June and July) during which streams flowing from the Park dry up.
Average rainfall is about 1650 mm per year (Werikhe 1991), but there is considerable
inter-year variability. The deep porous volcanic soils do not retain water through the
dry season and provide no water table accessible to hand-dug wells. Apart from two
small springs in Gisozi Parish, during the dry season, water has long had to be carried
from small swamps within the Park. Declaration of the Park ended access to these,
and necessitated an arduous trek to a lake below Kisoro town.

Various attempts were made from the 1940s onwards to extract water from
Kabiranyuma Swamp (on the Rwanda border) and convey it in ditches or pipes to
users (CARE 1997). The Park Management Plan proposed to re-establish secure
water supplies for villages below the Park, with minimal environmental disruption.
In 1994 the CARE-DTC project and UNP installed the Nyakagezi Water Scheme
to serve Gisozi Parish (Uganda National Parks 1996). A larger project, to rebuild the
1950s Kabiranyuma Water Scheme, is being developed (CARE 1997).

Investment has also been attracted to park-neighbour parishes for road
construction. Two roads serve the Park, running south into the hills from Kisoro.
Rehabilitation of these roads was an element in the Park Management Plan, and a
budget of US 41 million was allocated in 1995.[2] The district recognized the development value of these roads, as indeed did the farmers: 'opening of these roads will
not only promote tourism in the area but will also offer farmers easy access to
marketing areas for their produce'.[3]

Revenue Sharing

UWA has a revenue-sharing programme, based on visitor fees. In the gorilla parks
this programme has been developed with the International Gorilla Conservation
Programme (IGCP). Gorilla tracking began formally in 1994 at Mgahinga, a year
after Bwindi. During 1993 and 1994 20 per cent of gorilla trekking permit fees were
allocated to revenue sharing in the two 'gorilla' parks. From 1995, 12 per cent of all
visitor-derived revenues from the gorilla parks were placed into a revenue-sharing
fund. However, in 1996 MPs inserted a clause in the new Wildlife Statute[4] stipulating
that all parks should share 20 per cent of gate receipts. For the gorilla parks, gate
receipts represent a small fraction of overall income from visitors, and a decline in the
amount of visitor income to be allocated to revenue sharing resulted (US$12 instead
of US$150 per visitor in March 1998).

The key element in local benefits from the Park lies in the fees paid by tourists to
UWA for specialist activities. Several activities are available to visitors to MGNP: a
free evening birdwatching tour, and four accompanied walks and gorilla tracking for
which they must pay (Table 9.4). Almost all visitors are foreign nationals, the
majority non-resident. Almost all wish to see gorillas, and relatively few choose to
undertake walks. The importance of the high gorilla tracking fees is clear. There is
one group of habituated gorillas at Mgahinga, although they frequently depart to the
DRC for extended periods. Six people can track them per day. If all those were non-
resident foreign nationals, this would give a potential income of USh 810,000 per

Table 9.4 Activity fees at MGNP (March 1998)

	Foreign non-residents USh	Foreign residents USh	Uganda citizens USh	Local residents USh
Gorge Trail	22,000	17,000	4,000	3,000
Congo Border	28,000	21,000	5,000	3,500
Volcano climbing	57,000	48,000	20,000	17,000
Caving	28,000	22,000	6,000	4,000
Gorilla tracking	135,000	100,000	26,000	13,000

Source: UWA, Kisoro

day, or (assuming 20 days with resident gorillas a month), USh 16.2 million per month or USh 194 million per year. This is the equivalent of US$ 704 per day, or US$169,000 per year.[5]

In theory, park revenues must be sent back to Kampala, and can then be re-allocated. Owing to institutional problems both before and after the problematic restructuring of UWA, provision of funds from Kampala was unpredictable. In practice, therefore, the Park retains all visitor takings, only sending to Kampala any surplus on its agreed budget (up to USh 9 million per month). Equally, four of the six Mgahinga Gorilla Tracking Permits may be booked in Kampala, and are usually quickly snapped up by tour companies and foreign residents in Kampala. This money does not reach the Park. Of the money collected between 1993/4 and the creation of UWA in 1996 only about USh 12 million is available for revenue-sharing projects. The first disbursement of USh 7 million was made in October 1997.

Revenue-sharing money is supporting the construction of a classroom block in a primary school in each of the three park-neighbouring parishes. The plan is for a total of USh 12 million to be found for these community projects. To date, USh 2.3 million has been allocated to Rurembe Primary School, USh 0.89 million to Rukongi Primary School and USh 1.9 million to Gisozi Primary School.[6] This is popular and seen to be significant by local people. There seems to be no local perception yet that revenues on this scale may not be available in the future, and hence that this level of investment may not be sustainable.

Sustainable and productive management of land outside the Park

In 1992, CARE Uganda added the parishes adjoining Mgahinga to those neighbouring Bwindi Impenetrable Forest National Park further north to its 'Development through Conservation' (DTC) Project. Although the CARE DTC project does work to develop the institutional capacity of the Park itself (for example supporting the 1996 Management Plan), its main focus is on the productivity and sustainability of agriculture around the Park. A 'Mgahinga Community Training Centre' was built and staffed in 1995, working on agricultural extension, tree planting and agroforestry. Particular projects include development of a potato store suitable for household use, promotion of composting and seed multiplication work with farmers' groups.

Extractive use

The idea of allowing local consumptive use of resources (particularly plant resources) from Uganda's forest national parks is now well established (Cunningham et al. 1993; Cunningham 1996; Wild and Mutebi 1996 and 1997), although the principle of allowing access for consumptive use remains controversial for some conservation organizations. At Mgahinga, extractive use of bamboo has taken place legally in the past. Bamboo cutting was unrestricted in the Forest Reserve before 1951, and was then organized through a series of groups that were rotated (Cunningham et al. 1993). However, all cutting of bamboo, deployment of honey barrels and collection of forest products was stopped on the creation of the National Park in 1991.

The 1996 Park Management Plan, however, proposed establishment of a multiple-use programme for resources within the Park. A 'multiple use zone' was identified, stretching 500 m within the Park boundary (20 per cent of the total area of the Park). This followed extensive participatory research on the demand for, and probable environmental impacts of, such use (Cunningham et al. 1993; Uganda National Parks 1996). It was proposed that the programme should include provision of bamboo rhizomes, harvesting of water from the Park through a water scheme, beekeeping, harvesting of medicinal plants and collection of spear grass (Uganda National Parks 1996). In response park staff have begun to develop a programme of controlled access to the Park by farmers from adjoining parishes for the collection of bamboo rhizomes for planting on farms. An ethnobotanical survey of the Park was carried out in 1993 (Cunningham et al. 1993). In 1993 and 1994 farmers collected rhizomes from the Park on a number of specified days with the Community Rangers and the Multiple Use Team. By 1998, over 200 homesteads had been supplied with rhizomes, and bamboo clumps are springing up on farms (Hammett 1998). Some 2000 rhizomes had been supplied.[7]

Plans for more extensive resource-sharing programmes, for example the extraction of materials for making string and medicinal plants, and the placing of honey barrels are less well advanced (Cunningham et al. 1993; Adams and Infield 1998). A Mgahinga Beekeepers Co-operative met in January 1997, and resolved to place hives in three agreed spots within the 'multiple use' zone, to identify members to supervise the hives, and to make visits together, to minimize human presence in the Park, and to report all illegal use of the Park. The Management Plan also envisages organized arrangements for access to the multiple use zone for collection of spear grass and medicinal plants, but this has not yet progressed, while the experience at Bwindi is watched. Fear of the presence of *Interahamwe* within the Park is currently restricting local demand for access for consumptive use.

The Impact of Community Conservation

Fieldwork suggested three possible indicators of the effectiveness of the CC programmes at Mgahinga: first, the incidence of illegal entry and resource use in the Park; second, the degree of recognition of CC institutions; and third, local appreciation of the economic or infrastructural benefits of being a park neighbour.

Enforcement of regulations in the Park is done by the Law Enforcement Warden and Rangers. They report much reduced levels of illegal entry and resource use by local Ugandan people since the community programme developed. Data on the level of law enforcement activity (number of patrols) and of illegal activity (number of people arrested, number of snares removed, and number of cattle or goats found in the Park) from the Park's monthly reports for the years 1991 to 1997 suggest a decline in the level of illegal activities in the Park over time. The levels of arrests and snares removed during the years of 1996 and 1997 are low by any standards, and the reports suggest that many of these illegal activities were emanating from across the borders in the Democratic Republic of Congo and Rwanda, where civil disturbance was, and continues to be, high. The level of illegal use of the Park by residents of the parishes around the Park, would seem to be low.

However, it is not clear whether this is the result of the Park's law enforcement programme, or of the various CC programmes. It is also not clear whether these figures indicate the reality of illegal activities 'on the ground'. Dramatic changes in the levels of illegal activities patrols between months coincide with changes in park personnel, notably the chief warden, and may reflect changes in park management rather than changes in the behaviour of local communities. Reported declines in morale among park staff, resulting from removal of project paid bonuses or support, or failure of UWA to pay salaries on a regular basis, may be expected to cause changes in the frequency and diligence with which patrols are carried out by park rangers. Such changes might explain changes in the level of illegal activities reported. Locating snares in the Park, for example, requires a high degree of effort by rangers, and the numbers of snares found and removed might well be expected to fluctuate with the level of staff commitment.

The level of other illegal activities recorded in the monthly reports was surprisingly low given the former economic importance of forest resources. There were only eight reports of people entering the Park to collect water, although sometimes in large numbers (over 100), and only seven reports of bamboo cutting (just over one a year on average). Cultivation within the Park was only reported once during the six years for which reports were available.

Despite problems of interpretation, the monthly reports seem to suggest a growing acceptance over the years of the restrictions imposed by the Park authorities on community access to resources. This tends to confirm the effectiveness of the CC programme in helping to defuse tensions and persuading the communities to accept the existence of the Park. It also suggests that the concentration of DTC's work on the provision of water and bamboo is effective.

Parish meetings suggest high levels of recognition of CC organizations in park–neighbour parishes. Exercises to rank both the visibility of the organizations, and their perceived contribution in the inner parishes, gave first place to CARE, followed by the Ministry of Health and the Water Development Department (reflecting the perceived importance of the Kabiranyuma Water Scheme). The organizations connected specifically with the Park (park staff, PMAC and PPC) did not score particularly highly, although questioning made clear that they and the Community Rangers were well known.[8]

Venn diagrams were used to investigate local people's sense of the accessibility of the Park's own organizations, the Park Parish Committees (PPCs) and the Park Management Advisory Committee (PMAC). In Rukonge the PPC was placed in the group of organizations closest to the village, while the PMAC and the Park fell in the second group. In Gitendere the PMAC (with CARE-DTC) was listed in the second group of organizations, with the Park in group 3 (its appearance at all on a diagram of organizations 'helping' the village being vocally disputed). In Gisozi, the Park was recognized, but placed as far away as possible from the village (although this parish's contacts with the Rangers were frequent), reflecting the loss of land to the Park. MBIFCT was only recognized in Rukonge Parish ('because we see their vehicles passing by'), and then only following prompting.

Parish meetings were asked to identify positive impacts of the National Park. The question was phrased this way to see if the community conservation endeavours were cited as benefits. The question usually evoked much noisy incredulity, but eventually some benefits were identified (often following prompting, and often with dissent being strongly expressed). These included the construction of school buildings (sometimes explicitly 'revenue sharing') and of roads, and the water flowing from the Park in streams. Tourists were not seen to have brought benefits, although they did sometimes buy goods from markets on the road. In Mabungo Parish, people said 'only the nation benefits, the people do not'; noting that 'tourists pay a fee to government, but nothing to the people here'. One women's group chair volunteered the argument that tourists bring money, of which a proportion is taken and used to build classrooms in 'revenue sharing'. In Soko Parish it was argued that the gullies draining Mt Muhavura no longer deposit stones on the land and sweep people away because land is no longer cultivated in the Park. The benefits to individuals from employment were recognized.

The Batwa group identified two benefits of the Park, first the creation of their two 'schools' (open air teaching by two teachers funded by the Adventist Alliance Development Association) and, second, the availability of tips from tourists for those who live near the Park gates at Ntebeko.

Conclusion: The Sustainability of Community Conservation

Community conservation at Mgahinga has utilized most of the strategies outlined in Table 9.1. However, there has been little progress with the adjustment of park management to favour neighbours (although the 'multiple use zone' is perhaps evidence of this), and the PMAC and PPC offer little to neighbouring parishes in terms of an effective say in park management. Community conservation so far is almost entirely top-down.

Creation of the Mgahinga Gorilla National Park has created various benefit streams that are captured internationally, nationally and locally. International benefits derive from the maintenance of the existence value of the gorillas (and potentially other species such as birds). This benefit is not captured to any extent in the form of money. National benefits arise from the non-consumptive use of gorillas through gorilla tourism. These are expressed financially, and are captured principally by the tour companies (whom the tourists pay) and the Uganda Wildlife Authority (who are paid for permits), although secondary benefits are shared by the government (which gains foreign exchange from this tourist activity), the citizens of Uganda (who presumably benefit from the government's income), and the many other businesses that are involved in tourism (from tour companies to photographic film processors).

Although local people are slow to identify economic benefits from the Park, they do exist. They include benefits to all park-neighbour parishes in the form of money directed by the Uganda Wildlife Authority to revenue sharing, benefits for particular groups (e.g. those able to profit from local tourist facilities such as traders on the road from Kisoro to the Park gate in Gisozi Parish, and members of the Amajambere Iwacu Community Campground), and particular individuals (e.g. those local people employed as Park Rangers or labourers).

Most of the benefits of the creation of the Park, therefore, lie outside the local area. However, it is here that most of the costs are borne, in the form of loss of productive farmland, loss of grazing areas, loss of flows of commonly used resources (bamboo, water, thatching grass etc.) and loss of specialized resources (medicinal plants, sites for beehives). Hulme and Infield (Chapter 8, this volume) report similar findings from Lake Mburo National Park.

Money for community conservation is coming from two sources, donor support and revenue from tourists. Donor investment reflects the current (post-Rio) international priority placed upon biodiversity conservation, and the huge symbolic importance attached to the mountain gorilla. Much of the investment (especially that of CARE) is addressed at tackling problems of poverty and low agricultural productivity that are common across Uganda, and appear to be achieving productivity/welfare gains commensurate with such projects. However, CARE's investment around Mgahinga is obviously linked to the existence of the Park. This link is made directly and explicitly in all project documents and in communications with communities. Other donor investment in the area is also linked in this way. Revenue-sharing investment (e.g. in school buildings) has a less immediate economic benefit, although these are (perhaps quite rightly) valued extremely highly locally. The sums involved are small, but probably bigger than most other sources of community support, especially from government.

Community support for the Park is therefore being bought through continuous investment in the community conservation programme, at a fairly steep price. The goodwill that outside investment buys is directly related to the sustainability of the flow of revenue. This is dependent on two things. The first is the continued interest of donors (and the First World public whose expressed concerns they seek to respond to) in the 'biodiversity agenda', and especially forests and rare species such as mountain gorillas; the second is the buoyancy of the tourist economy.

The sustainability of tourist revenues as a source of income for both Park and local people at Mgahinga should not be taken for granted. Two problems are particularly important. First, tourist fee income is subject to powerful claims from UWA to meet urgent institutional needs (or wants), including the costs of managing other national parks which earn little revenue of their own. Gorillas are seen as a 'cash cow' within UWA for its own institutional survival, and also to subsidize biodiversity conservation elsewhere (i.e. meeting UWA's national mandate). Gorilla tourism is also viewed more widely by the Government of Uganda as the first-fruits of a much larger programme of tourist revenue generation. Second, tourist numbers are dependent on political stability in the region.[9] In the mid-1990s, regional instability worked somewhat in Uganda's favour, because Rwandan parks were closed, and the Congo border was intermittently closed. Uganda was the sole supplier of gorilla tourism! However, tourist arrivals nationally are not growing as planned, partly because of the regional picture. Moreover,

Mgahinga lacks resident mountain gorillas, and would hence take a lower place in tour companies' priorities (particularly at the more lucrative elite end of the market) if a choice of gorilla trekking destinations beyond Uganda were restored.

Community conservation at Mgahinga cannot therefore be assumed to be self-sustaining. It has achieved a remarkable job of finessing the controversial park boundaries, and buying time for the development of sustainable institutional mechanisms that can meet legitimate local economic needs and conservation goals. It is not clear how those institutions might be structured, nor who might be persuaded to consider what form they might take.

This research suggests that there is poverty and land hunger (and also a sense of the *threat* of poverty and land hunger) in settlements close to the borders of Mgahinga. Hardship in many households is directly related to the loss of the Park as a source of land for food production and (to a lesser extent) as a place of residence. It is also related to the inadequacy and/or inaccuracy of the 'compensation' paid (and, more widely, resentment at this loss and the inadequacy of compensation). All these represent considerable challenges to the legitimacy of the National Park in local eyes.

On the other hand, local people recognize the Park's boundaries, aims and objectives, and know the identity of the various actors involved in community conservation programmes. They recognize the potential economic benefits of the gorilla-related tourist industry, although they also realize that these benefits are focused on the main access road, and mostly captured by those with investments in infrastructure. Local people also acknowledge the value of the benefits of revenue sharing in the form of investment in classrooms, and appreciate other investments (for example in the road and water schemes) and the value of the DTC agricultural advice.

However, none of these benefits are seen to fully compensate for the real and perceived economic costs of actual and prospective resource use within the Park area. Furthermore, all community conservation efforts are focused either on those parishes immediately adjoining the Park boundary or those two-deep from the boundary, although it is likely that the negative economic impacts of the Park's creation are felt more widely than this. As Noss (1997) remarks, local 'community' work must be seen in the context of wider social, economic and political forces.

Community conservation is not something that can stand still. Over time, such programmes tend to evolve to embrace a larger range of activities (Table 9.1), moving from education to revenue sharing to consumptive resource use. As the local community is progressively taken more seriously as a potential partner in conservation, the feasibility of moving from 'outreach' to 'collaborative management' grows. However, so too does the demand for such a policy change. Parks and conservation organizations then no longer simply reach out to neighbours and surrounding areas, but neighbours start to reach in to seek control of the Park itself. In the context of Mgahinga, this transition would offer novel but exciting challenges.

Turning gorillas into a resource capable of yielding US dollars in quite large quantities[10] for community conservation is not a magic solution to conservation or local development problems. To use a medical analogy, the community conservation programme at Mgahinga is working at the level of emergency treatment, and has successfully stanched arterial flows of resentment. The patient is stabilized, but the harder tasks of surgery and post-operative recovery lie ahead.

Acknowledgements

This chapter draws on research at Mgahinga Gorilla National Park, in south-west Uganda, in March and April 1998 by Mark Infield and Bill Adams. We would like to thank David Nkuriyingoma, who guided us through the fieldwork and to whom we are very grateful for his wide advice and energy, the staff of the Mgahinga Gorilla National Park for their support in Kisoro, the staff of the Amajambere Iwacu Community Campground for looking after us and all those people who agreed to be interviewed. David Basanye (Population Officer, Kisoro District) supplied census data. Above all we would like to thank the people of Kisoro District for their tolerance and hospitality during our fieldwork.

Notes

[1]Werikhe notes that strictly these payments did not comprise compensation, since illegal occupancy (in the terms of the Game Act) could not be compensated for, and USAID was unwilling to pay formal 'compensation'; furthermore, payments did not relate to established government rates. Payments were intended to help people resettle (interview 1 April 1998).

[2]Memo from Jaap Schoorl, DTC Park Management Technical Adviser to CARE Uganda Director and Assistant Director, not dated; MGNP Files.

[3]District Executive Secretary Kisoro to Project Coordinator South West Agricultural Rehabilitation Project 14 August 1995; MGNP Files.

[4]The Uganda Wildlife Statute of 1996 established the Uganda Wildlife Authority through the merger of the Uganda National Parks and the Game Department. Members of Parliament took the opportunity during the debating of the Bill to insert a clause requiring that 20 per cent of park entry revenues be allocated to local authorities to be used for the development of communities living around the Park. The revenue-sharing policy of Uganda National Parks had shared 12 per cent of all park revenues. In the 'gorilla' parks, the legislation thus reduced the amount of revenue being shared with local communties.

[5]Conversion at US$1 = USh 1150, the rate at 13 March 1998.

[6]Interview, Chief Warden, 16 March 1998

[7]Interview, Chief Warden, 16 March 1998

[8]In Rukonge the Community Warden and Ranger were identified by name, but then the Ranger was a spectator at the meeting!

[9]After the completion of this chapter Mgahinga Gorilla National Park was closed for several months in early 1999 following the murder of tourists and rangers at Bwindi Impenetrable Forest National Park in February 1999. The 'gorilla' parks were re-opened in mid-1999 but this tragic event has been a great setback for international tourism in Uganda.

[10]New rates were set in April 1998 at US$250 per visitor per gorilla viewing trek; in theory this includes US$20 for local communities and a further US$20 to tackle the problem of 'problem gorillas' (crop raiding; a problem at Bwindi Impenetrable National Park). With six trekkers per day, this gives a possible revenue of US$1500 per day at Mgahinga (perhaps US$200,000–500,000 per year).

10

Conservation, Livelihoods
& the Intrinsic Value of Wildlife
Tarangire National Park, Tanzania

KADZO KANGWANA & RAFAEL OLE MAKO

Introduction

The last two decades have seen the application of considerable national and international resources to increase local participation in conservation initiatives. The outcome of such initiatives remains uncertain. Do people change their behaviour or attitudes towards conservation? Do benefits to local people increase and does conservation become more equitable? What are the social and ecological impacts of these projects?

Tarangire offers a rare opportunity to address these questions. Here, a concerted effort to work with local people was started by the Community Conservation Service (CCS) of Tanzania National Parks (TANAPA) as part of the *Ujirani Mwema* (good neighbourliness) programme, recognizing that the Park's continued existence is dependent on the support of the people living directly around it (see Barrow et al., Chapter 5, this volume, for a discussion of community conservation in Tanzania and Bergin, Chapter 7, this volume, for a detailed account of the CCS). TANAPA also recognized the threat of changing land use around the Park. Shortly after the first initiatives, and while the programme was still being designed, TANAPA conducted a survey of people's knowledge, attitudes and practices (KAP) with respect to wildlife around Tarangire National Park (TNP) in 1992. The survey provides baseline information for this study. Since 1992, activity has continued around the Park as part of the *Ujirani Mwema* programme and other programmes for community involvement in wildlife conservation have been initiated by the private sector and through NGO support.

This chapter describes the implementation of community conservation in Tarangire and analyses its major achievements. It examines the relationship between the National Park staff and the local people as the key variable in determining whether the CC programme of TANAPA has had any impact. The objectives of CC in Tarangire are focused on the conservation resource in the most general sense, and are summarized as the need to minimize negative impacts on the resource by reducing conflict and helping to solve problems (TANAPA 1994b).

Background

Tarangire National Park

Tarangire National Park (TNP) spans an area of 2642 km^2 in the Arusha Region of Tanzania and was gazetted in 1957 (Map 10.1). The Park is surrounded by the Mukungero Game Control Area (GCA) to the south, the Simanjiro GCA to the east, the Lolkisale GCA to the north-east and Mto wa Mbu GCA to the north. The park is savanna and covers a small portion of what has been described as the Tarangire ecosystem. It forms the dry season refuge for the migratory species in the ecosystem (Borner 1985; EC and TANAPA 1997). The fauna of TNP is characterized by a large mammal community that includes 58 species typical of the East African savanna. The Park hosts one of the most important populations of wild herbivores in eastern Africa and the largest populations of elephants in northern Tanzania. Studies (Borner 1985) have confirmed that most of the large mammals in the Tarangire ecosystem depend on the resources available outside the Park for more than six months of the year.

This is an area with a mixed land-use regime including GCAs and large pieces of land for agriculture. The GCAs are managed by the Ministry of Natural Resources and Tourism (MNRT) at the district level. Licenced hunting is allowed within GCAs, and other human activities, such as settlement and cultivation, are not restricted. TANAPA's control extends only over TNP and its influence on the surrounding area has to be negotiated with MNRT, private landowners, local governments and villagers.

TNP faces numerous management challenges. Of primary importance is the rapid demographic increase and consequent human impact on the areas around the National Park (EC and TANAPA 1997). Without careful land-use planning the key migratory routes for the wildlife stand to be lost and the park is in danger of becoming an island park with only resident species surviving. This could cause the ecological impoverishment of the Park and also the loss of a natural resource of significant economic value to Tanzania through tourism, and one potentially important to the economic development of the local people.

As part of the northern circuit of parks in Tanzania, and accessible from Arusha, TNP is a popular tourist destination. Tourist numbers have increased steadily during the 1990s (Table 10.1). Projections indicate a steady growth in the coming years, and the Park is reported to be one of four parks in Tanzania in which revenues are higher than the budget (EC and TANAPA 1997).

Table 10.1 Number of tourists visiting
Tarangire National Park 1992/93 to 1996/97

Year	No. of tourists
1992/93	31,852
1993/94	43,339
1994/95	38,746
1995/96	43,790
1996/97	54,454

Source: TNP headquarters.

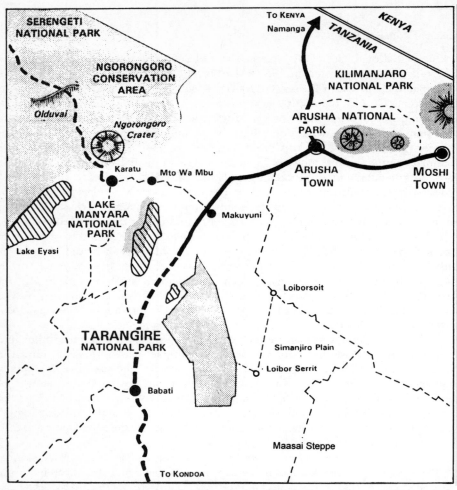

Source: Tarangire National Park Management Zone Plan/Environmental Impact Assessment,
April 1994. Tanzania National Parks

Map 10.1   Tarangire National Park, Tanzania

TANAPA and Community Conservation

TANAPA's CC initiatives began in 1985 when a working group recommended that a 'Rural Extension Education' programme should be initiated as a matter of priority (Bergin and Dembe 1996). The African Wildlife Foundation (AWF) was among the first to follow up on this recommendation by sponsoring a pilot project to support TANAPA and this set the stage for TANAPA's future extension work. In December 1990 AWF appointed a project officer to assist with the establishment of a Community Conservation Unit (CCU) at TANAPA headquarters working with TANAPA's Community Conservation Coordinator (see Bergin, Chapter 7, this volume, for a detailed discussion). TANAPA currently runs its CC activities around 12 National Parks through the Community Conservation Service (CCS) as a programme of park outreach. The Swahili term for the programme is *Ujirani Mwema* (good neighbourliness).

The objectives of the CCS are to:

• improve relations between individual parks and local communities;
• ensure that the interests of National Parks with regard to natural resource conservation and community welfare are presented at all levels;
• facilitate the sharing of benefits to target communities; and
• assist communities to gain access to information, resources and services which promote sustainable development.

The CCS is a department within the Directorate of Park Management and Conservation. Its activities around the different national parks are coordinated by the Community Conservation Coordinating Committee (C4) which meets quarterly. This forum brings together TANAPA staff, interested donors and NGOs. At the National Park level activities are guided by strategic action plans developed through participatory workshops, and TANAPA appoints a CC Warden to implement and coordinate CC activities. These now include a benefit-sharing programme which allocates 2.5 per cent of TANAPA's annual budget for community projects such as school buildings and dispensaries.

Community conservation initiatives around Tarangire

TANAPA
TANAPA currently has the most comprehensive and widespread programme of CC activities around TNP, although its initiatives have been complemented by those of the private sector and NGOs. CC activities around TNP had modest and informal beginnings through the initiatives of rangers in the early 1980s unofficially providing transport and other assistance to local people. As part of TANAPA's CCS programme, TNP was the first park to receive a full-time CC Warden in July 1990. The basic approach to community conservation at TNP has been what Barrow and Murphree (Chapter 3, this volume) term 'park outreach'. CCS field activities in TNP began in 1991 and a strategic action plan for CCS at Tarangire was developed in 1994. At that time Tarangire hosted the second largest CCS programme but this weakened in the mid-1990s. At the time of study in 1997 the CCW post had been vacant for one year and CCS activities were thus being overseen by the Park

Warden-in-Charge. They were implemented by one full-time CC Assistant in the western zone and a part-time CC Assistant in the eastern zone. A new CCW was appointed in December 1997.

Private sector

Since 1990 two tourist operators, Dorobo Safaris and Oliver's Camp, have been engaged in dialogue and in projects to get the benefits of wildlife tourism to the local community, while safeguarding their access to the resource that their businesses depend on. The experience of these private companies indicates promising results and the issues they have had to deal with are central to the issues of community wildlife management. Key informant interviews were held with owners and partners of the two companies and with village elders from target villages.

While the tourist operations of both companies differ on the ground, their shared principles and philosophies have meant that they were able to take a united approach in working with the communities. Both currently have legally binding contracts with villages, providing these companies with exclusive rights for tourist operations within the respective village, and allowing them to market a unique tourist experience. Oliver's Camp has an area set aside by Loibor Serrit village for a permanent camp and walking trips. Dorobo conducts mobile wilderness safaris and sets up temporary camps in the area of Emboret village. Central to the functioning of these agreements were issues of ownership and land tenure. Initial steps in these projects included villages securing title and seeking approval from the Wildlife Department for their wildlife enterprises.

Benefits distributed to the villages amounted to Tshs 10 million (US$16,670) between 1990 and 1993. Transparency and accountability have been encouraged through wide involvement of villagers in meetings after initial discussion with village councils. While the company directors are keen to see that funds filter down to the local level, they have also been sensitive not to dictate the use of funds and to encourage village-wide decisions on how these are spent (Oliver 1994). Encouraging transparency within villages remains a challenge, and the companies are seeking support for the time-consuming process of extension and negotiation with villagers from NGOs.

The Community Conservation Service Centre
and Wildlife Management Areas

The African Wildlife Foundation's Community Conservation Service Centre (CCSC) in Arusha has taken steps to support the establishment of wildlife management areas (WMAs) in high potential areas including the Simanjiro area east of TNP. The first step in the process of establishing WMAs has been the raising of awareness among community leaders and key actors of the potential for wildlife management on communal lands through a study tour. During this tour community leaders were exposed to four practical examples of community wildlife management. Fostering community support and seeking understanding within target villages formed the second step in the process. Thus far, two villages near TNP have gathered to form their own Natural Resource Committees. The CCSC has also facilitated links between the villages and their respective district governments and helped to have the WMAs recognized in the district level environmental plans. In the future WMAs may become an important adjunct to TNP's conservation goals.

Methods and Sources of Data

This study draws upon data from a number of sources. A Knowledge, Attitudes and Practices (KAP) survey carried out by TANAPA in conjunction with AWF in 1992 provided background information for the study. Primary data collection comprised a series of village meetings to the west of the park, and a series of key informant interviews and focus group interviews with TANAPA staff, local and district government officials, members of the private sector and NGOs. A meeting was also held with village leaders to the east of the Park. Primary data were gathered in September and October 1997 in TNP, in the area surrounding it and in Arusha. This study also draws extensively from the Tarangire Conservation Project (TCP), a study implemented by the University of Milan and TANAPA. This project collected extensive data on the east side of the park, including community interviews and participatory village maps. These are used to inform this study. Data on the status of the natural resource were obtained from Tanzania Wildlife and Conservation Monitoring (TWCM) and the TCP.

At the village meetings a structured participatory rural appraisal (PRA) exercise was held. The discussion was recorded on flip chart paper during the meeting, and reviewed with the villagers for accuracy. To reduce bias towards a wildlife or National Park focus among the villagers, village interviews were structured to begin with questions about livelihoods and natural resource use in general, focusing on wildlife and TNP only at the very end of the exercise. Given the extensive data available from the TCP to the east of the Park (see below), this study focused on villages on the western boundary. Of the five villages visited, three had been areas of focus for the CC programme.

The 1992 Knowledge, Attitudes and Practices Survey

To guide primary data collection in 1997 an analysis of the Knowledge, Attitudes and Practices 1992 survey (KAP) data was undertaken. KAP collected responses from 1256 people living around TNP on their knowledge, attitudes and practices regarding wildlife and the National Park. The survey instrument was a field coded questionnaire administered by trained local school teachers. Given the stated aims of the CCS, as well as the activities of the private sector and NGOs, the data were analysed to assess the problems incurred in living with wildlife; the wildlife–related projects being carried out or desired; and the contact and relationship between park staff and villages. While useful in guiding data collection in 1997, the data collected in 1992 and 1997 are not directly comparable, the latter being the result of village meetings while the former is the result of a questionnaire survey with individual respondents.

The survey indicated a fairly stable and ethnically mixed population. A significant proportion of the respondents (43.8 per cent) reported that they had lived in the village for more than 20 years and 39 per cent had lived in the village between 6 and 20 years. Only 13.3 per cent of the respondents had lived in their village for less than five years. The major economic activities of the respondents were farming (60.9 per cent), pastoralism (9.7 per cent), and a mixture of cultivation and livestock keeping

(27.0 per cent). Respondents were asked whether someone from TNP had visited their village. Nearly two-thirds (65.6 per cent) said their village had not been visited and 27.9 per cent reported they had been visited. On enquiring about the purpose of the visits, the response categories and the number of times each response was given were as follows: to educate villagers (84); to help with village projects (85); to patrol (86); to assess wildlife damage (87); to carry out research (88); to consult villagers (23).

Respondents were asked about the costs and benefits of both having wildlife in the area and living next to TNP (Table 10.2). On the benefits side for wildlife they reported seeing animals (42.4 per cent), getting game meat (23.4 per cent) and income from tourists. TNP was seen as beneficial in terms of providing transport (26.4 per cent), providing firewood (18.6 per cent) and creating business opportunities (13.8 per cent). However, high costs were reported because of the presence of wildlife. These included widespread destruction of crops (86.2 per cent), the death of livestock through predators or disease (38.4 per cent) and personal insecurity because of predators, elephants and buffalo (34.2 per cent). The main costs arising because of the Park were ranger harassment (32.7 per cent) and reduced access to trees (27.9 per cent), grazing (22.7 per cent) and farmland (18.3 per cent).

Table 10.2   Costs and benefits of living with wildlife at TNP

Questions	Response categories and number of times each was mentioned
What are the good things [benefits] of having wildlife in your area?	Able to see and know different kinds of animals (533) Get game meat (294) Income from the sale of items to tourists (104) Income from tourists camping in the area (104) Other (83) Money from photos tourists take (55) Get foreign exchange (5)
What are the good things [benefits] of living next to TNP?	Help with transport (332) Get firewood (234) Business opportunities (174)
What are the bad things [problems] of having wildlife in your area?	Destroy crops (1083) Kill livestock (482) Threat to safety and security of people (430) Spread diseases (163)
What are the bad things [problems] of living next to TNP?	Ranger disturbance (411) No access to trees (350) No access to grazing (285) Cannot expand farms (*shambas*) (230)

The Impact of CC around TNP

Village profiles

Of the five villages researched to the west of TNP, the Community Conservation Service had worked extensively with three (Minjingu, Sangaiwe and Mwikansi), and had not worked in two villages (Chubi and Itaswi). However, Chubi had received SCIP funds to finish a school. All village meetings were well attended with between 40 to 210 participants. Respondents at the meetings, apart from the youth, said that they had moved from elsewhere, the majority having moved to the area in the 1960s. Participants are therefore not people who were moved out of the Park when it was created.

All participants reported negative trends in the state of their environment. Primary concerns were decreased water, aridity and the loss of trees. While listing natural resources and their uses, the three villages CCS had worked with mentioned wildlife as one of their natural resources and listed its uses. Wildlife was not mentioned as a resource in the two villages where CCS had not worked. To the west of the Park the main problems of living with wildlife were the destruction of crops by wild animals, danger to humans and livestock and disease transmission from wildlife to livestock. The villages that had received funds from TANAPA's SCIP programme mentioned these benefits in their list of benefits of having wildlife in their area, with the exception of Chubi.

Data collected by the TCP study in 1996 provide an overview of the pastoralist context. Four villages were researched: Emboret, Kimotorok, Loibor Serrit and Terrat. Responses were markedly uniform within villages and between villages, and reflect the main challenges of keeping cattle alive at the wildlife interface. Interviewees reported the problems of competition with wildlife for water and grazing and the danger posed to themselves and their cattle by lions and buffaloes as the main problems incurred because of wildlife. Disease transmission from wildlife to domestic animals also poses constraints to livestock raising in the area. In particular, malignant catarrhal fever (MCF) and tickborne diseases were mentioned.

Park–people relationships

The visitor books of one of the villages researched to the west of the park provides empirical evidence for an increase in contact with TNP staff over time (Table 10.3). No visits from park staff are recorded between 1984 and 1992. The village had been visited by a member of TNP staff once in 1993 and 1994, four times in 1996 and seven times by October 1997. All villages visited in 1997 mentioned Park staff as one of the categories of people who visited their village and in Minjingu, Sangaiwe and Mwikansi villagers reported frequent visits by Park staff. Villagers in Chubi and Itaswi said they had no close relationship with Park staff. Numerous comments from the different village meetings and key informant interviews with villagers point to an improved relationship between local people and the Park staff. Reports of assistance given to villagers by the Park were consistent between interviews with Park staff and with villagers.

There is evidence that this short history of a Park working with the people is raising expectations and making people more interested in working with the Park. In Kondoa District, where TANAPA is starting to focus but has not yet worked with any intensity, people were willing to gather to talk about natural resource issues and were eager for the Park to address their problems as they had done in other villages. It cannot be ignored that relationships fostered between the national park and the local people are vulnerable to the personalities of the staff the Park recruits.

Table 10.3 Visitors to a village on the western side of the Park 1984–97

	1984	1985	1986	1987	1988	1989	1990	1991	1992	1993	1994	1995	1996	1997
Total visitors	20	50	74	77	49	56	99	93	62	68	100	45	39	62
Total park staff visits	0	0	0	0	0	0	0	0	0	1	1	0	4	7
% park staff/ visitors	0	0	0	0	0	0	0	0	0	1.5	1	0	10.3	11.3

Consistent reports of some staff being better than others were heard in three villages. In the words of one village elder from Sangaiwe: 'Some Park staff become part of our village life, they understand our problems and want to help us. Some, however, just have the job but are not interested in the people.' The term *Ujirani Mwema* is strongly embraced in the villages, but also raises questions of reciprocity frequently voiced during this research and reported in the TCP study: 'Why can our animals not go there [to the Park] while the Park animals can come here?'

In all villages, long descriptions were provided about the historical enmity between the park and the people. Points of contention were the fines imposed on villagers and the beating of people by park rangers. Villagers also felt they were not consulted on Park boundaries and were then punished for transgressing boundaries of which they were not aware. To TNP's credit, villagers felt they had a clearer understanding of the role of the Park since TNP efforts to educate them were started.

Benefit sharing

Budgets for Tarangire National Park SCIP funded US$93,800 of projects in 16 villages in the five fiscal years 1992/93 to 1996/97. The perception among villagers of receiving benefits from the park correlated closely with SCIP projects. The input to village projects seems to have provided much of the impetus in moving away from a history of negative relationships between the Park and the local people to the current more positive relationship. Furthermore, the impact of the SCIP projects seems to be broad. There is awareness of benefits in villages where CSS had not yet worked and villagers were eager for dialogue to attract TANAPA to their village.

Given the assistance requested from TNP by villages in 1992 – 'provision of clean water', 'health and education projects' and 'problem animal control'– the CCS has to some extent met these needs in the SCIP projects provided to target villages. Minjingu had received desks for a school in 1994; Sangaiwe had a classroom constructed in 1992 and a teacher's house constructed in 1995; Mwikansi had a classroom constructed in 1997; and Chubi had a classroom completed in 1996. The total value of these projects was approximately US$16,520.

An issue typically ignored in the implementation of CC programmes is the balance of resources between the implementing organization and inputs to the community. At the village meetings held in 1997 there was consistent mention that TANAPA was well resourced and benefits going to the community were small in comparison with TANAPA resources. Thus far the only benefits received by communities have been those received through the CCS, SCIP or the private sector initiatives. Opportunities for communities themselves to use wildlife resources on their land, such as the establishment of wildlife management areas, were still only at a planning stage at the time of the research.

Efforts at benefit sharing cannot be seen as a replacement for initiatives to minimize the problems people incur in living with wildlife. People reported the same problems of living with wildlife in 1997 that they reported in 1992, and there was little evidence of a concerted effort by TNP to address these. The request of most villagers in 1992 to 'make new efforts to prevent wildlife damage' does not appear to have received much attention, although Park rangers continue to assist with scaring crop raiding animals from people's cultivated plots of land.

Impacts on the conservation resource base

The impacts of the community conservation initiative on the resource base remain unclear, and an assessment is difficult without appropriate impact indicators determined at the outset. Given the stated aims of the CCS of reducing negative impacts on the environment, one of the clearest indicators would be a reduction in the incidence of poaching. Changes in the incidence of poaching have been used as an indicator of conservation impact elsewhere with success (Leader Williams et al. 1990a). Data collected from the TNP headquarters indicate a decrease in poaching since 1994. However, it is difficult to determine whether the observed trend in poaching reflects a true trend in incidents, particularly in the absence of data on the level of effort on the part of the park staff over time. It has been argued that a reduction in poaching has occurred since the inception of the CCS in Tanzania (Bergin and Dembe 1996), but the data to substantiate this claim were not available in Tarangire. Furthermore attributing any observable trend to CCS, as opposed to an increased effort in law enforcement patrols or any other factor, is problematic.

However, it was reported by four Park staff that villagers are increasingly informing park staff of poaching incidents and providing tip-offs on the presence of poachers on village land. It was also noted that since 1995 all poaching incidents have occurred outside the Park. Problems of poaching in Tarangire seem to be localized. Park records indicate that approximately 90 per cent of the poaching incidents occur to the west of the park. As relationships with the Park's neighbours improve it might be expected that poaching would decline further.

Institutional issues

The implementation of the CC programme around Tarangire National Park faces a number of constraints. While results are promising, it must be noted that the resources applied to CC around TNP are very limited. CC staff are spread thinly on the ground and the achievements of the CCS thus far are to their credit. The Park has operated with one CC warden (absent for one year 1996/1997) and one full-time CC Assistant. In comparison the Law Enforcement section has 50 rangers. The CCS also faces challenges in introducing CC as a legitimate approach to conservation in a Park where a more traditional 'law enforcement' approach to conservation prevailed. As a department CCS has yet to gain the support of all the other departments of

TANAPA. Doubt was also expressed about the impact of the CCS benefit-sharing programme. Several respondents argued that SCIP's focus on social infrastructure does not create a clear linkage between wildlife and benefits and does not encourage wildlife compatible land use.

At the Park level a lack of institutional support is manifested in doubts about the achievements of CC among senior staff at TNP. Some Park staff expressed doubt about the need for a separate department to deal with community issues. Law enforcement rangers expressed a lack of understanding of CC activities, although they did note that Park–people relationships had become more positive in recent years. Within the broader institutional framework, relationships with district level government, essential for the smooth functioning of TANAPA's activities outside the National Park, are mixed. Institutional jealousies based on differing levels of resourcing between TANAPA and the Natural Resources Departments of district government may compromise activities in the field.

Conclusion: Community Conservation, Livelihoods and the Intrinsic Value of Wildlife

Park–people relationships around Tarangire National Park have been improved by the concerted effort of the CCS extension work and the SCIP projects. In addition, the value of wildlife and the Park for local communities has been enhanced by TANAPA's benefit-sharing programme and the efforts of the private sector working to the east of the Park. A modest investment of manpower and funds has thus led to a significant change in attitudes towards the National Park: hostility and enmity have given way to dialogue and cooperation.

The evolving policy environment in Tanzania and initiatives such as wildlife management areas will increase opportunities for local people to benefit from the wildlife resources on communal and private land. However, models of conservation based on the argument that wildlife must 'pay its way', may be simplistic for TNP. Contrary to much current community conservation theory, which posits that wildlife will be conserved to the extent that it provides 'economic' benefits, conservation in TNP appears to be dependent on a complex and dynamic interaction between cultural values, livelihood issues, human relationships and economic benefits.

The evidence from TNP indicates that the people living around the Park hold cultural values which drive their desire to see that wildlife continues to exist in their surroundings. Wildlife is seen as having a value beyond its simple economic costs and benefits. These values are reflected in the responses from both the 1992 survey and the 1997 village interviews. Concern was expressed for the children who had not seen certain species of wild animal such as the rhinoceros. In both 1992 and 1997 interest in visiting the Park to see wildlife was high among village members. The most commonly stated benefit of living with wildlife in 1992 was 'We can see and know different kinds of animals'. In 1997 several villagers asked 'Where will we go to see wild animals if they are finished here?'. Further research is needed to determine the roots of this wildlife conservation 'ethos', and it is likely that the national value of wildlife, expressed in the Arusha Declaration, has influenced local attitudes toward wildlife.

This study also highlights the need to develop a conservation model in the context of secure livelihoods. The two sides of the park face different challenges in combining human livelihoods with conservation. In the west the main problem in securing a livelihood at the human–wildlife interface is the destruction of crops by wildlife. The danger posed to humans and livestock by some species of wildlife is also a problem. To the east of the Park the main problems are those of keeping cattle alive: securing grazing and water. Pastoralists also voiced concern over the threat posed to their livestock by lions and the danger of buffaloes to humans. In all villages wildlife is appreciated and wanted to the extent that it does not compromise livelihood. In 1992 the most commonly suggested wildlife-related project was 'new efforts to prevent wildlife damage', stressing the need to reduce the costs of living with wildlife.

It should be noted that land-use patterns around TNP are changing. An increasing amount of land is being cultivated to the east of the Park, expanding the extent of conflict between agriculture and wildlife. The single most important issue determining conservation possibilities in and around TNP is land use. Both the CC programme and private sector initiatives aim to expand the conservation constituency by having supporters outside the Park. Ways of influencing the land-use regime must also be sought. The desire of the local people to change their land use was stated by a Maasai elder: 'You cannot expect us to remain in history. Many projects come and recommend we remain pastoralists, but we have discovered the new foods. Now we want to grow crops and keep our cows.'

TNP, with its experimental approach to changing relationships with local people, shows promising initial results and answers some questions about community approaches to conservation. However, it raises further and more interesting challenges. Attempts at increasing dialogue, benefit sharing and problem solving are a step in the right direction, but the values, desired landscape and livelihood concerns of the local people need to be embraced as key variables in determining the design of conservation initiatives. Perhaps the biggest challenge for any implementor of CC around TNP will be to maintain the ability to adapt the CC programme in the face of the dynamic relationships between Park and people, the changing balance between the benefits and costs of living with wildlife, changing cultures and changing land-use patterns.

Acknowledgements

We would like to thank TANAPA for allowing us to carry out this study and providing useful data and insights. We would also like to thank all the staff of Tarangire National Park for their assistance and patience in providing information. Special thanks are owed to the villagers we met and interviewed for their time and perseverance with yet more researchers. We thank the staff of the African Wildlife Foundation and the Community Conservation Service Centre in Arusha for guidance in designing this study and for logistical and technical support throughout. Thanks are also due to all individuals who gave time to be key informants and generously provided information for this study. We are grateful to our driver, Lukas, for ferrying us from village to village. This paper has benefited from comments from David Hulme and Patrick Bergin.

PART FOUR
Devolving
Management

11

The Evolution of a Community-based Approach to Wildlife Management at Kunene, Namibia

BRIAN JONES

Introduction

The community conservation activities in Namibia's Kunene Region are an approach to community conservation based on the devolution to rural communities of responsibility and proprietorship over wildlife and tourism as resources.[1] Thus, they represent a relatively radical form of community conservation in terms of Barrow and Murphree's (Chapter 3, this volume) typology. As a case study, community-based conservation in the Kunene Region illuminates a number of key issues relevant to approaches which view wildlife as a sustainable natural resource. Five key issues are examined in detail.

1. The shifting balance between intrinsic and instrumental incentives for conservation.
2. Scale as a factor influencing the development of viable common property resource management institutions for wildlife and tourism.
3. The importance of external facilitation based on 'light-touch' adaptive management.
4. Modes of relationship between communities and the private sector.
5. The difficulties of reconciling intra-community differences.

The Kunene Region

The Kunene Region is situated in north-western Namibia (Map 11.1) and covers an area of about 70, 000 km². The region includes the northern Namib desert (100 to 600 m a.s.l.) and interior highlands (1000 to 2000 m a.s.l) divided by a steep and rugged escarpment. The climate is semi-arid to hyper-arid (350 mm of rainfall in the interior highlands to less than 50 mm in the Namib Desert). Wildlife in the region consists of a variety of arid savanna and desert-adapted species including elephant, black rhino, giraffe, Hartmann's mountain zebra, greater kudu, oryx, black-faced

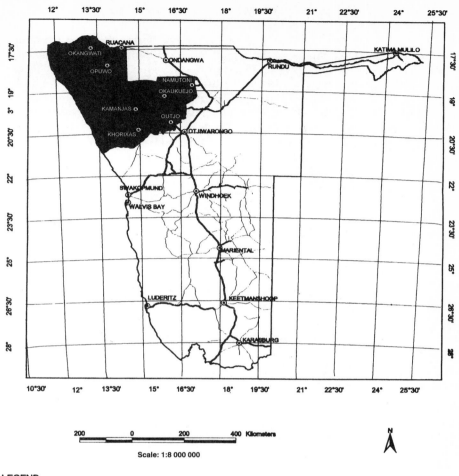

Scale: 1:8 000 000

LEGEND

☐ Namibia

■ Kunene Region and constituencies

⊙ Major Towns

∧ Main Roads

∧ Secondary Roads

Produced by the NRSC, MET

Produced for the Ministry of Lands,
Resettlement and Rehabilitation (MLRR)

October 1996

Map 11.1 The Kunene Region, Namibia

impala, springbok and warthog. Predators include lion, leopard, cheetah and spotted and brown hyena.

As a result of the low and erratic rainfall, combined with soils generally unsuitable for agriculture, the economy of the region is largely dominated by semi-nomadic pastoralism or sedentary livestock farming at low stocking rates. Tourism, based on the great scenic beauty, wildlife and cultural interaction with local residents, is increasingly playing a more significant role in the local economy. The western and northern parts of Kunene Region are inhabited by about 50,000 Herero, Himba, Damara, Nama and Riemvasmaker people who live in interspersed groups as a result of a series of forced removals and relocations imposed by successive colonial governments. The consequence has been frequent tensions between different groups, tenure insecurity and leadership instability, factors which make effective local organization difficult (Durbin et al. 1997).

Project History and Evolution

Poachers turned gamekeepers 1980–92

During the 1970s a number of factors resulted in heavy poaching and a major decline in wildlife numbers in Kunene Region. These factors were (WWF 1995):

- the increased availability of firearms during the liberation war;
- commercial demand for ivory and rhino horn as well as leopard, cheetah and zebra skins;
- subsistence meat and cash requirements after the loss of up to 85 per cent of residents' cattle during the severe drought of 1980–1.

Poaching came from a number of sources: government officials; South African Defence Force personnel stationed in the region; Portuguese refugees from Angola after 1975; and local residents on communal land (WWF 1995). While all of these groups were involved in commercial poaching for ivory and rhino horn, the biggest impact probably came from government officials and Defence Force personnel. Evidence exists of organized forays into remote areas with helicopters, the removal of elephant tusks with chainsaws and the hunting by senior South African officials of rare black-faced impala. While some local poachers were supplying tusks and horn to middlemen, most were hunting for the pot.

At the time, the region was afforded a low conservation priority by the South African government and the first conservation official did not take up station until 1978, with responsibility for a vast tract of remote and inhospitable country. Poaching continued and by 1982 the elephant population had been reduced to about 250 from an estimated 1200 in 1970. Black rhino numbers had been reduced from an estimated 300 in 1970 to about 65. Other large mammal populations declined by 60 to 90 per cent (WWF 1995).

In 1982 a local NGO, the Namibian Wildlife Trust (NWT), concerned at the lack of official response to the poaching, appointed its own conservator to work in the region. The NWT, supported by the Endangered Wildlife Trust (EWT) in South Africa, hired Garth Owen-Smith, a former agricultural extension officer and government game ranger. He had worked in the area in the early 1970s before being transferred out by the government for exposing poaching by high-ranking officials. Owen-Smith used his knowledge of the area and relationships with traditional leaders to open discussions with residents about the poaching and decline in wildlife. He established that the headmen and others were concerned at the situation, but were helpless to halt the decline as they had no authority over wildlife as game belonged to the government.

Teaming up with government conservator Chris Eyre, Owen-Smith proposed to the headmen that they appoint their own community game guards, who would be paid for by the EWT, but would be responsible to the headmen. The community game guards (CGGs) were initially part-timers who were expected to patrol their areas at least once a month. They were not there to apprehend poachers, but to monitor wildlife and any suspicious activities and then report to their headmen, who would decide upon a course of action. If there was a serious poaching incident, the headmen would hand the case over to the government.

Over the next ten years the game guards played an important role in reducing poaching. Game numbers were also helped by the end of the drought, increased anti-poaching activities by the conservation authorities and the rhino monitoring of the Save the Rhino Trust, another Namibian NGO (Durbin et al. 1997). Table 11.1 shows the increase in wildlife numbers in Kunene region since 1982. The support given to the game guards by the headmen during this period was considerable and came to symbolize community commitment to wildlife conservation.

Table 11.1   Wildlife statistics for key species in Kunene Region, 1982–97

	1982	1986	1990	1992	1995	1997 (est)★
Springbok	650	2000	7500			
Oryx	400	800	1800			
Mountain zebra	450	900	2200			
Elephant	250			384	415	
Black rhino	65	93		114		130
Giraffe	220		300			

★Estimate based on ground and air sightings.

Source: Durbin et al. (1997).

During the mid-1980s Owen-Smith teamed up with an anthropologist, Margaret Jacobsohn, who was studying the Himba semi-nomadic pastoralists of northern Kunene. Jacobsohn was living at a small desert village called Puros on the banks of the Hoarusib River. The people there, the Herero and the Himba, survived by moving their herds in response to rainfall and pasture growth. During her stay at Puros, Jacobsohn witnessed the beginning of tourism and the effects this was having on the local people. The regular passage of small groups of tourists 'on safari' resulted in people begging from the tourists, families moving their dwellings closer to the track to be first to the spoils and some families abandoning trekking with their herds. Social tensions developed as families competed for the handouts and tourists were unhappy at the 'beggars' they were encountering.

Jacobsohn and Owen-Smith held a number of meetings to discuss these problems with the residents at Puros. The result was an agreement with two safari operators, who regularly took tourists through Puros, that they would pay the community a US$5 head levy per tourist. The residents of Puros decided among themselves how the income should be spent and who should benefit. The Puros Project, as it became known, had a number of significant results. Members of the community realized that their access to the benefits of tourism was secure and resumed their normal grazing patterns and lifestyles. Competition for benefits from tourism was reduced. The benefits were regular and, although relatively small in terms of the earnings of the safari operators, were significant in a cash-starved community. The link that people made between the cash income from tourism and the wild animals tourists came to see affected people's attitude towards wildlife, particularly dangerous species such as lions and elephants. Jacobsohn (1990) relates how young men of the community tracked down a lioness so that conservation officials could capture and relocate it away from the village. Previously men of the village would have tracked and killed the predator as a threat to their families and their livestock.

During its early years the game guard programme received little support from the conservation authorities. The close association of Smith and Eyre with local black communities was viewed suspiciously by the South African administration, which was implementing apartheid policies. Pressure was brought to bear on the organizations funding the Namibia Wildlife Trust and support for Owen-Smith was cut off. In order to continue working in the area he raised funds by taking tourists on safari tours. The authorities moved Chris Eyre to work with hardbitten white commercial farmers in Keetmanshoop, a move interpreted by many in Namibian conservation circles as a punishment for his involvement with black communal area residents and 'liberal' NGOs. Owen-Smith had to wait until Namibian independence in 1990 before his work was recognized by government.

By 1991, the community game guard programme had become firmly established as a means of successfully involving rural people in conservation in Namibia. Owen-Smith and Jacobsohn, encouraged by success in Kunene Region, had started a similar programme in Caprivi in the north-east of Namibia in 1989. In order to cope with the increasing demands of supporting the game guards across the country, they formed an NGO called Integrated Rural Development and Nature Conservation (IRDNC).

From gamekeepers to proprietors 1992–7

During 1992, Owen-Smith and Jacobsohn collaborated with officials of the then Ministry of Wildlife, Conservation and Tourism in drafting a new policy for the conservation of wildlife in communal areas. The policy proposed that if residents of communal areas formed a common property resource management institution, called a conservancy (see Jones and Murphree, Chapter 4, this volume), they would be granted conditional ownership of certain game species, the right to use others through a permit system, and the right to buy and sell game. A conservancy would need a defined boundary, a defined membership, a representative committee, and a constitution recognized by government (MET 1995). Much of the work of IRDNC over the next five years focused on helping communities to prepare themselves for the passing of legislation that would put the conservancy policy into effect.

IRDNC supported communities by informing all residents about the opportunities and operation of conservancies and encouraging them to choose representative committees. It also provided training and capacity building in social survey techniques and provided logistical support for household surveys and community meetings (Durbin et al. 1997). A number of women were employed from various communities to focus on women's issues, but with the shift to supporting emergent conservancies, the women 'community activators' became part of the team that undertook household surveys. They also provided a mechanism for integrating women into the conservancy process.

IRDNC, building on experience gained during the Puros Project, also worked to bring increased benefits to local communities from tourism as at Etendeka Mountain Camp where the community was paid bed-night levies for tourists. They also helped in the communities of Bergsig and De Riet (who together form a proto-conservancy) in negotiating a joint venture tourist lodge development, Damaraland Camp, with a large safari company. IRDNC assisted community committees to carry out household surveys to ascertain who should benefit from the levies and who should have a say in how the income was used. This provided a foundation for these communities to meet one of the government conditions for conservancy registration, that of having a plan for the equitable distribution of benefits and income.

Another income-generating activity supported by IRDNC was community hunting carried out in 1993 and 1995. Previously MET staff had hunted surplus game and given the skins and meat to the community. This became too expensive for MET and so the Ministry allowed the communities themselves to hunt according to agreed quotas. IRDNC provided logistical support, loans for ammunition and advice to the communities. By 1994 the Puros community had graduated from receiving levies from passing tour groups to running its own campsite.

Self-sustaining community institutions, 1998 onwards

By mid-1998, the Ministry of Environment and Tourism had registered two conservancies in Kunene Region, one of which, the Torra Conservancy, represented the Bergsig and De Riet community that had been supported by IRDNC. Another community supported by IRDNC, in the Sesfontein area, was about to submit its application to the MET. A number of the activities currently carried out by IRDNC and funded by them, should ultimately become the responsibility of the conservancies themselves. Its role will diminish as the conservancies begin to earn sufficient revenue to take over, for example, the funding of community game guards and vehicles required for organizing meetings and radio communication between committees and members. Indeed, in August 1998 the Torra Conservancy took over 40 per cent of its own running costs using income from its joint venture. As the conservancies become self-sustaining, both in terms of finances and human resources and capacity, IRDNC staff will be able to shift their attention to other communities requiring support in conservancy formation.

Key Issues for Community Wildlife Management Raised by the Kunene Case Study

The shifting balance between intrinsic and instrumental incentives for conservation

At the heart of attempts to promote sustainable management of natural resources in southern Africa is a belief that local communities will respond to economic incentives that can be established or enhanced through government policy and legislation. The hypothesis is that if local communities have secure rights (proprietorship) over the resource, can retain the benefits of use, and these benefits outweigh the costs of managing the resource, then sustainable use is likely (Steiner and Rihoy 1995; SASUSG 1997).The Communal Areas Management Programme for Indigenous Resources (CAMPFIRE) in Zimbabwe, for example, places considerable emphasis on the revenues from trophy hunting and tourism as incentives to local communities for conservation of wildlife and wild habitat (Steiner and Rihoy 1995). Wildlife policy in Botswana enables local communities to gain rights over tourism and hunting concessions in designated areas and a crucial part of Namibia's communal area conservancy policy and legislation is that communities will retain the full amount of income generated by their wildlife and tourism enterprises.

Much emphasis has been given to these instrumental incentives, but there are other incentives, based on intrinsic cultural and religious values, which affect the way in which Africans respond to wildlife. Like many Westerners, many Africans value wildlife for its existence and wish their children and grandchildren to be able to enjoy seeing the wild animals they and their parents witnessed. As George Mutwa, chairperson of the Salambala Conservancy in eastern Caprivi states: 'They are also looking for cultural, indirect benefits. In the old days people attached great importance to wildlife' (Mutwa, pers. comm., 1998). Religious beliefs in many African societies promote respect for wildlife and have contributed to the development of systems of use and non-use (Matowanyika et al. 1995).

The experience of community-based natural resource management in Namibia's Kunene Region has helped to focus attention on intrinsic incentives for conservation and on the dynamic relationship between intrinsic and instrumental incentives. The activities initiated by IRDNC in the early 1980s were based on the realization that local communities had an ethic of conservation and sustainable use which could be built upon to halt the large-scale poaching of that time. While individuals were poaching for a variety of reasons, there was evidence of community-level concern at the disappearance of wildlife from the area. Furthermore, traditional leaders, important figures within the community, wanted to do something about the situation.

Local communities today might be suspected of mouthing what they think donors, NGOs and others want to hear in the hope of getting some benefit. When Owen-Smith and Eyre first discussed conservation and poaching with community leaders, there was nothing on offer in return except the knowledge and satisfaction that the community was doing something itself to halt the decline in wildlife. It became clear in the early 1980s that communities in the Kunene Region 'could and would take responsibility for resources before benefit flows' (Durbin et al. 1997: 2). The community game guards, while having certain functional responsibilities, were an expression of community responsibility 'which can be interpreted as ownership on a cultural rather than an economic level' (ibid. 13). People defined 'ownership' in terms of a connection to wildlife based on cultural values rather than property rights derived from the state. Owen-Smith and Jacobsohn (1991: 19) conclude of the Game Guard and Puros Projects: 'Although much attention has been given to the cash benefits generated by these projects, an equally or possibly more important benefit has been the social re-empowerment that has resulted from local communities regaining some control over the management and conservation of their wildlife resource.'

From the early days of the game guard programme there has been a clearly discernible evolution of community-based natural resource management activities in Kunene Region. Through the game guards the poachers collectively (if not all individually!) turned gamekeepers accepting responsibility for a resource which they felt some cultural ownership over. Once the principle and practice of responsibility had been established, this was reinforced by the prospect and realization of benefits flowing from the results of taking responsibility. The third evolutionary stage was moving from responsibility and benefit to proprietorship once government policy and legislation had changed.

Durbin et al. (1997) suggest a number of reasons why this development took place.

- Communities themselves recognized the evolutionary nature of the process and while the conservation ethic was an appropriate starting point, there was also a time frame in which there was an expectation that conservation investments would produce financial benefits.
- Pressure from younger people demanding jobs and wages meant that if the programme was to retain popular support it would have to give more emphasis to the generation of income.
- Wildlife and tourism needed to become more economically competitive because increased human population and schemes for other land uses were resulting in increased competition for land.
- The increase in wildlife as a result of community efforts (and other factors noted earlier), resulted in increased competition between wildlife and livestock for water and grazing, increased damage to water points by elephants and stock losses to predators. The increased costs of conservation demanded a compensating increase in benefits.

Another important factor which facilitated the evolution from responsibility through benefit to proprietorship was the timely intervention of government through the conservancy policy and legislation. The shift in emphasis from responsibility to benefit increased communities' expectations of gaining full 'economic ownership' of the resource. These expectations had been fuelled by the rhetoric of government and conservation NGOs which had promoted the notion of community 'ownership' particularly since Namibia's independence in 1990. By 1996, for community-based conservation to be maintained in Kunene Region, and much of the rest of the country, it had become crucial that government deliver on its promises. The involvement of IRDNC in a national programme which included policy and legislative reform provided the opportunity for its own and community experiences to influence policy development and to help government provide the policy and legal context within which community resource management institutions could evolve.

The Kunene Region in Namibia provides examples of people who embraced the idea of wildlife management and conservation before there was a realistic expectation that significant revenues would accrue from utilization. At the same time, the prospect of improved livelihoods and perhaps a diversification of the rural economy, has sustained community commitment to wildlife conservation, particularly in the face of a dire need for jobs and cash income. Through a change in government policy and legislation, communities have been able to move from responsibility and benefit to proprietorship.

Scale and the development of viable common property resource management institutions for wildlife and tourism

The emerging conservancies in Kunene Region demonstrate some of the problems of matching appropriate sized social units with appropriate sized ecological units, when designing effective common property resource management institutions. Conventional wisdom in common property resource management theory is that 'small works' (e.g. Ostrom 1990; Murphree 1993) in terms of social units because decision-making is easier and transparency and accountability are more likely to be achieved. However, given the 'fugitive' nature of many wildlife resources and the arid ecological conditions of Kunene Region, the optimal ecological unit is very large, probably encompassing several conservancies. Elephants, for example, move over vast areas responding to the stimuli of rainfall and vegetation growth. The fugitive nature of some species also presents problems of 'ownership' between neighbouring conservancies and/or conservancies and non-conservancy communities.

Turner (1996) has analysed proto-conservancy development in four communities in northern Namibia. He points out that 'principle and practice suggest that a successful conservancy, as a successful venture in common property resource management, would have a strong natural resource base (in which wildlife is prominently represented), and form a compact geographical and social unit, with a large enough population to sustain robust social institutions – including a strong and respected leadership and a localised system of justice'. However, he sees conservancies developing with different degrees to which this 'perfect' match is achieved. One pattern is socially stronger conservancies in relatively compact areas developing on weak natural resource bases, and with relatively large human populations. Another pattern is a stronger natural resource base spread over large areas with very sparse human populations, among whom leadership is less strongly developed and poverty levels high. A third pattern, illustrated by the Kunene Region, is where distances are great, the resource base promising and the population small, but social and institutional cohesion stronger.

Conservancy policy and legislation in Namibia leaves communities to define themselves. The communities of Kunene region are using a number of strategies to overcome the problems inherent in self-definition. To some extent they have agreed to use a pre-independence system of headmen's wards as the basis for defining conservancy boundaries and the people who are included and excluded. The headmen's wards nominally contain groups of people who accept the authority of a headman and share a sense of 'community' in other respects. However, in practice, there are people living within wards who look to other wards for their sense of community and most wards contain people of different ethnic background. The use of the ward system has therefore caused some problems. Some families, while living on land accepted to be in a particular ward, have seen themselves as falling under the headman of another, adjoining ward. In another case, on the same area of land were people who wished to be in different conservancies. The MET informed the communities concerned that it was prepared to approve their conservancies if the land on which the disputes were taking place was excluded from all conservancy applications, pending adjudication.

At Kunene wards are large and, for more sedentary species, might be viable ecological units. But for elephants, springbok, oryx and mountain zebra in particular, they are too small. The large wards and scattered settlements present communications problems for community leadership and management institutions and make information and accountability between conservancy committees and members costly and difficult. The larger the unit, the more the issue of representation becomes problematic. For example, a committee elected by majority vote of all residents might yield a geographically or ethnically skewed representation, leaving some people with the perception that their voices will not be heard in decision-making.

A number of factors lead to the expectation that at Kunene and other conservancies the boundaries will change over time as communities adjust to the different requirements of social cohesion, practical organizational constraints, and viable areas for resource management. In some cases, conservancies will opt for further devolution of authority to sub-areas within the conservancy, particularly over localized tourism enterprises. In other cases, perhaps with elephant management and elephant-generated income, conservancies might need to collaborate with each other at a regional level. In this last case, localized units of proprietorship would bring together their rights over wildlife and tourism and agree to co-operate at a higher level and broader scale of common property resource management. Future adaptations and adjustments might lead to smaller conservancies with more socially cohesive human populations and sub-units within the conservancy, with these conservancies forming the building blocks for co-operative management across larger resource management units. However, the direct and indirect costs of managing such 'nests' of institutions are high in areas of dispersed populations and poor communications. Some attempts by government to bring community level representatives together at a regional level are already foundering because of these problems.

Importance of external facilitation based on 'light touch' adaptive management

Rural communities know about their environments (Matowanyika et al. 1995). They are also often shrewd negotiators with outsiders. However, to meet the conditions set by government policy, and to negotiate joint venture wildlife-based enterprises with the private sector, communities need additional skills and information. They also need practical assistance in the form of funds and equipment to carry out key activities such as holding meetings, electing office-bearers and disseminating information. But there are dangers in providing large-scale externally funded assistance to local communities. External assistance needs to be such that communities are able to wean themselves off it and eventually afford to maintain and replace equipment and other infrastructure provided for them.

The approach of the NGO that has worked with specific Kunene region communities over a period of about 15 years demonstrates the importance not only of persistence and consistency, but of a real commitment to a 'bottom up' philosophy based on flexibility and adaptation in the face of the contingencies of communities, governments and environments. IRDNC has founded its activities at Kunene on a number of key principles. These principles have helped shape the way in which it has supported communities, and can be described as 'facilitation based on light touch adaptive management'.

IRDNC has recognized the intrinsic values that wildlife have for local people and has built upon this conservation ethic through other more instrumental incentives. The recognition of a local conservation ethic has had major significance in the way that IRDNC has approached its work. Many conservation programmes begin with the premise that local people need to be taught that conservation is necessary and hence develop a 'top down' environmental awareness approach, trying to teach locals that a set of conservation problems defined by outsiders needs addressing (Brown and Wyckoff–Baird 1992). By contrast IRDNC has built a set of activities upon a problem which was also defined by the local community, which wanted to act to solve the problem. The NGO believes strongly that local people are knowledgeable about their environment and its problems. Outside assistance therefore needs to focus on issues where communities' own knowledge and experience is lacking.

IRDNC's support has been flexible, adapting to changing needs and circumstances within communities and within the emerging policy and legal framework for community-based conservation, while retaining integrity of approach. This is seen in the transition from the game guard programme, with its emphasis on responsibility, through projects emphasizing benefit creation and finally to support for conservancies as proprietorial units. As this transition has taken place, IRDNC has focused on building community capacity at each stage. Inherent in the game guard programme has been the phased handover of responsibility to the community. IRDNC has helped communities build their own offices from where the game guards can be administered and other conservation activities planned, such as community hunting of surplus game. IRDNC has facilitated the formation of local conservation committees or worked with existing development committees which have increasingly taken over the administration of the game guards. These committees negotiated relationships with tourism concessionaires and handled the distribution of income. They then drove the conservancy formation process and are now evolving into representative conservancy committees. The light touch approach of IRDNC has meant leaving communities to get on with their own decision-making processes and accepting their decisions, even where IRDNC staff might believe unwise choices have been made.

IRDNC has also tried to relate the level of its support to the degree to which a conservancy can generate its own revenue. Thus funding for game guards, community conservation offices and vehicles is not provided unless there is evidence that conservancies will later be able to cover their own costs and make a profit for members. At the same time, this prudence has to be balanced against the practicalities of communities trying to mobilize and organize themselves over vast distances. In order to hold meetings, respond to the demands of government and other outsiders and for leadership to provide feedback, communities need faster means of transport than the traditional donkey cart. For strategic reasons, strict considerations of sustainability often have to be balanced against the practical problems of organization in areas of very dispersed population.

The ability of NGOs to work closely with local communities is often dependent upon the attitude of government to NGO activities. In Namibia, generally, NGOs are free to operate as they wish within the laws of the country and are not regulated by government. The relationship between IRDNC and government has, however, been a mixed one for a number of reasons. The organization's strongest relationship with a government agency has been with the Directorate of Environmental Affairs (DEA) in the Ministry of Environment and Tourism (MET). The DEA developed a partnership with IRDNC in establishing a national CBNRM programme, based on the acknowledgement that MET did not have the necessary institution building and community development skills and that it would be costly and time-consuming to build this capacity up. The DEA saw the role of government as being to provide the enabling framework within which communities could gain rights over wildlife and tourism while NGOs could facilitate and support community action.

However, other branches of government were not so sanguine about the role of NGOs. Within MET some Directorate of Resource Management (DRM) staff felt that IRDNC was undermining the Ministry and was so pro-community that it did not share MET's conservation objectives (also see Jones and Murphree, Chapter 4, this volume). Other field personnel have resented NGOs that appear to have more money and better equipment than government conservation staff and who are viewed by communities as the 'good guys' while the MET conservators are thought of as the 'bad guys'. Some of these perceptions might have been avoided if senior MET staff had shown a greater commitment to community-based approaches to wildlife management, thus giving clear direction to their personnel. Often, individual conservators have been willing to work with communities and develop a partnership with IRDNC, but have been hindered by institutional constraints. The situation has begun to change with new leadership within DRM and agreement on the shift of responsibility for community-based wildlife management from the DEA to DRM. Despite the frictions between some MET personnel and IRDNC, senior DRM staff acknowledge the contribution that local communities and NGOs have made to conservation in Kunene Region.

Modes of relationship between communities and the private sector

The private sector can play an important and positive role in community conservation, provided the power relations between the two can be equalized as far as possible. Community conservation activities in Kunene Region illustrate some of the contradictions inherent in community relationships with the private sector and some of the ways in which successful partnerships can be developed. In their attempts to create sustainable use regimes for wildlife and tourism, local communities in Kunene Region have forged different types of partnerships with the private sector. These relationships have not always been straightforward or easy and have reflected the dual nature of the private sector as potential partner and potential competitor for resources, markets and profits.

The nature of relationships between communities and the private sector has been shaped by many factors. In some cases, such as at Puros and the Etendeka Mountain Camp, private sector operators have entered into a relationship with the community out of enlightened self-interest. The Etendeka concession agreement, for example, does not explicitly exclude members of the community from using the land for grazing livestock, an activity which the concessionnaire views as conflicting with the natural wilderness product he is selling. He is happy to raise a bed-night levy for payment to the local community in excess of the rent he pays to the government because he realizes he is vulnerable (Liebenberg, pers. comm.). He took IRDNC advice on aspects of levy distribution and accepted its recommendation that communities be left to decide themselves how to use their income. He has a good relationship with his neighbours because they have seen a tangible demonstration of his goodwill. By contrast, another concessionnaire collected a levy but would only hand it over if the community identified a specific project for which the funds would be used which the concessionnaire approved of (Gruttemeyer, pers. comm.). His relationship with neighbours was uneasy for some years until recent facilitation by the MET.

The joint venture partnership between a southern African safari company and the Torra Conservancy at Damaraland Camp represents a different mode of relationship between community and business. The company has an ethos of developing partnerships with rural communities, no doubt out of self-enlightenment, but it also links this to a belief that community involvement is important in conservation. The real difference in the Damaraland Camp joint venture, however, is that the community have a type of lease from government on the land on which the lodge is situated. This strengthens the community's position in its negotiations with the company and establishes a more equal partnership. With support from IRDNC, a public interest legal firm and government resource economists the community have negotiated a deal which includes managerial level training for community members and an option for the community to take over the full running of the camp after a certain period with a guarantee by the company to maintain the supply of tourists to the camp. The same community has taken out a similar lease on another prime site in the area and has turned down one potential investor who was not prepared to meet its conditions.

In this mode of relationship, communities are dependent upon the private sector being willing to invest time in developing such a relationship. But the important factor which changes the relationship from that of the voluntary bed-night levy mode is that, through a lease from government, the community controls an asset that the private sector wants. A larger amount of income is generated for the community (about US$35,000 by August 1998 for Damaraland Camp), and the sense of empowerment is stronger because of the status afforded the community in the joint venture and the managerial training being provided.

Once conservancies are registered by government in Kunene Region a third mode of relationship between community and private sector can be established. Because conservancies include concessionary rights to tourism within the conservancy boundaries, communities will have full control over resources that the private sector wants to exploit. Communities will be able to gain maximum financial return through competitive bidding for their concessions. NGOs and government will continue to play an advisory role to communities, ensuring that they have sufficient information and understanding of business practices and tourism requirements to negotiate with confidence.

In many respects the private sector also needs some 'capacity building' when it comes to relating to local communities. There are a number of inherent differences between the style of doing business of the private sector and of communities. The pace at which communities make decisions is usually far behind the pace at which the private sector wants to move. If the private sector and communities are to successfully conclude joint venture partnerships both will need to adjust to the style of the other. The best way for communities to ensure the private sector will enter into a partnership is by combining rights with marketable assets. Communities in north-west Namibia that form conservancies will by and large be able to bring together these two criteria. The combination of spectacular desert scenery and desert-dwelling large mammals, such as elephant and black rhino, provides the assets. The rights come with the granting of conservancy status. But this will not be enough to ensure that the private sector is 'community friendly'. In Namibia, community-based tourism enterprises (CBTEs) have combined to form their own NGO, the Namibian Community-Based Tourism Association (NACOBTA). This association has opened a dialogue with private sector tourism umbrella organizations to provide information about CBTEs and promote community friendly approaches. Perhaps ultimately, however, it is market forces that will convince many private sector operators that working with communities is worthwhile. The Damaraland Camp joint venture was in 1997 given a major international award by the British Travel Writers Association, sending a clear signal to the industry that discerning tourists are looking for ecologically and community friendly safari experiences and will pay more to find them.

The difficulties of reconciling intra-community differences

Rural communities are heterogeneous. They are made up of a variety of different groups distinguished by age, gender, ethnicity, socio-economic status and other factors. These groups compete in different ways for the rights, revenue and resources which are available. Within Kunene Region local communities have been using different means to try to ensure that particular groups do not become dominant.

A number of conflicts between group interests have become discernible during the process of conservancy formation. In both the Bergsig/De Riet proto-conservancy and at Puros, the youth had expressed opinions which were different from those of other groups within the community, creating problems and delays in the establishment of conservancies (Durbin et al. 1997). At Bergsig/De Riet, until the last moment before the community was due to hand in its conservancy application to MET, a group of young people wanted to delay the process, claiming the conservancy committee was unrepresentative. The committee felt confident in its own representativeness and that the youth were in a minority in terms of the rest of the community and went ahead with the application. A difference between younger and older members of many rural communities in Namibia is that the youth are in a hurry to get jobs for wages so they can acquire the material goods associated with a higher standard of living. Older people tend to be more patient and to seek indirect cultural benefits rather than money alone. In the case of Bergsig/De Riet a specific youth project emerged aimed at providing information to young people about conservancies and natural resource management.

Ethnic conflict has arisen in different ways among the communities forming conservancies in Kunene Region. The Bersig/De Riet community is made up of mostly Damara speaking people and the Riemvasmakers, people who were moved from South Africa to Namibia as one of the quirks of South Africa's apartheid system. During 1997 there were allegations that the conservancy formation process was being dominated by Riemvasmakers and that Damara people were being left out, for example, of the proto-conservancy committee. There were newspaper reports that the Damaraland Camp joint venture was employing only Riemvasmakers and not Damaras. Regional councillors used the ethnic issue to delay their endorsement of the Bersig/De Riet application. Responding to the allegations, the committee held new elections for office bearers, resulting in a Damara speaking person becoming chair of the committee. The committee was able to show that Damaras were also benefiting from the joint venture and there was no discrimination in employment policy. The ethnic issue was probably one of perception, rather than reality in the sense that many Damara people had been very actively involved in conservancy formation, but were not on the 'high profile' committee. A pragmatic and quick response by the conservancy committee in ensuring that Damara involvement became visible was able to prevent a potentially divisive conflict from developing.

In the Sesfontein proto-conservancy, there has been conflict between different factions within one ethnic group, with each faction owing allegiance to competing headmen. One faction has held up the establishment of the conservancy for many months by delaying agreement on crucial issues. The Sesfontein community had tried to deal with the issue of competing interests among geographically dispersed settlements by allocating committee seats to each settlement according to its size. The faction in dispute perceived themselves to be a minority group on the conservancy committee and wished to have greater representation so that they would not be swamped by the majority. This issue remains unresolved at the time of writing.

With regard to gender issues, the experience of communities in Kunene Region has been interesting. The programme began based on the involvement and commitment of male headmen and male community game guards. At the time this was the appropriate (and successful) entry point for the discussion and implementation of active wildlife conservation by the community. Over time, however, the involvement of women has grown, particularly with the process of conservancy formation. During 1993, the author attended an all-male meeting at the community of Warmquelle. When asked if we could not call the women to attend, our interpreter told us 'That might be your way, but in our culture, it is the men who take the decisions.' Yet by 1997, women community activators were playing an important role in informing community members about the conservancy, women were present and participated at conservancy meetings, were well involved in committee elections and were represented on the committees (Durbin et al. 1997). This shift in the level of involvement by women reflects both the dynamic nature of the facilitation provided by IRDNC and the adaptability of the communities themselves. It should also be noted that a focus on large mammals may have led to a neglect of other natural resources that are mainly used and managed by women and that this may have reduced opportunities for women's involvement on conservancy committees (Sullivan 1999 and 2000). The experience of women's involvement also illustrates the clash between different cultural views. The strong Western agenda of equality for women is reflected in development programmes led by Western donors and NGOs, some of which try to force the issue, for example by setting quotas for women on community committees. At times this has generated resistance from community leaders.

The equitable distribution of benefits from wildlife management is a key issue from both social and resource management perspectives. If there is inequitable benefit distribution, there could be conflict, leading to the collapse of collective management institutions such as conservancies. If groups or individuals within a community perceive they are treated unfairly, they will no longer have incentives to adhere to rules about use of the resource, and are likely to become free-riders. The damage they inflict will be in inverse proportion to the authority and ability the management institution has to enforce rules.

The bed-night levy collection and distribution was an important learning experience for the emerging conservancies in Kunene Region, particularly as the establishment of a method for equitable distribution of benefits is a requirement of the conservancy legislation. IRDNC assisted communities in undertaking a consultation process among their members in order to decide how the income could be equitably distributed. For the Etendeka bed-night levy a household survey was conducted by a bed-night levy committee. Durbin et al. (1997) conclude that although the negotiations with the Lodge owner and the community surveys were time-consuming, they appear to have been very useful. The surveys explained the source of the income, thus reinforcing its links with tourism and wildlife, and ensured that all households had a vote on how the money would be used and could express their views on the distribution process.

Conclusion

The Kunene case demonstrates a number of innovative and positive responses to the challenges posed by community-based wildlife conservation on communal land. The case study also demonstrates the dynamic nature of a set of community-based activities which have evolved over a period of 16 years. These activities have influenced national policy development and, in their turn, had to respond to the opportunities presented by new policy and legislation. The pioneering work of IRDNC, along with the commitment of community leaders, was crucial for the development of national policy, while the establishment of an enabling framework by government was crucial for community conservation in Kunene Region. The significance of intrinsic incentives for conservation in Kunene Region suggests that the level of instrumental benefits required to achieve sustainable use of the wildlife resource is not always as high as a purely economic analysis would indicate. It also suggests that policies and practices are required that will favour the retention, and passing on to future generations, of intrinsic values.[2]

As government begins to register the first conservancies in the Kunene Region there are exciting new opportunities for communities to begin integrating wildlife and tourism with their other land uses, and to realize significant economic benefits. Conservancies also provide the potential for the social and political empowerment of rural communities through planning and group action. There are also potential pitfalls. In some communities, factional differences have delayed the process of conservancy formation as existing intra-community conflicts have been re-exposed. The new conservancies, driven often by younger people conscious of the need for employment and wages, are not necessarily in tune with the aspirations of the older leaders. Conservancies confer resource rights, but not land rights. Local communities throughout Namibia await the tabling of a communal areas Land Reform Bill, which may or may not make provision for secure community land tenure. Without secure land tenure, conservancy land-use regimes can be undermined by the influx of people and livestock from elsewhere. There are question marks over the capacity of government to provide the necessary extension and support on wildlife management to the conservancies. The same innovative and positive spirit which served well in the past will need to be demonstrated well into the future as conservancies struggle for recognition and legitimacy among different interest groups competing for rights, revenue and resources.

Notes

[1] This paper has benefited from comments from David Hulme and Marshall Murphree.
[2] Kangwana (Chapter 10, this volume) has similar findings from Tanzania where local residents place an intrinsic value on wildlife.

12

Community, Council & Client
A Case Study in Ecotourism Development from Mahenye, Zimbabwe

MARSHALL MURPHREE

Introduction

In Zimbabwe's CAMPFIRE Programme, revenue generation from wildlife has been largely derived from safari sport hunting. Over 90 per cent of CAMPFIRE income between 1989 and 1996 has come from sport hunting leases and fees (see Bond, Chapter 15, this volume). The emphasis on safari hunting, rather than on photographic and other forms of non-consumptive ecotourism, is the result of a combination of factors. Hunting safari enterprises do not require high levels of capital investment in lodge development nor extended lease periods to recover initial investment. They are less dependent on a well developed road, air transport and energy network than most other forms of ecotourism and can more easily accommodate the relatively undeveloped infrastructure characteristic of most CAMPFIRE districts (Map 12.1). They can be successful in areas which have no immediate exotic or photogenic appeal. Also, although in common with other forms of ecotourism they are critically dependent on an effective marketing network, the client network involved is highly specialized and more closely linked to professional operators rather than to specific sites. The combination of these industry characteristics – flexibility, mobility, relatively low initial capital outlays and relatively high revenues – has made safari hunting the inaugural entrepreneurial choice in most of CAMPFIRE's districts. This is likely to continue for many districts as long as this market remains strong.

Safari hunting is not necessarily the highest value use of wildlife and natural resources in all contexts. Particularly at sub-district levels, some wards are endowed with micro-environments of scenic or recreational attraction or of particular ecological interest which have potential for the ecotourism market. The financial value of these assets varies widely. In many cases they are sites which are primarily of attraction to a local tourist market, often for the weekend recreation of city dwellers. In response to this market a number of initiatives have been taken by communities or district councils to develop camping sites, often with simple accommodation in huts or bungalows and with a facility for the sale of drinks and snacks. Start-up capital has

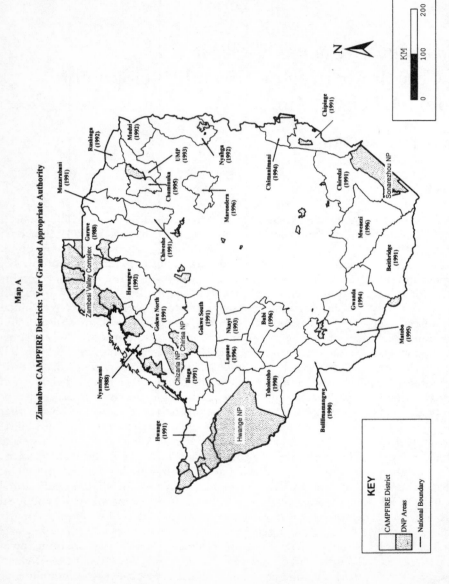

Map A

Zimbabwe CAMPFIRE Districts: Year Granted Appropriate Authority

Map 12.1 Zimbabwe CAMPFIRE districts: year granted appropriate authority

typically been provided by loans or grants from donors or councils. Locally managed, they are referred to as 'non-lease' tourism sites. They have the advantage of encouraging the development of new forms of local collective management and entrepreneurship. At the same time they operate at the 'cheap' end of the market and face the problems which collective management tends to exhibit everywhere. A 1998 study of three of these enterprises concluded that they all were operating at levels of marginal financial viability due to managerial and marketing problems. The study also points out however that 'the low budget international, national and regional market remains largely untapped and is looking for new destinations' and suggests that with improved managerial and marketing structures this mode of communal enterprise has the potential for growth (Murphree and Nyika 1998).[1]

There are also a number of wards in CAMPFIRE districts which possess prime sites for upmarket international tourism. These include a number of locations on the shoreline of Lake Kariba, and sites adjacent to Zimbabwe's major tourism destinations such as Victoria Falls. They also include micro-habitats for rare floral and faunal species, which are particularly important for the growing interest in specialist niche ecotourism. For such wards the revenue potential from non-consumptive tourism is significant and may well exceed that of safari hunting. If this potential is realized a transition over time from hunting safari to other modes of ecotourism could well take place. The case study presented in this chapter provides a pointer in this direction.[2]

Mahenye Ward: The Socio-historical Background

Mahenye Ward lies at the extreme southern end of the Chipinge District, covering about 210 km² in the Ndowoyo Communal Land. Its eastern boundary is the Mozambique border. Its western boundary is the Save River, separating it from the Gonarezhou National Park and the Sangwe Communal Land in the Chiredzi District. To the north its neighbour is the Mutandahwe ward of Ndowoyu Communal Land (Map 12.2). Average rainfall is low (450–500 mm per annum) supporting dry land cultivation of grains only in good seasons. Most of the ward is covered by mixed mopane and combretum woodland but along the Save River dense riverine forest occurs supporting a broad range of floral and avian species, some of them rare in Zimbabwe. Ngwachumene Island, within the borders of the ward, is particularly noted in this regard.[3] The alluvial soils in and around this riverine forest are used for the cultivation of vegetables and dry season grains.

This brief biophysical description of the ward reflects a defining characteristic of Mahenye: discreteness and isolation, which is replicated in its socio-political location. Its neighbours to the east are in a different country. Administratively its neighbours to the west across the Save River are not only in a different district but also in a different province of Zimbabwe. In contrast to the heavily populated, overgrazed wards of the Ndowuyo Communal Land to the north, Mahenye represents a lowveld habitat in relatively good health, with a population density of about 20 persons per km² in contrast to a district average of 43 persons/km² (Booth 1991: 9–10).

Finally and perhaps most importantly the people of Mahenye are, within the Chipinge District, ethnically discrete. All the other wards of the district comprise primarily Shona-speaking Ndau peoples. The Mahenye people are a segment of the

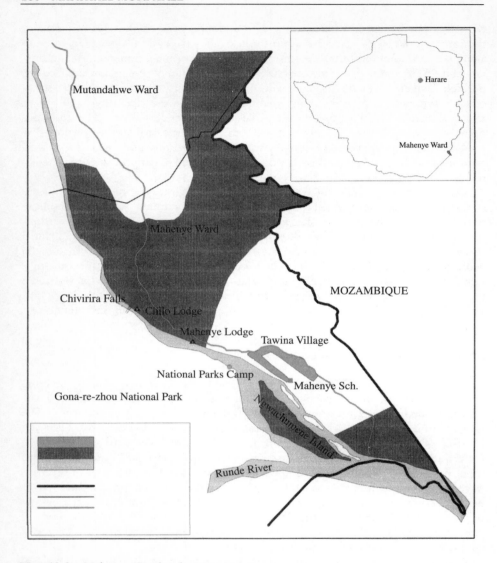

Map 12.2   Mahenye Ward and ecotourism sites

Shangaan-speaking peoples who in precolonial times occupied the south-east lowlands of Zimbabwe, the north-east lowlands of what is now South Africa and much of what is now the Gaza and Inhambane Provinces of Mozambique.[4] In South Africa and Zimbabwe colonialism brought displacement and compression to these peoples, and both the Kruger and Gonarezhou National Parks were carved out of Shangaan territory. In Zimbabwe the Shangaan were forced on to communal lands in the Chiredzi District and into Mahenye Ward in the Chipinge District. Some emigrated to Mozambique.

Thus for the people of Mahenye the double expropriation of rights to land and wildlife brought by colonialism was an acute reality (see Jones and Murphree, Chapter 4, this volume, for a discussion). Evicted from their traditional territory and forced to live on its perimeter they were furthermore denied the right to use wildlife. This exclusion was not a minor denial as hunting had been a major component of Shangaan livelihood strategies and their culture had evolved well-defined regulatory practices to make hunting offtakes sustainable.[6] Their eviction from Gonarezhou had taken place in stages, the latest being in 1966 when the area between the Save and Runde rivers, which included the community's store, mission station and school, was taken over by the Park. These events were thus not simply part of a transmitted history, they were part of the personal history of the elders who, at the time of independence in 1980, pressed the new government to restore their lost lands. Peterson (1991b: 6) comments that 'For the people of Mahenye, the land issue in the War for Independence was seen as their right to regain their homes in the National Park. Indeed, clear promises were made to the Shangaan people that Independence would mean a restoration of their hunting rights.'

In the event such promises were not honoured. The new government reinforced its hold on the Park and park officials intensified their anti-poaching raids in the Mahenye Ward. In response to questions as to why the Park had not been returned to the Shangaan, government officials suggested that government needed foreign exchange brought in by international visitors to the Park. The people of Mahenye retorted that this gave them an added incentive to poach within the Park: if there were no animals there would be no tourists, no revenue and thus no reason for government to retain the Park. Furthermore, elephant and buffalo from the Park raided their gardens and fields regularly, threatening their remaining means of subsistence. As one elder put it to Peterson (1991b: 10), 'We were displaced and we don't have the game we used to have. We have to depend on our agriculture. We must grow our crops to survive. Their animals cross over the river and eat our crops. We have no food when our crops are eaten, so we have to eat their animals or we would starve. If they would control their animals, we could grow our crops. Then there would be no poaching.' The language as well as the substance of this quote is significant. Wildlife, previously an important aspect of subsistence, had become 'their animals'. A spiralling dialect of confrontation had developed which resulted in the abrogation of the Shangaan ethic of sustainable hunting and an increasingly zealous, if ineffective, campaign of anti-poaching incursions by park staff into the Ward.

This alienation between the Shangaan, wildlife and the wildlife authorities was paralleled by an alienation between the community, government and the district council. Mahenye's ethnic discreteness had always distanced it from the rest of the district. But the new government's policy of reducing the power of hereditary chiefs and introducing elected councils at both ward and district levels exacerbated this. This policy was seen as a threat to the cultural distinctiveness of the community, and when asked to elect a councillor to represent the ward at district level they elected a cousin of the chief to demonstrate the solidarity of popular and traditional legitimization within the community. This political cohesion within Mahenye, which has generally prevailed over the past 15 years, was matched by political segregation at the district council level, where Mahenye's councillor stood out as the one member in a council of 22 (now 30) from an ethnic minority.

Mahenye and Hunting Safari Tourism

Although Mahenye is now a part of the CAMPFIRE Programme, it is not, historically speaking, a product of it. In a sense the reverse is true. Mahenye's initiation of a communal natural resource management regime antedates CAMPFIRE and was a precursor to it.[6] In early 1982 the Mahenye leadership, through their councillor, arranged to have a meeting with the Gonarezhou warden in an effort to improve their relationship with the Park. Anticipating a difficult meeting, the warden, a white Zimbabwean, asked a local rancher and safari operator, Clive Stockil, to accompany him and provide translation. Stockil's grandfather had established the mission at Mahenye. Stockil had learned Shangaan as a child, was well known and liked in the Mahenye community and respected in both local farming and government circles.

The warden's anticipation of a difficult meeting was fulfilled as the Mahenye people put their case aggressively. Stockil changed his role from that of translator to instigative facilitator. With his grasp of the importance of wildlife to Shangaan culture and his personal experience with wildlife proprietorship as a private rancher through the 1975 Act (see Jones and Murprhee, Chapter 4, this volume), he seized on the importance of the pronoun in the complaints to park officials about 'your wildlife'. Was it possible, he speculated, to effect a similar change of proprietorship over wildlife on communal land for the Mahenye community? He put this to the meeting along the following lines: If government were to agree that wildlife within the ward would be regarded as the property of the community, with community rights to sell this wildlife on the safari hunting market and keep the proceeds, would Mahenye be willing to accept a degree of crop damage and co-operate in the repression of poaching?

The proposal was received with both interest and scepticism. It seemed like a step towards the re-appropriation of wildlife but would the government really implement such a suggestion? Stockil was not a representative of government and could not say. The warden had no personal objections, but would have to refer the matter to headquarters. Nevertheless agreement was reached to proceed with negotiations. Subsequently the Director of the Department of National Parks and Wild Life Management (DNPWLM) was approached and agreed to a one-year trial. Permits for two trophy elephant to be taken in Mahenye by clients found by Stockil would be issued for 1982. Both clients would have to pay for their hunts in foreign currency. Provided that the community co-operated with park officials in anti-poaching efforts, DNPWLM would insist that the concession fees for the hunts would be paid to the Ward.

In August 1982 the hunts took place and the people of Mahenye celebrated success through the ritual distribution of meat which followed. With a renewed hope of being given the authority to manage their natural resources, the community leadership persuaded those living on Ngwachumene Island (approximately 100 people in 7 hamlets) to move to the mainland, thus leaving this prime habitat free for wildlife. At the same time the anti-poaching unit from National Parks reported that poaching in the ward had decreased (Peterson, 1991b: 14).

There remained, however, the matter of the concession fees promised by the Department of National Parks. Not for the last time, Mahenye was to learn that in dealing with government it had to deal with a number of different branches. The money had been received and lodged with the Treasury, which insisted that it could only be returned via the Ministry of Local Government and the Chipinge District Council, which would have the right to determine its use. DNPWLM (and its parent ministry, the Ministry of Environment and Tourism) remained adamant that it had been promised to Mahenye. An impasse resulted and safari revenues for 1982 and the following three years accumulated as the bureaucrats procrastinated. At Mahenye suspicions increased that the whole affair was a scheme to clear Ngwachumene Island of settlement, deceive them into compliance and line a few private pockets.

By 1986 DNPWLM was in the final stages of preparing its proposals for a national CAMPFIRE Programme and the Mahenye case was an embarrassment to the Department. It pressed the District Council for a resolution of the matter, stating that Z$30,461[7] had accumulated to this account. During meetings held in October and November 1986 the District Council debated the use of this money, with a majority of the councillors arguing that it had accrued from wildlife which should be regarded as the common property of the district, and thus distributed throughout the district. The Mahenye representatives retorted that they regarded their wildlife as livestock, with the management and opportunity costs that livestock entails. If the District Council wished to regard all livestock in the district as common property they would be content with the approach and assume that they would share in the proceeds of all livestock sales in the district in the future. It was left to Chief Musikavanhu, from the northern end of the district, to clinch the argument. 'My children', he said, 'What we have heard is the truth. We have no claim on this money. We did not sleep in the fields to protect the crops from elephants, as the people from Mahenye did. The elephants are theirs, not ours.'[8] The District Council agreed that the funds should go to Mahenye Ward. This was in effect an agreement to the CAMPFIRE principle of linking wildlife costs and benefits prior to its promulgation.

In February 1987 the Z$33,461 was presented to the community in the form of a cheque, to be used (as agreed by the Mahenye people) for a school building, a grinding mill and teachers' accommodation. The cheque returned to Chipinge with District Council officials and three months later construction commenced. While the District Council had not completely relinquished its involvement in the distribution and use of Mahenye's wildlife revenues, the community was gaining the sense that their wildlife programme could bring both material and political benefit to the ward. Of this period the councillor at the time, Phineas Chauke, had this to say: 'When the cheque finally came, the people's patience was very thin. The people were also a little alarmed when the cheque was presented and then it went back to Chipinge. But then three months later, when the materials finally began to arrive for the construction of the school, the people were very happy. The people looked at Stockil as their security in this project, and after the materials began coming, they were no longer suspicious of him.'[9]

Safari hunting continued during 1987–90 under an agreement between Stockil, the ward wildlife committee and the district council. However, once again the proceeds were held up by bureaucracy, and it was not until 1990, when the Chipinge District Council was granted Appropriate Authority status under the CAMPFIRE Programme, that Mahenye could once again be in receipt of wildlife revenues. From 1990 Mahenye's safari hunting and wildlife management activities have been carried out under the CAMPFIRE arrangements (see Chapters 4 and 15). A locally elected ward wildlife committee plans and carries out management functions, employing local field staff to monitor wildlife, poaching and the hunting activities of the professional hunter. The committee sets budgets and is responsible to general community meetings for its activities and planning. The district council formally awards the hunting concession, lease having advertised for and considered tenders. According to a process developed by the CAMPFIRE Programme, tenders are evaluated both in terms of amounts offered and also on qualitative considerations. It is an expectation that district councils will take into consideration the views of wildlife-producing wards in awarding contracts. Stockil, supported by the Mahenye wildlife committee, continued to hold the hunting concession at Mahenye from 1990 through 1996.

The revenue-generating potential of the Mahenye hunting concession is almost entirely dependent on trophy elephant. Other 'huntable' species, such as leopard, buffalo, bushbuck, grysbok and impala, are present only in low numbers. There is thus a close correlation between the presence of trophy elephant in the ward and revenue accrued in any given year. This is linked to the health of elephant populations in the neighbouring Gonarezhou National Park. In the 1991/2 rainy season a severe drought produced a crisis in the Park and a culling and translocation exercise radically reduced elephant numbers in the areas adjacent to Mahenye,[10] impacting on concession revenues. While the elephant quota in the ward from 1992 to 1996 was four per annum, this quota was not achieved after 1992 (Table 12.1). Total hunting revenues (which include per diem rates and trophy fees for other species and thus do not bear a one-to-one relationship to elephant trophy fees) to a degree track the elephant offtake and levelled off after a high in 1992 to a plateau of between Z$138,000 and 163,000 per annum. A recovery of the elephant population in Gonarezhou and increases in the price of trophy elephant could improve these figures in the future. However, it is clear that the capacity of the ward to expand its safari hunting revenues is finite and unlikely to grow significantly. Increasing the ward's wildlife-related income thus required the diversification of activities.

Table 12.1 Mahenye hunting safari revenues, 1992–6

	Elephant quota	Elephant shot	Revenue (Z$)
1992	4	4	180,000
1993	4	1	158,000
1994	4	2	163,736
1995	4	1	138,445
1996	4	1	138,495

Source: Adapted from DICE (1997: 174)

The Development of Non-Consumptive Ecotourism in Mahenye

Planning and initiation

The Mahenye Wildlife Committee had considered early on other possible enterprises to develop the earning potential of their natural resources. In 1991 when the safari concession was advertised an additional game-viewing safari concession was added. Stockil successfully bid for both and worked with the Wildlife Committee to develop a joint venture proposal which was presented to the District Council in 1991. The proposal included the following components:

- a safari camp at Chivirira Falls, to be used both for hunting safaris and game viewing visitors to Gonarezhou National Park;
- safari hunting on Ngwachumene Island;
- the development of a wildlife management area in the north of the ward to include fencing, water points and the further training of game scouts;
- the development of a small–scale irrigation scheme below the Chivirira Falls;
- the development of a crocodile and ostrich farm on Gombe Island, in conjunction with the neighbouring Chitsa Ward.

This scheme, integrating wildlife and agricultural development in two wards, was a product of Mahenye's wildlife committee interacting with Stockil rather than the initiative of an aid agency or NGO.[11] Unfortunately neither the community nor Stockil had the capital to put the scheme into operation at the time, and the proposal in its local joint venture form was stillborn.

However, Stockil subsequently entered into a partnership with Zimbabwe Sun Hotels which involved lodge development at his own ranch in the Save Valley Conservancy in the Chiredzi District and at Mahenye. At Mahenye the partnership resulted in a lease agreement between Zimbabwe Sun Ltd and the Chipinge Rural District Council[12] for the construction and operation of two tourist lodges: the Mahenye Safari Lodge on Gayiseni Island and Chilo Lodge, approximately 3 km upstream, overlooking the Chilo Gorge. Smaller and more intimate, Mahenye Lodge accommodates l6 guests and was opened in February 1994. Chilo Lodge, larger and more luxurious, accommodates 28 guests. It was officially opened by Zimbabwe's Vice-President, Simon Muzenda, in November 1996.

The formal agreement

The agreement under which these developments proceeded, signed in 1996, is for a period of ten years, with provisions for the negotiation of extension. Entitled a 'Memorandum of a Lease Agreement for communal land for trading or other purposes made and entered into and between CHIPINGE RURAL DISTRICT COUNCIL and ZIMBABWE SUN LIMITED', the document runs for 21 pages and was the subject of extensive negotiations, drawing the wry comment from one legal reviewer that 'This should stand as the most mulled over agreement in existence'.[13] Its major provisions require Zimbabwe Sun Limited (ZSL) annually to pay the Council 8 per cent of its gross trading revenue in the first three years, 10 per cent in the next three and 12 per cent in the remaining four years. Gross trading revenue is defined as 'all amounts paid to ZSL as a consequence of any of its activities within the Unit including sales of accommodation, sales of food and beverages, and sales of non-consumptive safari or photographic activities less sales tax payable' (Clauses 3.1, 3.2). The agreement also stipulates a minimum annual payment by ZSL to the Council of Z$220,000. In addition ZSL is required 'wherever possible to utilize and pay for labour available from the Mahenye Community for purposes of constructing the required accommodation and supporting infrastructure' and to subsequently utilize 'wherever possible the work-force potential of the Mahenye Ward Community' (Clauses 5.5 and 5.6).

The Council is required by the agreement to ensure that the 'areas within the Unit at which any safari camp, lodge, resort or hotel is constructed by ZSL is (sic) rendered free of any other human habitation and further in this regard shall ensure that any such site is free from any disturbance arising either from human settlement or live-stock' (Clause 6.5). The Council is required to pay for access permits for ZSL clients to enter Gonarezhou National Park, up to a maximum of Z$120,000 per annum (Clauses 6.2, 3.1).

In the agreement the Council undertakes to 'use its best endeavours to ensure the continued popular support of the Mahenye Ward Community for the projects and/or activities undertaken by ZSL in terms of this agreement' (Clause 6.6). This clause reflects the paternalism of CAMPFIRE's current position in which wards have no legal persona in themselves: interestingly, however, the agreement does go on to formally bind the council to CAMPFIRE guidelines regarding revenue. The Council can retain from ZSL revenues 'a portion thereof to cover administrative expenditures incurred by it in relation to the Unit, which portion shall be in accordance with guidelines set by the Campfire Association but which shall not exceed 20 per cent of the total revenues paid to it by ZSL. The balance of such revenues shall be made available by it to the Mahenye Community and distributed to the latter in accordance with the principles and procedures established by the Campfire Association from time to time it being understood by the parties that the payment of such revenues is of fundamental importance to this agreement' (Clause 6.8).

Collectively, the agreement binds both council and ZSL to 'jointly endeavour to administer the Unit so as to ensure that the activities of ZSL are rendered as efficient and as profitable as possible and so as to ensure the proper and efficient preservation, management, responsible usage and protection of the natural habitat and wildlife found in the Unit, and further to ensure that the usage by ZSL is as unobtrusive and beneficial to the Mahenye Ward Community as possible' (Clause 4.1).

Company perspectives

ZSL estimates the costs of the construction and equipping of Chilo Gorge Lodge at Z$16 million and Mahenye Safari Lodge at Z$7 million. In addition, a 45 km electricity supply line from the national grid at Quinton Bridge had to be built, the gravel road from Quinton Bridge to Mahenye had to be improved, a water purification, pumping and reticulation system had to be installed and a telephone line was erected. An airstrip was built near the lodges. These are estimated to have added Z$1.9 million to the capital start-up costs, totalling Z$24.9 million. To recover this initial investment and provide profits Zimbabwe Sun projected revenues based on prevailing international rates and with bed occupancy rates of between 50 and 60 per cent. Performance figures through 1997 show occupancy rates below this and a smaller proportion of international visitors than anticipated. Performance in 1998 had improved and management is optimistic that bed occupancy and tariff levels will continue to improve. The company has restructured its operations and the two Mahenye lodges now fall under an independent subsidiary, Safari Lodges of Africa. Under this new arrangement greater emphasis is being placed on international marketing operations and niche tourism, for which Mahenye is considered ideal. The initiation, in conjunction with other operators, of a tourism circuit including Victoria Falls, Great Zimbabwe, the wildlife ranches of the Save Valley Conservancy and destinations on the Mozambique coast, is anticipated to boost client demand.

Even if this optimism is justified it is clear that the Mahenye venture is a long-term investment for ZSL. The investment is being made primarily as a business gamble on the future of the upmarket Zimbabwean tourism industry which is currently performing well (see Bond, Chapter 15, this volume). However, as an international company in an industry where environmental image is important, ZSL's involvement in a community-based natural resource management enterprise enhances its image of being an environmentally responsible business. The company has a mission statement which asserts its commitment 'to participate responsibly in the controlled social and environmental development'[14] of the regions where it operates, and its Mahenye operation is seen as an example of this. Finally, there is an element of political investment in the involvement. Within Zimbabwe CAMPFIRE is popularly seen as a programme for rural, black development and any large multinational which associates itself with this does its political image no harm.

Community perspectives

The community's assessment of the tourism lodge development is generally highly positive. Interestingly, community infrastructural development related to the lodge enterprise is usually mentioned first in any listing of benefits, followed by comment on local employment generation. Five major benefits are cited:

- *Improved road transport.* The improvement in the road from Mahenye to Quinton Bridge is considered a great asset, something which the community had been asking for from the Council for many years without success. The building of the airstrip is also mentioned in this connection, as a means for the emergency evacuation of critical medical cases.
- *Mains electricity.* The community seized the opportunity to arrange an extension of mains electricity from the lodge sites to the main centre of the settlement. This cost Z$140,500, which was advanced to the community against annual payments, the first repayment instalment to be Z$30,239. Currently electricity connections are to the clinic, the school, the grinding mill and the police post. One trader has also connected his store to the mains, and it is expected that other private users will have electricity installed. All supply is metered and charged to the respective users. The community take great pride in having electricity in their remote location.
- *Telephone connections.* The telephone extension to the lodges was extended to the community centre, with handsets at the clinic and the police post.[15]

- *Water reticulation.* One of the conditions of the lease was that livestock would be excluded from areas immediately adjacent to the lodges. This was a provision with conflict potential and to reduce this possibility ZSL agreed to provide livestock watering points away from the river. The community then requested that this reticulation be extended to the village centre. An agreement was reached whereby ZSL provided the PVC water pipe line and supply, and the community dug the trench.
- *Employment.* The lodges provide employment and local people staff 63 per cent of posts (Table 12.2). However, only six employees (15.8 per cent of local staff) were women. Furthermore local employment is skewed towards lower paid categories of employment: no local persons are employed as managers, guides or drivers. The community is aware of this and is pressing for the training and employment of local people at higher grades. At the same time they are aware that local salaries are a significant contribution to the community economy at Z$34,438 per month.

Table 12.2   Employment at Mahenye and Chilo Lodges, 1997

	Mahenye	Chilo	Total
Beds	16	28	44
Total staff	18	42	60
Local staff total	11	27	38
Local staff female	03	03	06
Monthly local staff wage bill	Z$11,400	Z$23,038	Z$34,438

Source: Adapted from DICE (1997: 178).

Overall, the local assessment of lodge development is strong but not unqualified. There are complaints that the lodges have restricted community access to bathing and fishing points on the river and disturbed livestock grazing and watering patterns. There are suggestions that the lodges bring in outsiders and that petty thievery has increased. Cultural concerns are also expressed. The behaviour and forms of dress of lodge visitors are regarded by some as inappropriate and there are worries that wage structures giving younger workers higher salaries than their elders will upset traditional hierarchies of respect. These are, however, seen as minor problems compared with the benefits that have accrued.

Revenue generation

Much as the Mahenye people emphasize employment and infrastructural development as the benefits of lodge development, the cash revenues of their ecotourism enterprise remain a critical factor in their collective assessment. The inclusion of non-consumptive ecotourism in their exploitation of natural resources has lifted revenues significantly above the plateau of income revenues that can be expected from safari hunting in their context (Table 12.3). As this table indicates, after a slow start-up period in 1994–5, when the lodges were being built and prior to the opening of Chilo Lodge, lodge revenues overtook hunting revenues in 1996 and far exceeded these in 1997, representing 69.5 per cent of total revenues in that year. The figure of

Table 12.3 Mahenye Ward tourism revenues by category, 1991–7 (Z$)

Year	Hunting safari revenue	Lodge revenue	Total
1991	68,800	—	68,800
1992	180,000	—	180,000
1993	158,000	—*	158,000
1994	163,736	—*	163,736
1995	138,445	5,940*	144,385
1996	138,495	140,484	278,979
1997	188,740	429,804	618,544†

Notes: *Revenue from Mahenye Safari Lodge not formally entered in RDC reports for the period 1993–5, prior to signing of Memorandum of Agreement. Monies were advanced directly for community projects or included in 1996 payment.
†Z$30,000 deducted from actual payment for previous advances.

Source: Chipinge RDC Annual Reports and files of the Zimbabwe Trust.

Z$429,804 does not, however, represent the amount received by the community since council administration fees are deducted from this figure. For a clearer picture we examine revenue disbursement in the following section.

Revenue disbursement

Table 12.4 shows the disbursement of ecotourism revenues generated in Mahenye over the period 1992–7 by four categories, household dividends, management expenditure, administrative fees and community projects. Management expenses are those incurred by the Ward Wildlife Committee and include the salaries and expenses of locally employed wildlife monitors, and Committee expenses. Figures listed under administration include the Council levy and membership dues to the CAMPFIRE Association. Budget allocations to administration are 'fixed' in the sense that they are set by standard formulas and beyond the control of the community. The community determines all other allocations after debate on the recommendations of the Ward Wildlife Committee.

Table 12.4 CAMPFIRE revenue disbursements, Mahenye Ward, 1992–7 (Z$)

Year	Household no.	Share	Household payouts	Management	Admin	Projects	Total
1992	484	140	87,120	10,850	30,600	51,430	180,000
1993	581	138	80,178	27,962	26,860	23,000	158,000
1994	647	126	81,229	27,380	35,367	19,760	163,736
1995	751	105	78,855	28,930	29,920	6,740	144,445
1996	768	183	140,544	36,700	49,761	51,974	278,979
1997	770	442	340,499	58,260	129,536	57,320	588,594*

Note: *Revenue was Z$618,594, from which a lease rental advance of Z$30,000 was deducted.

Source: Chipinge RDC Annual Reports on CAMPFIRE.

The percentage of total revenue taken for administration is fairly consistent, ranging from 17 to 22 per cent. Of this the amount paid to the CAMPFIRE

Association is relatively small, calculated at 2 per cent of revenue plus a fixed annual subscription of Z$3000. In 1997 this amounted to Z$14,771. In the same year Council administration took 20 per cent of the balance of revenue or Z$114,764. It is difficult to argue that this figure represents actual administrative expenses by the Council for the Mahenye enterprise and this figure can more properly be considered a council tax on Mahenye revenues. Secondly, we can note that allocations to community projects show considerable variance from year to year. This relates to the costs of the particular project or projects of contemporary focus. The 1997 expenditure of Z$57,321 was for the electrification of the Chipote grinding mill.

Allocations to household dividends are consistently around 50 per cent of total budget, ranging from 48 per cent in 1992 to 55 per cent in 1997. The actual amount of household dividends is of course determined by the size of annual budgets and the number of households which qualify for payments. This number has grown from 484 in 1992 to 770 in 1997, but growth has slowed down over the period 1995–7.[16] A significant rise in the size of household dividends has coincided with the introduction of tourism lodge development in the ward. This suggests that the development of this type of non–consumptive tourism may modulate the correlation between human population density and revenue generation discussed by Bond (Chapter 15, this volume).

Ecotourism in Mahenye: Retrospect and Prospect

This chapter began by noting that safari hunting, the predominant mode through which CAMPFIRE has been initiated in Zimbabwe, may in the evolution of the programme and in certain local contexts have limitations which set an upper threshold to the revenue which can be derived. For certain localities, non–consumptive ecotourism could shift this threshold and provide the basis for further development in the efficiency and profitability of natural resource-based community enterprise. The Mahenye case study provides evidence to corroborate this. On the basis of several criteria – financial performance, community infrastructural improvements, community institutional development and community satisfaction – Mahenye's venture into non–consumptive ecotourism must be judged a success. It is an all-too-rare success in the CAMPFIRE portfolio and it is tempting to see the Mahenye case as the triumph of entrepreneurial hope and ingenuity over legal and structural constraints. There are, however, aspects of the Mahenye case study which make it something more than a story of random and fortuitous achievement and which contain generalizable lessons for progress in similar contexts elsewhere.

Firstly we should note two legal and structural constraints which have inhibited success in CAMPFIRE generally (mentioned in Jones and Murphree, Chapter 4, this volume) and which have impinged on the developments mentioned in this case study. The first is the attenuated devolution of authority and responsibility which lies in the legal status of a ward such as Mahenye. As things stand in Zimbabwe's current legislation formal authority over Mahenye's land and natural resources is vested in the Chipinge Rural District Council, not with the ward's people and their leadership. As mentioned earlier, they are not only *a ward* in the district, they are also *wards* of the District Council. Although the Chipinge Rural District Council has generally complied with CAMPFIRE guidelines and given a *de facto* authority to the ward in respect to its natural resource management and use, the *de jure* situation intrudes at critical points. Thus the community cannot formally interact with its client, ZSL, but has to deal with it through the Council. This has three negative effects. Firstly, the arrangement is administratively ponderous, and sometimes formal interaction does not take place when it is critically needed. The Memorandum of Agreement, for instance, seeks to provide a mechanism for interaction by stipulating the creation of a Management Committee 'to meet on a regular basis' (Clause 4.2). This Committee is, however, an organ of 'both parties to the agreement', i.e. ZSL and the Council, whereas the need for such a mechanism lies in the relationships between ZSL and the Ward Wildlife Committee. Wrongly focused and awkward to orchestrate, the Management Committee has not met with regularity and cannot address the functional needs for which it has been designed. By default these have to be addressed by informal links between the lodge management and the Wildlife Committee. Secondly, the arrangement perpetuates an adversarial relationship between the community and the Council, in which the community sees the Council as financially predatory and manipulative. Regarding the latter, the community cites the Council award of the hunting concession contract in 1997 to another professional hunter, rather than Stockil. Thirdly, the arrangement perpetuates a sense of uncertainty in the community regarding the future, inhibiting its planning and decisiveness.

The second major constraint to Mahenye's entrepreneurial development is the multifaceted nature of the government. Its primary relationship is with the Council, but the Council itself is under the Ministry of Local Government and these two do not always act in concert with each other, or indeed with other organs of government. Thus, for instance, the Memorandum of Agreement has a 'Condition Precedent' that it will not come into operation until it is endorsed by the Senior Minister of Local Government, Rural and Urban Development. However, the Ministry of Local Government was so delinquent in providing this endorsement that the development of the Mahenye lodges commenced without this step and the Chilo Lodge was officially opened by the Vice President of Zimbabwe while endorsement was still on the desk of the Ministry.

However, Mahenye's relationships to government are not confined to the Council and the Ministry of Local Government. The vertical compartmentalization of government's line ministries means that, in its natural resource-based enterprises, the community must also deal with the Ministry of Agriculture and the Departments of Physical Planning and Water Affairs, all of which have their own plans for Mahenye. This list is only illustrative; there are a host of other government departments and ministries which potentially can intrude on Mahenye. Most importantly DNPWLM can critically affect what transpires in Mahenye. Aside from its statutory powers to control wildlife use in Mahenye, DNPWLM is the manager of Gonarezhou National Park across the river from the ward. Lodge development in Mahenye was predicated on access to the Park by ZSL for its clients at discounted rates. In the earlier years of CAMPFIRE, DNPWLM pursued such a policy to encourage the development of wildlife enterprises in neighbouring communal lands. More recently, with a change of DNPWLM's status to that of being a Statutory Fund with responsibility to raise its own budgets, DNPWLM now gives no such concessions. Entry fees have been raised, and these are a cost both to the community and to ZSL. The payment of these fees remains a matter of contention between the Council, ZSL and the community on the one hand and DNPWLM on the other, and this makes budgeting difficult for the enterprise.

Given these legal and structural constraints, it is surprising that community-based ecotourism has fared as well as it has in Mahenye. The case history is one of success in the face of adversity, achieved by the presence of a number of significant factors.

- *Intra-communal cohesiveness.* Mahenye's in-group solidarity, rooted in history and reinforced by perceptions of external differences, has already been discussed. Like any community Mahenye has its internal differentiations but these have been contained by a sense of collective communal interest. The importance of this condition cannot be over-stressed. Without it, and regardless of the presence of other positive elements, communal enterprises have little chance of success.
- *Resource richness.* Mahenye has a resource endowment which is adequate to support an ecotourism enterprise yielding significant inputs to community infra-structure and annual revenues. This is not the case for many other communities, and in such cases the Mahenye experience has little relevance. However, there are a large number of localities in Zimbabwe and elsewhere which have potential for this kind of development. The larger lesson here is that the right mix of incentives for communal regimes of natural resource management and use will vary with context and must be tailored for this context.
- *Social energy.* Mahenye's entrepreneurial history demonstrates the importance of social energy (Uphoff 1992): the insights, ingenuity and commitment of socially dedicated individuals in positions of influence or leadership. Mahenye has been fortunate in having a local leadership demonstrating these characteristics. These include the chief, a number of respected elders, the school headmaster and an elected leadership which has included councillors and the members of the Ward Wildlife Committee. Collectively these have provided a leadership structure which has been balanced in its sources of traditional and popular legitimation. Added to this structure of local leadership has been the influence of Stockil, who has brought to the community the combination of his own particular and personal location in the community, his experience in wildlife ranching, and his network of contacts in private enterprise. Most institutional analyses tend to ignore the personal factor but it is this component which frequently determines success or failure.
- *Enlightened private sector involvement.* ZSL's involvement in Mahenye ecotourism development has been done from a long-term investment perspective, and for reasons which have been discussed earlier in this chapter. The involvement stems from self-interest, but corporate size and time-scale induce a perspective which links the interests of the resource base and its proprietors with those of the company. This community/client coincidence of interest produces a synergy which has impacted positively on the enterprise.
- *Flexibility and evolution.* Mahenye's ecotourism started with safari hunting which rapidly reached a threshold set by resource limitations. A shift to non-consumptive tourism has demonstrated a flexibility which has moved the threshold of revenue generation upwards. This shift was a response to insight and opportunity rather than a response to imposed policy. It was planned and implemented by local management and was the product of organic institutional growth in the rela-tionship between the community and its clients.

- *Acceptance of risk.* Innovation involves risk. In this case study successful entrepreneurship required initiation and implementation in a context inhibited by legal and structural constraints and in a time frame far shorter than that dictated by the pace of bureaucratic procedures. The community and its client took a calculated risk, with the concurrence of the Council. Thus lodge development was initiated prior to the endorsement of the Ministry of Local Government, on the basis of what was in effect an operational agreement rather than a legally binding document. At more detailed and daily levels, the enterprise continues to proceed operationally on this basis.

These factors explain Mahenye's success in ecotourism to date in the face of serious legal and structural constraints. They continue to drive Mahenye's forward planning, which includes the development of a fenced game viewing area for tourists and greater emphasis on specialist tourism packages to exploit the floral and avian resources of their riverine border with Gonarezhou. Less reliance on tourist access to the Park is one objective, given the increasing cost of Park entry fees.

The future is, of course, uncertain. Much will depend on the status of the international tourism industry, over which neither the community nor its private sector client has control. Within Zimbabwe, Mahenye's enterprise would be greatly facilitated if legal changes were to be effected conferring appropriate authority status on wards, bringing community and client formally into a much tighter relationship. Until this takes place, however, Mahenye's enterprise will have to continue on the basis of the energizing factors identified above. That they have shown the potential to produce success in the face of legal and bureaucratic constraints is the positive message of the Mahenye story for community-based conservation elsewhere, where the right combination of resources, social energy and private sector involvement exists.

Notes

[1] See also Bond (1998).

[2] Fieldwork for this case study was carried out during the period April–August 1998. I acknowledge with gratitude the generous assistance of the following: Fungai Manyau, Silas Makanza and Miriam Rukweza of Zimbabwe Trust, SE Lowveld Regional Office, Councillor Javani Phineas Jauke of Mahenye Ward, Clive Stockil, Simon Rowson of ZSL, D Simbini, J Khosa, S Mhlanga, E Mhlanga, J Simango, P M Chauke, all members of the Mahenya Wildlife Committee, wildlife monitors L Chauke, M Masuke and J Sithole, and other members of the Mahenye Community. I am also grateful to Ivan Bond and Abel Khumalo of WWF, Harare, for assistance in preparing the two maps incorporated in this chapter.

[3] Booth (1991: 31) makes the following observations: 'The Mahenye Ward is well known, from an ornithological point of view, because of the unique habitat that occurs there. The main area of ornithological interest in the Ward is Ngwachumene Island, which is one of the only two true lowland evergreen forests occurring in Zimbabwe. The other forest (the Haroni/Rusitu and Makupine complex) is rapidly disappearing in the face of human settlement, with the result that the Island, and the Save/Runde confluence area, will become the only place in Zimbabwe where those species endemic to the lowland evergreen forests of Mozambique can be viewed. This will make the area a particularly valued venue for bird-watching tourism. The following species of particular interest have been recorded in the area: southern banded snake eagle (*Circaetus fasciolatus*); Madagascar squacco heron (*Ardeola idae*); green coucal (*Ceuthmochares aereus*); barred cuckoo (*Cercococcyx montanus*).'

[4] Ethnographically the Shangaan are Hlengwe peoples who were over-run by the Nguni under Soshangana in the early nineteenth century and who adopted elements of Nguni culture and the name 'Shangaan'. Junod and Earthy provide early ethnographies with excellent detail (Junod 1927; Earthy 1933).

[5]See Junod (1927) and Wright (1972) for further detail.

[6]The early history of Mahenye's proto-CAMPFIRE experiment is well documented, see Peterson (1991b), Stockil (1987).

[7]The Z$ has slipped from US$1 = Z$2.13 in 1989 to US$1 = Z$10.03 in 1996. Further devaluation continued in the late 1990s.

[8]For an extended account of this meeting, see Stockil (1987).

[9]Further comment from Chauke is to be found in Peterson (1991b).

[10]The Mahenye people consider the elephant cull in Gonarezhou to have been wasteful and unnecessary. For further detail see Peterson (1991b) and DICE (1997: 173—174).

[11]AGRITEX, the extension arm of the Ministry of Agriculture, had developed its own land-use plan for the ward. This had been incorporated in the ward's proposals (cf. Booth 1991: 12, 35). The inclusion of an irrigation scheme in the ward's proposals is interesting. The ward saw this as compatible with tourism, as a rational use of the water in the Save River and as a substitute to the extension of dryland agriculture into the wildlife area. Their interest in game farming through the use of crocodile and ostrich is also note-worthy. This aspect of their planning has not yet materialized and is unlikely to do so while the ostrich and crocodile markets remain depressed.

[12]With the reorganization of local government in 1993, the District Council became the Rural District Council.

[13]The comment quoted is from a note attached to the draft Memorandum, prepared by a legal adviser (n.d.).

[14]For an extended statement of ZSL's environmental stance, see DICE (1997: 178).

[15]The attitude of the Mahenye community to the police is strongly positive. In part this is due to the protection they provide to the community against stock theft from Mozambique.

[16]See Murombedzi (Chapter 16, this volume) for further discussion on in-migration to successful CAMPFIRE wards.

13

Old Ways & New Challenges
Traditional Resource Management Systems in the Chimanimani Mountains, Mozambique

SIMON ANSTEY & CAMILA DE SOUSA

Introduction

This case study looks at traditional natural resource management and the institutions and systems that have evolved, and are evolving, outside the formal framework of conservation policies, projects and programmes.[1] It explores 'community conservation' in a context in which the community has autonomy. The focus is on an area in central Mozambique which has a relatively low human population, a high degree of resource richness and a history of limited intervention by external management regimes. It is also an area which has experienced over 30 years of armed conflict and has been buffeted by the extremes of Mozambique's political and economic lurches from extractive colonialism, to centrally planned socialism, to the new credo of market forces, decentralization and democracy (see Anstey, Chapter 6, this volume for a discussion of the country's history and conservation policies).

The emphasis in many community conservation initiatives has been on devolving some measure of tenurial rights over natural resources, and developing the capacity of community level institutions to have legally recognized, democratic and technically functioning systems to manage and to distribute benefits from natural resources (see Barrow and Murphree, Chapter 3, this volume). The implicit assumption is that such rights and management institutions do not already exist among local communities or are not appropriate for the complexity of the modern world. For many countries this assumption may hold true, as during the past century state control over natural resources and their management has marginalized indigenous regulatory systems or 'traditional' conservation to the point that such systems have either been criminalized or are unable to function effectively (see Matowanyika 1989; Sithole 1997). However, even in countries with high state control over wildlife, recent studies of the wild meat trade (TRAFFIC 1999) in eastern and southern Africa have shown the complex access, use and trade systems which function outside formal institutions and frameworks of law and order and which involve millions of US dollars.

In contrast to many of the countries discussed in this volume, Mozambique has had a history of relatively limited intervention by the state and formal administrative structures in the management of wildlife in most of the country. Because of the recent 30 years of conflict, a number of areas have had very minimal contact with government and, in the absence of alternatives, pre-existing social institutions have retained their authority. During the civil war period from 1979 to 1992 in which both the government and the armed opposition (Renamo) alienated local communities and were unable to provide effective administration, in certain areas traditional institutions have dominated local governance. Vines (1996), for example, discusses the establishment of neutral zones in southern and central Mozambique where spirit mediums established areas in which neither the government army nor the armed opposition could carry arms or harass the local people. In the Gorongosa Massif the spirit medium Samantanje persuaded Renamo commanders that violence to people or extraction of wildlife and forest products would be met by spiritual retribution.

This study focuses on the relatively isolated Chimanimani mountain range.[2] The reason for this selection was that previous reconnaissance studies for proposed wildlife conservation areas in the early 1970s and then again in the mid-1990s had reported it as being strongly influenced by traditional management systems (Dutton and Dutton 1973; Hatton 1995; Hughes 1995). In addition, this area is one of the proposed Mozambican Transfrontier Conservation Areas (TFCA) and developments are underway to implement formal conservation and development programmes involving the local community. It thus offers the opportunity to look at an area which is in transition from relative isolation to incorporation in formal conservation programmes.

The conceptual basis for the study was developed by Ostrom (1990). These principles (Table 13.1) are frequently used to assess and assist in the development of formal community institutions to manage common property resources and are used as a basis for identifying the prerequisites for effective institutions for such management.

Table 13.1 Design principles for long enduring common property institutions

1. Clearly defined boundaries
2. Congruence between appropriation and provision rules and local conditions or appropriate rules for exploiting the resource and conserving it
3. Collective choice arrangements or the people affected by the rules must be able to participate in changing them
4. Monitoring: effective monitoring procedures must be in place and monitors of rules must be resource users or accountable to them
5. Graduated sanctions: resource users who violate rules will be liable to sanctions graduated in terms of degree of the violation
6. Conflict resolution mechanisms: rapid access to low cost arenas to resolve conflicts
7. Minimal recognition of rights to organize: or the right of resource users to devise their own institutions should be recognized by external (government) authorities

Sources: Ostrom (1990) and IIED (1994).

The Chimanimani Mountains

Geography and natural resources

The Chimanimani mountains in Mozambique are located in the central province of Manica bordering eastern Zimbabwe and the study took place in the District of Sussendenga (see Map 13.1). The central Chimanimani covers an area of around 1750 km² and is made up of a core massif at over 1000 m altitude. The area overseen by Regulo Mahate is one of the less accessible areas in the central foothills of the massif and on the western side of the Rio Massapa. There are no direct roads to this area. Regulo Gudza is located some 15 km from the administrative post of Rotanda on the northern margin of Chimanimani foothills close to the border of Zimbabwe and in a less isolated position than Mahate. The majority of the people live in scattered settlements along the major river systems and valleys at lower altitude. The area has little in the way of schools, roads, clinics or shops and people generally look to the Zimbabwe side of the border for trading, schooling or health services. It is thus relatively poorly integrated into Manica Province.

The area has diverse natural resources and spectacular mountain scenery. Higher areas are dominated by open grasslands and open woodland with dry montane forest in the higher valleys and moist forests in the foothills and valleys at lower altitudes. The area has a high degree of biodiversity (although still poorly studied) with over 1000 species of plants of which 44 are endemic, over 160 bird species and a rich set of mammal species. The adjoining area in Zimbabwe is a National Park and since the first assessments in the 1970s there have been plans to put this area under some form of protection status (Dutton and Dutton 1973; Hatton 1995). Chimanimani is one of the top five areas in terms of importance for the conservation of biodiversity in Mozambique (Tinley 1990).

History and people

The people of the central Chimanimani are of the Ndau group and part of the broad family of Shona speaking people who occupy parts of central Mozambique and much of Zimbabwe. The Ndau have held this area since at least the fifteenth century and thus have a long-standing relationship with the land and its resources. They have a reputation in Mozambique for their spiritual powers and their cultural independence from external influences. They were among the least integrated within the Portuguese colonial structure. Ndau speakers also formed the original core leadership of Renamo, the armed opposition to the Frelimo Government.

Appendix 13.1 presents a general history of the area and key events in order to put into context the traditional leadership structures and institutions discussed in later sections. This area has had a history of external influences that can be divided into four main periods:

- A period prior to the 1890s of limited external influences in which the waves of the Ngoni empire, Portuguese authorities and Afro-Portuguese merchant traders and warlords eddied around the Chimanimani but had little direct impact.
- A period from the 1890s to the 1970s in which increasing formal administrative structures began to influence the area initially through the proxy administration,

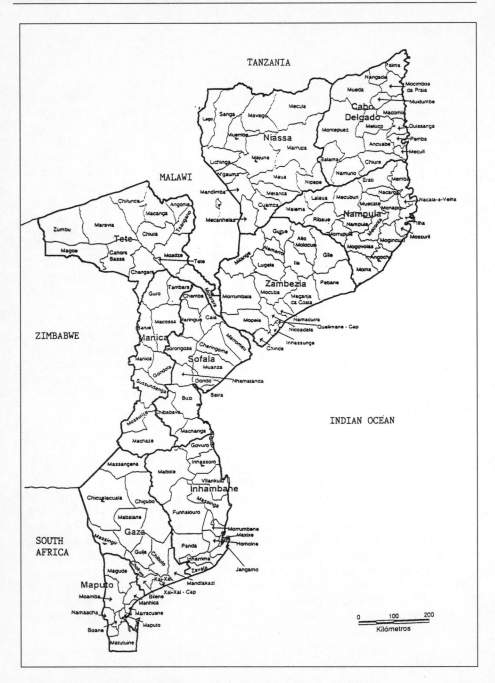

Map 13.1   The Republic of Mozambique

taxes and forced labour of the Mozambique Company and later under direct Portuguese colonial control. However, these impacts were less powerful than across the border in Rhodesia as traditional leadership structures were used as the local administration and the Portuguese bureaucracy had a very limited role.

- The period from the 1970s to early 1990s in which three wars were occurring (two simultaneously). This was the main period when significant steps were taken to directly impose formal administrative structures as part of the Frelimo policy of state and party control, collectivized agriculture and suppression of traditional systems and authority. As Alexander (1997) notes, 'Frelimo prohibited chiefs from participation in the new structures of state and party and condemned beliefs and practices deemed "traditional".

- The period from the early 1990s to the present characterized by the end of war and the process of transition and reconstruction. In this period traditional leadership and systems have been functioning as the lower tier of administration for decisions on land or resource allocation and settling local disputes. They are either informally recognized by government systems, or are acting in parallel to them, or function simply because of the absence of anything else. 'Traditional leaders' have increasingly been courted by political parties and the bureaucracy as 'chiefs seemed to offer a cheap, willing and apolitical means of extending state authority' (Alexander 1997). In short, there is a crisis of authority and within this crisis government administration and traditional structures function in an uneasy and complex set of compromises.

What is particularly relevant for this study is that throughout the four periods noted above (and only severely challenged in the 1970/80s), traditional institutions at local level have remained in place and have been the main form of governance.

Proposed community conservation programmes

There have been proposals since the early 1970s to establish some form of conservation area in the central Chimanimani. The first was based on a study which argued for the declaration of the core area as a protected zone given its biodiversity importance, scenic beauty and watershed protection role (Dutton and Dutton 1973). The study noted the importance of traditional management systems (the protection of certain areas and species for sacred reasons) and the degree of local knowledge of plants and animals. It reported that the main threats to the area were external, especially timber cutting, and it argued for protected status on the grounds of these increasing external threats and to control fires and hunting pressures. The study rejected a National Park designation, as existed over the border in Rhodesia, and emphasized community participation: 'the local tribespeople should be informed that the area is to be used entirely for their benefit and involvement', and income from ecotourism should be returned to the local population. It was also suggested that 'the local tribesmen should be trained to perform the duties of administrators and guardians of the proposed conservation area'. The proposal was never implemented as it was overtaken by the independence war and then the civil war.

More recently, further studies were undertaken in the area as part of the government's Transfrontier Conservation Areas programme (Hatton 1995). Despite the passage of 20 years and three wars the description of the area, its biodiversity importance and the significance of local traditional structures, was virtually identical to that of 1973. The conclusions and recommendations, both in terms of the need to create a conservation zone and to have the involvement of the community, were also remarkably consistent, despite considerable changes in the policy and agendas of conservation and development agencies over this period.

The programme for the area, which started implementation in early 1997, involves a government agency (Manica Provincial Forestry and Wildlife Service, SPFFB), a local development NGO (ORAM) and a Mozambican cultural and historical research institute (ARPAC). Funding is from the Ford Foundation and GEF/World Bank. The basic objectives of the programme are to conserve the biodiversity in the central Chimanimani, and to provide benefits to the local community through their participation in the management of the area. At the time of our research the programme was only in the preliminary phase and few direct field activities had been undertaken. This was reflected in the rather vague concepts of how and in what ways local communities would 'participate' in the programme.

Case Study 1 – Regulo Mahate

In the preliminary studies undertaken for the Chimanimani community conservation programme, *Regulo* (or Chief) Mahate was identified as one of the key traditional leaders whose involvement in the process of proceeding with the community component was critical (Hatton 1995). Regulo Mahate lives in one of the most isolated areas of the Chimanimani, accessible only on foot. This area has relatively little contact with government structures. He lives with his immediate family (wife and two daughters) in a small agricultural clearing with other scattered households two hours or more walk away. The area has a low population dispersed in settlements along river valleys. Regulo Mahate resides in this area as the spirits have indicated he must live there in order to be close to a sacred mountain and to sacred forests where former chiefs are buried. His way of life requires remarkably few external inputs: his family cooks in earthen pots, grinds maize and millet by stone and lives in simple housing with no obvious material signs that he is a powerful administrative and spiritual figure.

Regulo Mahate (or Elias Panyika) was born in 1946 of the totem Ngombe and became the chief (Regulo) in 1986. The boundaries of his area of influence are the Rio Mussambudzi in the north, to the west the Rio Marepa and to the east the Rio Mussapa. The watershed of the Rio Lucite forms the southern boundary. In the past his area extended into Zimbabwe. The customary administrative structure as described by Mahate, for this area is as follows. As a paramount chief (or *mambo/Ishwe*) he has a counterpart female chief called a *Nyadombe*. Both have other officials to communicate, monitor and enforce their decisions. Lower level chiefs administer smaller units, referred to as *sabhuku* (a term introduced during Portuguese colonial time for the official responsible for tax collection) and *samatunhu*. Under Mahate are six *samatunhu/sabhuku* who are largely responsible for basic administration, the settling of disputes and the allocation of land. Only in serious cases are issues referred to Mahate and only in very serious cases does he visit the site of the problem.

While such administrative functions mirror formal local government, the major difference is that Mahate also has a spiritual role. He is the secular contact with the spiritual world and his derivation of power and even his selection to be Regulo depend on decision-making by ancestral spirits. He is the main secular instrument to bring problems to, and receives guidance from the area's spirit medium (*ciquero* or *mudzimu*) who has been in place for 18 years. Chimedzi, the spirit medium, lives near Mahate and the spirit boundaries are approximately the same as Mahate's. Mahate's position of respect and his authority largely rest on this spiritual role, rather than on his administrative role.

Rules and regulations relating to the use or protection of the environment and the allocation of land and resources are mediated through a combination of spiritual considerations and customary law. Most wild animals can be hunted although the customary rules are that the hunter should first get permission from Mahate and take a portion of the meat of the hunted animal to Mahate. In return Mahate gives prayers to the spirits as thanks. In the case of large animals the hunter cannot eat the meat in the bush, but must take it to the Regulo who is given the bottom foreshoulder (or in the case of elephant the side tusk). For crop pests, such as baboons or wild pig, such rules are not necessary. There are also some animals which are restricted from hunting including the pangolin (which can only be eaten by chiefs on special occasions with the shells used in spiritual divining). Other rules apply to reptiles, birds and fish with some species being protected (e.g. black eagle and owl species). Methods of harvesting are also regulated, for example, some fish pools and rivers are sacred and cannot be fished, and the poisoning of fish pools is prohibited as it is against the wishes of the spirits. Forest resources are managed through rules with some areas protected as sacred forests and additional rules to prohibit the destruction of medicinal plants and fruit trees.

While the area appears to be rich in resources and under relatively low population pressure there are emerging pressures resulting in the adoption of new regulations. The increasing use of forest, wildlife or fish by people from outside a sub-chief's area has resulted in the application of the rule of the proximate, i.e. access being increasingly limited to those living closest to a resource. These new regulations were agreed at meetings with the sub-chiefs: access to outsiders is still possible if approached through the *Regulo* or *samadunhus*. The sanctions for breaking these rules are largely mediated through the spirits rather than through temporal punishment. For example, ignoring the rules relating to fishing will result in the fish turning into snakes, while misuse of forest resources or un-sanctioned entry to sacred forests will result in the transgressors being attacked by leopards or disappearing. To emphasize this point Mahate recounted that recently a group of seven people had entered a sacred forest for timber extraction and subsequently six of them died. He also reported that during the civil war the high level of meat hunting by soldiers, not following the proper rituals and rules, resulted in many being punished by the spirits through psychological and navigational troubles.

The allocation of land is also mediated through Mahate and the spirits. Immigrants wanting land must first go to the Nyadombe and then to Mahate with ceremonial gifts. He will then take the matter to the spirits through the spirit medium and relate back to the immigrants the rules and the area where they can settle. Rituals to ensure success must then be followed (e.g. with the first crop of maize they must call on the spirit medium and brew beer). In general the sanctions for transgression of rules relating to land, resources and the environment are meted out through the spirits (as the 'owners') and Mahate's main role in disputes is related to judgments on human conflicts such as adultery and stealing. However, it is interesting to note that some measure of 'spiritual adaptive management' exists in relation to changing pressures and threats, such as the response by Mahate that although all tree species could be cut outside sacred forests, should a road be built and large-scale extraction by timber companies occur, then 'maybe the spirits will bring new rules'.

The political conflict between Frelimo and traditional authority in the 1970s to early 1990s was discussed in terms of the response of the spirits rather than the response of the people or Mahate. Mahate's father was killed by Frelimo in the early 1970s and shortly after his own accession to Regulo in 1986 he was arrested by Frelimo and held in Sussendenga town until 1993. The environmental problems of this time (the drought) and the harsh life for the people was presented as a result of disrespect being shown to the spirits. The drought only ended when he was permitted to return to the area and, with the spirit medium, conduct the necessary ceremonies. He continues to live in this isolated spot in order to retain the harmony between the temporal and spiritual world and thus ensure that 'life is peaceful and life is good'.

Mahate's attitude towards the proposed community conservation programme was that he welcomed the idea of devolution of power to local communities and increased development prospects such as schools and clinics. However, he had considerable reservations about the conservation objectives. His view was that outsiders knew nothing about the sacred places and that such schemes would shut people out and not be in accordance with tradition and the spirits. The spirits had rejected the concept of a TFCA when approached in 1997 with the issue. His concerns appeared to be based on what he knew of the Chimanimani National Park in Zimbabwe and the conflicts over resources and the restrictions on traditional functions there.

Most of Ostrom's design principles (Table 13.1) for robust common property management institutions (boundaries, conflict resolution, graduated sanctions, monitoring and collective choice arrangements) were being met through the existing traditional institutions at minimal cost to Regulo Mahate. However, the question remains as to whether such institutions could still be effective if population increases. Also the last principle, 'minimal recognition of rights to organize' by external authorities remains to be resolved. To test whether these design principles were evolving in traditional institutions for natural resource management a further study in the area, in a section where population pressures were higher and resources more limited, was undertaken.

Case Study 2 – Regulo Gudza

Regulo Gudza (or Chinoyi Robson) lives near the administrative post of Rotanda in the fertile valley of the Rio Mussapa. This is a relatively densely populated zone concentrated along the river valleys with easy accessibility to Zimbabwe. He has been

Regulo since the death of his father in 1993. He has spent considerable parts of his life working over the border in Zimbabwe. He lives in a large concrete house by a road and is an affluent farmer. In short he presents a considerable contrast to Mahate and his surroundings.

Regulo Gudza disputed Mahate's presentation of his boundaries and believed that they both fell under the overall authority of Regulo Moribane. While this issue was not discussed in great detail, it does indicate the current degree of dispute within and between lineages and traditional leaders.

As in Mahate's area there are sacred forests where it is forbidden to cut trees. However, there was far less emphasis on spiritual issues in relation to natural resource management or society in general and sanctions could be applied by secular as well as spiritual mechanisms. This may reflect both the greater dependence of the people on sedentary agriculture in the fertile river valleys, lower dependence on common property natural resources and also the greater integration of the area into the 'modern world': schools, clinics and the cash economy. During Gudza's father's time there was a spirit medium in the area but for the past seven years there has been no manifestation of the spirit in a new medium.

However, there were very clear and detailed customary rules and institutions relating to the main natural resource in the area: water for crop irrigation. This is examined below in relation to Ostrom's design principles (Table 13.1). The Rio Mussapa valley is broad and has intensively farmed fields irrigated by the river. Farmers are settled along the valley sides. These irrigated fields have been tilled for a long time and clear rules have evolved for the management of the common property. The plots are controlled by families and range in size from one to ten hectares. Some families own more than one plot. Large plots are worked by tractor or draught power.

Principle 1 Clearly defined boundaries

The boundary of the area is clearly divided by the valley sides and the extent from the Zimbabwe border to an identified point on the lower reaches of the river. There are three main canals for irrigation in the upper zone. The first canal has three family plots, the second two family plots and the third ten family plots. Each plot has access to water in rotation. No one is permitted to open a new canal on their own, they have to be part of a group. At both macro and micro levels the boundaries and authorization for access are clear.

Principle 2 Congruence between appropriation and provision rules and local conditions or appropriate rules for exploiting the resource and conserving it

The main canal is maintained by everyone, with the sub-canals maintained by groups of owners of the related plots. In dry years collective agreement is reached to limit water extraction up river to permit some water to reach tail-enders (see also examples under Principle 6). There is hereditary ownership of plots and water rights but plots cannot be bought or sold. The size of the plot varies with the technology available to the owner (oxen/tractor or hand labour).

Principle 3 Collective choice arrangements or the people affected by the rules must be able to participate in changing them

Decisions on the plot use and canals are negotiated at meetings of the people directly involved. The leader of the group (the first person to open the plot) makes the final decision. Empty plots (i.e. after the civil war) or plots made available when people are expelled are distributed by the Regulo based on advice from elders and collective meetings.

Principle 4 Monitoring: effective monitoring procedures must be in place and monitors of rules must be resource users or accountable to them

Neighbours talk with each other and monitor each other's use of water.

Principle 5 Graduated sanctions: resource users who violate rules will be liable to sanctions graduated in terms of degree of the violation

Failure to participate in maintenance of the canals results in being denied access to water until maintenance has been done. If people waste water, then their water access is interrupted for a day or in proportion to their degree of waste. If people waste water in the dry season they can be expelled from their plots but there is usually a three-stage gradation of punishment: a warning; restricted access to water; and finally expulsion.

Principle 6 Conflict resolution mechanisms: rapid access to low cost arenas to resolve conflicts

Gudza knows each valley and plot and is the ultimate judge on conflicts. There is a graded level of conflict resolution. First within the family from the head of household, secondly through meetings of the groups of householders (with the first plot holder making final settlement) and thirdly through the local headman or *sabhuku*. If the conflict is still not resolved the final stage is presentation and judgment by the Regulo (Gudza).

Principle 7 Minimal recognition of rights to organize or the right of resource users to devise their own institutions should be recognized by external (government) authorities

There is *de facto* acceptance by government authorities of this traditional institution but little direct involvement. The community are currently trying to formalize their institutions and rights through land titling under the new Land Law. However, during 1975 and 1976 the Frelimo administration took over the area and created three co-operatives and this has complicated claims.

Conclusions

The case studies of the two sites in the Chimanimani show in both high resource/low population and limited resource/high population cases the potential of indigenous institutions to effectively manage and distribute benefits from natural resources. In

Regulo Mahate's area the situation is almost analogous to that of the pre-colonial situation in much of eastern and southern Africa. Natural resources are managed by long-standing customary institutions in an area with relatively low human population densities, high resource richness and limited external influences. It also illustrates the complexity arising from the collision of two almost mutually incomprehensible systems: the formal bureaucratic administration of the modern state and a customary institutional framework that recognizes both the temporal and spiritual worlds. The study in Gudza's area demonstrated that traditional institutions can evolve more complex institutional arrangements for the management of scarce natural resources and as technological change occurs. These are far more robust, efficient, equitable and requiring lower inputs than those preferred and introduced by formal programmes of the state, donors and NGOs.

As regards the TFCA programme in Chimanimani, the field research illustrates that it will not be simple to undertake a conservation programme based on direct participation by local communities. A long-term process of dialogue and the building up of mutual trust will be needed to break down community concerns about getting involved with the government and external donors, given their knowledge of the problems local people face across the border in Zimbabwe because of conservation. On the government, NGO and donor side there is a need for greater recognition and respect for the aspirations, beliefs and philosophies of local people. These are very different from their own. To take a case in point, a recent report by a development NGO involved in the programme described Regulo Mahate in the following terms: 'Mahate is not considered a good administrator ... he never thinks of development. He is considered by the population as past it and a drunkard who doesn't even look after his own house and even lets his own family starve' (ORAM 1997). This attitude reflects a continued ambivalence to the role of traditional leaders and structures by both government agencies and NGOs.

For the broader questions tackled in this volume this study might be regarded as atypical and of limited relevance to areas with histories of official administration. However, the lengthy start-up time, high cost, bureaucratic complexity and also the fragility of the community level institutions built by governments, NGOs and donors argue for more attention to customary institutions and their capacity to evolve as robust mechanisms to manage natural resources where the state is weak and the bureaucracy poorly functioning.

The challenge thrown down by this study is how to to design community conservation around the potential of these robust traditional institutions. Otherwise Regulo Mahate's fears that formal 'community conservation' will result in the loss of both natural resources and spiritual values may come true and with this loss the assurance that 'life is peaceful and life is good'.

Appendix 13.1   The history of Chimanimani and key events for areas of Regulos Mahate and Gudza (based on Newitt 1995 and this fieldwork)

1500s to 1800s
- Karanga states of Manica, Barue and Kiteve of the Shona/Ndau speaking people
- First entry of Portuguese traders and armed incursions in mid-1500s and establishment of trading posts for gold with the interior of the Zimbabwe plateau
- Establishment of the crown estates or *prazos* run by Afro-Portuguese in the area between the Chimanimani and the coast from the 1600s to mid-1800s. Portuguese influence limited to indirect rule via the *prazos* and trading with interior

1800s to 1940s
- Entry of the Gaza Empire of the Ngoni group moving up from South Africa between the 1830s and 1860s subjugating the existing Ndau speaking people but not greatly influencing the local level traditional authorities or culture. Establishment of the Gaza capital in southern foothills of Chimanimani. Decrease of Gaza influence from 1870s as capital moves to Limpopo area
- Establishment of Rhodesia in 1890s and increasing conflict between Portugal and Britain over boundaries of control or influence (Berlin Conference). Border dispute settled by division of the Chimanimani massif between Rhodesia and Mozambique. The first establishment of Portuguese administration presence in area (Rotanda post)
- Establishment of the Mozambique Company; a private company given the concession to manage and administer central Mozambique between 1891 and 1941. Imposition of hut taxes and forced work (*chibalo*) often via indirect rule through Regulos. Little direct influence or development in Chimanimani area. Increased migration of people out of central Mozambique to escape *chibalo*/taxes or to find improved prospects elsewhere. Process continued up to 1970s

1940s to 1960s
- Cessation of the private concessions (Mozambique Company) and increased involvement of Portuguese state in administration and development. However continuation of largely indirect rule via Regulos in collection of taxes and forced labour. First entry of Portuguese settler farmers on eastern frontier of the Chimanimani and of timber companies. Still very little development within Chimanimani in terms of schools, roads, clinics etc.
- Independence war starts late 1960s (Frelimo vs. Portuguese state)
- *Five Mahate – Regulo in central Chimanimani dies and succeeded by Fernando Mahate.*

1970s
- Independence conflict enters Chimanimani area in early 1970s with increasing presence of Frelimo
- *Fernando Mahate killed by Frelimo soldiers (accused of collaboration with Portuguese). Succeeded as Regulo by Edison Mahate*
- Mozambique independence in 1975. Increasing promotion of new administration structures based on socialist models and antipathy to traditional rulers and institutions
- *Creation of co-operatives and promotion of communal villages in the fertile agricultural valleys of Regulo Gudza area. Resistance to this by local communities and then abandonment in late 1970s as impact of war increases*
- 1975 to 1980, use of Chimanimani as transit route for Zimbabwe independence fighters (ZANLA) and increase in impact of war in the area

1980s
- Increased impact of Renamo – Frelimo civil war in Chimanimani and reduced influence of government administration (rural areas under Renamo influence, towns under Frelimo)
- *Edison Mahate dies and succeeded as Regulo by Elias Panyika Mahate (1986 to present). Elias Mahate arrested by Frelimo in 1986 and held in prison/house arrest in Sussendenga town*

1990s
- Peace agreement between Frelimo and Renamo signed in October 1992
- *Mahate released from house arrest in 1993 and returns to central Chimanimani*
- *Regulo Gudza succeeds as chief on death of his father Malingate in 1993*
- National elections held in 1994. Frelimo wins overall but Renamo gains most votes in central Mozambique. Municipal (decentralized) elections held in 1998 but boycotted by Renamo. Increasing role and respect for traditional authority and institutions 1993 onwards
- 1995 onwards. Increasing promotion of Chimanimani area for some form of conservation zone with local community participation. Basic programme developed with funds from Ford Foundation and GEF supporting government agencies, development NGO and research institutions

Notes

[1]The authors would like to thank Pedro Garikai and Candida Lucas for assistance in the field work and translating, Eng. Ana Paula Reis for her assistance with reports, Eng. Serra for logistical help. Particular thanks to Regulo Mahate and family and Regulo Gudza and family for their time and hospitality.

[2]The fieldwork for this case study was undertaken in May 1998. Background information reports and publications were first collected and discussions held with a variety of the NGOs, government agencies and research institutions based in central Mozambique involved in the Chimanimani area. A week was then spent visiting two areas: the first being the settlement of Regulo (or Chief) Mahate in the Chimanimani foothills near Nyamabonda mountain and then that of Regulo Gudza near the administration post of Rotanda. Information was collected in both cases through semi-structured interviews conducted in ChiNdau with translation into English or Portuguese.

PART FIVE

Economics, Incentives & Institutional Change

14

The Nature of Benefits & the Benefits of Nature
Why Wildlife Conservation has not
Economically Benefited Communities in Africa[1]

LUCY EMERTON

Introduction

Community-oriented approaches to wildlife conservation usually have a strong economic rationale. They are typically based on the premise that if local people participate in wildlife management and economically benefit from this participation, then a 'win–win' situation will arise whereby wildlife is conserved at the same time as community welfare improves. While most community conservation activities have the ultimate goal of maintaining wildlife populations, they simultaneously aim to improve the socio-economic status of human communities in wildlife areas. Although less common, some community wildlife conservation initiatives reverse these goals, primarily aiming to contribute to sustainable local development and only trying to conserve wildlife in order to achieve this end.

This chapter describes how most attempts to conserve wildlife carried out in East and southern Africa over the last decade have been at least partially based on this economic rationale. In order to achieve the joint ends of conservation and human welfare improvement such projects and programmes have followed a common approach to generating economic benefits for the people who live in wildlife areas. In combination with other forms of local participation in wildlife management, benefits have tended to be provided by returning a proportion of the revenues earned by the state from wildlife back to them through indirect benefit-sharing arrangements and grass-roots development activities: mainly the provision of social infrastructure such as schools, water supplies and health facilities.

The economic rationale behind such benefit-based approaches to community conservation – that communities must benefit from wildlife if they are to be willing and able to conserve it – is sound. It constitutes a major advance from traditional exclusionist approaches to wildlife conservation which were largely based on denying community access and gain from wildlife, and has undoubtedly resulted in the more equitable distribution of wildlife benefits. This chapter, however, argues that such benefit-based models are based on an incomplete understanding of the economics of community conservation and of the nature of wildlife benefits. Over the long term they may neither lead to community welfare improvement nor contribute to wildlife conservation.

Benefit distribution is a necessary, but in itself may not be a sufficient, condition for communities to engage in wildlife conservation. Whether or not communities have economic incentives to conserve wildlife, and whether or not they are economically better off in the presence of wildlife, goes far beyond ensuring that a proportion of wildlife revenues are returned to them as broad development or social infrastructure benefits. It also depends on the economic costs that wildlife incurs, on the form in which wildlife benefits are received, on the costs and benefits of other economic activities which compete with wildlife, on the intra- and inter-household distribution of costs and benefits and on a range of external factors which all limit the extent to which communities are able to appropriate wildlife benefits as real livelihood gains (see Murombedzi, Chapter 16, this volume). Community incentives to conserve wildlife, and the conditions they depend on, vary at different times for different people. Additional economic considerations need to be incorporated into community approaches to wildlife conservation, and form a part of whether such approaches can be judged to have been successful in development and conservation terms.

Wildlife Benefits and Community Conservation

The total economic benefit of wildlife

A starting point in the economics of community conservation is to recognize that wildlife – defined in its widest form to include all kinds of wild plant and animal resources – yields economic goods and services.[2] The high economic value of wildlife, and the need to maintain it for the benefit of present and future generations, provides a major justification for wildlife conservation. The fact that wildlife can generate revenues in turn forms a precondition for community-based conservation. There are multiple economic benefits associated with wildlife (Figure 14.1). The direct value of such products as meat, hides and trophies and of activities such as tourism, research and education have conventionally formed the focus of economic analysis. Wildlife is now widely recognized by economists to also support a range of ecological services and ecosystem functions, to allow for the option of carrying out economic activities in the future, some of which may not be known now, and to provide considerable intrinsic cultural, aesthetic and existence value to human populations. The total economic benefit of wildlife is the sum of all these values, which accrue at global, national and local levels.

The national economic benefit of wildlife

Wildlife benefits accrue at many different levels of scale and to many different groups. Assessing the national economic value of wildlife forms an important step in the

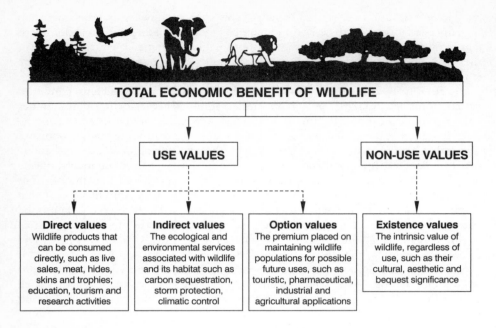

Figure 14.1 The total economic benefit of wildlife

economics of community conservation. Unless it can be demonstrated that wildlife resources contribute to development and economic goals at a whole-country level, governments are unlikely to be willing to allocate scarce resources to their wildlife sectors or to engage in community-based forms of conservation. This national economic value of wildlife is demonstrably high, as in the case of Kenya (Box 14.1). Wildlife can make an important contribution to national income and also help to

---

Box 14.1 The national economic value of wildlife tourism to Kenya

In national economic terms, direct income from wildlife tourism contributes about 5 per cent of Kenya's GDP. It also accounts for just over a tenth of national wage employment and over a third of total annual foreign exchange earnings. Gross income from tourism was worth about US$420 million in 1989 of which approximately 50 per cent or US$210 million could be attributed to wildlife. This produced a net return of 21 per cent or US$27 million to the Kenyan economy.

Gross revenues from tourism 1989	US$419 m
Tourism revenues attributed to wildlife sector (50 per cent)	US$210 m
Foreign exchange retention (82.4 per cent)	US$173m
Operating surplus (30 per cent of retained foreign exchange)	US$52 m
Gross capital charges (12.5 per cent)	US$58 m
Foreign exchange premium (20 per cent)	US$35 m
Net returns to wildlife tourism sector	US$27 m

Adapted from Emerton (1997a) and Norton-Griffiths and Southey (1995).

meet national development goals, and plays an important economic role in East and Southern African countries where sources of income, employment, public sector earnings and foreign exchange are all limited.

Although there is little quantified information about the indirect and non-use values associated with wildlife – which, as we will discuss later, may have constrained both wildlife revenue generation and attempts at community conservation – the fact that the direct products and services associated with wildlife can provide national income, employment and subsistence opportunities is well documented (Table 14.1). Most economic approaches to wildlife conservation to date have focused on demonstrating this economic value and on finding ways in which it can be captured as national economic benefits.

Table 14.1   Examples of the national economic value of wildlife

Country	Economic contribution	Value (US$ million)	Source
Botswana	Government earnings	3	(Modise 1996)
Kenya	Net annual economic gain	27	(Norton-Griffiths and
	Contribution to GDP	5%	Southey 1995)
	Contribution to formal sector employment	10%	(Emerton 1997a)
	Contribution to foreign exchange earnings	>1/3	
Namibia	Net value added to the national economy	68	(Ashley and Barnes 1996)
South Africa	National Park revenues	40	(Wells 1996a)
Tanzania	Wildlife utilization	130	(Leader–Williams 1996)
Zimbabwe	Direct wildlife uses and products	139	(Muir et al. 1996)

Wildlife benefits as an economic rationale for community conservation

The economics of community conservation depends on the fact that wildlife can generate national benefits. If there is no domestic economic gain associated with wildlife then there will be insufficient arguments – as well as insufficient local incentives – either for conserving it or for communities becoming involved in conservation activities. The contributions of wildlife to national economies provide a powerful – and much needed – argument for allocating scarce financial, human and natural resources to conservation. It is, however, necessary to move beyond merely stipulating that wildlife contributes to national economic goals. The main concern in economic approaches to community conservation is not the total economic value of wildlife but rather the extent to which wildlife benefits actually reach the local residents of wildlife areas. Surprisingly, given their importance as a rationale for community-based forms of wildlife conservation, little analysis of local-level benefits accruing from wildlife is available in existing literature.

This concern with distribution arises from the fact that although wildlife contributes substantially to the national economies of many East and southern African countries, a high national economic value alone is not enough to ensure that it will be conserved. Wildlife economic benefits are unequally distributed, with community benefits typically accounting for only a small proportion of the total value of wildlife, as illustrated for the case of the Maasai Mara (Box 14.2). Similar instances of low community

Box 14.2 Distribution of wildlife tourism revenues to communities in Kenya

In 1988 the 122 500 visitors to the Maasai Mara National Reserve accounted for over a tenth of all tourist bed-nights in Kenya. In addition to spending money on accommodation and Reserve fees, tourists also directly supported a range of other enterprises, including balloon safaris, sales of handicrafts and various travel and transport-related purchases. Total tourist expenditure for the area was over US$26 million. However, although almost twice as many tourists visiting the Maasai Mara stayed (and most wildlife was found) on communal lands rather than in the Reserve, less than 1 per cent of cash income accrued to local Maasai and under a tenth remained in the district as council revenues or wages to local employees.

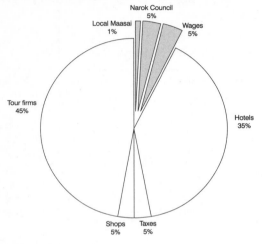

Adapted from Douglas-Hamilton and Associates (1988).

wildlife benefits exist in other areas; for example only a quarter of Namibia's wildlife income accrues to private farmers and less than 3 per cent to communal landholders (Barnes and de Jager 1996); local communities received less than 1 per cent of all tourist revenues from Amboseli National Park in 1990 (Norton-Griffiths 1995), and only just over half of the revenues earned by government from hunting in communal areas of Zimbabwe in 1988 (Muir et al. 1996).[3]

This skewed distribution of wildlife benefits away from local communities is not only inequitable, it can actually discourage wildlife conservation. The majority of wildlife in East and Southern Africa is found on private and communal lands; for example in Kenya it is estimated that between 65 and 80 per cent of wildlife is outside National Parks and Reserves (Ouko and Marekia 1996), and less than 10 per cent of Namibia's wildlife is found inside formally protected areas (Yaron et al. 1996). The survival of wildlife ultimately depends on the action of these landholders.

Benefit-based approaches to community conservation are based on the economic rationale that although wildlife has a high economic value, local communities – who are often already economically marginalized – receive little of this value, and therefore have little incentive to conserve wildlife because they do not economically gain from doing so (Figure 14.2). Benefit-based approaches require that wildlife

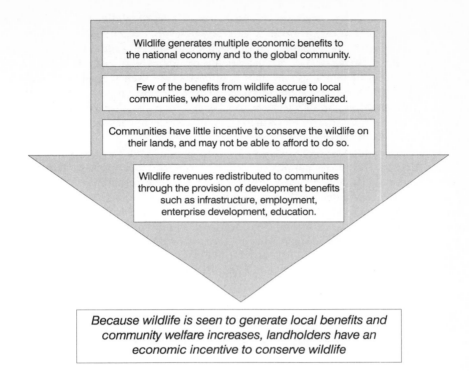

Figure 14.2 Benefit-based economic model of community wildlife conservation

conservation simultaneously generates national benefits (which will justify wildlife conservation overall), government revenues (which will provide funds to distribute to communities) and community benefits. This requires a redistribution of wildlife benefits, which are currently balanced in favour of the people who live outside wildlife areas and often outside wildlife-rich countries. If wildlife has little or no value to local communities, there is no reason why they should conserve it. It is not in their economic interests to do so. At best they may be wildlife-neutral, at worst they may actively destroy wildlife. If wildlife cannot contribute sustainably to local livelihoods then it stands little chance of survival.

The implementation of benefit-based approaches to community wildlife conservation

The majority of wildlife conservation activities implemented over recent years in East and southern Africa have been at least nominally community-based, aiming to overcome inequities in wildlife benefit distribution. Most rely on indirect methods for distributing wildlife benefits to landholders, sometimes in combination with other community incentives such as permitting limited wildlife resource utilization or employing local people as wildlife workers. They primarily operate in protected areas and their buffers in East Africa, where income is collected by the state or some other authority through such mechanisms as entry charges, sales of wildlife products, or fees and levies raised on hunting, tourism and other wildlife-based activities. A percentage of these revenues are then channelled through some kind of fund, usually administered by local authorities or the national wildlife agency, which is earmarked for local community development activities such as infrastructure improvement and maintenance, educational bursaries or micro-enterprise development, and sometimes partially distributed as cash dividends to local landholders. In southern Africa there is a contrast and community wildlife management most often focuses on communal lands (see Jones and Murphree, Chapter 4, this volume).

This type of arrangement is typified by Kenya Wildlife Service's approach to benefit sharing (Box 14.3). Other examples of benefit sharing and its impacts on community welfare and wildlife conservation are discussed in detail elsewhere, and include arrangements made under the Kenya Wildlife Service (Barrow et al. 1996), South African Parks Boards (Wells 1996a; Davies 1993), Tanzania National Parks (Dembe and Bergin 1996; Leader-Williams 1996; Kangwana and Ole Mako, Chapter 10, this volume) and Uganda Wildlife Authority (Barrow 1996b; Chapters 8 and 9, this volume) as well as under LIRDP and ADMADE in Zambia (Kapungwe 1996) and CAMPFIRE in Zimbabwe (Muir et al. 1996; Bond, Chapter 15, this volume).

Box 14.3 Community benefit sharing in Kenya

Kenya Wildlife Service's revenue-sharing policy uses a Wildlife Development Fund as a mechanism to distribute some of the revenues earned from protected areas to local communities. Initially this was based on a quarter of gate fees, subsequently revised. Between 1991 and 1995 over US$1.25 million was allocated to community-related activities in protected area buffer zones, including water, education, health, livestock and enterprise development as well as the provision of famine relief. Such revenue-sharing mechanisms currently operate in 33 districts of the country.

Adapted from Barrow et al. (1996).

Limits to Benefit-based Economic Models of Community Wildlife Conservation

Because most approaches to community wildlife conservation are based on sharing income as broad development benefits, their success has mainly been evaluated in terms of the total value of revenues and range of development projects initiated among the residents of wildlife areas. That benefit-based approaches have allocated substantial sums of money to community development activities, and have managed to involve local people in wildlife conservation at the same time as contributing to local development is well-documented (see for example Barrow et al.'s (1996) discussion of community conservation policy and practice in East Africa, Siachoono's (1995) discussion of the impacts of ADMADE in Zambia, Thresher's (1992) discussion of the impacts of revenue-sharing around Amboseli National Park in Kenya and Davies' (1993) discussion of the impacts of community involvement in conservation around Pilaniesberg National Park in South Africa, also illustrated in Box 14.4).

Box 14.4   Community benefit sharing in South Africa

Pilaniesberg National Park in Bophuthatswana was one of the first efforts in South Africa to integrate community development with wildlife conservation. In an attempt to compensate local people for the loss of residence, grazing land and access to wild resources caused by the fencing of a large area as a National Park and to encourage them to support wildlife conservation, a range of benefit-sharing arrangements were set in place by the park authorities through the formation of a Community Development Organization. Activities undertaken included the development of local enterprises such as vegetable growing and clothing manufacture, the establishment of a community game reserve, employment, use of local contractors and infrastructure development. Surveys carried out before and after these arrangements were effected show a shift from an initially hostile reaction to the Park to a situation of strong support where almost 90 per cent of local community members approved of the use of public funds to maintain the Park, nearly a third had visited it and half expressed willingness to occasionally work in the park on a voluntary basis.

Adapted from Davies (1993).

For reasons which will be discussed below, it is, however, not self-evident that sharing wildlife revenues as development benefits will alone lead to a net economic gain for communities living in wildlife areas or encourage them to conserve wildlife. The provision of benefits to communities is undoubtedly necessary, but may not in itself be a sufficient economic condition for wildlife conservation; there are a number of other economic impacts of wildlife conservation which may counterbalance, or even negate, the gains from revenue-sharing arrangements. Benefit-based approaches only partially address the economic issues involved in community wildlife conservation.

Most importantly, purely benefit-based approaches to community wildlife conservation neglect the local economic forces motivating wildlife loss. Disbursing broad development benefits such as infrastructure construction and maintenance, the provision of educational opportunities, employment generation and enterprise development can and does improve community welfare, and lead to short-term improvements in public attitudes to wildlife. However, the assumption that this will change community behaviour over the long term, and lead to a downturn in activities which impact negatively on wildlife, is seriously flawed because it fails to address the reasons why people engage in economic activities which destroy wildlife. Three important factors, addressed below, must be incorporated into economic approaches to community wildlife conservation because they help to explain the underlying forces motivating wildlife loss at the local level. These include the nature of livelihood systems in wildlife areas and the form in which wildlife benefits are received by communities; the costs that wildlife imposes on local livelihoods; and the broader policy factors which influence local land use and economic activities.

The nature of livelihood systems in wildlife areas and the form in which wildlife benefits are received by communities

The physical and socio-economic conditions in wildlife areas generally mean that sources of employment, income and subsistence are scarce and livelihoods are insecure for the majority of the population. People engage in a range of economic activities in the search for secure livelihoods, and these activities in turn impact on wildlife – for example through resource over-exploitation, hunting and the clearance of habitat for agriculture. Benefit-based approaches to wildlife conservation uncritically accept that broad development benefits are not only what communities need and want, but will somehow put people in a position where they do not need to destroy wildlife to achieve livelihood security. Yet the form in which benefits are shared under these arrangements – usually in the form of the provision of social infrastructure – rarely provides subsistence, income or secure livelihoods to the majority of community members in wildlife areas and thus may not generate incentives for community conservation (illustrated for the case of Zambia in Box 14.5). These forms of benefit-sharing arrangements rarely meet people's day-to-day needs for income, consumption goods and employment which cause them to engage in activities which damage wildlife.

Box 14.5 Community benefit sharing in Zambia

Two forms of benefit sharing operate in seven of the protected areas in Central, Copperbelt and Luapula Provinces of Zambia. ADMADE retains hunting rights and concession fees and half of animal licence fees from hunting in Game Management Areas through a Wildlife Conservation Revolving Fund, 35 per cent of which is allocated to local community development activities. LIRDP sets aside 40 per cent of revenues from culling, hunting, park entry and leases for community development activities. Together these funds helped to finance community development projects worth nearly US$0.25 million in 1996. Communities benefited from these developments, but it is not clear that they provided sufficient incentives for wildlife damaging activities to decrease. Although the major motivating forces for wildlife loss in these areas are clearance of habitat for agriculture, unsustainable wild resource use and pressing local needs for cash income, there is only one case of community cash income generation and livelihood development through wildlife in all three provinces: the community-managed Nsobe self catering camp in Bangweulu Swamps, Luapula Province.

Adapted from Kapungwe (1996) and Emerton (1997c).

As well as the form in which wildlife benefits are shared with communities, the level of benefits generated may not be enough to compensate people for economic activities which interfere with wildlife. People may be unable to cope with the loss of income and subsistence generated by wildlife-depredation. The small amount of wildlife revenues allocated to communities is frequently not of a sufficient value – especially when shared between many community members – to allow people to be in an economic position to forgo wildlife damage. People may also be unable to afford the high transaction or compliance costs of participating in community conservation, for example the time involved in attending meetings and carrying out conservation-related activities. Contrary to popular belief, that levels of underemployment are high and that time and labour are not binding constraints in rural subsistence economies, the opportunity cost of people's time in wildlife areas is high. In poorer regions, at times of stress, or for more marginal social and economic groups people tend to pursue multiple and continuous strategies in order to generate sufficient food and income and may be unable to afford the time to participate in community conservation activities unless they are directly compensated for these productive activities forgone.

It is thus unlikely that sharing wildlife benefits as community development projects will lead to an overall decrease in wildlife-damaging activities, or increase in welfare, unless they meet livelihood needs and generate real income and subsistence products. These needs will vary within and between communities, and a single set of development benefits provided at the level of whole communities is unlikely to significantly improve individual or household economic welfare.

Community wildlife costs

Benefit-based approaches assume that converting a proportion of wildlife revenues into community development benefits will mean that wildlife becomes a positive economic asset for landholders. Yet wildlife benefits can never be seen as absolute. They can only be used as an incentive for community wildlife conservation if they are seen in relation to the costs that wildlife incurs. As illustrated in Figure 14.3, as well as the direct costs which have formed the focus of conventional economic analysis – the physical inputs required to conserve wildlife – the presence of wildlife gives rise to costs by interfering with other components of community livelihood systems.

Direct costs include the staff, equipment, infrastructure and maintenance associated with wildlife management. These costs can be substantial; for example total costs to Kenya Wildlife Service were over US$14.5 million in 1992, of which over half was spent directly on wildlife management and conservation, and annual expenditure on

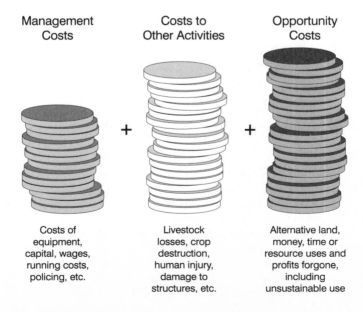

Management Costs	Costs to Other Activities	Opportunity Costs
Costs of equipment, capital, wages, running costs, policing, etc.	Livestock losses, crop destruction, human injury, damage to structures, etc.	Alternative land, money, time or resource uses and profits forgone, including unsustainable use

Figure 14.3 The total economic cost of wildlife

rhino and elephant conservation alone were US$0.4 million and US$1.9 million respectively (Mwamadzingo 1992). The cost of managing Uganda's protected area network was over US$12.7 million in 1993 (Howard 1995), and direct expenditure on South Africa's National Parks was US$71 million in 1994 (Wells 1996a). Wildlife benefits must at least cover direct costs for conservation to be economically viable.

Wildlife areas in East and southern Africa are primarily agricultural zones, supporting livestock and sometimes arable production. Wildlife competes with crops and livestock for land, water and other resources. Wild animals also cause direct damage to agricultural enterprises through the transmission of disease to livestock, kills of domestic stock and crop destruction. As well as having a high overall economic cost, as illustrated in Table 14.2, wildlife damage to agriculture also has major impacts on the production base of landholders. It can serve to make already insecure livelihoods even more marginal in economic terms. The livestock and crop losses caused by wildlife impact heavily on individual ranchers, pastoralists and arable agriculturalists, as illustrated in Table 14.3.

Table 14.2 Examples of the overall economic cost of wildlife damage to agriculture

Country	Scale of wildlife cost	Value (US$)	Source
Malawi	National cost	17.3 million	(Deodatus 1996)
Namibia	East Caprivi villages	757/village	(Ashley and Barnes 1996)
Uganda	National cost	20 million	(Howard 1995)

Table 14.3 Examples of the local economic cost of wildlife damage to agriculture

Country	Type of wildlife cost	Value (US$)	Source
Kenya	Laikipia disease transmission to livestock	37/km^2	(Grootenhuis 1996)
	Maasai Mara agricultural production costs	35–45%	(Norton-Griffiths 1996)
	Maasai Mara livestock disease, kills and injury	104/km^2	(Mwangi 1995)
	Maasai Mara crop damage	200–400/household	(Omondi 1994)
	Shimba Hills elephant crop damage	100/household	(PDS 1997)
Zambia	Mumbwa Game Management Area crop damage	122/household	(Siachoono 1995)

The land, labour, funds and other resources allocated to wildlife conservation have alternative uses elsewhere; for example protected areas could be given over to agriculture or used for other economic activities (as illustrated for the case of Kenya in Box 14.6). Conservation typically precludes certain levels and types of wild resource utilization; funds used to develop wildlife enterprise could be invested elsewhere in the economy. The opportunity costs of wildlife are the income and profits forgone from those activities which are precluded or diminished by allocating resources to wildlife conservation. In East and Southern Africa, where wildlife areas predominantly lie in subsistence agricultural zones, agricultural production and local resource utilization forgone are major components of the opportunity cost of wildlife conservation, as illustrated in Table 14.4.

Box 14.6   The opportunity costs of wildlife conservation to Kenya

The net agricultural opportunity cost of alternative land uses and earnings forgone to the Kenyan economy from maintaining nearly 61,000 km² of land under protected areas is US$203 million, some 2.8 per cent of GDP and equivalent to support to 4.2 million Kenyans. The combined net returns from wildlife and forestry of US$42 million is inadequate to offset these costs, at the national or household level. Because the chief value of Kenya's conservation activities is indirect and external, it is inappropriate that the costs should be wholly borne by the Kenyan government and domestic economy.

Protected areas	60,600 km²
Potential human population	4.2 million
Potential livestock population	5.8 million
Potential cultivated area	0.8 million ha
Potential gross revenues	US$565 million
Potential net returns	US$203 million
Net returns from protected areas	US$42 million

Adapted from Norton-Griffiths and Southey (1995).

Table 14.4   Examples of the agricultural opportunity cost of wildlife

Country	Type of opportunity cost	Value (US$)	Source
Kenya	National opportunity cost of biodiversity conservation	203 million	(Norton-Griffiths and Southey 1995)
	Local opportunity cost of Maasai Mara wildlife conservation	27 million	(Norton-Griffiths 1995)
	Local opportunity cost of Mount Kenya forest and wildlife conservation	75 million or 5700/household	(Emerton 1997b)
South Africa	Local opportunity cost of Kruger National Park wildlife conservation	6 million or 5000/household	(Engelbrecht and van der Walt 1993)
Uganda	National opportunity cost of forest and wildlife conservation	110 million	(Howard 1995)

Wildlife conservation also typically precludes a certain level of wild resource use, and protected areas often permit no extractive activities whatsoever. This can impose significant opportunity costs on adjacent communities and take away vital sources of subsistence and income including basic needs such as food, water, shelter, medicines, fuel and pasture as well as emergency fallback goods and services. As illustrated in Table 14.5 the value of local wild resource use is high throughout East and Southern Africa, and loss of part or all of this utilization imposes high costs on communities in cash and livelihood terms.

As is the case with benefits, wildlife costs tend to accrue unequally. Whereas communities often receive few direct wildlife benefits, they typically bear the full burden of the damage wildlife causes to other economic activities and the opportunity costs of alternative land uses forgone or diminished by the presence of wildlife. For example, at Lake Mburo National Park in Uganda, park 'neighbours' suffer very high levels of crop damage because of the high numbers of bush pigs (Hulme and Infield, Chapter 8, this volume). Communities in wildlife areas are often already

Table 14.5 Examples of local resource utilization values

Country	Type of wildlife value	Value (US$)	Source
Kenya	Aberdare Forest local use	165/household	(Emerton and Mogaka 1996)
	Arabuko Sokoke forest local use	135/household	(Mogaka 1991)
	Kakamega forest local use	160/household	(Emerton 1992)
	Mau forest local use	350–450/household	(Lubanga 1991)
	Mount Kenya forest local use	300/household	(Emerton 1997b)
	Oldonyo Orok forest local use	100/household	(Emerton 1996)
South Africa	Natal Parks local resource use	0.5 million	(Wells 1996a)
Zimbabwe	Local bushmeat consumption	1 million	(Bojö 1996)

economically marginalized and least able to bear these costs. Even if they are willing to conserve wildlife, the costs to them of doing so may be insurmountable.

Consideration of wildlife costs thus forms a central part of the economics of community conservation. It also strengthens the argument for building community benefit-sharing arrangements into wildlife conservation. Benefit sharing will, however, have only marginal impact on either community welfare or wildlife conservation unless it directly offsets wildlife costs. It is not enough to merely allocate a fixed proportion of wildlife revenues to community development activities; the level and type of benefits provided must be closely tied to the magnitude of wildlife costs accruing to communities. Not only must benefits be provided to a sufficient level to balance the value of wildlife costs, but they must also be generated in a form which directly compensates for the economic activities precluded or diminished by the presence of wildlife. For local communities to be willing and economically able to conserve wildlife, conservation must generate broad benefits and fulfil the additional conditions that wildlife benefits exceed wildlife costs, and that such benefits accrue to communities in the form of real financial or livelihood benefits which offset the financial and livelihood costs caused by wildlife.

Policy influences on community wildlife benefits and costs

Even where wildlife can generate high returns which accrue to local communities it still may not be considered a desirable use of land, resources or funds. Benefit-based approaches, while aiming to provide community conservation incentives by imbuing wildlife with economic value, ignore the fact that there simultaneously exist a range of wider and pervasive economic disincentives to community wildlife conservation. In particular, a range of market, policy and institutional distortions in East and southern African countries have discriminated against wildlife (Figure 14.4), by increasing the opportunity cost of alternative land uses (Pearce 1996) and denying rights to own, manage or utilize wildlife to groups other than the state (Child 1996; Emerton 1997a; Muir et al. 1996; Yaron et al. 1996). These distortions have the net effect of decreasing the absolute and relative economic profitability of wildlife for landholders, as illustrated for the case of Namibia in Box 14.7. Giving communities in wildlife areas sufficient economic incentives for conservation is not just a matter of providing them with wildlife benefits, but also of recognizing the perverse incentives which encourage them to engage in activities which deplete or destroy wildlife.

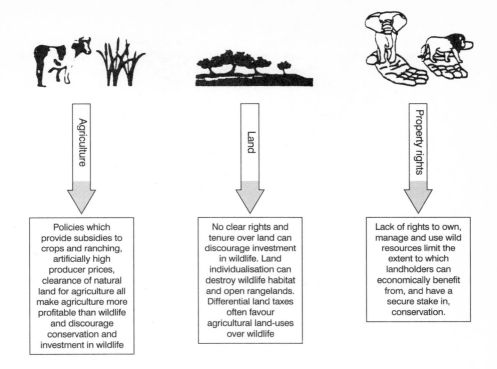

Figure 14.4   Major economic policy disincentives to community wildlife conservation

---

Box 14.7   The impact of market and policy distortions on wildlife profitability in Namibia

Although the level of agricultural sector protection has decreased in Namibia over recent years, there still exist a range of taxes, subsidies and foreign exchange manipulations which influence the profitability of wildlife-based land uses by driving a wedge between the financial profits landholders face and true social and economic values. These policy and market imperfections have a net negative effect for landholders by decreasing profits and increasing costs. The results of financial and economic analysis show that even where financial returns are low or negative for landholders, wildlife is socially and economically profitable. This demonstrates that policy and market distortions discriminate against wildlife-based land uses, and that wildlife deserves public policy support.

	Sheep/game ranch	Cattle/game ranch	Game lodge
Financial NPV/ha	US$ -4.3	US$ -10.1	US$ -13.5
Economic NPV/ha	US$ +5.1	US$ +1.4	US $ +18.1
Effect on costs/ha	US$ +4.0	US$ +4.6	US$ +6.2
Effect on cash income/ha	US$ -2.2	US$ -2.7	US$ -2.7

Adapted from Barnes and de Jager (1996).

Identifying and overcoming these policy distortions forms an important part of the economics of community conservation.

The dominant mode of production among communities in wildlife areas is livestock or arable agriculture. Macroeconomic and sectoral policies in sub-Saharan Africa have long been biased towards agriculture, imposing a range of price distortions which mean that wildlife is rarely able to compete fairly with agriculture because it is less profitable in financial terms. A range of subsidies and taxes have been set in place aimed at stimulating domestic crop and livestock production, with the aim of promoting national food security and foreign-exchange earning agricultural exports. Although the agricultural sector has been undergoing liberalization in most parts of East and southern Africa over the last decade, it is still protected in comparison with wildlife. Wildlife inputs are still more expensive in market terms, and their outputs cheaper, because they lack many of the subsidies provided to agriculture and are subject to many of the taxes from which the agricultural sector is exempt.

Heavy subsidies to the livestock sector, as well as export-led veterinary regulations which encroach on wildlife habitat and migration routes, have in Botswana (McNeely 1993), Namibia (Yaron et al. 1996) and Zimbabwe (Muir et al. 1996) encouraged the incursion of ranching into wildlife areas and diminished the relative profitability of wildlife-based land uses. In Kenya differential land-use taxes have made wildlife less profitable compared with crops and livestock (Vorhies 1996), reinforced by other subsidies to the agricultural sector such as duty and tax exemptions on imported agricultural equipment, low interest credit facilities, agricultural price fixing and protection against imported agricultural commodities (Emerton 1997a).

Forms of land tenure also tend to be biased towards settled agriculture, and have thus discouraged wildlife conservation. Throughout East and southern Africa there has been a shift in land tenure systems towards consolidation and individualization (Woodhouse, Bernstein and Hulme 2000). Many wildlife areas which were formerly large, communally owned lands are now being sub-divided into small, individually owned farms or settlement schemes. The extensive tracts of land required to support wild animal populations are being physically demarcated and split into agricultural units which threaten wildlife, for example around the Nairobi National Park dispersal area (Gichohi 1996), the Maasai Mara National Reserve (Norton-Griffiths 1996), and the Amboseli-Tsavo region in Kenya (Southgate and Hulme 1996). Many land units are now smaller than the minimum viable area for wildlife populations (Howard 1995; Mwau 1996).

Policy factors which limit private property rights in wildlife and natural resources can also severely constrain the extent to which communities can benefit from the wildlife on their lands (Ashley and Barnes 1996; Child 1996; Emerton 1997c). The traditionally heavy regulation of the wildlife sector in most East and southern African countries, and the impact of lack of community rights to own, manage or utilize wildlife are discussed in other chapters and provide strong economic disincentives to community wildlife conservation. Even where wildlife can in theory generate high financial returns and compete with alternative land uses, local communities are often not permitted to legally capture these benefits.

Going Beyond a Benefit-based Approach to the Economics of Community Wildlife Conservation

Several attempts have been made to go beyond a benefit-based approach to community conservation and to incorporate these additional economic considerations. An important element of these approaches has been their efforts to capture wildlife benefits as real cash values or livelihood support for local communities, in order to directly offset the tangible costs incurred by wildlife and enhance the ability of wildlife-based activities to compete with other land uses and livelihood elements. Most of these approaches also recognize the need to involve community members directly in conservation and grant some form of rights to manage and use the wildlife lying on their lands (see Chapters 3, 4, 11, 12 and 16 in this volume for discussions of tenure and proprietorship).

Rather than the one-dimensional benefit-based approach described in Figure 14.2, these approaches to community conservation are based on the multi-causal economic model summarized in Figure 14.5 which recognizes the need to overcome the many economic forces leading to wildlife loss at the community level and to see conservation within the context of providing secure livelihoods to the communities living in wildlife areas. These approaches accept, but go beyond, the single condition that wildlife conservation must generate national economic benefits, government revenues and community benefits. They also require that a number of additional conditions are fulfilled: that community economic benefits from conservation are as a whole greater than the total costs incurred to communities by wildlife; that the net benefits accruing to participants from complying with a community approach to wildlife conservation exceed the transaction costs of their forgoing other productive opportunities in order to allocate time to wildlife-related activities; that community

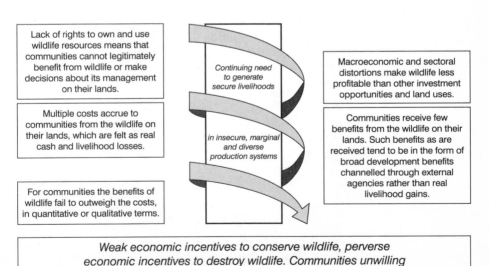

Figure 14.5 Multi-causal economic model of community wildlife conservation

wildlife benefits accrue as real financial and livelihood benefits to households; and that no community member whose economic activities impact on wildlife is made tangibly worse off as a result of conservation.

Maximizing wildlife values and using them as a direct means of livelihood support forms an important part of such approaches to community conservation. However great the demonstrated total economic benefit of wildlife is, these approaches require that a sufficient portion of this benefit is captured as financial benefits – such as income, consumption goods and employment – which are received by all land-holders in wildlife areas to a level which exceeds the costs borne as a result of wildlife. Increasing the economic gain from wildlife for communities has also been achieved by moving away from traditional benefit-sharing arrangements, as illustrated for the case of Namibia in Box 14.8. Although most benefit-sharing activities are currently carried out by wildlife agencies or local government authorities, there is no particular reason why they should always be indirect or externally implemented. The trans-action costs of these arrangements tend to be high, the public sector is often already over-burdened and under-resourced, and benefits do not always reach all sectors of communities. Enhancing the ability of communities to directly generate income or livelihood benefits from wildlife themselves may be a more cost-effective and economically efficient way to implement benefit-sharing arrangements.

Because many wildlife values are unvalued or undervalued by the market, increasing the real benefit of wildlife for communities has also meant finding new markets and diversifying or improving existing markets for wildlife products and

---

Box 14.8   Community wildlife income in Namibia

In four communal areas of Namibia communities gained benefits in excess of US$0.5 million in 1995 from wildlife through a series of arrangements including locally controlled enterprise, employment and partnerships with government and the private sector. Income from wildlife is up to four times as high as the costs wildlife incurs at the household level. Potentially, community economic benefits from wildlife may become three times higher as community enterprises develop.

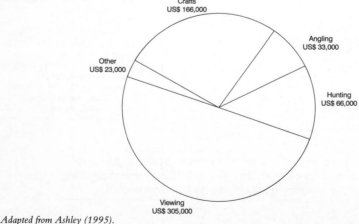

Crafts
US$ 166,000

Angling
US$ 33,000

Other
US$ 23,000

Hunting
US$ 66,000

Viewing
US$ 305,000

Adapted from Ashley (1995).

services. The direct products of wildlife such as tourism, hunting and cropping currently form the major source of cash revenues and provide the major finance for community benefit sharing. The demand for these products is limited, and their revenues are not always enough to provide community benefits to a sufficient value, especially to balance the high cash costs of wildlife. Direct community involvement in wildlife income generation can take many forms, ranging from pure community wildlife enterprise management to a range of partnerships and arrangements with commercial companies. That a variety of wildlife enterprise and sustainable wild resource utilization arrangements can be profitable for landholders is well-documented (Ashley 1995; Barnes and de Jager 1996; Emerton 1997a; Muir et al. 1996; Mwau 1996). Landholders in wildlife areas have often been excluded from wildlife markets for financial, human resources and institutional reasons. Enabling this kind of arrangement means providing local communities with the training, credit and market information to allow them to fairly compete or co-operate with other, more established, commercial and private-sector companies.

The privatization of wildlife resources and enterprise has already occurred, albeit to a limited extent, in several East and southern African countries. Although much of the direct participation in wildlife income-generation is still confined to large landholders and commercial farmers, the results of community forms of wildlife income generation are positive. Experiences of direct community participation in wildlife income generation demonstrate that these arrangements can be an effective way of both increasing community welfare and conserving wildlife. For example, under the Chobe Enclave Project in Botswana communities have entered into a joint partnership with a local safari operator to manage their wildlife quota, earning cash returns of over US$100,000 in 1996 (Modise 1996). It has been estimated that in Namibia direct revenue-sharing and partnerships between local communities and tour operators can generate for a single village up to US$20,000 in wages, up to US$20,000 in other local income and between US$150 and 250 per household in sales of handicrafts and souvenirs (Ashley 1995). In Namibia (Yaron et al. 1996) and Zimbabwe (Muir et al. 1996), much of the recovery of wildlife populations over recent years has been attributed to the shift in wildlife management and utilization from the state to the commercial sector and landholders in wildlife areas.

Conclusions: Assessing the Economic Impacts of Community Wildlife Conservation

One-dimensional, benefit-based approaches have formed the guiding principle for many of the community wildlife conservation activities implemented in East and southern Africa over the last decade (see Chapters 8–10, this volume, for examples). Most of these activities aim to redistribute wildlife revenues to local communities as broad development benefits. This chapter has argued that although the economic rationale of benefit-based approaches to community wildlife conservation is sound – if local communities do not benefit from wildlife they are unlikely to be willing or able to conserve it – it is incomplete. Generating broad development benefits does not ensure that the presence of wildlife generates a net local economic gain and is not the same as providing economic incentives for conservation.

Because of their narrow conceptualization of wildlife benefits, it is difficult to assess whether such conservation initiatives actually have made communities in wildlife areas economically better off. There are few cases where detailed economic analysis of the impacts of wildlife conservation has been carried out. It has merely been assumed that generating benefits for local communities is an indication that such activities have been successful in conservation and development terms. In order to assess the economic impacts of conservation initiatives it is necessary to go beyond assessing the magnitude of benefits distributed to communities in wildlife areas.

Benefit sharing forms a necessary, but rarely sufficient, condition for local communities to economically gain from wildlife conservation. Judging the success of community conservation in terms of development benefits generated may indicate neither that community welfare has improved nor that the local economic conditions which will lead to wildlife conservation have been set in place. Even when the people in wildlife areas are furnished with community development benefits, frequently they still lose out in economic terms from the presence of wildlife.

There are multiple economic conditions which are necessary for successful community wildlife conservation, of which benefit sharing is but one. A range of other economic factors need to be incorporated into benefit-based approaches to community wildlife conservation, and used to evaluate their success. At the least these factors include consideration of the costs associated with wildlife and their distribution, the level and form in which community benefits are received, the degree to which communities have economic choice and control over wildlife management, use and benefit generation and the wider policy factors which discriminate against wildlife as a profitable land use for communities. Which combination of conditions is sufficient to ensure that people are economically better off in the presence of wildlife and have economic incentives to conserve wildlife will vary between and within communities. Communities are heterogeneous in their composition, their aspirations and in the wider economic conditions they face.

Community approaches to wildlife conservation can be judged to be economically successful if they not only generate benefits but also ensure that these benefits are of a sufficient value, and accrue in an appropriate form, to offset the costs that wildlife imposes on communities and to make wildlife an economically viable land use compared with other wildlife-displacing livelihood alternatives. Providing communities with economic incentives to conserve wildlife means ensuring that they are better off in financial and livelihood terms with wildlife than they would be without it, at the same time as overcoming the root economic factors which cause them to engage in economic activities which threaten or deplete wildlife resources.

Notes

[1]This paper has benefited substantially from comments made by Mike Norton-Griffiths and Ed Barrow.
[2]Local currency values have, throughout this document, been converted to current US$ (1998).
[3]See Bond (Chapter 15, this volume) and Murombedzi (Chapter 16, this volume) for detailed examinations of the benefits and costs of CAMPFIRE. Murphree (Chapter 12, this volume) provides an example of a CAMPFIRE project that has increased income by diversifying into tourism.

15
CAMPFIRE & the Incentives for Institutional Change

IVAN BOND

Introduction

CAMPFIRE and other community-based natural resource management (CBNRM) programmes seek to create the necessary conditions for institutional change in the management of wildlife, wildlife habitat and other natural resources. Central to CAMPFIRE, and common to all of the community wildlife management programmes in Southern Africa, is the role of economic incentives for institutional change. These incentives and the resulting changes in relative prices are considered by economic theorists to be the most important factors influencing institutional change (North 1990).[1] This chapter considers the financial benefits derived from wildlife and the incentives these create for institutional change. It has been proposed that institutional change will only take place when the net benefits of the new institution are much greater than the net benefits of the old institutions (or lack of institutions) which they seek to replace (Ostrom 1998). However, when the difference between the two sets of rules is small or there is no difference then institutional change is unlikely.

Because institutional change is a gradual and incremental process (North 1990) many of the initial analyses of CAMPFIRE were constrained by a lack of time–series data or restricted by a narrow geographical focus (Murindagomo 1997). The analysis presented here is based on the data from the first eight years (1989–96) of CAMPFIRE drawn from 12 to 16 districts.[2] It considers the sources of CAMPFIRE revenue and then traces the allocation and the relative incentive for institutional change at district, sub-district and household level. The chapter concludes with the policy implications derived from the analysis for CAMPFIRE and other CBNRM within sub-Saharan Africa.

Physical description of rural district councils (RDCs) with wildlife

Those districts which have significant populations of large mammals are, in conventional terms, the least developed. Of the 16 primary wildlife districts, six are in the top ten of the least developed districts in Zimbabwe (derived from Eilerts 1994). Until recently the absence of rural infrastructure, most notably roads, and the presence of tsetse fly have restricted human settlement and cultivation. Within the past 18 years, the construction of roads, the widespread eradication of tsetse fly and central government settlement projects have resulted in substantial increases in human populations in many of those 'wildlife' districts (Derman 1997).

Most of the wildlife producing districts are located towards the margins of the country and all but one border state protected wildlife areas (see Map 12.1). The status of wildlife populations varies considerably between districts. The abundance of elephant and other large mammals is positively correlated to the area of wildlife habitat in each district, and negatively correlated to human population density (Taylor 1998). Nearly all the wildlife producing districts lie in the agriculturally marginal natural regions and more than 90 per cent of the wards which have received wildlife revenue are located either in Natural Regions IV or V (Bond 1999). Although all are constrained by low agro-ecological potential, there are major regional differences in agricultural productions systems. Generally in the southern (Lowveld) district communal land farmers rear livestock and cultivate small grains, while in the northern districts agricultural production is dominated by large grain and cotton production. In both systems, cattle provide an important source of draught power together with other goods and services appropriate to an agro-pastoral economy (Bond 1993). Since the inception of CAMPFIRE, communal land production systems have been affected by poor rainfall.[3] The annual requirement for government and donor funded drought relief in most communal lands is indicative of the poor agro-ecological potential and the inability of many households to grow sufficient food.[4]

The CAMPFIRE Model

Although the RDCs with Appropriate Authority are characterized by considerable bio-physical, social and economic variability, it is possible to describe a general model for the income earned from the use of wildlife and the allocation of wildlife-based revenue. Usually, the consumptive (sport hunting) or non-consumptive (tourism) rights for the use of wildlife are leased to a private sector entrepreneur by the RDC. The terms and conditions of the lease, such as its financial structure, its length and the area covered are determined primarily by the RDC. The number and mix of leases per district vary according to the area of wildlife habitat and the estimated wildlife populations. By either temporal or spatial zoning of activities, districts have combined both sport hunting and tourism leases. Lessees pay all their fees to the rural district council. The extent to which representatives of the communities living with the wildlife are involved in the allocation of leases to private sector partners varies substantially between districts (see Jones and Murphree, Chapter 4, this volume). However, the devolution of Appropriate Authority from central government to district level has resulted in greater use of market-based mechanisms for the allocation of leases and greater efficiency of resource use (Bond 1999; Child, GFT 1995).

The gross wildlife revenue received by districts is allocated to wildlife management activities, district council levies and to wildlife producer wards (Figure 15.1). There is

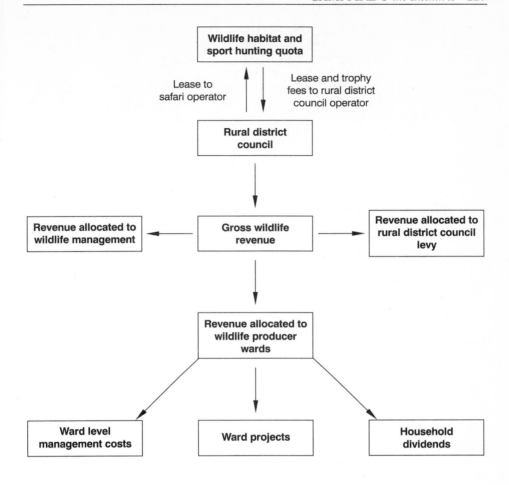

Figure 15.1 The CAMPFIRE finance model

considerable diversity in terms of wildlife management activities between districts. However, most districts have a small core team of personnel whose duties involve law enforcement, problem animal management and wildlife (including sport hunting) monitoring. CAMPFIRE coordinators and trainers which support sub-district CAMPFIRE and/or wildlife committees are generally also paid from this revenue.

The revenue devolved to sub-district levels, mostly to wards, provides the financial incentive for individuals and households to participate in the common management of wildlife. Most districts pay ward dividends annually in arrears. Wards allocate this revenue to management, ward projects and household dividends. Management at the ward level consists of salaries for ward employees (fence and resource monitors), allowances and costs for meetings and travel by committee members, and repairs and maintenance to ward facilities (for example, electric fences). The types and the value of the projects undertaken at the ward level using money from wildlife vary considerably between wards. Projects can usually be classed as either income-generating projects (for example, grinding mills) or the construction of social facilities (for example, school buildings and clinics). Depending on the potential cash dividend per household, the past agricultural season and the attitude of district officials, some wards have paid cash dividends directly to households.[5]

Income Earned at District Level from Wildlife (1989–96)

Between 1989 and 1996 the revenue earned and retained by RDCs with Appropriate Authority exceeded US$9.3 million (Z$66 million). More than 90 per cent of the total revenue has been earned from the lease of sport-hunting rights to commercial safari operators (Table 15.1). Income from the lease of tourism rights, the sale of hides and ivory and other minor resources (crocodile and ostrich eggs, firewood) provided the balance of the income earned. The future role of tourism in CAMPFIRE is interesting. On receipt of Appropriate Authority status many RDCs were able to roll over existing leases with safari operators. For those with low wildlife densities sport-hunting was the obvious entry point into the commercial use of wildlife. However, as shown by Mahenye Ward, sport hunting and international tourism activities can be integrated at a local level. This has substantially increased both their direct (financial) and indirect (facilities, employment) incentives for institutional change (see Murphree, Chapter 12, this volume). There are other wards in a similar situation and with effective local level planning, links with a strong and motivated commercial sector partner and co-operation from DNPWLM, they too could diversify into international tourism. However, it must be noted that tourism projects in communal lands face strong competition from commercial operations located in strategic positions within the parks and wildlife estates (e.g. Hwange and Mana Pools National Parks), the commercial farming sector (Save Valley Conservancy, Gwaai Valley ICA) and prime wildlife-based tourist destinations elsewhere in the region (e.g. Okavango

Table 15.1 Income earned by RDCs with Appropriate Authority for wildlife between 1989 and 1996

	Sport-hunting leases	Tourism leases	Sale of hides and ivory	Other	Total income
1989–96 (US$)	8,653,211	176,970	147,741	395,044	9,372,966
1989–96 (Z$)	61,783,227	1,342,801	867,637	2,252,390	66,246,055
% of total by activity	93	2	1	3	100

Source: WWF, Harare, CAMPFIRE database.

Delta, Botswana). Unfortunately, current examples of community-based tourism or non-lease tourism, have proved not to be financially viable and seem unlikely to drive processes of institutional change.

There is significant variation in the revenue earned by participating districts. Since 1990, more than 50 per cent of the total recorded revenue has been earned by three RDCs: Binga, Guruve and Nyaminyami. At the national level, the substantial nominal increases in revenue earned through CAMPFIRE are largely attributable to the increase in the number of districts with Appropriate Authority between 1989 and 1996, the 372 per cent devaluation of the Zimbabwean dollar[6] and marginal changes in the number of animals on sport-hunting quotas. In addition, the competitive and market-based methods adopted by districts for allocating wildlife leases resulted in a real increase of approximately 11 per cent in the efficiency of the use of sport-hunting leases (Bond 1999).

The tourism and sport-hunting markets

The comparative economic advantage of wildlife lies with its aesthetic uses, either in the form of sport hunting or wildlife-based tourism (Child 1988). Sustainable rural development, however, is predicated on stable and strong markets (Gittinger 1972). It has been argued that the markets for hunting and wildlife-based tourism are both thin and risky and may compromise the conservation and development objectives of CBNRM (Barrett and Arcese 1995).

Tourism in Zimbabwe is primarily 'nature based' (Kaufmann 1992). The number of visitors to Zimbabwe is determined primarily by domestic social, economic and political stability (Moore 1990; Exa 1992; Heath 1992; Child, GFT 1995). Between 1980 and 1994, the gross number of visitors to Zimbabwe increased by 325 per cent, from 268,000 to 1.2 million (Bond 1997). This is frequently used to support the argument that tourism is a 'boom industry'. However, other indicators depict a much more uncertain environment for the demand for Zimbabwean tourist products. For example: the average length of stay of visitors declined from 12 to 5 days over the same period while real visitor expenditure per capita declined by 9 per cent between 1980 and 1991 (ibid.). Investment in the tourism sector has resulted in a 63 per cent increase in the total number of bed nights available in the country between 1980 and 1994, which is consistent with the general proposition that tourism has been the fastest growing sector of the economy in recent times (Muir et al. 1996).

The analysis of the demand for sport-hunting is constrained by the limited data on the sector. Between 1984 and 1993, the recorded value of sport-hunting in Zimbabwe increased from US$2 million to US$12 million per annum and the total number of recorded days of sport-hunting increased from 4,255 to 14,142 (Bond 1997). The average daily rate paid by visiting sport hunters increased in real terms by 16 per cent between 1987 and 1993, while the annual average trophy fees for animals killed or wounded increased by between 34 per cent and 183 per cent depending on the species. Overall the value of the average hunt paid by visiting sport hunters increased from US$6078 in 1986 to US$9970 in 1993 (ibid.).

The limited data available appear to indicate that at the national level the markets for tourism and sport hunting have strengthened over the 1990s.[7] Previously, international (CITES) and national (US Endangered Species Act) legislative changes posed a significant threat to elephant sport hunting which constituted approximately 54 per cent of total sport hunting revenue to RDCs with Appropriate Authority (Bond 1997). These have receded substantially due to the de-listing of elephant from Appendix I to Appendix II by CITES, in 1997. Maintenance of domestic, political and social stability, especially in the context of the current economic depression and regional political instability, appears to be the primary factor which will determine the demand for both tourism and sport-hunting products in the medium term.[7]

The Allocation of the Revenue Earned from Wildlife (1989–96)

Five categories have been defined for the analysis of the allocation of revenue earned by RDCs from wildlife. These are: revenue disbursed to sub-district levels (wards), revenue allocated to wildlife and programme management, revenue retained by RDCs in the form of levies, other CAMPFIRE and/or wildlife-related uses and unallocated revenue. As the holders of Appropriate Authority, rural district councils are not obliged to devolve revenue to sub-district levels but are encouraged to do so in the 'spirit of CAMPFIRE'. The CAMPFIRE Guidelines (1991 and 1992) have sought to ensure that producer communities are the primary beneficiaries of the revenue earned. The 1991 Guidelines recommended that at least 50 per cent of gross wildlife revenue should be devolved to ward level, up to 35 per cent could be allocated to wildlife management and that up to 15 per cent could be retained by the RDC for programme management. Between 1989 and 1996 just over 53 per cent, or Z$35 million of the total revenue earned, has been allocated to wards, some Z$14 million to wildlife management and a little over Z$8 million has been retained in the form of a RDC levy (Table 15.2). Significantly, over Z$6 million remains unallocated. It is generally assumed that this revenue has been allocated to activities not related to wildlife and CAMPFIRE.

Table 15.2 The allocation of revenue from wildlife by RDCs between 1989 and 1996

	Disbursed to sub-district levels wards)	Wildlife and programme management	Council levy	Other uses	Unallocated
1989–96 (US$)	4,895,527	2,060,913	1,210,545	217,996	987,985
1989–96 (Z$)	35,187,665	14,443,401	8,807,320	1,252,310	6,303,700
% of total by activity	53	22	13	2	10

Source: WWF Harare, CAMPFIRE database.

The financial benefit measured at the district and household level

Within the current CAMPFIRE framework where revenue is collected and then disbursed by the RDC, the incentives for institutional change need to be considered at both the district and the household level.

District level incentives for institutional change

RDCs are financed by a combination of locally generated revenue and grants from central government. Characteristically they are cash-strapped organizations whose responsibilities usually exceed their total incomes (de Valk and Wekwete 1990; Owen and Maponga 1996). On average, for those district councils with Appropriate Authority, central government grants accounted for 35 per cent of total revenue with 65 per cent being locally generated (derived from Hlatshwayo 1992). This is substantially higher than the national average of locally generated revenue to total revenue, which has been estimated at 15 per cent (de Valk and Wekwete 1990).

The modal class of wildlife income compared with both total and locally generated income from sources other than wildlife was 0–24 per cent (Table 15.3).[8] However, the comparison shows that in two cases the income from wildlife exceeded all other income to the RDCs and in eight cases exceeded all other locally generated income. The data suggest that wildlife is an important and significant source of revenue to some districts which justifies the substantial investments at district level in wildlife management and production (Murindagomo 1997). This finding is supported by other data.[9] It has been proposed that the proportion of wildlife revenue disbursed is inversely proportional to its relative importance to the district *fiscus* (Hasler 1994) but statistically there is no significant relationship between the variables, suggesting that the proportion of revenue devolved is determined by a complex, dynamic and constantly changing set of variables (Bond 1999).

Table 15.3 Annual wildlife revenue as a proportion of total district income and of locally generated revenue between 1989 and 1993

	0–24%	25–49%	50–74%	75–100%	>100%
Total district income	26	10	6	2	2
Total local income	21	9	2	6	8

Source: Bond, 1999.

Actual benefit per household from wildlife

The total number of households resident in the wards which have received wildlife revenue has increased from approximately 8280 in 1989 to 102,000 in 1995 (Figure 15.2). The financial benefit per household (ward dividend/number of households) between 1989 and 1996 is low and positively skewed. In real terms the median benefit per household from wildlife declined from US$19.40 in 1989 to US$4.49 in 1996. In part the decline is caused by the decreasing wildlife production potential

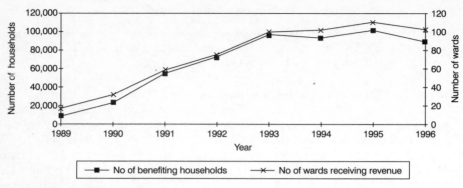

Source: WWF, Harare, CAMPFIRE database.

Figure 15.2   Number of wards with households benefiting from wildlife revenue 1989–96

in the growing number of wards participating in CAMPFIRE. The results show that in 50 per cent of wards which received wildlife revenue in 1996, the financial benefit per household was US$4.49 or less (Figure 15.3).

The financial benefits from wildlife relative to gross agricultural production
At the household level the financial viability of wildlife, and implicitly the necessary conditions for institutional change, have most commonly been defined with

Year	1989	1990	1991	1992	1993	1994	1995	1996
Upper Quartile	34.47	14.91	9.95	13.73	13.48	10.97	12.36	11.41
Median	19.4	7.75	5.97	5.89	5.63	3.88	5.19	4.49
Lower Quartile	14.73	4.07	2.8	3.4	1.08	1.79	3.1	2.17

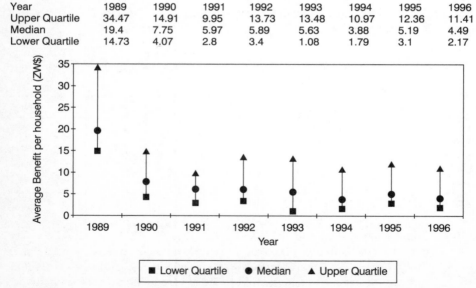

Source: Ibid.

Figure 15.3   Frequency distribution of actual average benefit per household by ward 1989–96

reference to other sources of household income. It has been suggested that for wildlife to be viable, it must satisfy the criteria of peasant accumulation (Murombedzi 1994; Chapter 16, this volume). An alternative definition proposes that under conditions of weak proprietorship the financial benefits from wildlife need to exceed agricultural income for it to be considered viable (Murphree 1991). Muir et al. (1996, p. 17) focus on the opportunity cost of unsettled and uncultivated land and propose that 'if agricultural incomes cannot be improved with wildlife then the best option is to eliminate wildlife and encourage immigrants and cattle'.

The distribution of the comparison of the financial benefit per household and an index of gross agricultural income[10] across all wards between 1989 and 1993 is positively skewed (Figure 15.4). In 1990, 1992 and 1993, the median of wildlife benefit as a percentage of gross agricultural income was less than 10 per cent. In 1989, when CAMPFIRE consisted of only two districts and 15 wards, the median was 17 per cent. Significantly in 1991, following one of the severest droughts on record,[11] the median was 21 per cent. In this year the relative importance of wildlife revenue increased due to the severe decline in agricultural production. The implication is that in most wards the financial benefit per household from wildlife revenue is low and in most years constitutes less than 10 per cent of gross agricultural production. In terms of the proposed definitions of the financial viability of wildlife it appears that in most wards wildlife is not financially viable at the household level. Consequently, in most wards, the current financial incentives for institutional change for sustainable management of wildlife and wildlife habitat are low.

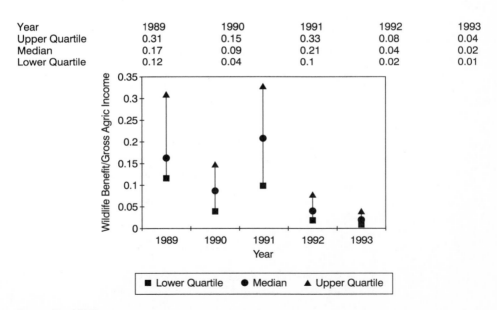

Year	1989	1990	1991	1992	1993
Upper Quartile	0.31	0.15	0.33	0.08	0.04
Median	0.17	0.09	0.21	0.04	0.02
Lower Quartile	0.12	0.04	0.1	0.02	0.01

Source: Bond 1999.

Figure 15.4   The distribution of the financial benefit from wildlife as a percentage of gross agricultural income at household level by year

Factors Constraining Financial Incentives for Change

Institutional change under CAMPFIRE is predicated on the financial incentives earned from wildlife. As illustrated above in many wards these are low. This is the result of both institutional and bio-physical factors.

Institutional constraints to maximizing financial incentives for change

The conditions under which Appropriate Authority was granted to district councils were: that they demonstrate sufficient capacity to manage wildlife; that communities should be fully involved in decision-making; and that the benefits would accrue directly to those communities which produced the benefits and incurred the costs of management (Peterson 1991a).

The CAMPFIRE Guidelines (1991 and 1992) for the use and allocation of wildlife revenue were issued by DNPWLM to protect wildlife-producer community interests in the absence of strong and well-defined property rights over wildlife. At the national level approximately 53 per cent of total wildlife revenue has been devolved from district to sub-district levels since 1989 (see Table 15.2). However, the district level analysis of the proportion of wildlife revenue devolved is characterized by a high level of inter-district variability (coefficient of variation 39 per cent). Further, within districts there is also a high degree of variability in the proportion of annual wildlife revenue disbursed (coefficient of variability 37 per cent). The implications of the high inter- and intra-district variability are twofold. Firstly, there has been a substantial reduction in the financial incentive at the household level to participate in collective decision-making and management. Secondly, the variability implies that there is still only weak ward level proprietorship over the financial benefits derived from wildlife, let alone the wildlife resource itself.

The conditions of Appropriate Authority also required district councils to devolve wildlife revenue to those communities which produced the benefits and incurred the costs of management. This has been termed the 'producer community principle' and operationally it means that hunting revenue is allocated to the wards in which animals are shot. Nationally, the number of RDCs using the producer community principle, or a derivative thereof, increased from one in 1989 to nine by 1996. Thus, contrary to the weak proprietorship indicated by the high levels of inter- and intra-district variability, the adoption of the producer community principle implies some level of sub-district proprietorship. This is particularly important within the context of the policy often advocated by the Ministry of Local Government Rural and Urban Development (MLGRUD) that 'wildlife revenue should be used for district-wide development' (Chiwewe 1994).

It can be concluded that the CAMPFIRE Guidelines have been largely ineffective at protecting sub-district organizations in the management of wildlife and wildlife-based revenues and that they are not a substitute for strong and well-defined legislation giving sub-district organizations control over wildlife revenue. Consequently, the incentives for institutional change at the household level have been substantially reduced by the resistance of RDCs to devolve wildlife revenue. Further, the failure to devolve legal authority over wildlife to sub-district levels has meant that most producer communities have remained largely passive recipients of revenue transferred to them by RDCs. Recently, this weakness has allowed government to attempt to implement a substantial and significant recentralization of CAMPFIRE and proprietorship over wildlife and wildlife revenue at the RDC level (see Government of Zimbabwe SI 38/98).

Bio-physical constraints to maximizing financial incentives for institutional change

The loss of wildlife habitat to human settlement has consistently been identified as the major factor contributing to the decline of African wildlife populations (Parker and Graham 1989). The relationship between human population (independent variable) and elephant densities (dependent variable) in Zimbabwe has been postulated as a linear relationship.[12] It predicts that at human population densities greater than 19 persons km² there will be no elephants (ibid.). Investigations of the relationship between human population density and wildlife-derived revenue (a proxy for wildlife populations and corrected for production) between 1989 and 1993 showed no statistically significant linear relationship. An alternative but statistically weak (r^2=0.38) non-linear model between human population density and wildlife-derived revenue at the ward level has been proposed (Bond 1999). The model suggests that at very low human population densities and all other factors being held constant, the producer wards can earn very high levels of wildlife income (Figure 15.5). However, a marginal increase in human population density can cause a substantial fall in wildlife revenue. Beyond a point of transition at approximately 9–10 persons km², revenue derived from wildlife appears to be independent of human population density. The first section of the model implies that in the semi-arid communal lands there is intense competition between people and wildlife, particularly mega-herbivores, for key resources. Spatial analysis of settlement patterns in the Zambezi Valley between 1963 and 1993, shows that new settlement tends to be concentrated along the alluvial soils of the major drainage lines (Cumming and Lynam 1997). The model suggests that at human population densities greater than 10 persons km² revenue earned from wildlife is largely based on opportunistic use of wildlife populations of adjacent state protected areas or other communal lands of low human population density.

The model suggests that wards in CAMPFIRE can be differentiated into wildlife producers and wildlife users. This has important implications for land-use planning and re-organization for these wards. Planned settlement and mechanisms to restrict illegal settlement in those wards which currently have low human population densities will have a very high benefit:cost ratio. If wildlife is to continue as an important part in the development and future economies of these wards, then human population issues and particularly immigration and settlement pattern will have to be planned. However, in those wards which already have a high human population density, even substantial reductions in human population density are likely to have only a marginal impact on the revenue earned from wildlife. Thus, the allocation of land for wildlife will have a very low or even negative return.

Organizations supporting CAMPFIRE need to recognize the implications of this finding. Most importantly it implies that different approaches are needed between those wards which are genuine wildlife producers and those wards which are opportunistically harvesting wildlife produced in adjacent state protected areas. In these

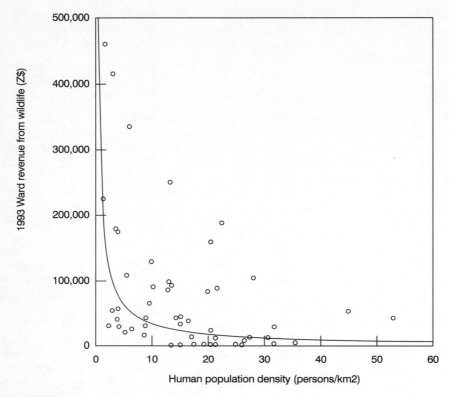

Source: Bond 1999.

Figure 15.5 Population density and ward revenue from wildlife (1993)

latter wards an approach closer to standard park outreach approaches may be most effective (see Barrow and Murphree, Chapter 3, this volume, for a discussion of park outreach). However, these programmes will only succeed if the DNPWLM adopts a more conciliatory approach to private and communal wildlife producers than is currently being witnessed (Bond 1998). Tangible steps which could be taken include concessionary pricing agreements for private sector development in communal lands adjacent to protected areas and usufruct rights over certain resources (i.e. thatching grass) in the protected areas. While such policies might reduce revenue to DNPWLM in the short term, the long-term benefits of an effective park outreach policy should be reflected in lower law and order costs.

Land-use Decisions: The Primary Indicator of Institutional Change

It has been proposed that, in the Zimbabwean context, one of the most important indicators of institutional change for the management of wildlife and wildlife habitat is the allocation of, or maintenance of, land for wildlife production (Bond 1999). Since the devolution of Appropriate Authority to RDCs substantial areas of land have been allocated or maintained under wildlife management. The total area under some form of wildlife management in the communal areas has been estimated at 36,000 km² (Taylor 1998). However, many of these land–use decisions have been made and enforced by RDCs with little or no support from sub-district levels.[13] Examples of these are: Mavuradonha Wilderness Area (Muzarabani RDC) and the Gokwe Wildlife Corridor (Gokwe North RDC). In other districts, areas demarcated by RDCs for wildlife production have been subject to intense pressure from immigrants and settlement, for example: Omay Communal Land (Nyaminyami RDC), Dande Communal Land (Guruve RDC) and Mukwichi Communal Land (Hurungwe RDC). For RDCs the danger of this approach is that it could easily lead to the creation of RDC-managed protected areas on communal land. While the short-term returns on this might currently be positive, the alienation of communal land residents would ultimately lead to law enforcement costs which exceed the benefits and destroy both the potential financial and the conservation benefits.

The paucity of sub-district land-use decisions which favour wildlife suggests that in many wards the economic incentives for institutional change are weak. Consequently, a wide spectrum of stakeholders, including the residents, perceive wildlife habitat to be under–utilized. Additionally, the wildlife present in these areas results in direct and indirect costs for those living on the wildlife–settlement interface (see Emerton, Chapter 14, this volume for a discussion). As a result, in many parts of Zimbabwe, and especially in the Zambezi Valley, wildlife habitat continues to be converted for settlement and cultivation as Murombedzi (Chapter 16, this volume) describes.

Within CAMPFIRE, Kanyurira Ward (Guruve RDC) and Mahenye Ward (Chipinge RDC) are frequently cited as two successful examples of local level land-use planning and institutional change for wildlife (Peterson 1991b; Murphree 1995, 1997a and, Chapter 12, this volume). The social (homogeneity, leadership) and bio-physical (location, isolation, population density, settlement patterns and wildlife numbers) characteristics of the wards are atypical, and unlikely to be replicated elsewhere in Zimbabwe (Cutshall 1989). In addition, and in part due to the unique combination of bio-physical factors, the average benefit per household from wildlife revenue exceeded the index of gross agricultural production in four out of five years between 1989 and 1993 (Bond 1999). There is little doubt that there has been significant institutional change within these wards towards the management of both wildlife and wildlife habitat. Indicators of this change are: an effective constitution defining community membership; a substantial investment in local monitoring of wildlife abundance, sport hunting and illegal activity; graduated sanctions for those violating the rules; and an increased capacity for self-organization and self-determination (Murphree 1997a).

Exogenous constraints to institutional change

This chapter has proposed that institutional change is primarily a function of relative economic returns. There are, however, numerous other endogenous and exogenous variables which also affect the rate and direction of institutional change (Bromley and Cernea 1989). Examples of endogenous variables which may influence institutional change are leadership, population growth, social and economic stratification. Two key exogenous variables are the enabling legislative framework for institutional change and the challenges to nascent community-based organizations that arise from macro-economic performance.

The probability of institutional change without strong and well-defined property rights at the community level is very low (Bromley 1994; Hanna et al. 1995). The enabling legislation for the use and control of most natural resources in the communal lands is fragmented, resource-specific and vests control in either central or local government. The legislation does provide for subsistence use of resources by households but criminalizes most commercial uses of natural resources. Consequently local communities have no commercial rights to natural resources on any land owned by the state, which includes the communal lands (Wood 1991).

As argued earlier, the enabling legislation for CAMPFIRE primarily empowers the RDC and the devolution of wildlife revenue to producer communities takes place only under the 'spirit of CAMPFIRE'. The result of vesting Appropriate Authority at the district level is that the units of responsibility and rights are not consistent. Thus while communities are expected to be responsible for the management of wildlife and wildlife habitat, they have few if any legal rights over that wildlife (see Barrow and Murphree, Chapter 3, this volume, for a discussion).

The importance and significance of land tenure reform for the success of CAMPFIRE was noted in the original CAMPFIRE proposal (Martin 1986). The legacy of the racially biased allocation of land by colonial governments is that the distribution of land between large-scale commercial farming and communal sectors generally overshadows the issue of land allocation and tenure within the communal lands (World Bank 1991). However the latter is arguably as great, if not a greater problem, than the distribution of land between sectors (Ncube 1996). Land tenure has been politicized to such an extent by successive governments that the current status of communal tenure does not reflect the land-holding practices of black Zimbabweans. Consequently, throughout the communal lands the allocation and use of land in the communal areas is characterized by conflict which has been exacerbated by the 'acute breakdown in administrative structures and the erosion of authority and responsibility' (Rukuni 1994).

Current macro-economic conditions together with the high population growth rate and the failure of the government to adequately address the issue of resettlement has meant that the demand for land is very high. Consequently, in many communal areas *de facto* access to land and the control of natural resources varies from open access to weak common property. This does not represent the conditions necessary for institutional change: for institutional change that strengthens common property, strong and well-defined property rights are required.

In Zimbabwe, the weakening macro-economic performance poses one of the most significant challenges to the institutional change that CAMPFIRE seeks to promote. A simple macro-economic land-use model predicts that under conditions of increasing population, cultivation and settlement will expand into low potential lands until the marginal returns from the rural home base (agriculture and natural resources) are lower than the marginal urban wage rate (Hartwick and Olewiler

1986). Between 1980 and 1994, the proportion of the total population of Zimbabwe in formal employment fell from 14 per cent to 11 per cent. Within the four main sectors (agriculture, manufacturing, domestic and administration) and over the same period real wages have declined by between 24 and 65 per cent. As a result, since 1989 the proportion of employees by sector, earning less than the minimum consumption needs of a family of two adults and four children, has increased from 39 per cent to 67 per cent (derived from Mundy 1995). Under such economic conditions, a secure rural home base from which the household's labour pool can be managed and income supplemented by harvesting natural resources is essential to its survival (Low 1986).

The uncertain and conflicting legislation governing the allocation of land has facilitated the expansion of unplanned settlement into many areas previously considered as wildlife habitat. In the Zambezi Valley between 1983 and 1993, the annual average rate of increase in the area of settlement and agriculture was 12 per cent (Cumming and Lynam 1997). It has been predicted that the conditions which will reduce the demand for land in the communal areas, namely greater industrialization and lower population growth, is 'still three or so decades away' (Reynolds 1991). The high demand for land and natural resources constitutes the major exogenous challenge to the emerging institutions for the management of wildlife and wildlife habitat under CAMPFIRE.

Conclusions and Policy Implications for CAMPFIRE

This chapter has pointed out that the role of economic incentives is central to the process of institutional change under CAMPFIRE and other CBNRM programmes (see also Emerton, Chapter 14, this volume). The financial data presented have shown that there are significant incentives at the district level for the management of wildlife in the communal lands of Zimbabwe. The observed increase in the investment in wildlife management by RDCs supports this observation. However, positive examples of substantive institutional change at sub-district levels (i.e. the ward) are very few. At this level the common limiting factor appears to be the marginal economic incentives derived from wildlife. The implication is that the net benefits which would be realized from institutional change either do not exceed, or only marginally exceed, the benefits from the old institutions (or lack of institutions). In contrast, the experience of Kanyurira Ward and Mahenye Ward (Murphree, Chapter 12, in this volume) has shown that under conditions of very high financial incentives institutional change is both possible and may be sustainable. For such wards it is probable that the net benefit of the new institutions is much larger than the net benefit from the old institutions. The proposed relationship between human population density and the revenue earned from wildlife at the scale of the ward implies that substantial increases in the economic incentives derived solely from wildlife are severely limited. However, it is important to recognize that the institutional changes required for the effective management of wildlife and wildlife habitat are also being constrained by the limited proprietorship granted to sub-district levels and the poor performance of the Zimbabwean economy.

These observations have important policy implications for CAMPFIRE and for other CBNRM programmes.

1. It is only under a combination of exceptional circumstances that the financial incentives from wildlife alone are likely to be sufficient to promote institutional change. This implies that the diversification of CBNRM programmes into other natural resources which can realize both market and non-market incentives is essential to raise the incentives for institutional change.
2. The enabling legislation for CBNRM programmes must aim to achieve a much higher level of proprietorship at the community level. Under CAMPFIRE, Appropriate Authority has allowed RDCs to tax wildlife producer communities at a rate close to 50 per cent. The non-binding 'CAMPFIRE Guidelines' have not been effective in controlling proprietorship over wildlife revenue to sub-district levels. Despite the progress and lessons learned from CAMPFIRE, natural resource legislation still invests proprietorship in the state thereby marginalizing those living with and using natural resources. Consequently, there is a poor fit between the units of management, benefit and responsibility.
3. High population growth and declining economic performance have placed almost unbearable pressure on the process of institutional change. Falling real incomes have forced, and will continue to force, both rural and urban house-holds to exploit natural resource capital as their only possible alternative. Under these conditions effective institutional change for the management of natural resources will be very difficult to achieve.

Despite this negative, economics-focused assessment of the potential of CAMPFIRE to achieve institutional change, it is still important to recognize that due to the programme the rate of loss of wildlife habitat has been substantially reduced in many areas. This has effectively maintained the option for institutional change for the management of wildlife and other natural resources which was being rapidly fore-closed before CAMPFIRE was initiated.

Notes

[1] This chapter differentiates between institutions and organizations as follows: institutions include any form of constraint that human beings devise to shape their interaction. They constitute the 'rules of the game'. Organizations are groups of individuals bound by some common purpose to achieve a given objective (North 1990).

[2] Effective Appropriate Authority status was granted to Nyaminyami and Guruve Districts in 1989 by the Minister of Natural Resources. In 1991, Appropriate Authority was formally granted to 12 districts (SI 12 and 61 of 1991). A further 15 districts received Appropriate Authority between 1991 and 1996; however, of these only three have recorded revenue from wildlife.

[3] Between 1989/90 and 1996/97 there have been five agricultural seasons in which the national rainfall has been below the 90-year national mean (Department of Meteorological Services).

[4] Between 1982/83 and 1992/93 the Government of Zimbabwe distributed more than 1.2 million tonnes of drought relief maize in communal lands (Ministry of Social Welfare 1994).

[5] Between 1989 and 1993, approximately 10% of the total revenue devolved to sub-district level was paid in the form of cash household dividends in six districts. The payment of household dividends has been the subject of significant controversy between DNPWLM and the Ministry of Local Government Rural and Urban Development (Bond 1999).

[6] Average annual exchange rate (Z$: US$)

1989	1990	1991	1992	1993	1994	1995	1996
2.126	2.472	3.751	5.112	6.529	8.212	8.724	10.027

[7]Since writing this paper Zimbabwe's political stability has declined. The country has become a participant in the conflict in the DRC, inflation and unemployment have risen, commercial farms have been seized and President Mugabe is seen as increasingly out of touch with socio-economic conditions by many commentators.

[8]In the absence of financial data for all districts with Appropriate Authority, both local and total income has been extrapolated from 1989/90 income derived from Hlatshwayo (1992). The model assumes revenue to have remained constant in real terms. Tested against actual income for selected districts the model had an r^2 of 0.82 and was thus considered valid.

[9]Statements such as 'in every financial year since 1980 game proceeds have constituted between 45% and 50% of the district council budget (pp2) ... council is further confident that the Mavuradonha Wilderness Area (MWA) would be viable and will ultimately be the largest money spinner for the council' (Chipadza, SEO, Muzarabani DC, 03–06–1991) or 'this area [the wildlife corridor] is so valuable as a goldmine for the council and the wildlife should not be disturbed' (Gokwe North RDC, Wildlife Board of Management, WBOM 23–09–95).

[10]The index of gross agricultural production was derived from the AGRITEX second estimate of areas and yields by communal land. The index is of gross agricultural production and does not consider the costs of crop production. The index also assumes an income of 5% of the total value of livestock held. A similar methodology has been used to determine the vulnerability of communal lands to drought (see Eilerts 1994; Eilerts and Vhurumuku 1997). The index was preferred to alternative sources of agricultural data (for example the Annual Ministry of Lands and Agriculture *Household Survey*, 1990, 1991, 1992, 1993) because it allowed comparisons to be made across all the benefiting CAMPFIRE wards using a standard methodology.

[11]National average rainfall for 1991/92 agricultural season was 49% of the 90-year mean.

[12]These relationships are scale-dependent. At a micro level the relationship between human settlement and the presence of elephant has been shown to be exclusive, i.e. the settlement precludes the presence of elephant. However, given undisturbed habitat, elephant will live in very close proximity to human settlements (Hoare 1997).

[13]Patel (1998) cites such examples as a case of 'the CAMPFIRE Programme' breaching fundamental human rights. While many people associated with CAMPFIRE believe that the argument she makes is both inaccurate and whipped up to raise emotions, they are equally concerned about RDCs imposing decisions on rural people, such as forced relocation, that adversely affect their rights and livelihoods.

16

Committees, Rights, Costs & Benefits
Natural Resource Stewardship & Community
Benefits in Zimbabwe's CAMPFIRE Programme

JAMES MUROMBEDZI

Introduction

In the CAMPFIRE formulation, the resource management problems of the communal areas of Zimbabwe are the result of a lack of both the institutional capacity and the incentives to effectively manage natural resources. The CAMPFIRE solution is to introduce new systems of tenure and rights to natural resources for communities, and develop local institutions for resource management for the benefit of these communities (Martin 1986). The implementation of this solution was attained through an amendment to the Parks and Wild Life Act of 1975, which enables the government to delegate *appropriate authority* over wildlife to 'communal representatives'. The CAMPFIRE programme constitutes a transfer of the notion of non-state wildlife ownership, previously only availale to freehold landowners, to the residents of communal land (Farquharson 1993).

This chapter tests the extent to which CAMPFIRE has been able to devolve ownership of wildlife to people in the communal areas, and thereby promoted stewardship of wildlife through the production of benefits for the participating communities. To achieve this, I first evaluate the extent to which CAMPFIRE has succeeded in eliciting stewardship of the wildlife resource by participating communities through the devolution of clear rights to wildlife to these communities. This is critical, given that stewardship itself is a direct result of the nature of rights that communities have in the resources in question. To what extent, then, has CAMPFIRE successfully constituted resource tenure reform for the people on communal lands?

The second test seeks to establish the extent to which, in addition to rights and control, benefits generated in the CAMPFIRE programme have made wildlife management a part of local household economies. Thirdly, while individual household benefits are themselves important in determining investment decisions at the household level, typically these benefits are mediated by other factors such as community and other investments in infrastructure that affect the efficiency of the household economy. To this end, it will be necessary to evaluate how households invest the benefits they derive from wildlife, and assess the implications of these investments.

Zimbabwe's Communal Lands

The CAMPFIRE programme is designed for the 'communal' lands of Zimbabwe, and assumes that its goal will be achieved by creating strong communal tenure regimes over wildlife resources in those areas. Communal lands refer to those areas, formerly known as Reserves and later as Tribal Trust Lands, that were created for the African population when the colonial authorities expropriated lands for white settlers, sought to create labour reserves and sought to undermine African agriculture (Phimister 1986).

There continues to be considerable debate in Zimbabwe about the exact nature of the tenure system operating in the so-called communal areas today. According to Cheater (1989), the current definition of communal tenure in Zimbabwe is largely normative and based on an ideological construct, starting in the colonial era, to rationalize the racial division of land. It created an effective basis for the indirect control of land and natural resources by the colonial state through the chiefs. This has been continued by the post-colonial state to justify continued state control over land. It has also been observed that the current idea of communal tenure resulted from the colonial usurpation of land, and power over land, from the traditional chiefs, which created a power vacuum which the state was not anxious to fill, thus leading to local and consensual systems of land allocation and use (Ranger 1985, 1988). Drinkwater (1991) comments that the growing power of the colonial state from 1893 onwards was based on state control of land use and land tenure in a process in which land allocation was the state's central concern. Bruce (1998), and Scoones and Wilson (1989) maintain that the current system of allocating land to communities originated with the colonial government, rather than prior to it. In this view, the attachment of communities to a discrete piece of land was a function of the colonial system of indirect rule, which passed control over land to chiefs and headmen. Precolonial self-allocation of land (Bruce 1990), significant and recurring inequalities in land holding size among the indigenous African population (Ranger 1985, 1988), and African readiness to purchase land in freehold areas (Bourdillon 1987), are cited to argue that the communal nature of land tenure in Zimbabwe's communal areas may have been overstated.

The Communal Lands Act of 1982 vests ownership of communal lands and resources with the state and assigns rural district councils (RDCs) the power to regulate land holding and land use in the communal areas under their jurisdiction. According to the Act, access and occupation of communal land is in terms of the customary law. Rural district councils regulate land use in terms of communal land by-laws produced by the Ministry of Local Government, which provides for the planning and control of land use within council areas. In some RDCs, the constituency also includes owners and occupiers of alienated lands, held under private freehold or leasehold tenure. In such cases, the RDC has a very different relationship with the private landholders. In particular, private landholders have full control over the planning and use of the land to which they hold title or lease. The role of the RDC in this system is merely to provide services.

The CAMPFIRE Programme

The National Parks and Wild Life Act (1975), as amended in 1982, gives appropriate authority over wildlife to the RDCs for the communal areas, and to the landowners for the private/leasehold tenure sector. Communal residents typically do not determine how wildlife is going to be 'produced' and how the 'benefits' generated are to be utilized. These decisions are usually made by the RDC and other 'outsiders'. The level of benefit is thus affected by policy decisions over which the 'wildlife producers' themselves have little or no control (see Jones and Murphree, Chapter 4, this volume for a discussion of the history and characteristics of CAMPFIRE).

Moreover, communities also have to pay a variety of taxes and charges to the RDC for the management of 'their' wildlife (see Bond, Chapter 15, this volume for details). Communities do not have the right to use wildlife, only the right to benefit from the use of wildlife by others. Owners and occupiers of private lands, on the other hand, can decide on wildlife uses without any external influences, and are free to appropriate all the benefits of use, or to share some of these benefits with their communal lands neighbours in the case of 'conservancies'. In practice, appropriate authority has come to represent the decentralization of authority and control over wildlife only to the rural district councils.

A significant component of CAMPFIRE has been an institutional development programme aimed at creating new forms of communal organization for wildlife management. In practice, this has been implemented through the creation of village, ward and district wildlife management committees in a process led by the Zimbabwe Trust, a local NGO that has become the lead implementing agency for CAMPFIRE. The new committees are in effect sub-committees of the local government units, the Village Development Committee (VIDCO), the Ward Development Committee (WADCO) and the RDC. As such, they get their authority over wildlife through both the Parks and Wild Life Act and the Rural District Councils Act.

While this evolving institutionalization of wildlife management at the local level devolves some authority over the resource, it has not developed into a process for defining local rights over the wildlife resource. Management is based on RDC control over wildlife. As such, wildlife management has been completely divorced from other local systems of rights to communal resources. The institutional development programme has not attempted to identify existing ways by which communities manage other communal resources to which they have rights, and to define a place for wildlife management in this system of communal rights. Partly because of this, evidence suggests that most local people still do not view themselves as the joint owners of wildlife, but rather continue to see it as a resource belonging to either the government or the RDC (Murombedzi 1994). Because CAMPFIRE has focused on creating new 'formal' institutions, it has tended to ignore the important pre-existing 'traditional' institutions for land and resource management that exist in many communities in Zimbabwe. This is largely because, in the absence of clear rights to wildlife for the local communities, institutional development has been defined outside of the communities themselves, rather than responding to the internal micro-political dynamics within these communities. This lack of regard for local resource management decision-making mechanisms has contributed to the alienation of communities from the CAMPFIRE initiative.

Traditional authorities continue to play a leading role in managing and regulating the use of communal resources. Where resources are critical to the household economy, communities invest in their management (Scoones and Wilson 1989) and usually such management is undertaken through the operation of diffuse systems of rights, adjudicated locally by traditional leaders and authorities. Lack of recognition from government and programmes like CAMPFIRE has not compromised traditional leaders' authority, particularly over land and natural resources (Ahmed 1998). 'Traditional leadership draws much of its legitimate authority from its embeddedness in the social and cultural life of rural communities, where discourses of "tradition" associated with cultural identity are still persuasive for many' (Cousins 1998).

To the extent that institutional development in CAMPFIRE virtually ignores local rights and knowledge systems, it is informed by a centralizing and 'modernizing' ethic. This constitutes a huge contradiction in a programme that is supposedly creating community forms of resource ownership. Attempts are currently underway in CAMPFIRE to stimulate the further devolution of authority over wildlife from the RDCs to the 'producer communities' (CAMPFIRE News 1998: 8). The Tenure Reform Commission of 1994, for instance, recognizes that communal land tenure in Zimbabwe gives all rights to communal lands to the government. It recommends that new village assemblies be created as communal property associations with clear and unambiguous rights to communal lands and their resources. The Commission bases this recommendation on the operation of the CAMPFIRE programme, and its demonstration of the capacity of communities to control and manage resources over which they have clearly defined rights. However, as the foregoing section has demonstrated, the CAMPFIRE programme would itself benefit from the implementation of this recommendation if rights for local communities to wildlife were more clearly defined.

It would further appear that CAMPFIRE has not sufficiently devolved rights in wildlife to local communities to the extent where these communities can use these rights to gain an increased stake in the wildlife utilization enterprise at its multiple levels of value. Thus communities have little control over wildlife management, little or no equity in wildlife utilization, and very few opportunities to provide goods and services to the wildlife utilization industry. From this perspective, community participation in CAMPFIRE can be seen as constituting little more than the receipt of handouts.

The Benefits of the CAMPFIRE Programme and Population Growth

The quantification of the financial and economic benefits generated from wildlife utilization under the programme has been the subject of enquiry. Firstly, the general conclusion has been that CAMPFIRE revenues have contributed significantly to the well-being of participating communities. With a few exceptions (Bond 1997b;

Chapter 15, this volume; Murombedzi 1992, 1994), these conclusions have generally not compared the CAMPFIRE benefits with potential benefits from other land uses, nor have the opportunity costs of participating in the programme been questioned (see Emerton, Chapter 14, this volume, for a discussion of the full economic costs and benefits of community-based wildlife management). Secondly, very little empirical data exist on the costs that individual households in CAMPFIRE communities actually incur through wildlife predation, opportunity and transaction costs. Thirdly, individual households need to receive direct financial benefits from wildlife production as: 'unless the revenues from wildlife are translated into disposable individual or household incomes decisions on wildlife/livestock options will be skewed towards livestock even in situations where it is apparent that the wildlife option is collectively more productive' (Murphree 1997a: 22).

Benefit in CAMPFIRE has tended to be used to refer to the revenues that accrue to communities and RDCs from the utilization of the wildlife resources in specific geographic areas. Utilization usually takes the form of safari hunting with game cropping, photographic safari, and ecotourism ventures as minor sources of income (see Bond, Chapter 15, this volume). Typically, calculations of benefit do not include the revenues accruing to safari operators themselves, nor do they refer to the rights (or loss of them) accruing to communities. Obviously, the level of household benefit is affected by several factors, chief among which is population density. Wildlife populations are most dense in those areas where human population is sparse. Human population densities are also lowest in those areas where the pastoral and arable agricultural potential of the land is severely constrained by natural climatic factors, or by inadequate physical and other infrastructure, or both. These tend to be the marginal lands that are adjacent to national parks and other protected areas. Consequently, those wards with the lowest human population density and the highest wildlife densities also tend to have larger safari hunting operations. Because of this combination of factors, the households in these wards have, at least potentially, the highest revenues from safari hunting and other wildlife utilization operations (see also Bond, Chapter 15, this volume). Other factors that affect the level of revenue include the amount of the land available to the community, and especially the amount of community land that is 'wilderness'.

Masoka Ward in the Dande Communal Lands is regarded as the prime CAMPFIRE ward. Because of the extremely low population density and very high wildlife density (due to its proximity to the Mana Pools National Park) Masoka ward has one of the highest revenues of all the wards participating in the CAMPFIRE programme. However, a small increase in human population density is likely to reduce earnings considerably as humans compete with wildlife for key resources such as arable land and water and disturb elephants (Bond 1997a; Chapter 15, this volume). Consequently, households with significant proportions of their incomes accounted for by wildlife earnings would be expected to be motivated to manage population size. However, the contrary appears to be the case in CAMPFIRE wards with low human population densities and high wildlife revenues.

Because of the historical distribution of land in Zimbabwe, and also because of the shortcomings of the land reform programme in the first 18 years of independence, there has been a high rate of inter-rural migration between communal lands and, in particular, from the higher potential, more densely populated communal lands to the more marginal, less densely populated communal lands. While accurate figures on inter and intra-communal lands migration are not available, it is likely that more households have resettled themselves in other communal lands than have been officially relocated through the government resettlement programme. Spontaneous settlement in communal lands has occurred against official government policy and attempts by the RDCs to regulate land settlement and land use. The extent of such settlement is most marked in the CAMPFIRE programme areas.

Masoka, with one of the highest wildlife revenues per household in the programme, also has one of the highest rates of in-migration compared with other CAMPFIRE wards (Nabane 1997). Although the potential impacts of migrants on wildlife habitat have been stressed to the people of Masoka, they continue to strive to attract more people to come and settle in their ward, fully aware that this will have the effect of reducing the amount of revenue per household. Similar dynamics have been observed in the Dobola ward in Binga communal lands, which until recently was one of the major wildlife producing areas for Binga's CAMPFIRE programme. Between 1990 and 1993, this ward experienced an influx of more than 300 households (Dzingirai 1994). What are the implications of such dynamics and how do we explain the apparent anomaly between revenues and wildlife stewardship?

The people of Masoka argue that those who are settling in the area today are not new immigrants, but are mostly descendants of Masoka families who are 'coming back home' from wage labour employment. They also state that the few non-indigenous people settling in the ward are accepted mainly on compassionate and humanitarian grounds. However, field research revealed that most of the settlers are not descendants of Masoka families, and in many cases are retired immigrant labourers from Malawi and Zambia, or their descendants, who have decided to settle in Zimbabwe. When confronted with this evidence the people of Masoka admit that this is so, but argue that they are a very small community of only a few hundred households. Their children have to leave home to attend secondary school more than 100 km away because they are too few to warrant government investment in a secondary school. Their nearest neighbours are at least 60 km away, and no bus operator will send a bus to Masoka because there are just too few travellers to warrant a 120 km round trip. In any case, the road itself is impassable in the wet season as the government will not invest in its improvement because there are so few cotton growers in Masoka.

To initiate the CAMPFIRE programme, Masoka community erected a solar powered electric perimeter fence around an area of some 18 km² in 1991 to safeguard crops and livestock against wildlife predation. Today, the community wants to realign the fence to accommodate village expansion. Masoka people actively encourage settlement in their ward because it is the only way that they can quickly establish a large enough constituency to leverage 'development' from the government. The settlers themselves are agriculturalists, and so they open up land for agriculture and encroach into wildlife habitat. The long-term residents are fully aware of the potential impact of this human population on wildlife habitat, and therefore on their own wildlife revenues, but the 'development' option is more attractive to them as shown by their choice to encourage immigration despite the advice of researchers and development practitioners. From this example, we may argue that at least at this stage in the development of CAMPFIRE, participating communities view the programme as a temporary windfall to finance long-term development. Thus, even in those wards where CAMPFIRE revenues constitute a significant proportion of household incomes, wildlife habitat continues to be lost to agricultural expansion.

Immigration has also been occurring in other CAMPFIRE wards. The extent of immigration into the CAMPFIRE wards of Binga district, and the role of powerful politicians in facilitating this movement of people, is well documented (Dzingirai 1994). Earlier immigrants into Dobola ward in Binga subdivide their land to facilitate the settlement of new immigrants in order to minimize their own wildlife predation-related costs by displacing the wild animals. The Nyaminyami Rural District Council continues to launch paramilitary style raids, using armed CAMPFIRE game guards, to evict settlers from council lands. North Gokwe is rapidly becoming a very densely populated district, from a very low population density only a few years ago. In all these cases, the long-term residents not only encourage, but actually facilitate immigration, because of the perceived developmental benefits of higher population densities. If anything wildlife is perceived as the archetype of under-development for villagers, rather than a potential development resource.

The settlers are attracted into the CAMPFIRE areas by the eradication of tsetse fly, which makes agro-pastoralism less risky. The tsetse fly eradication programmes opened up roads in these previously unserviced areas, and thus provided some rudimentary infrastructure for potential colonists. Despite the low and erratic rainfall and poor soils of the Zambezi valley, overcrowding in other communal lands and the slow pace of land reform, there appear to be sufficient incentives for farmers to resettle into these marginal areas. Such farmers are attracted by the relative abundance of land in the valley and, like all settlers, they view wildlife as an asset that can be mined: valuable in subsidizing the process of settlement, but constituting an impediment to long-term investment. It also appears that long-term residents of the valley do not consider wildlife to constitute an important part of their own livelihoods, and as such they are prepared to forgo wildlife revenues by promoting immigration into their wilderness areas.

Another critical factor in many CAMPFIRE wards where there is a high rate of in-migration (Gokwe, Binga and Dande communal lands) is that all the areas are high cotton production areas. There has not been any attempt in CAMPFIRE research to measure systematically cash crop production in any of these wards and to compare it with wildlife revenues (with the exception of Bond's work in this volume). What has been demonstrated, however, is that most migrants into these areas are enterprising frontiersmen and women who wish to invest in cash crop and livestock production. Most of these settlers originate from other communal lands, where their own capacity to meet livelihood needs and accumulate capital through expanded cash crop and livestock production is severely constrained by land shortages due to the higher population (both human and livestock) densities in those lands. They thus see the 'less developed' and sparsely populated communal lands of the Zambezi valley as a place that offers both the land for cotton production as well as grazing for livestock (Dzingirai 1994; Derman 1990).

Migrants prefer to spontaneously settle in other communal lands rather than be formally resettled as a way of avoiding the perceived bureaucractic constraints of the resettlement programme. Surprising as it may seem, in all the CAMPFIRE communal lands, agricultural extension services continue to be geared towards encouraging the expansion of arable agriculture, rather than realigning land use to favour wildlife production. The tsetse fly eradication programmes of the Zambezi valley are justified on the basis of their potential to open up land for settlement and agricultural production. The huge mid-Zambezi Valley settlement scheme, for instance, was a policy response to spontaneous settlement in areas in which the fly had been eradicated. The scheme never had a wildlife production aspect until much later in its life (Derman 1990).

The relationship between the state and the communal landholders means that the state has retained control over communal lands. The implication of this for CAMPFIRE is that for such programmes to be effective, there has to be complete and unambiguous devolution of control over communal tenure to the residents themselves. In effect, the continuation of migration into communal lands, without the sanction of the RDC as the land authority (in fact even against the intentions of the RDCs), means that while the state may have retained putative control over communal lands, the communities themselves are able to determine land use. Given the inability of the state to control land use and land transfer in the communal lands, then, it would be logical for policy to promote increased community control over so-called communal lands, as recommended by the Land Tenure Commission of 1994.

Immigration into CAMPFIRE wards also demonstrates that even in most of the successful CAMPFIRE wards, wildlife benefits themselves are viewed as insufficient to permit residents to achieve their development goals. People participating in CAMPFIRE are prepared to degrade the wildlife resource in return for greater human population densities which in turn will result in central government policies that provide roads, schools and other infrastructure. Bond (1997b; Chapter 15, this volume) demonstrates that since 1989, CAMPFIRE revenues per household have actually been declining. The decline has been due mainly to the increase in the number of households participating in the programme. Case studies of household investment strategies demonstrate that most households in communal areas invest significant amounts of income into agricultural production (Murombedzi 1994). This study also demonstrates that, typically, household investment in agricultural production far exceeds the CAMPFIRE revenues, and that CAMPFIRE revenues tend to be significant only to the extent that they are invested in agricultural development. Thus most CAMPFIRE wards invest their revenues not to improve wildlife management and therefore increase wildlife revenues, but rather to improve agricultural productivity. Typical ward investments of CAMPFIRE revenues include purchases of tractors and the construction of warehousing facilities for agricultural inputs and produce, as well as investment in agricultural processing technology such as grinding mills.

It has been observed that attempts to entice people's participation in conservation through the distribution of revenues from resource utilization without at the same time devolving rights to these resources to local people will not necessarily improve local stewardship of resources, regardless of the scale of these revenues. In this view, 'such benefactions exacerbate the landowners' belief that they do, as an aspect of common sense and natural justice, have a prior right to both use and benefit from the natural resources on their land. Further, such benefit is inseparable from the powers of decision regarding general use that go with ownership' (Parker 1993: 3). Thus, for as long as local landowners do not have these powers of decision, wildlife utilization in CAMPFIRE will also be inferior to other forms of land and resource use over which the local communities and individual households exert significant levels of control. It is also evident that the implementation of CAMPFIRE alone cannot resolve the long-standing land problem in Zimbabwe. Instead, the immigration problem in CAMPFIRE should serve to highlight the need for effective land reform programmes to be implemented if conservation-based development is to succeed.

In addition to the problem associated with land distribution and the slow pace of land reform in Zimbabwe generally, it is evident that CAMPFIRE needs to start developing programmes by which those communities living on the boundaries of, and that can claim prior rights in, protected areas should participate in the management of such protected areas and directly benefit from them. Finally, the costs of loss of rights of access to the wildlife resource itself need to be considered in the equation. The focus of CAMPFIRE on high value forms of utilization continues to marginalize other local needs for wildlife utilization, such as hunting. Even when wildlife is cropped for local communities, the actual cropping is done by 'professionals' in orgies of butchery as in the Nyaminyami annual impala cropping programme (Murombedzi 1994). Such game cropping programmes should be community-based, which will cut costs and offer the communities opportunities to directly utilize the wildlife themselves. This can be done through licencing and monitoring systems that are controlled by the participating communities themselves.

Communities, Councils and the Safari Industry

Because of the weak tax base for most local authorities, wildlife has been treated as a taxable commodity. For this reason, and also because of the mistrust of local people by local government staff, it has become increasingly difficult to further devolve proprietorship of wildlife to local communities. The taxation of wildlife by district councils has significantly reduced the scale of local level financial and economic benefit, while at the same time facilitating continued local authority control over wildlife management (Bond, Chapter 15, this volume). The inevitable result has been that nowhere in CAMPFIRE has wildlife come to represent a viable mechanism for household level accumulation. Consequently, CAMPFIRE is not seen as significant for household incomes: its main economic role is to subsidize the local authorities.

In CAMPFIRE wildlife management continues to be driven, in the main, by external policy interests rather than responding to local dynamics stimulated by proprietorship. The RDCs with appropriate authority use this authority to provide services to a broad range of residents, as well as to control potentially negative local community activities such as livestock grazing and arable expansion. RDCs also serve to mediate conflicts between local and other resource users, as well as to regulate the conditions under which outsiders actually access the wildlife resources. In addition, the mitigation of local conflicts for access to the wildlife resource, expressed mainly through poaching, is a major function of the appropriate authority.

The CAMPFIRE focus on financial benefits emphasizes wildlife management for the purpose of supplying market demands for safari hunting and tourism. It thus focuses exclusively on large mammals while the management of other natural resources on which household livelihoods depend (perhaps even more so than on large mammals) is ignored. The greatest beneficiaries of the wildlife management services provided through CAMPFIRE are the safari operators who gain increased security of access to the wildlife, as well as protection from local community threats to wildlife through agriculture, poaching and so on. Yet communities do not manage natural resources in isolation. Systems of rights determining the management of natural resources are diffuse, yet CAMPFIRE attempts to introduce an exclusive wildlife management regime without reference to these diffuse and nested systems of rights and management.

Employment is often cited as one of the benefits of CAMPFIRE. However, there has been no attempt to document the number of jobs created in the different communities participating in the programme and it is evident that the safari industry is capital-intensive rather than labour-intensive. Furthermore, the actual management of wildlife by communities is undertaken by elected committees, rather than by dedicated organizations employing staff to undertake routine tasks. Thus most local people volunteer, rather than get employed, in wildlife management in the CAMPFIRE programme. The methods of wildlife utilization under CAMPFIRE are patently racist and alienate and humiliate local populations. The safari industry continues to be dominated by whites, with very little participation of blacks in the skilled worker categories (hunters and guides). The majority of black employees in the safari industry are cooks and camp attendants. The success of most safari hunts depends on the tracking skills and knowledge of the local trackers, who are an integral part of every safari operation. Yet these trackers are treated as unskilled labourers rather than recognized as qualified guides. Besides constituting another instance of the devaluation of local environmental knowledge, this treatment of local trackers also demonstrates the contempt with which local people tend to be regarded by white safari operators.

The historical reasons for the domination of the safari industry by whites go back to the appropriation of rights from the local population by the colonial state. The racist conditions under which the safari industry in Zimbabwe developed exist to this day almost unchanged. Further, in their desire to perpetuate the myth of a wild, pristine African experience for their clients, most safari operations prohibit all local access into the safari hunting camps except as lowly paid labourers. The livestock and dogs of local people are shot if they are seen as interfering with hunting operations (for they indicate the presence of human life in the 'pristine' wilderness). Individual safari operators also impose restrictions on local activities in the hunting areas, ranging from total prohibition of any form of access to some forms of negotiated access. This is only possible because of the lack of clarity of the nature of local rights to these resources in the CAMPFIRE programme. In the hunting operations themselves, where locals have insisted that members of the local communities should be attached to these hunting operations for monitoring or training purposes, there is no evidence that the so-called training programmes have resulted in any skills acquisition by the local people. To date, not a single community trainee in any of the CAMPFIRE training programmes has qualified as a guide. Locals attached to monitor the hunting operations are typically left stranded in the village due to lack of space for them in the hunting trucks, and consequently the communities remain suspicious about what actually goes on out in the bush. Where local guides and monitors actually participate in the hunt, the treatment they receive is often deplorable; they are viewed as a nuisance rather than an aspect of co-operation between safari operators and community.

The poverty facing rural households in Zimbabwe has been well documented. What are not as well documented, however, are the differential impacts of poverty on different households. One determining factor of such differentiation is micro-climatic conditions. The CAMPFIRE programme postulates that wildlife management is the most productive form of land use in marginal ecosystems. CAMPFIRE is thus being implemented predominantly in marginal ecosystems, where there continue to be viable wildlife populations, and where there are climatic limitations to arable agriculture and pastoralism. If CAMPFIRE is to become a viable land use in such areas, it must offer a potential solution for the crisis of accumulation to the residents of these areas. Accumulation means assigning social and economic resources to improving the production process, and has both qualitative and quantitative aspects. Quantitatively, accumulation means more implements, more land for arable agriculture, more marketing points, more inputs, and so on. Qualitatively, accumulation means the adoption of new and more sophisticated production technologies (mechanization, improved seed varieties, fertilizers, etc.), better land protection, and the allocation of land to more productive uses (Barker 1989).

Viewed through the lens of household accumulation the CAMPFIRE premise is that it will foster accumulation by allocating land to a more productive land use (wildlife utilization) and ensuring that the benefits of such land use accrue directly to the individual household. Consequently, the success of CAMPFIRE in stimulating household accumulation in the marginal ecosystems has to be tested against this premise. Wildlife management in CAMPFIRE, at least for the communities involved, means local programmes to enable the RDCs and communities to control arable expansion of agriculture, grazing and livestock, through collaboration in land-use planning. In a few cases, such as in Masoka, land-use planning is itself devolved to the local community, although this has been insufficient to stop the expansion of arable agriculture. Thus wildlife management defined in this way appears to entail the imposition of limitations on quantitative accumulation. There is evidence from the investment of CAMPFIRE dividends to demonstrate that accumulation for most households in the CAMPFIRE wards continues to be seen as a function of the expansion of arable agriculture and livestock. In most communal areas, this accumulation is dependent on access to off-farm incomes. Wildlife incomes on average are too small to constitute a source of capital for most CAMPFIRE households. However, at the community level, wildlife revenues can constitute a source of capital for qualitative accumulation, mainly through the investment of revenues in the provision of agricultural services (marketing points, warehouses, sources of inputs and food processing technology).

In quantitative terms the available evidence suggests that CAMPFIRE implementation has actually constituted a constraint on the ability of households to accumulate through arable expansion or the acquisition of livestock. This has occurred through restrictions on the importation of cattle and donkeys (for draught power) into those CAMPFIRE districts that did not have them because of tsetse fly infestation, as well as through restrictions on arable agricultural expansion through RDC land-use planning. Wildlife revenues have been used as a carrot to encourage individuals to conserve wildlife while land-use planning has been used as the stick to prevent the expansion of agriculture and to control domestic livestock.

Conclusion

In small, discrete, and relatively homogeneous communities with access to extensive wilderness, CAMPFIRE has been a success in terms of stimulating communities to demand more secure rights to the wildlife resources with local authorities. In such communities, it is evident that as community rights over resources become clearer and control enhanced, communities also begin to exert considerable influence over the actual utilization of the resource itself. The cases of Mahenye (see Chapter 12, this volume) and Masoka are especially instructive. According to Bond (1997b), 'there are a relatively small number of wards in which benefit per household is very high and comparable with average household income figures for households in semi-arid communal lands'. In such cases, CAMPFIRE appears to have been particularly successful as a means for qualitative accumulation. Wildlife revenues have been invested in the development of agricultural infrastructure and equipment, which in turn are seen as having the potential to improve the conditions for individual household quantitative accumulation.

Local valuations of CAMPFIRE relate to the ways in which CAMPFIRE revenues become available for individual household accumulation. Bond (1997b) further observes that 'in at least 50 per cent of the wards the revenue earned from wildlife can at best only be considered supplementary to other sources of income'. In such cases, it is debatable whether land-use allocation will be determined by local economic imperatives. It is more likely that the households in these wards are constrained by RDC policies to participate in wildlife management, and that the CAMPFIRE programmes in such wards are heavily contested. It is doubtful that in situations where wildlife management only contributes marginally to the local and household economies, individuals will be motivated to manage the wildlife beyond a certain minimum threshold, and that minimum threshold is determined by existing coercive measures through the appropriate authority, rather than by individual commitment to the resource. Where wildlife costs continue to be greater than the benefits, management of wildlife will continue to be top-down, authoritarian and coercive, and communities are not likely to seek greater rights to the wildlife resource. In such cases the top-down preferences of central government on communities have merely been replaced by the top-down preferences of local governments on communities.

PART SIX

Measuring & Monitoring Conservation

17

Can Community Conservation Strategies Meet the Conservation Agenda?

KADZO KANGWANA

Introduction

The last two decades have seen the evolution of conservation strategies from largely protectionist efforts to those which encourage the participation of local people in conservation (Anderson and Grove 1987; Kiss 1990; West and Brechin 1991; Western and Wright 1994b). This paradigm shift arose from the recognition that in many parts of the world the conservation of biodiversity is unattainable without the support of the people living in close proximity to the resources in question (McNeely 1984, 1989; Mackinnon et al. 1986). This rationale continues to provide strong argument for channelling resources into a myriad of conservation projects which encourage local participation and aim to meet local economic needs.

Attempting to increase support for and equitability of conservation is a step in the right direction. The ideal landscape would probably include people managing and using resources sustainably. However, in linking local communities with conservation, careful scrutiny of the assumptions being made is required to ensure rigour of action and to inform practice. Studies that do this are emerging. Wells et al. (1992) identify the lack of coherent links between development activities and the achievement of biodiversity conservation objectives as a recurrent weakness of Integrated Conservation and Development Projects (ICDPs) which aim to combine conservation with local economic development. Other programmes have been criticized for lack of adequate reflection on the circumstances in which biodiversity conservation and sustainable economic development are compatible (Wells 1994). The World Wide Fund for Nature (WWF 1997) concludes that to date there is little measurable conservation benefit in ICDPs and outlines ways to improve conservation impact monitoring. This chapter addresses the question of whether the involvement of local people can promote the conservation of biodiversity for a subset of community conservation (see Barrow and Murphree, Chapter 3, this volume, for a definition of community conservation) interventions known as protected area outreach (PAO). These interventions have biodiversity conservation as their primary goal. They also characterize the main strategies adopted by protected area authorities in East Africa to gain the support of the people living around protected areas (Barrow et al., Chapter 5, this volume).

The chapter begins with an examination of the hypotheses and assumptions of protected area outreach initiatives and their implications. It then discusses the methodological challenges of measuring conservation impact, and ends with a case study of the conservation impact of PAO in Lake Mburo National Park in Uganda.

The hypotheses and Assumptions

Protected area outreach 'seeks to enhance the biological integrity of parks by working to educate and benefit local communities' (Barrow and Murphree, Chapter 3, this volume). The protected area authority strives to secure conservation and enlist the support of local people through project activities which range from extension and education to benefit sharing and resource sharing. Commonly, it aims to reduce pressure placed on the protected areas by creating a 'buffer zone' around the protected area where wildlife is tolerated. In protected area outreach conservation objectives are of primary importance and development objectives are secondary (for example see AWF 1993). There are many definitions of conservation. All of them imply maintaining, enhancing or using sustainably the biological component of an ecosystem or biodiversity. For the purposes of this study biodiversity is defined as the composition of natural variation found in genes, species, communities and ecosystems (Wilson 1989).

The main conservation hypothesis of PAO could be stated thus: the support of people surrounding a protected area will enhance the conservation of biodiversity. Since its inception in the early 1980s, protected area outreach has focused on distributing benefits to park neighbours (Western 1982; KWS 1991); working with local communities or extension work (Berger 1989; Bergin 1995b); institutionalizing PAO within protected area authorities (Bergin and Hulme and Infield, Chapter 8, this volume); and improving park–people relationships (Barrow et al., Chapter 5, this volume). Thus, nested within the main conservation hypothesis of PAO are the hypotheses that i) economic or social project gains; ii) good relationships; and iii) awareness, make people more inclined to protect biodiversity and the protected area. A further hypothesis associated with PAO states that local support for a protected area reduces the cost of law enforcement (Western 1989). All these hypotheses depend on strong linkages between the development and/or livelihoods of local people, their behaviour and the resource base. These links are, however, largely untested.

Some controversy surrounds the linking of human development goals with conservation. At one extreme, it can be argued that human use and occupation of an area almost always leads to a reduction in biodiversity. At the other, is the view that humans form an integral part of some ecosystems, and their actions enhance biodiversity. Between these two extremes, proponents of rural development within a conservation context postulate that development comes at some cost to biodiversity. They recommend that in multi-use landscapes, adequate regions of undisturbed and unmodified habitat should be protected, creating a mosaic of disturbed and undisturbed habitat. Barber et al. (1996) conclude that communities and situations can be found to support all these perspectives.

Another implied assumption of PAO is that one of the greatest threats to biodiversity or the integrity of a protected area comes from the people living closest to the protected area. However, a strong argument has developed that attributes the depletion of biodiversity to current macro-level economic and environmental policies and global population growth (Carley and Christie 1997). Action by a protected area authority at local level may therefore have little impact on biodiversity conservation.

In light of the above hypotheses and assumptions, the real test for whether or not PAO meets the conservation agenda would lie in clear evidence of biodiversity benefiting from PAO activity. This chapter examines the extent to which practice meets this ideal.

The Methodological Challenges of Determining Conservation Impact

Conservation theory offers no end of indicators or methods to determine whether or not biodiversity conservation is taking place. In examining the conservation impact of PAO initiatives, it is the interaction between the project activities and biodiversity that presents challenges. Despite the large number of reviews that exist on community conservation initiatives (West and Brechin 1991; IIED 1994; Western and Wright 1994a; Redford and Mansour 1996), no coherent set of indicators with which to measure conservation impact has been proposed. This section outlines the theory of measuring changes in biodiversity and examines the methodological challenges of attributing these changes to PAO. Rather than presenting detailed methods, it outlines the principles of appropriate conservation monitoring, and provides a framework for the case study (see below).

It is argued that the most effective means of measuring conservation impact are based on conservation biology theory (GEF 1992). Three guidelines have been developed for determining conservation impact and monitoring and evaluating conservation projects using these principles (GEF 1992; WWF 1997; WCMC 1996). All guidelines recommend that biodiversity be monitored at three levels (see Table 17.1). The three guidelines are not purely theoretical models but are designed as practical guidelines for implementors. Their three-pronged approach ensures that changes at each level are seen within the context of the overall status of biodiversity. For example, an anti-poaching programme may reduce direct exploitation of a species, and indicators at species level would show an increase in the species' population, while the ecosystem as a whole may continue to deteriorate (WWF 1997).

Within the above framework, assessment of conservation impact of protected area outreach can focus on the status of that biodiversity or on the threats to it. A number of techniques for the evaluation of the status of biodiversity have been developed. Many

Table 17.1 Levels at which biodiversity should be monitored

WWF (1997)	GEF (1992)	WCMC (1996)
Sensitive species	Species or population	Genetic diversity
Critical habitats	Community or ecosystem	Species
Ecological problems	Regional or landscape	Habitats

include the use of indicator species whose presence or absence provides information on the status of biodiversity (Stotz et al. 1996). Data on population trends also give some indication of what is happening to biodiversity. Where human use or hunting of any species has been identified as a key threat, one can examine trends in the level of threat by examining either human use of the protected area or trends in illegal activity.

A comparative approach offers the potential for measuring the conservation impact of a PAO initiative. For example, the target area of an initiative could be compared with a similar site where no protected area outreach programme is being implemented. However, few places exist that would make suitable controls for PAO initiatives, and confounding biological variables would make it difficult to draw comparisons between two sites. In addition, variables at community level would need to be considered, and the time and resources to assess 'controls' are usually not available.

Conservation biology also lends itself to a clear methodology of the establishment of a biological baseline and subsequent evaluation at the end of a project or intervention. However, a review of community initiatives in East Africa indicates that little thought is given to the establishment of biological baselines at the start of PAO initiatives. It is also the case that the funds available and field conditions may mean that at project inception priority is given to conflict resolution between communities and protected area authorities rather than biological inventory.

A number of practical factors need to be considered in assessing conservation impact, the most important of which are the time and spatial scales of the intervention or project activity (GEF 1992). In general, the assessment of trends in indicator variables, particularly those addressing long-term threats to biodiversity, will be detected on a time scale beyond the life span of most interventions. For example, the recovery of an endangered species may require monitoring that spans more than a decade. PAO initiatives are generally shorter than this. The time frame of these projects also limits the possibilities for establishing causal links between community action and conservation. Biological systems typically change within a time frame much longer than the three to five year life span of a PAO initiative.

With respect to scale, PAO initiatives which focus on a specific site should address how the initiative promotes conservation and maintains biodiversity across the entire regional landscape or ecosystem. In many cases PAO activity focuses on a specific site while threats to biodiversity occur on a broader scale. For example, Tarangire National Park in Tanzania is threatened by the cutting down of trees many miles away for charcoal to supply urban markets in Arusha (Kangwana and Ole Mako, Chapter 10, this volume). Associated with the issue of scale, any achievements in terms of biodiversity conservation will be limited by the constraints of protected area design. Research points to poor design as a key factor in the ecological impoverishment of protected areas over time (Leader Williams et al. 1990b). The history of parks indicates they were created for reasons other than biodiversity conservation and thus have inherent design problems. Amboseli National Park, for example, protects only the dry season concentration area for its migratory wildlife species, while the wet season dispersal areas outside the Park are threatened by changing land use and human population growth. In this case, while PAO sought to expand the area available to wildlife by sharing tourist revenues with the local people (KWS 1991), possibilities for biodiversity conservation are constrained by Park design.

The design and articulation of PAO conservation goals have the potential to limit the monitoring of conservation impact. To a large extent PAO has been supported by a series of projects which link its activity to the overall goal of conserving biodiversity through project logic and a hierarchy of aims. The logical frame approach to project design and management, while seeking to ensure logical links between project activities and overall objectives, has the potential to introduce tenuous links dependent on many assumptions. Logical frames can thus make it difficult to determine whether a lower level objective is indeed contributing to the overall objective of biodiversity conservation. The conservation goals of PAO initiatives can also be articulated such that links with the resource base are general and not specifically related to biodiversity. Tanzania National Parks, for example, states that the aim of PAO around Tarangire National Park is to reduce conflict between wildlife, the Park and local people. While this goal can and is being met, benefits in terms of biodiversity are unclear (see Kangwana and Ole Mako, Chapter 10, this volume).

Even when it is possible to detect and monitor changes in the level of biodiversity threats and the status of biodiversity, it is difficult to determine whether these changes are the direct result of a PAO intervention. The fact is that the time frame over which biological change takes place is well beyond the duration of most PAO initiatives, and the number of variables affecting natural systems make a minefield of linking PAO with biological change or establishing causal links. As WWF (1997) states, 'determining causality between ecological indicators and project interventions is fraught with methodological difficulties'. The challenges of using conventional conservation biology theory and methodology to assess the conservation impact of PAO are therefore great, particularly in light of the time frames of PAO initiatives and the resources normally available for monitoring purposes. The next section explores these challenges through a case study of PAO in Lake Mburo National Park, Uganda.[1]

Lake Mburo National Park: A Case Study

Background and project goals

This section examines whether conservation goals have been met after six years of the implementation of PAO around Lake Mburo National Park (LMNP) in Uganda. The LMNP Community Conservation Project was initiated around LMNP by Uganda National Parks (UNP) and the African Wildlife Foundation (AWF) in February 1991 (Hulme and Infield, Chapter 8, this volume). This three-year project ended in January 1994 and was extended for one year by a No-Cost-Extension. The SIDA funded project was followed by a three-year USAID-funded project, also implemented by AWF, to consolidate the achievements of the first phase of PAO in Lake Mburo. The USAID-funded project is continuing.

The Community Conservation (CC) Project was developed to secure the future of the Lake Mburo Ecosystem, which is too small to survive without the support of the local people (AWF 1992). The project started against a backdrop of hostile feelings toward the National Park. The gazettement of the Park in 1982 was followed by the forced removal of numerous families, many of which had legitimate claims to land within the former Game Reserve. The manner of evictions and the imposition of the Park provoked much hostility among the local people.

The first phase of the project was structured to address park–people relations; increase awareness of the Park's values; and encourage people to participate in conservation and sustainable wildlife-based development. The project also provided funds to improve the infrastructure of the Park and promote tourism. Project goals were to be met within the context of the Park objective 'to preserve and develop the values of LMNP by conserving biodiversity, maintaining ecological processes, promoting the sustainable use of its resources, and safeguarding Uganda's aesthetic and cultural needs for present and future generations'. This objective is to be met through the pursuit of three specific objectives:

a) Biodiversity conservation: To ensure the preservation of all species within LMNP, especially endemics and those for which LMNP is the only sanctuary.
b) Sustainable development: To promote the sustainable use of LMNP's resources to safeguard Uganda's aesthetic, cultural and development needs.
c) Maintenance of ecological processes: To maintain the ecological processes on which the park's biodiversity depends and which provide ecological services to surrounding communities.

Both project and Park objectives are articulated at a level of generality which makes the task of determining whether or not they have been achieved a difficult one. However, it is clear that the CC project and the Park aim to conserve biodiversity, and conserving wildlife is articulated at both levels.

Assessment strategy

Data for this study were collected by a small research team during fieldwork in January and March 1997. Fieldwork comprised a series of participatory rural appraisal exercises in villages surrounding the LMNP and key informant interviews with Parks staff and government officials (see Hulme and Infield, Chapter 8, this volume for a detailed examination of the social and institutional findings). While the LMNP community conservation project was designed with biodiversity objectives in mind, a comprehensive biodiversity monitoring system was not set up, nor was a baseline assessment done against which impact was to be measured. The project did, however, set out a socio-economic baseline through a socio-economic survey (Marquardt et al. 1994). The absence of biodiversity baseline data at the start of the LMNP Community conservation project limited the options for using direct measures of biodiversity status. This study therefore selected the most appropriate indicators against which project impact could be measured, within the conservation biology framework. The resources of the study precluded the use of large-scale biological inventories typically used for such assessments. The study therefore used existing data to assess trends in large mammal populations.

Observing trends in pressures on biodiversity held some potential for providing the information needed for evaluating the conservation impact of the CC Project. An assessment of pressures on or threats to biodiversity was carried out with the assumption that a reduction in the pressures affects biodiversity positively. The short-term threats to biodiversity at the time of the LMNP project design were the illegal offtake of wild species by poachers and the intensive use of the park by people (AWF 1992). Long-term threats lay in the changing land use around the National Park and the increasing isolation of LMNP within the broader ecosystem. Short-term and long-term threats are, of course, not mutually exclusive.

The findings of this study are presented as follows: trends in illegal activity; trends in human use of the Park; land use around the Park; trends in large mammal numbers; and perceived changes in the ecosystem. The first three examine pressures on biodiversity, while the last two examine the status of biodiversity more directly.

Trends in illegal activity

One of the central hypotheses of PAO is that as community support for conservation increases through PAO activities, the cost of law enforcement will be reduced. For this study, it was hypothesized that the advancement of the PAO programme in the area, with its aims of building partnerships and sharing the park benefits, would decrease illegal encroachment into the park and the poaching of park resources by local people.

To assess whether a change in behaviour had occurred, patrol records of the park rangers were examined. Park rangers maintain law and order in the park, make arrests and generally strive to maintain the habitat integrity of the Park. Data were analysed in two time-blocks: 1991 to 1992 covers the pre and early PAO project period and 1996 to 1997 covers a period six years after the inception of PAO activities. Data extracted from the records were: the start and end time of patrol; number of men; number of arms; area patrolled; purpose of patrol; observations; action taken; number of people arrested; and number of livestock seized. The level of effort in man-hours spent in the field was correlated with the numbers of encounters with humans; signs of human activity; arrests made; encounters with and seizure of cattle.

These data indicate that catch per unit effort has decreased over the course of the PAO project. Arrests were 6.3 times more likely to be made in 1991 and 1992 than in 1996 and 1997 (coefficients of catch per unit effort 0.022 and 0.0035 respectively). Over this time period the purpose of patrol expeditions also changed from evictions to general surveillance patrols. Whether this decrease in arrests is the result of the PAO project is difficult to infer from the patrol data alone, and qualitative data must inform. Rangers reported positive relationships with local people to the extent of receiving tip-offs from community members on the presence of poachers. This in turn may have resulted in a decrease in illegal activity. On the other hand, the data indicate a much stronger presence of law enforcement rangers in the Park in 1996 and 1997 than in 1991 and 1992. In 1997 patrols went out daily and were eight men strong whereas in 1990 the patrol team was five men and patrols went out on average every other day. Although the analysis of number of arrests controls for the effort, just the fact of a stronger law enforcement team present in the field could have deterred poaching. While this analysis of the patrol data implies a positive change in behaviour of people surrounding the national park, it is clear that there is difficulty in directly attributing this trend to the activities of PAO in LMNP.

Trends in human use of the Park

The gazettement of Lake Mburo as a National Park in 1982, and its change in status from Game Reserve, contains the implicit statement that one of its conservation goals was to create an area for the exclusive use of wildlife. This is the interpretation of a 'National Park' as per IUCN protected area categories (IUCN 1984). When the LMNP project began in 1991, there was a significant number of people living in the area gazetted as a National Park and a high level of human activity in the Park (for further details see Hulme and Infield, Chapter 8, this volume). At that time human use was identified as the main pressure on biodiversity in LMNP.

An assessment was made of the use of the Park prior to CC project activity and comparison drawn with patterns of human use of the Park in 1997. Data on levels of human use are derived from key informant interviews with senior park staff, the AWF Community Conservation Project Officer, project reports and other project documents.

In 1991 there was settlement and cultivation in central and western parts of the Park. There was a trading centre near the present-day Ruizi Track to the extreme west of the Park, and a weekly market was held in the centre of the park at Kashara. Livestock was found throughout the park. Monday (1993) reported, 'At present 150 cattle-keeping families, 180 cultivator families and 30 fishing community families are residing in the Park'. This is in stark contrast to the situation in 1997 where only three areas inside the Park, held by private title, had residents. Access to resources within the Park is also negotiated with Park management. For example, livestock are allowed access to water sources within the Park at times of drought through the CC project. Otherwise encroachment on the Park is illegal and dealt with severely.

Patrol reports from 1991 and 1992 indicate that much ranger activity involved evicting people from within the Park to create a central core area free of people. Huts were burnt and people's belongings moved outside the Park. During this period care was taken to separate 'legitimate' (i.e. pre-1983 residents) from 'illegitimate' squatters. Pastoralist squatters had presidential authority to reside in the present-day Park area on a temporary basis, while 196 cultivators were identified as legitimate and compensation and land were provided for them. The negotiation with people to move outside the Park took place as a result of the PAO project in LMNP. The project thus directly contributed to the creation of an area for the exclusive use of wildlife and facilitated the Park's ability to negotiate with local people and handle disputes through the creation of a CC unit within the Park.

Land use around the Park

In the case of LMNP, the spatial context is of particular importance. Theory holds that the long-term viability of the protected area rests ultimately upon the extent to which regional planning efforts integrate a park into a larger area where management is compatible with conservation (GEF 1992). An assessment of land uses around LMNP was made through a combination of key informant interviews with planners and local government officials as well as the land-use patterns observed by carrying out participatory and rapid rural appraisal exercises in eight villages surrounding the Park. Community mapping exercises were also carried out.

The area immediately surrounding LMNP is a mosaic of human settlement, cultivated areas and livestock grazing land. As people have turned to the cultivation of crops around the Park, the resulting conflict over crop raiding by wild animals has given rise to animosity between local people and park staff. A large development project adjoining LMNP, funded by German Technical Assistance (GTZ), includes as one of its objectives the settlement of pastoralists on ranches and agricultural development. Interviews with the agricultural officer for the area also indicated that the government was actively promoting mixed farming around the park. The encouragement of land uses conflicting with the Park objectives directly outside the Park boundaries compromises the future integrity of the Park. It directly conflicts with the biodiversity conservation objectives of the Park. Any benefits gained by securing the Park as a zone free of human use are undermined by the creation of an island Park surrounded by incompatible land use. Conservation biology theory predicts species extinctions in such island parks in the long term. Park outreach activity at LMNP has not been able to influence the land-use patterns of park 'neighbours' in ways that support LMNP's conservation goals.

Trends in large mammal numbers

Qualitative data provided conflicting views on the status of wildlife populations in LMNP. Interviews with rangers and other Park staff indicated that wildlife numbers in the Park are increasing. On the other hand, there was a consistent view that the number of wild animals had decreased since times of early settlement in four out of seven villages around the Park. A number of sources provided large mammal popu- lation data for the Lake Mburo Ecosystem (Monday 1991, 1993; Olivier 1992), but the determination of trends proves difficult because each of these covers a different census zone. Surveys carried out in 1995 and 1996 for the Ministry of Tourism, Wildlife and Antiquities (MTWA) do, however, examine trends in wildlife and live- stock populations between 1992, 1995 and 1996. The 1995 and 1996 wildlife counts were carried out using systematic reconnaissance flight methods and were part of a series of surveys conducted to determine the level of human encroachment and appraise the status of the protected area (MTWA 1996a).

Data were available for comparison between 1992 and 1995 for cattle, shoats (sheep or goats), impala, zebra, huts and kraals. The surveys indicated that the number of cattle in the whole LMNP ecosystem had increased by 69 per cent. They also confirmed the finding that encroachment of the present-day Park area had decreased over the period 1992 to 1995. The number of cattle in the Park had declined from 14,000 head in 1992 to 9500 in 1995. The number of huts in the Park had reduced from 2000 in 1992 to 700 in 1995 (MTWA 1996a). The surveys showed that impala populations decreased by 61 per cent in the Park. This finding was confirmed in a repeat survey of the same area carried out in 1996 (MTWA 1996b). The degree to which these trends in numbers can be attributed to PAO is ques- tionable but the MTWA (1996b) does attribute the reduction of human use of the Park directly to PAO. Park staff have thus been successful in reducing pressures to the core area of the ecosystem, but cattle have increased in the wider ecosystem to the point where severe habitat alteration is taking place (MWTA 1996b). This brings into question the long-term viability of the Park.

Perceived changes in the ecosystem

Research carried out in villages surrounding LMNP permitted an assessment of change in the environment as perceived by local villagers. Group interviews were conducted in which villagers were asked what changes they had observed in the envi- ronment since their arrival in the area. Villagers commented on a reduction in soil fertility and stated that there were fewer trees than there had been in the past. Villagers also reported that changes had occurred in the type of pasture available for livestock –

they consistently reported a change from a predominant palatable grass species to an unpalatable grass species in recent times. The clearing of bush to eradicate the tsetse fly in the 1960s was referred to in the timelines of two villages. There was also mention of the fact that rainfall patterns had changed. Such perceived changes are unlikely to be correlated with PAO activity in the area, and are probably the result of broader environmental change and increases in human population in the area, with movements and influxes of people over time. They may, however, indicate an overall trend of environmental degradation in the context of the Park's conservation objectives.

A Summary of the Conservation Impact of Protected Area Outreach at LMNP

Determining the conservation impact of PAO activity at LMNP is problematic because of the lack of a clear baseline and conservation targets. As a Park it has suffered the limitations of Park design: its present-day borders are the result of political expediency more than they are the result of ecological rationale. The Park encloses a dry season concentration area for wildlife, many species of which range beyond the Park boundaries. The Park therefore is not a 'self-contained' ecological unit, a factor which puts LMNP at risk of losing biodiversity regardless of measures taken to conserve it within the Park. Conservation activity in the Park is therefore significantly dependent on efforts to secure wildlife dispersal areas outside the Park.

Illegal activity in LMNP decreased over the course of the PAO project. Qualitative data indicate that this may be associated with PAO activity and better park–people relationships, but a causal link between PAO activity and fewer illegal incidents is hard to establish. While there has been a significant decrease in the number of arrests per unit effort, the mere presence of a stronger law enforcement team may be exerting an unquantifiable influence in deterring poaching in LMNP. Whether or not human use of an area affects biodiversity positively or negatively is controversial. Human use of LMNP decreases over the course of the CC project as a direct result of project activity. However, the impact of this action on biodiversity is unclear. A core area of the Lake Mburo ecosystem is retained with little human use, but the pressures outside the Park are probably causing significant depletion of the ecosystem as a whole.

This case study of LMNP demonstrates that setting up the means for the assessment of conservation benefit of PAO needs to form an integral part of the project design. Some information can be gleaned from assessments done without appropriate baseline information, but the complexity of establishing causal links and confounding variables renders severe limitations to these data and their interpretation.

Conclusion

The history of PAO indicates that the social dimension and strategies for working with local people have been given priority, probably as a result of two factors. First, PAO developed from a recognition that the hostile relationship created with local people in the establishment of protected areas gave rise to little local support for protected areas. PAO has thus focused on increasing local support and distributing the benefits of conservation more widely. Second, the immediate threats to the biological integrity of protected areas are thought to arise from the depletion of resources within and around the protected area by local communities lacking alternatives. The East African experience shows that significant advances in thinking have been made on institutional arrangements and policies for PAO, resource access and tenure, park–people relationships and benefit sharing (Barrow et al. 1995a; Chapter 5, this volume). Each of these is a benefit of PAO initiatives in its own right, but cannot be deemed a conservation strategy unless the link between community action and biodiversity outlined in the hypotheses of PAO holds true.

Conservation biology lends itself to a clear methodology of establishing baselines and the subsequent evaluation of conservation impact. However, this is difficult to apply to PAO initiatives with their short time frames and limited resources for monitoring and evaluation as illustrated by the LMNP case study. Invariably, PAO implementors have not paid attention to the collection of adequate biological baseline data nor selected key biodiversity indicators against which to measure conservation impact. The links between PAO activity and biodiversity conservation thus remain largely unproven. The findings from the LMNP community conservation initiative were paradoxical. While CC appeared to have assisted in the conservation of the Park itself it had not succeeded in influencing environmental change outside of the Park. This suggests that, at best, the Park will become an 'island' and, as a consequence, its biodiversity will be depleted.

In continuing to use PAO as a conservation strategy, greater rigour is required in the articulation of conservation goals and in project design. Specific conservation targets should be set and monitored, and resources must be allocated for whatever biological inventory or baseline setting is deemed appropriate. The selection of appropriate indicator species would reduce the need for extensive biological surveys. Taylor (Chapter 18, this volume) proposes the use of participatory census methods as an intermediate between the use of high quality census data, which are generally not available, and the random setting of hunting quotas. Similarly, the selection of indicator or keystone species could serve as an intermediate step between the realities and constraints of PAO implementation and the conservation biology theoretical ideal. Research could then focus on the relationship between the species selected and the status of biodiversity in the target area.

The need for a long-term perspective to determine biological change should also inform the approaches taken in trying to conserve and monitor biodiversity at the human–park interface. Short-term projects with no follow-up are unlikely to affect biodiversity positively, given the time scales over which ecosystems change. PAO might also address the spatial requisites for conservation. Reducing the immediate and urgent threats such as human and livestock use in a protected area needs to be balanced with efforts to influence land use around protected areas and to secure the future of ecologically viable conservation areas. The methodological challenges of linking PAO with biodiversity conservation are significant. They must, however, be addressed if resources available for conservation are to be used effectively.

Note

[1]The study was made possible by the kind permission of Uganda Wildlife Authority and the Park staff of Lake Mburo National Park, Uganda. This chapter has benefited from comments from David Hulme, Mark Infield and Marshall Murphree.

18

Participatory Natural Resource Monitoring & Management
Implications for Conservation

RUSSELL TAYLOR

Introduction

Although the history of resource management is replete with spectacular failures, policy or practice is rarely changed in response to these bad experiences (Ludwig et al. 1993). Ludwig (1993) concludes that such failures are a consequence of an inherent contradiction between human desire and human capability. For example, although fisheries managers need to control the amount, distribution and technique of fishing effort for sustained yield, this has never been achieved (Larkin 1977). The history of forest management and exploitation is no more encouraging with widespread wastage and loss as a consequence of inappropriate policies (Repetto and Gillis 1988). Describing a somewhat different but parallel situation in African conservation, Bell (1987) asks the question 'Can human nature be trusted to maintain equable access to resources, either between sectors of society or between generations in time?' Conventional wisdom answers in the negative and endeavours to maintain centralized control, in the belief that our environment is on the brink of man-induced ecological collapse (Bell 1987). These arguments are pivotal to issues of sustainability and in particular how science relates to sustainability and resource management (Holling et al. 1997). They are equally pertinent to a new conservation paradigm presently emerging in Africa where conservation strategies are moving from an earlier emphasis on state-enforced protection of wildlife and natural resources to promoting increased participation of local people (Chapters 2 and 3, this volume).

Ecology, including wildlife management and conservation, deals with systems about which we know little, yet want to manage or exploit. Moreover, there are severe limitations in our ability to experimentally manipulate, in a scientific sense, these systems and thereby gain the knowledge supposedly needed for such management (Macnab 1983; Hilborn and Ludwig 1993). Failure to recognize that the management treatment is itself an experiment, which can be used to test the assumptions on which the treatment is based, reflects many a lost opportunity (Macnab 1983).

Adaptive management (Holling 1978), in the context of African wildlife conservation and management (Bell and McShane-Caluzi 1985), has a pre-eminent role to play as an important learning tool in both the biological and social sciences.

This contribution[1] examines current limitations in conventional wildlife management methodologies for large mammal census and the establishment of harvest rates. It argues that these are fundamentally flawed, biologically and institutionally. Consequently, either inefficient use or overuse of resources can result, with potentially adverse impacts for ecology, livelihoods and conservation. Invariably, such approaches are centralized, non-participatory, expensive and usually remote from the resource user or manager. They are unlikely to provide sustainability, biologically or institutionally, and intended beneficiaries are largely passive recipients of a management decision flowing from inappropriate policy formulation. Alternative and innovative approaches which reverse the role of local communities and resource managers to that of active participants are described and discussed. The Zimbabwean example of CAMPFIRE and trophy hunting is used but the approach has a much wider applicability to resource management and conservation, in Africa and elsewhere.

Community-based Natural Resource Management and Conservation in Southern Africa: The Example of CAMPFIRE

Throughout pre-independent southern Africa, conservation policy and practice, based on centralized and racial lines, alienated most rural people from their wildlife resources. Over the past decade, however, a number of initiatives in the region have sought to return rights of access to these natural resources through legislative change, devolved responsibility and economic empowerment (Jones and Murphree, Chapter 4, this volume). In Zimbabwe, the CAMPFIRE programme (Communal Areas Management Programme for Indigenous Resources, Martin 1986) is an innovative example that seeks to place the proprietorship of natural resources, especially wildlife, with the people living most closely with them. A 1982 amendment to the 1975 Parks and Wild Life Act gave rural district councils (RDCs) in the communal lands Appropriate Authority over wildlife. Such authority allows RDCs to manage and benefit from wildlife resources occurring in them. This decentralization of authority (Figure 18.1), although not yet complete, and to which I will return, reflects a crucially important step in the institutional reform necessary for effective resource management (see also Chapters 4, 15 and 16, this volume, for discussions on this issue).

In Zimbabwe internationally marketed sport hunting for trophies is an important form of wildlife use and particularly so in the CAMPFIRE programme (Taylor 1994). Most districts have chosen to lease hunting rights to commercial partners and such use generates over 90 per cent of the revenue presently earned by these districts (Bond 1994; Chapter 15, this volume). The CAMPFIRE 'guidelines' for wildlife-derived revenue require that at least 50 per cent of gross income is devolved to communities (in wards and villages) living with wildlife, the so-called 'producer' communities (Child 1995b). Up to 35 per cent can be allocated to expenditure on wildlife management activities in the district with the remaining 15 per cent being

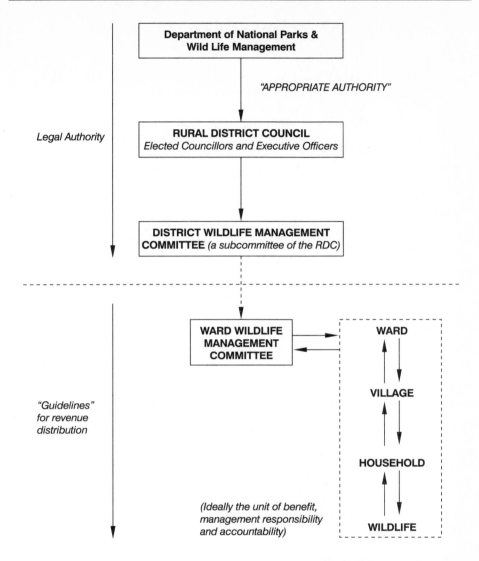

Figure 18.1 The legal and administrative framework for CAMPFIRE in Zimbabwe

retained as a district levy. The financial benefits derived from wildlife are central to the CAMPFIRE programme. The devolution of these benefits to communities living with wildlife is intended to stimulate both collective and individual resource management, thereby providing rural communities with an alternative or complementary land use to agriculture and livestock. For most districts, however, the benefit at household level has been very low, compared with other sources of income (Bond, Chapter 15, this volume), another important point to be returned to.

The Conventional Wildlife Monitoring and Management Model

Offtake quotas for wildlife harvests

Conventionally, offtake quotas for wildlife harvests are usually established by a centralized management authority with overall responsibility for wildlife administration and management. The quota is based on surveys conducted by biologists or ecologists who feed back their information to the management authority which then issues a quota for use. Two important points emerge from a review of this model: (i) surveys are invariably inadequate, spatially, temporally and in respect of the species enumerated; (ii) the decision-making process is limited institutionally, with little or no consultation with the end users of the quota, to what is essentially a bureaucratically dominated decision-making process. Implicit in this approach is a paucity of knowledge, based on limited lines of evidence which must undermine confidence in the decisions taken and the quotas issued. Any lack of confidence on the part of the management authority is invariably well disguised in bureaucratic jargon and ambiguous scientific language. Any lack of confidence resource managers or conservationists may have in the quota (too high, too low) is usually expressed loudly but often uncritically due to a lack of knowledge.

The application of the conventional model to CAMPFIRE

Legal, administrative and institutional arrangements

Although the deficiencies inherent in the conventional management model have been increasingly recognized in Zimbabawe (Child, GFT 1995), the country's wildlife management authority, the Department of National Parks and Wild Life Management (DNPWLM), has continued to apply this approach to managing wildlife, but with important differences. The Parks and Wild Life Act of 1975 vested the custody of wildlife in the landholder, be it the state, private landowner or communal land occupant, all of whom can derive benefits from the wildlife on their land (Cumming 1983; Taylor 1990; Child, GFT 1995). Although communal management of wildlife thus became possible, especially after 1982, legal responsibility still remains vested in RDCs (Figure 18.1). It is to this institutional level that DNPWLM devolves the administration of communal wildlife, with accompanying benefits but very little management responsibility.

Wildlife survey and census

In African wildlife management, aerial census using sampling procedures and accompanying statistical analyses provides the primary index of wildlife abundance and distribution (Jolly 1969; Norton-Griffiths 1978). While generally effective for large dark-bodied herbivores, such as elephant, buffalo and sable antelope in Zimbabwe, such censuses are inefficient for many of the smaller-bodied antelope and predators (Taylor and Mackie 1997). This is especially pronounced in heavily bushed and wooded savannas where sampling and observer biases become increasingly problematic (Caughley 1977). Although satisfactory and cost-effective for the objectives of protected area management at a coarse scale of resolution (1000–10,000 km^2), the method becomes increasingly unsuited for the purpose of estimating animal abundance at a finer scale (<1000 km²) or for establishing offtake quotas. Apart from the fact that harvestable species may remain undetected, the error associated with the estimate of population size for most species is invariably greater than their likely growth rate so as to make the detection of population trend almost impossible, at least on an annual basis, if not longer. The high variability associated with population size estimates over relatively small areas, typical of CAMPFIRE districts and wards, is also linked to the wide-ranging nature of herbivores such as elephant and buffalo, which function spatially at a scale somewhat larger than the average size of a ward or census stratum. Aerial wildlife censuses in CAMPFIRE districts are undertaken by, or on behalf of, DNPWLM annually during the dry season in Zimbabwe. These surveys are technologically sophisticated, centrally managed and directed, expensive and remote from resource managers and wildlife producer communities. Moreover, recent aerial surveys in support of the CAMPFIRE programme have all been undertaken with donor support which brings into question their longer-term sustainability.

Decision-making process

In Zimbabwe, management decisions, especially those involving the killing of large mammals, are regulated by the country's wildlife legal and administrative framework. Overall offtake quotas for sport hunting, and other management activities, are centrally established by a DNPWLM management committee comprising senior research, management and administrative personnel. Offtake quotas for CAMPFIRE districts, until very recently, have been established at this level as well as decisions relating to other wildlife matters such as problem animal control.

There is no formal involvement of resource managers or users outside of DNPWLM in this decision-making process, although occasional informal discussion may take place, for example with RDCs or safari operators. Once the quota is established, this is issued to the RDC which then allocates the quota to different uses, primarily sport hunting but which may also include cropping, culling and capture and translocation. The sport, or trophy hunting quota, is marketed through a commercial safari operator who has the hunting rights, negotiated with the RDC, in the district. Revenue thus earned accrues to the RDC which then distributes the revenue according to the CAMPFIRE guidelines (Figure 18.2).

Although it has been strongly argued that the institutional profile for successful management must bring together ownership, management, cost and benefit of wildlife in one unit (IIED 1994; Murphree 1994a), this profile is absent in the conventional model described above. Ideally that unit could be found at a sub-district level at the ward, village and household level, and usually represented by a Ward Wildlife Management Committee (WWMC). It is also the unit that interfaces most directly and frequently with the wildlife it supposedly bears responsibility for. In the conventional model communities at the local level are largely passive recipients of an imposed wildlife management regime which has become re-centralized at a district or equivalent level (Murombedzi 1992; Chapter 16, this volume; Gibson and Marks 1995).

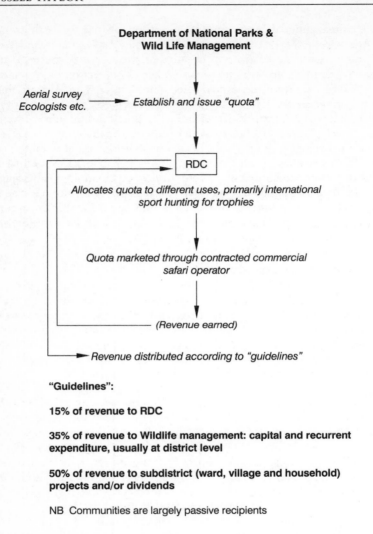

Figure 18.2 The conventional approach to establishing offtake quotas for large mammals in Zimbabwe's CAMPFIRE programme

The participatory wildlife management model

Participatory resource management

The fugitive nature of wildlife and the multiple stakeholders involved in its management and use favour a participatory management approach. In the conventional model, the role of the producer communities in CAMPFIRE was restricted to that of passive recipients of wildlife revenue. Under such conditions wildlife utilization as a long-term sustainable land-use option can be considered unlikely unless two important changes are implemented. Firstly, a stronger and more clearly defined enabling environment for the use of wildlife is required, namely that Appropriate Authority status or some such similar instrument, be devolved from district to ward level. This is discussed again later.

Secondly, participatory resource management methodologies have to be developed to allow community wildlife producers to participate more meaningfully in wildlife management activities and optimize their role in a wider decison-making framework. Such changes would provide incentives for the development of common property management regimes and for land uses supporting wildlife and wildland. Underpinning the development of these methodologies is their use as tools with which to involve local communities as active participants, rather than passive recipients, in natural resource management. Participatory technology development (PTD) brings together technical specialists, in this case ecologists or biologists and local communities, to design, implement, test, monitor and refine locally applied management activities (Sutherland et al. 1998).

Wildlife survey and census

The development of participatory methodologies builds on local community knowledge and assessments of wildlife resources which are both simple and robust. To ensure that census principles of rigour, standardization and repeatability are met, however, it is necessary to consider census techniques (Table 18.1) and establish criteria for their selection (Collinson 1985). This important first step is all too often missed or ignored in our haste to implement a technique (Caughley 1977). The most important criterion is the objective of a wildlife census and its goals. In the case of trophy hunting, the objective is sustained yield harvesting of high quality trophy animals. Ideally, if hunting quotas are to be based on census data alone, then the goal of the census is an absolute estimate of population size. Important properties of the estimate would be moderate accuracy, a high level of precision and a high level of repeatability over time.

PTD is used to design a first approximation to developing an appropriate participatory technique. In this way different participatory approaches to ground-based census methods have been developed with producer communities and include annual censuses, 'random walks'(see below) and fixed transect counts (Mackie 1993). The goal of these methods has been an index of population abundance where accuracy is less important, but a high level of repeatability is required. Precision improves with that repeatability. Because measurement of distance, commonly used in ground census methods (Buckland et al. 1993), has proved difficult to apply, time provides the unit of measurement for the indicator of wildlife abundance in participatory methods (Marks 1994). Generally, and because they do not know where the animals are, biologists stratify and systematically count the census area across ecological gradients. Local resource managers, such as subsistence hunters, find this difficult to understand and tend to sample only where they know animals to occur (Marks 1994). This is a form of obligatory sampling (Collinson 1985) not well appreciated by many biologists who undertake road strip counts, for example, in the belief that their sampling is at least representative if not random. Obligatory sampling has been adapted to produce the 'random walk' sample count over which there is no

Table 18.1 Participatory census: classification and selection of techniques.

Options in **bold** type are those most likely to be appropriate for the development of community-based census methods

Classification	Options	Activity/Comments
Set of objects		
animals		Direct; highly appropriate
animal sign	Dung, spoor	Indirect; unsuccessful
Tactics for location		
ground or air		Ground–day–mobile
day or night		Static placement e.g. waterhole
static or mobile		Count an option
Tools and/or instruments		
mobility	Vehicle, aricraft, horse, boat, **foot**	Walked patrols, transects
location	Binoculars, scanners, GPS, **eyes**	Use eyes for sightings
enumeration	Camera, video, tape, **visual**	Visual sightings recorded
measurement	Rangefinder, compass, **watch**	Time is recorded (catch/effort)
analysis	Calculator, computer, **pencil and paper**	Pencil and paper for calculations
Estimation strategies		Greatest potential
numerous		difficulty; measurement of area
sampling	Area, **time**, ratio/regression	problematic; use time as unit of
non–sampling	Total count	measurement
Survey design		Obligatory and/or
obligatory		representative design to begin
random		with; refinements can follow
systematic		
representative		

Source: Adapted from Collinson (1985).

technical control other than the recording of wildlife sightings. When compared with abundance indices from standard transect counts in the same area, there is little or no difference in results (Taylor unpublished data). Participants either analyse records immediately following the census (in the case of annual counts) or quarterly for those counts undertaken more frequently. Counts over three years have yielded consistent results, i.e. within the same orders of magnitude, providing usable indices of abundance and trend for those large mammal species important to management (Taylor unpublished data). These results are now being used, together with other trend indices, by WWMCs and RDC officials to establish offtake quotas for trophy hunting (see below).

Undertaken by community members themselves, the application of these census methods reflects local perspectives and adaptations to site specific requirements and conditions, rather than the development of a standard methodology. PTD cannot be hurried and time is needed to develop locally workable and sustainable methodologies. The needs and abilities of people must take precedence over the method and its results. Long sessions of repetitive observations are avoided, as is undue physical discomfort and undertaking work at inconvenient times. While intellectual ability must be taken into account, it should not be assumed that local people have no knowledge of the subject. Simple and robust methods which minimize subjective decisions are preferable to those which are highly sensitive to violations of underlying assumptions. Furthermore, methods that rely on highly accurate measurement, sophisticated technology and complicated analyses should be avoided. Census must be seen as a means to an end rather than an end in itself. Thus, data collection, storage and analysis are all undertaken locally by community members, either ward-employed appointees (game guards, wildlife monitors) or, in the case of annual counts, volunteers. The information and knowledge gained is locally owned, provides learning and develops confidence. WWMCs are provided with feedback by their community members or employees which can then feed into subsequent management decisions and action. This contrasts with other CBNRM initiatives where survey and census methodologies are more extractive in nature (Goodman 1996; Tagg 1996) and disempower local resource users.

The quota setting process

The development of a participatory quota setting methodology, commencing at the producer community level, is viewed as a process. It brings together, in a workshop setting, all the key stakeholders involved in the establishment of the quota and its subsequent use, and recognizes the importance of data, information and knowledge that each stakeholder can offer to a decision-making process. Thus aerial census data, participatory ground counting results and trophy quality measurements, together with the local DNPWLM warden's opinions, safari operator's 'catch-effort' and community perceptions (e.g. illegal offtakes) provide a set of indices which are trian-gulated and combined in a matrix used to adapt the previous season's quota (Figure 18.3). The methodology makes use of data (kill date, location, trophy size) provided by a hunt return form administered by the CAMPFIRE Association and RDCs for each hunt undertaken during previous and past seasons, and which participants have access to at quota setting workshops. Trend data are assembled by participants and

SPECIES	THIS YEAR'S QUOTA	AERIAL SURVEY TRENDS	Community GROUND COUNT TRENDS	TROPHY QUALITY TRENDS	INPUT FROM Safari Operator	COMMUNITY ESTIMATES	PROPOSED QUOTA FOR NEXT YEAR
Elephant (M)	7	⟺	⟺	⟺	⇓	⇑	7
Buffalo (M)	20	⟺⇓	⟺	⇑	⟺	⇑	20
Lion	3	X	X	⟺	⟺	⟺	3

KEY TO FIGURE		
⇑ Indicator shows a general population increase	⇓ Indicator shows a general population decrease	⇓⇓ Indicator shows a medium decrease in population
⟺ Indicator shows a stable population	⟺⇑ Indicator shows a stable but increasing population	⟺⇓ Indicator shows a stable but decreasing population
X Information not available or irrelevant		

Figure 18.3 The participatory triangulation matrix summarizing trends in key indicators for individual species in relation to the existing and proposed offtake quota

graphically represented for each species and entered into the matrix. The existing quota is assessed against the available data and information and the proposed quota adaptively determined using the full set of indices.

Crucially, the information and data are collated and analysed in a highly visual, interactive manner, thereby allowing full participation by all stakeholders regardless of educational background. Built into the workshop methodology is a training component based on a series of participatory exercises (games, simulations, role plays) which provides greater understanding and simplifies data analyses. These inform producer community representatives, allowing them to actively participate in determining the quota (Figure 18.4). The completed matrix and quotas produced are forwarded through the RDC to DNPWLM as recommendations for final approval. Over time, and with further experience and confidence, quotas from a number of sub-district wards or villages can be pooled for the district as a whole. An important

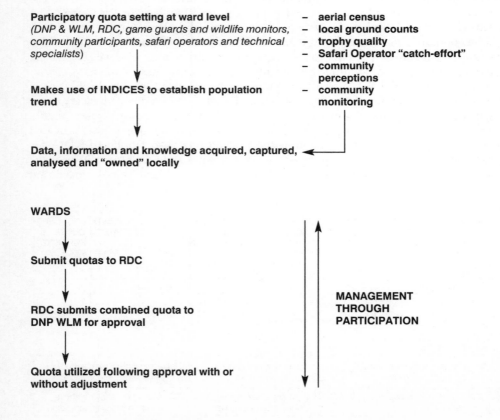

Figure 18.4 The participatory approach to establishing offtake quotas for large mammals in Zimbabwe's CAMPFIRE programme

aspect of the methodology is that domination by one stakeholder (e.g. DNPWLM personnel) over others is minimized, especially when local participants are able to provide abundance data not available elsewhere.

The recommended quota is reviewed by DNPWLM ecologists, taking into account, where necessary, the population dynamics of each species, permissible offtake rates and ecological relationships between the district and/or ward and adjacent protected areas e.g. cross-boundary animal population movement. Following final approval, the quota is returned to the RDC for use in the coming hunting season by the contracted safari operator. Hunting during the season is monitored by RDCs and/or WWMCs using community game guards and wildlife monitors. Compliance with the Parks and Wild Life Act and regulations by safari operators and professional hunters continues to be the responsibility of DNPWLM while the CAMPFIRE Association ensures that hunt return forms are completed for each hunt by safari operators and RDCs. The hunt return form allows the key variables to be captured for input into the national database and provides further feedback for subsequent quota setting exercises.

Participatory Natural Resource Monitoring and Management: Conclusions

There are numerous points of fundamental importance that this example of participatory census and quota setting provides for community participation and natural resource management.

Biological sustainability

Measuring biological sustainability using conventional tools and methods is complex, difficult and uncertain. No one single index will provide absolute confidence in a management decision but an informed set of quantitative and qualitative indices applied rigorously and adaptively improves confidence in the recommended quota, since it is derived from a set of data and information that are more reliably based than previously, when only a limited knowledge base was used. Monitoring repeated assessments and offtakes based on this approach improves understanding and subsequent management action over time. It provides for incremental changes in offtakes and avoids crisis reactions such as stopping all offtakes or pressures for massive culls.

Institutional and organizational capacity

All parties interested in the resource and quota have been involved in the decision-making process in a participatory manner. Because these parties have been involved in establishing the quota themselves, consensus is reached at an early stage so that final approval of the recommended quota should rarely require adjustment by the management authority. The institutional conditions necessary for successful resource management are thus strengthened to include all necessary stakeholders, provide an enhanced decision-making framework unit, greater organizational efficiency and management through participation. Implicit in the approach is its demand for accountability by all stakeholders.

Ownership and incentive

Much of the information and data used to establish the quota is compiled locally by WWMCs and safari operators, giving participants a strong sense of ownership and direct involvement in the management of the resources being utilized. In particular, local communities are no longer passive recipients but rather active participants, thus ensuring their longer-term commitment to resource management. This is especially important when viewed against the marginal monetary benefits realized from wildlife at the household level (Bond, Chapter 15, this volume). Incentives are not only financial and those such as ownership, participation and learning can contribute to effective institutional development. Although the need for greater local participation and ownership in resource management is becoming increasingly recognized in southern Africa (Lewis 1995), Gibson and Marks (1995) point out the numerous pitfalls and assumptions present in many CBNRM designs especially about ownership, control and benefit. While there has been no change legally in the status quo of the enabling environment in Zimbabwe, with appropriate authority status not yet devolved to ward level, the development of participatory methodologies not only allows communities to increase their management role within the set of rules presently pertaining; they also allow the rules to be challenged.

Implications for the conservation of wildlands and wildlife

In the CAMPFIRE programme the retention of wildlands and associated conservation values has relied on the return of financial benefits from wildlife use to those people who live in these wildlands. An analysis of the 12 primary wildlife-producing districts in CAMPFIRE shows that revenue earned was positively and significantly correlated with both the proportion of wildland and elephant density present in these districts (Taylor 1999). The proportionality of these financial returns to resource abundance provides considerable incentive for local communities to conserve and maintain wildlands and wildlife. This incentive is strongly linked to resource management activities such as participatory census and quota setting, since these activities reinforce the linkages between resources assessment and subsequent benefits, for conservation authorities and local communities.

In this example the management authorities (DNPWLM and RDCs) are beginning to accept the strengths of the participatory census and quota setting methodologies. The local resource managers at a community level are becoming empowered through learning and gaining knowledge by action, and the resource user (safari operator) is intimately involved and a committed participant, contributing market information linked to sustainable benefit. It is in the interests of all to participate. Nevertheless, participatory natural resource management has much wider application, across institutional and organizational levels and between disciplines, with important and far reaching consequences for the conservation and sustainable use of the environment. Participatory census and quota setting reflects the practical integration of social and natural sciences which combines multiple sources of evidence (historical, comparative and experimental) well described by Holling et al. (1997). Conservation must endeavour to focus on social and ecological processes which invest in the maintenance of natural systems, and the use of their components. By making knowledge creation and decision–making a less elite activity, trust and confidence can be built among the range of stakeholders directly and indirectly involved in the use of natural resources. The importance of participation in natural resource management and the implications for conservation policy and practice are only just beginning to be appreciated in the developed world (Forum 1993; Hanna et al. 1996). Developments in African community-based natural resource management are providing insightful examples of approaches that might be replicated elsewhere.

Note

[1]Numerous participants in the CAMPFIRE programme have contributed to the concept and practice of participatory census and quota setting. Ivan Bond and Charles Mackie must take credit for their innovative approaches to the early development and implementation of the methodology while Norman Rigava has continued to refine and improve it. David Hulme and Marshall Murphree commented on an earlier draft of this paper.

PART SEVEN
Conclusions

19

Community Conservation as Policy
Promise & Performance

DAVID HULME & MARSHALL MURPHREE

Introduction

It is evident from the chapters in this volume that the recent move towards more community-oriented approaches to conservation in Africa has taken many different forms and that precisely assessing the various costs and benefits associated with specific initiatives is problematic in terms of both methodologies and the resources that would be needed. Generalizing about such 'impacts' (adopting a term and concept widely used in development policy) might seem a foolhardy task but in this chapter – and at the risk of oversimplifying information that is not only diverse and complex but sometimes contested – we attempt to assess the achievements of community conservation. This is based on the case studies presented in earlier chapters, the findings of the country level and cross-national studies, the chapters that focus on economic and conservation issues and the wider academic and professional literature. The concluding sections explore the future of community conservation and outline ideas about how it might make a greater contribution to the evolution of effective institutions to manage the African environment.

It might be asked: 'why attempt to generalize at such a high level?' The answer, for us, is quite simple. Policy processes are shaped by many factors, an important one being the highly generalized contemporary accounts of whether certain policies are 'successful', 'problematic' or 'failing' (see Adams and Hulme, Chapter 2, this volume). We wish to ensure that our findings shed some light on the relative importance that is credited to community conservation approaches within conservation and development policies and on ways of making such approaches more effective. Initially, we consider impacts in terms of the varying perspectives of different stakeholders in community-based approaches. Subsequently, we tackle the questions of whether the 'move to the community' is more equitable, more efficient, more conservatory and more developmental than alternatives. The final section draws out the policy implications.

Stakeholders in Community Conservation: Who Wins, Who Loses?

Taken at face value community conservation promises to create benefits (economic and intrinsic) and reduce costs for people who live on or adjacent to wild lands and wildlife. By doing this it seeks to achieve the goals of people at other levels (regionally, nationally and internationally) who wish to conserve species, habitats or biodiversity. As revealed in the case studies, however, community conservation can take many different forms and, when implemented, community-oriented approaches can differ markedly from stated policies and plans. Individuals and groups often seek to manipulate the meaning of the concept and its practice to serve their personal, group or organizational interests. Here we explore the evidence concerning 'who wins and who loses' when community conservation is introduced. The stakeholders that we examine are the communities, conservation bureaucracies, local government authorities, conservation NGOs, aid donors and private businesses. Each of these categories represents an aggregation of many different individuals and collectivities (be they informal groups or formal organizations). Clearly the experiences of the entities within any one of these categories vary. While it is not possible to capture all of this variation within our summaries we do attempt to cover some of the most important 'within category' variations.

'The communities'

The evidence from our research indicates that shifts to community conservation have generally been beneficial in aggregate terms for communities, relative to the pre-existing regimes of 'fortress conservation' or purely 'coercive conservation' (Peluso 1993). However, the scale of improvement is generally very limited. The main gains have been improved relationships between local residents and conservation agency personnel, increased access to material and/or financial resources and improvements to social infrastructure (such as schools and water supply). In rare cases (for example the Mahenye case study, see Murphree, Chapter 12, this volume) the economic benefit of 'new' income or resources is significant. In the vast majority of cases the evidence indicates that the additional economic benefits generated by community approaches are not at a scale that would adequately compensate local residents for the aggregate direct costs (crop raiding by animals, livestock predation and the physical threat of large animals) and opportunity costs (loss of access to natural resources and disrupted transport systems) caused by conservation. Emerton (Chapter 14, this volume) reviews this situation and provides examples in related case studies (Emerton 1997a and 1998). Overall, community conservation has only made official conservation policy marginally more acceptable to rural people in Africa; it is a step in the right direction but there is a long trek ahead if communities are eventually to view conservation and wildlife management as preferred forms of land use in appropriate contexts.

At the individual and household level the 'new' patterns of benefits and costs vary greatly. In many cases (for example our Ugandan, Namibian and Zimbabwean studies) the project or programme attempts to 'spread' benefits throughout the community by directing revenue shares to social infrastructure (especially primary schools).[1] This is a partially effective mechanism in terms of equitability and has high instrumentality as it means that relatively small volumes of additional benefits can be argued to have benefited large numbers of households. However, the distribution of benefits does vary between households with successful local entrepreneurs and those who gain employment (i.e. game guards) through community conservation programmes often gaining most. It seems clear, however, that financially significant benefits at household level, deriving from sustainable wildlife use, are only possible in contexts where the ratio of wild resources to human populations is very high as is illustrated by Bond (Chapter 15, this volume). Such contexts are very rare in contemporary Africa.

While the narrative of community conservation is of 'consensus', 'partnership', 'co-operation' and non-conflictual 'participation', the experience of our case studies reveals the ways in which the initiatives generated or reinforced forms of local competition and conflict. Those who hold power at the local level – traditional leaders, local officials and business people – are likely to use that power to capture new sources of income and resist any erosion of their position. That said, it must be observed that in our case studies there was no evidence of large-scale capture by local elites of the revenues and resources generated by community conservation. Conflicts did arise, however. At Kunene (Jones, Chapter 11, this volume) younger men have begun to challenge the authority of elders to control wildlife-generated revenues. At Lake Mburo (Hulme and Infield, Chapter 8, this volume) there was keen competition for fishing permits and great doubts about the fairness of their allocation. In the Cameroon (Sharpe 1998), and probably many other locations, 'community' access to resources has led to attempts to ethnically distinguish between 'indigenes' and 'strangers'. The former argue that they are the community and should thus receive all benefits: the latter often have a quite different account of their history, identity and rights to access local resources. Community conservation is no panacea for intra-communal differentiation or conflict. By raising economic stakes or creating new modes of access to resources it may exacerbate such tensions. The same can of course be said of virtually all other forms of local economic development initiative.

Conservation bureaucracies

For conservation bureaucracies (within the civil service or as parastatals) community conservation has often involved a reluctant move out of well-established roles and behaviours. As a warden in Uganda (Hulme and Infield, Chapter 8, this volume) commented, it has been '...a bitter pill to swallow'. It complicates the simple to operate 'hands off' rule (Budiansky 1995: 247) under which local residents in national parks or people carrying hunting equipment can be automatically treated as criminals. It also reduces the opportunities for staff to trade in wildlife products or illegal hunting or access rights where conservation agencies, or the state more generally, are 'criminalized' (Bayart et al. 1999).

There have been benefits, however. At least for our Tanzanian (Chapters 7 and 10) and Ugandan (Chapers 8 and 9) examples, community conservation has reduced the hostility of local communities towards rangers and wardens and thus made parks more manageable and life more congenial. In such cases it has created, or expanded, the local socio-political space for conservation bureaucracies to operate. Community conservation has been an effective strategy for conservation bureaucracies in another sense. It has facilitated their access to foreign aid and the vehicles, travel allowances and overseas trips that this generates. For most donors in the 1990s financing a conservation agency that does not have a 'participatory' or 'community' focus in its strategy would have been very problematic.

The case studies present contradictory evidence about the commitment of conservation agencies to community-based approaches. In Tanzania, TANAPA has institutionalized community conservation and there are signs of organizational cultural change (Bergin, Chapter 7, in this volume). In contrast, the promising initial experiments in Uganda are likely to stall as UWA responds to its financial problems by dramatically reducing resources for community conservation and as the tourist industry slumps following the murders at Bwindi in 1999 (see Chapters 5 and 9). In Zimbabwe, CAMPFIRE has encouraged radical changes in approaches to DNPWLM management of wildlife on communal lands, but it has allowed the agency to retain its 'fortress conservation' strategy for the country's protected areas.

Clearly, an emphasis on 'the community' is an idea that is still only being absorbed by most conservation bureaucracies and policy direction does 'oscillate' over time (Jones and Murphree, Chapter 4, this volume). Whether it will become embedded in these agencies remains to be seen, but this will require a broader political environment that fosters devolution and local level management, and not merely a change within an agency.

Local government authorities

Across sub-Saharan Africa local government structures are in a relatively sorry state and have limited capacities (Tordoff 1994). The role that local government plays in community-oriented initiatives varies greatly. In Zimbabwe, the rural district councils (RDCs) are the legal entity to which authority is devolved. This proves attractive to them as it provides them with legal control of the wildlife resource and an additional source of revenue. However, it has proved problematic for the 'producer communities' at ward level who find that while they are the *de facto* management unit for wildlife, and bear the costs that wildlife imposes, they are reliant on RDCs for their revenue. RDCs have behaved in different ways to producer communities, but for many analysts of CAMPFIRE (see Chapters 12 and 16), the programme is doomed if devolution does not proceed to a lower level than the RDC. In Namibia, the legislation to establish conservancies has occurred before the legislation to create local authorities (Jones, Chapter 11, this volume). By chance, this seems likely to mean that wildlife management will bypass local government structures.

In cases where community conservation has focused on protected areas the situation has usually been quite different. The conservation agencies that run PAs are usually part of central government structures and show a preference to work directly with the 'community' and minimize contact with local government as in Kenya, Tanzania and Uganda. This allows them to avoid the problems that have arisen in Zimbabwe, where there is conflict between RDCs and producer communities. It also puts them in a powerful position vis-a-vis local people: not needing to formally negotiate with council chairmen or executive officers who are likely to be connected with patronage networks linked to national politicians and political parties. In effect, PAs are usually alienated from the formal political landscape at the local level. As a senior local government official in Uganda told us '...parks are a state within a state'. This is 'good' if, as most wardens argue, local politicians are purely mischief-makers looking for bribes or deals. It has the disadvantage, however, of stifling any debate about conservation that is formally linked to local politics. In the short term, and given the context in most countries, keeping local government 'out of conservation' is logical. In the longer term it means that conservation is likely to remain a central government function with little or no focus on accountability to local residents. This creates a structural situation in which the legitimacy of PAs and conservation activities for local residents is likely to remain low.

Conservation NGOs and movements

Our case studies indicate that the main 'civil society' actors in community conservation are international conservation NGOs and groups (e.g. AWF, FFI, IUCN, Conservation International and WWF). At times they are accompanied by international development NGOs, such as CARE at Mgahinga Gorilla National Park in Uganda (see Adams and Infield, Chapter 9, this volume) using the banner of 'sustainable development'. The predominance of international NGOs, as against regional, national and local associations, may be a result of our case selection methods: however, we believe it is a reflection of the more general situation in which international (i.e. North American and European) public concern about the African environment leads to NGOs based in those countries having a high profile in conservation policy and practice in Africa.

While our sample is small, and may be biased, somewhat different processes appear to be operating in southern and East Africa. In Zimbabwe and Namibia national development NGOs (The Zimbabwe Trust, Africa Resources Trust, IRDNC) have played an important role in introducing, developing and promoting community-based approaches,[2] reflecting their interests in local economic and institutional development, and a belief that people on communal lands should have the same rights as commercial farmers. In Kenya, Tanzania and Uganda long-established international NGOs (see previous paragraph) have taken the lead in promoting community approaches. One of the factors behind this is the importance of aid donors in the public finances and development policies of East Africa (see Adams and Hulme, Chapter 2, this volume). For international environmental NGOs the move to community conservation has proved useful in terms of giving them a 'human face' (Anderson and Grove 1987: 10) and responding to charges of 'eco-imperialism'. It has also greatly increased their access to development aid. They may have been insensitive to the costs that conservation has imposed on Africans in the past but now they can promote local development, alongside conservation, to make amends. However, the shift to community conservation is more than just moral restitution or an exercise in public relations. For many of these, it reflects a professional policy shift to approaches seen as being more pragmatically and systematically responsive to conservation constraints in the developing world: they believe that it is the best policy to pursue.

Aid donors

For aid donors community conservation has been an ideal policy, permitting environmental and developmental (particularly, anti-poverty) goals to be combined into 'sustainable development' (Adams and Thomas 1993) and 'sustainable rural liveli-hoods' (Carney 1998). Such concepts present the achievement of development and conservation goals as being almost fully compatible. Community conservation is also compatible with the 'post-top-down' and participatory approaches that are a mandatory aspect of the donor social development and good governance agendas that have emerged in the 1990s. By these means aid-financed programmes can be presented as a 'win–win' scenario that provides a response to both development and environmental lobbyists in OECD countries.

Some donors have recently begun to develop reservations about community conservation, however. They want results within the short time frames of project cycles but are finding that community conservation is a long-term process (Kiss 1999). Its results, particularly in terms of conservation objectives, are difficult to quantify and demonstrate in a manner that satisfies the bodies and publics to which they have to account (ibid.). They are now pressing for tight monitoring and evalu-ation systems to justify their investments in the approach.[3]

Private businesses and entrepreneurs

It is difficult to summarize the effects on private business. In Zimbabwe and Namibia the shift to the community has opened up new opportunities for tourism and safari-hunting; for some operators this has been profitable and sometimes very profitable. In East Africa the impacts are less clear as the opportunities have not developed so extensively, but they are beginning to emerge (see Kangwana and Ole Mako, Chapter 10, this volume). The idea of community conservation does permit some tour operators to present an image to tourists of conservation as being people-friendly, but this is in a context of mass tourism where few visitors are aware that conservation (or indeed tourism) has costs for the people of rural Africa. Clearly for those businesses that are involved in illegal activities there is a possibility that community conservation will reduce opportunities. Arguably, community-based approaches have been part of a strategy that has reduced ivory and rhino horn poaching by creating incentives that are 'anti-poaching' (but more effective law enforcement and trade bans may be the larger part of the story). The evidence from Mahenye (Murphree, Chapter 12, this volume), Kunene (Jones, Chapter 11) and Tarangire (Kangwana, Chapter 10) illustrates how community conservation can open up productive partnerships between formal businesses and communities. However, a key gap in present knowledge is of the nature of business–community relationships, the ways in which income is shared and the extent to which relation-ships can be established in which the community is more than a powerless bystander (see later).

The Conservation and Development Achievements of Community Conservation

In all of the countries researched the move to more community-oriented conser-vation strategy was linked with the achievement of both conservation and devel-opment goals. The relative prioritization of these goals varied between countries and projects (see Barrow and Murphree, Chapter 3, this volume). In Zimbabwe,

CAMPFIRE emphasizes economic development through the sustainable utilization of wildlife. In contrast, our East African examples highlight biodiversity conservation while augmenting local livelihoods. How effectively are community conservation strategies meeting their conservation and development mandates? We examine this in terms of their effects on the environment, efficiency, poverty reduction (equity) and institutional development.

Environment

As Kangwana (Chapter 17) points out, knowledge of the environment or conservation impacts of community conservation approaches is meagre and, at least in terms of scientifically reliable data,[4] is likely to remain that way. There are a number of reasons for this. The yardstick against which to compare 'outcomes' is difficult to construct. It requires a judgement of what would have happened 'without' the intervention which must be set against the background of a moving baseline. The ecosystems and/or species that are to be conserved are in relatively unpredictable states of dynamic change, not at equilibrium or moving towards an identifiable 'climax' state (Botkin 1990).[5] The scientific capacities and finances needed to assess actual change and generate quasi-experimental 'without intervention' models are also beyond the resources of probably all of Africa's conservation agencies. To compound this the time scales needed would almost certainly mean that findings would have little influence on the present generation of initiatives.

While the direct effects of community conservation on the environment are unclear, there is evidence from our case studies that it can shape the behaviours of local residents in patterns that are more compatible with conservation goals. For example, the deep antagonisms between residents and conservation bureaucracies have been partly addressed in Uganda and the economic incentives to convert 'wild' land into farmland have been reduced a little in Namibia and Zimbabwe. But, even in cases where the ratio of economically valuable wildlife and wild land to human demand has led to significant rises in financial returns at community or household levels, it is clear that rural people regard these resources as only one component in their diversified investment and livelihood strategies (see Murombedzi, Chapter 16, this volume).

When measured against the goal of conservation as preservation (or conservation as the reconstruction of some imagined nineteenth century environment) then community-based approaches are almost certain to fail. The profound economic change that has been underway in Africa since colonization is not going to disappear. Growing populations with rising aspirations integrating into a global economy will continue to modify and intensify their use of natural resources. Why should Africa or Africans be any different from the rest of the world? However, if a more pragmatic and relative goal is set for conservation – a scenario of environmental change in which resource users are motivated to include wildlife and wildlife habitats as assets available for present or future benefit rather than liabilities (a 'least worst' scenario) – then community conservation is a belated step in the right direction, permitting some rural people to view wildlife as a potential benefit rather than a set of externally imposed costs. From this perspective conservation becomes a choice between different forms of human-modified ecosystems. Should those with maximum biodiversity be favoured or those with particular species or attractions (e.g. large, rare mammal populations or areas of natural beauty)? Conservation in Africa has not yet begun to concern itself with policy issues in these terms.[6]

Efficiency

Contemporary development seeks to promote economic growth (often prefaced by the term 'pro-poor'). Proponents of community conservation argue that it can contribute to this goal: rather than alienating natural resources from economic utilization or proscribing use, a community approach integrates natural resources into local, national and international markets so that the economic value of these resources can be realized. For larger wildlife this breaks down into four main activities: the production of bushmeat/gamemeat (for subsistence or sale), the sale of other products (especially ivory), safari-hunting and tourism. The use of wildlife for bushmeat is a long-established economic activity across Africa and it continues today both where it is permitted and where it is banned. Some variants of community conservation emphasize the legalization of local hunting to permit 'sustainable offtake'. This can increase the value of bushmeat if quotas are raised (because unnecessary restrictions are removed) and reduce the costs of hunting (as rangers no longer have to be bribed and public paths can be used). Such a change can make a contribution to economic growth but in most contexts this will be relatively marginal and has the distinct disadvantage of being a use that soon reaches a ceiling because of the limitations of sustainable offtake (Barrett and Arcese 1995). Other products can augment the economic value created by offtake but, with certain exceptions, these have relatively low values (though they can be important to livelihood provision at the local level as discussed later).

The main economic promise of community conservation lies in its capacity to expand the 'high value added' activities of safari hunting and tourism. The economic success of CAMPFIRE has been built on the extension of safari hunting into communal lands. In areas with low agricultural potential where elephant and other 'game' species are plentiful this may well be an economically optimal use, providing that the expansion of supply does not flood the safari hunting and wildlife tourism markets and reduce margins. Interestingly, most safari hunting management has focused on the supply side and relatively limited attention has been paid to developing demand. If economic returns are to be increased then serious market research and 'new product development' will be needed. A number of possibilities are emerging in both elite and middle market niches (Box 19.1). If these are wide-eyed speculation then the 'value added' by hunting may soon reach its limit. If 'new markets' can be created, then Africa's comparative advantage in having large wildlife populations might yield considerable financial dividends.

Wildlife-related tourism is already on a vast scale in East and Southern Africa. Whether the move to community conservation can expand this market remains to be seen. Our Mahenye example (see Murphree, Chapter 12, this volume) illustrates the potential for the development of tourist facilities associated with community-based initiatives, and there may well be an 'enlightened' tourist demand for tourism that is 'good for the animals and good for the people'. This is likely to remain a small, high cost niche market unless consumer attitudes can be changed in the low cost mass market for wildlife safaris.[7]

Box 19.1   New product development and safari hunting

In South Africa 'green hunting' has been trialled. Wealthy, pro–wildlife hunters pay US$25,000 to dart an elephant with anaesthetic. Subsequently the elephant is radio-collared or sterilized, according to wildlife management needs, and then released (*Horizon*, BBC2 television, 11/2/99).

A large volume, 'middle price range', hunting holiday market could be developed for the millions of middle income hunters in North America, Spain, Italy, Germany and France. For example, a fortnight in East Africa involving a safari (to see the 'Big Five'), shoot an impala (and/or a zebra) on a community conservancy, catch a Nile Perch and spend the last few days at a beach resort. The 'shoot' could generate an additional charge of US$300 to 1000 (pers.comm., Brian Heath).

The above sections have focused on how to increase the revenue generated by wildlife. It must be noted that, even if aggregate income is increased, the costs of wildlife, particularly in terms of damage to crops, need to be considered (see Emerton, Chapter 14, this volume). In some cases even greatly increased income flow might still not offset the direct and opportunity costs of wildlife.

The shift towards more community-oriented approaches has begun to integrate wildlife products and services more effectively into the economy and reduce the policy-based comparative disadvantages from which it has suffered. However, our findings (see especially Chapters 8 and 14–16) indicate that only in relatively rare circumstances is wildlife likely to fully 'pay its way' in open competition against agriculture and cattle grazing. New product development (see Box 19.1) and more effective community–business partnerships (see below) will improve the economic prospects for wildlife and its habitats but long-term external financial support (from national or international sources), increased employment opportunities in urban areas and improved national macroeconomic performance will be needed if rates of habitat loss are to be stabilized at some future time.

Poverty reduction

For governments, donors and most commentators, development is not merely about economic growth and efficiency but also poverty reduction. The complex debates about poverty and the means by which it may be reduced[8] are beyond the scope of this work and so we adopt a rather simple framework. The move to community conservation promises to reduce poverty, indirectly by contributing to local, regional and national growth, and directly by providing poor people from the local 'community' with additional sources of income, improved access to resources, upgraded social infrastructure and employment. In addition, the costs imposed on poor people by wildlife may be reduced. While the data required to comment precisely about the 'poverty impacts'[9] of community conservation are not available to us, a number of general points can be made with a reasonable degree of confidence.

The evidence from our study indicates that community conservation has been associated with positive changes in terms of the poverty-reducing activities and resource flows identified above. Revenue sharing in Uganda, Kenya and Tanzania means that some income which would have gone to the conservation bureaucracies is now re-directed to local residents. The legislative changes in Namibia and Zimbabwe permit community members to derive income from hunting and tourism that was not accessible before and, through tenurial reforms, have extended their entitlements over natural resources. Jobs have also been created through the new activities. In Uganda resource sharing gives some park 'neighbours' access to resources that were previously unavailable. Donor funds for conservation (that would usually have gone into conservation bureaucracies and NGOs) have been partly re-directed to local social infrastructure in Kenya, Tanzania and Uganda. Given that in virtually all of our study areas local communities are likely to experience poverty at levels above national averages (as they are rural and occupy marginal land or border national parks), a case can be made that the move to more community-oriented approaches has led to a redistribution of income and resources to poorer people. This said, it must also be noted that in all except the rarest cases (low human population density with high levels of hunting or tourist activity) the additional flows of income and resources are at a scale of magnitude that means that, at best, they are a welcome increment to the livelihoods of the poor. In some parts of Africa wildlife-related economic activity could be an element of a poverty-reduction strategy, but it would be disingenuous to pretend that it could form the basis for comprehensive poverty reduction even under the most favourable conditions. Bond's work (Chapter 15, this volume) indicates that, even for the high-performing CAMPFIRE project, the additional benefits generated by wildlife utilization are relatively small.

Moving to distributional issues, at the local level it is evident from the studies in this volume (in particular see Anstey, Chapter 6) and the wider literature that distribution of 'new' benefits (and also new and/or reduced costs) is greatly influenced by the operations of local and national political economies. In Kenya there is fierce competition to 'grab' natural resources by local elites with political connections (Southgate 1998). In Cameroon (Sharpe 1998) complex political processes surround attempts to let communities manage forests. Key issues concern the definition of 'who' is community, what forms of benefit the community should receive and the processes for decision-making.

While many academics pontificate about community conservation initiatives treating local people as an undifferentiated collectivity, our fieldwork indicated that project managers are keenly aware of the ways in which rural and urban elites, lineages, ethnic groups and men try to capture benefits. Because of this there are concerted attempts to use participatory procedures, have representatives selected by electoral processes and to deliver benefits in an indivisible form (schools, health centres, village water supplies, and protective fences) that makes elite capture less likely. Such techniques can still be undermined by those with local power, but interestingly examples emerged of strong community pressure to see that benefits were shared equitably. In particular, at Lake Mburo (see Hulme and Infield, Chapter 8, this volume) the members of the Park Management Advisory Committee rejected the Park's proposed system for allocating revenue shares. The rationalistic approach proposed (the screening of submitted parish project proposals in terms of a scoring technique) was perceived to be too complex and manipulable. The members preferred simplicity and transparency: each parish gets its school rebuilt in rotation and parishes with poor school buildings are redeveloped ahead of others. While Western-trained professionals pointed out that this was 'unfair' (as low population parishes get bigger per capita shares) for local residents it was seen as both fair and transparent.

Finally, in this section, we return to a point made earlier. The nature of contemporary economic processes in Africa (as indeed in most of the world) means that established businesses can generally capture the lion's share of new business opportunities in their sector. For community conservation this is particularly significant as the high value-added activities that are emerging are in safari hunting and tourism, sectors in which national and international companies have a strong comparative advantage and in which 'the community' (as individuals or collective enterprise) has little experience. In Zimbabwe, most safari operators are part of the small elite which largely controls the sector and concentrates benefits in its own hands (see Murombedzi, Chapter 16, this volume). At Lake Mburo plans for a community campsite collapsed during the planning stage but an expatriate businessman, based in Kampala, runs the lodge with all staff recruited from outside the Mbarara District. Forging more equitable community–business 'partnerships' will be necessary if relatively poorer local residents are to gain a larger share of the benefit created by wildlife-related businesses.

Institutional development

A final 'impact' question is to ask whether community conservation has fostered the evolution of institutions that have a greater capacity to achieve development and conservation goals in the future. At the policy level a positive answer could be offered. The policy changes associated with the shift to community conservation have started to remove 'distortions' in the markets for wildlife products and services. This has already raised the economic value of wildlife (and wildlife habitats) so that as a form of land use it no longer carries all of the disadvantages that it used to do compared with agriculture and cattle-rearing. In terms of livelihoods this is a clear advance, giving rural residents greater choice in the way that they earn a living. For conservation goals this will be seen as an advance by those who believe that for wildlife it is 'use it or lose it'. Those who have less faith in the invisible hand of the market to promote conservation, or ethical concerns about the rights of wildlife, would hold a contrary view.

For conservation bureaucracies the initial experience of community-oriented approaches to conservation has introduced new ideas about the role of communities, new methods and techniques, such as participatory appraisal and monitoring (see Taylor, Chapter 18, this volume, for a concrete example) and advisory committees (Hulme and Infield, Chapter 8, this volume). In some cases this may have led to attitudinal change among staff and, arguably, organizational cultural change (see Bergin, Chapter 7, this volume). In others, most obviously from our field experiences in Kenya, the changes have been token; waxing and waning with the volume of foreign aid funds that can be won by temporarily signing up to the donor fashions of 'community' and 'participation' and with changes in agency leadership.

The impact on local institutional development is also mixed: capacities only slowly evolve and are subject to many contingencies. For individuals and agencies new to the field this may have come as a surprise. For those with experience in local institutional development in rural development programmes the recognition that local institutions gradually evolve, and cannot be rapidly 'built', has long been known (Uphoff 1986). The clearest examples of effective local institutional development are in Namibia, where communities are directly involved in wildlife management, and in some parts of Zimbabwe where RDCs have been supportive to VIDCOs and WADCOs in CAMPFIRE areas. In the cases where community conservation is essentially a park outreach strategy then institutions are less developed and remain heavily dependent on the organizational capacities and personal energies of the staff of conservation agencies. Our Ugandan case studies illustrate this (see Chapters 8 and 9).

Such findings might disappoint donors who plan to establish financially and managerially 'sustainable' institutions in two to five year periods. However, these time scales are simply unrealistic during the experimental stages of institutional development.[10] They derive from the donor fixation with projects (Kiss 1999) rather than an analysis of goals, tasks and contexts. It is thus too early in the history of community conservation in Africa to reach conclusions about the approach's influences on institutional development.

Implications for Policy and Practice

The practical lessons that are derived from our findings are inevitably of a relatively general nature. This is partly because of the nature of the findings which point to the infeasibility (and undesirability) of proposing blueprints for interventions in which context is crucially important and in which the process of programme design may be as important as the design features themselves. It is also due to the different ways in which the projects and programmes we have studied can be assessed. At one level, they can be viewed technically as sets of inputs that have produced outputs and impacts and about which judgements can be made by relating the value of inputs to the value of achievements. This approach has the strengths of providing a precise logic for analysis and prescription and of emphasizing the efficient use of resources. It does, however, decontextualize intervention.

An alternative is to view community conservation initiatives as one element of broader social processes concerning the use and governance of natural resources and the spread of democractic ideas into conservation. From this stance our comparative findings would treat the initiatives as an early stage in the evolution of a more society-based concept of conservation. The implications would relate to how to improve and speed up the diffusion and development of this process (because of the 'rightness' of its principles), rather than make judgements about whether specific initiatives represent 'value for money' in the short term. Such a view permits the experience of community-oriented approaches to be more deeply contextualized, but provides an analytical framework that is 'fuzzier' and lacks precision.

Policy makers and policy influencers in Africa find themselves having to operate within both of these perspectives with donors demanding a narrow, technical focus while the broader socio-political environment requires that policy be closely related to contemporary social processes.

The future of community conservation policy

Are community-oriented approaches 'good' policy? Should policy elites (politicians, bureaucrats, aid donors, NGOs and researchers) support them, continue to promote them but with significant changes, or abandon them and return to purely protectionist strategies?

For those who adopt a narrow technical perspective (particularly aid donors) it seems likely that in the next few years 'disenchantment' (Agrawal 1997) will occur as the outcomes of community conservation initiatives are judged against the 'objectively verifiable indicators' of their logical frameworks (and similar devices). The critique of ICDPs in Africa is already well advanced (Barrett and Arcese 1995; Stocking and Perkin 1992; Wainwright and Wehrmeyer 1998); in Indonesia disillusionment with community-based approaches appears to be well underway (Wells et al. 1999) and calls for a return to protectionist policies are becoming more voluble (Struhsaker 1997; Kramer et al. 1997). Cycles of enchantment and disenchantment are characteristic of programmes that attract aid funds when donors pile into an apparent panacea and then pull out when it does not deliver miracles[11] (e.g. small farmer credit, community development, integrated rural development projects and farming systems research). There is a distinct likelihood that some donors may decide to 'exit' from community conservation: this could lead to other donors following and, at least in aid-dependent countries (i.e. most of sub-Saharan Africa), national governments eventually losing interest in community-oriented approaches.

Technical analyses that move beyond the simplistic logic of linear cause and effect chains and that embrace ideas about institutional learning and change will produce a more optimistic view. Over the last decade community-oriented approaches have generated learning on an unprecedented scale (through both good and bad experiences) about how to involve local residents in conservation activities and about how to convert conservation resources (species, habitats and landscapes) into flows of economic benefits for local people and the wider economy. They have also revealed the importance of retaining and building on the intrinsic values that rural Africans hold for their environment (Chapters 10 and 11, this volume). Analyses from this perspective will lead to the conclusion that community conservation initiatives should be continued, but with significant changes.

Our judgement, taking this longer-term perspective, is that the shift to more community-oriented approaches has been worthwhile and should be continued and extended. It has helped to introduce three particular changes into conservation in Africa that raise the prospects for retaining key species and habitats while reducing the economic burden placed on rural people:

- in *economic* terms the initiatives have demonstrated the possibility of increasing the benefits, and reducing the costs, that wildlife imposes on its human neighbours;
- in *socio-political* terms it has made conservation slightly less socially illegitimate for African citizenries and provided pointers for ways in which conservation might one day be socially rehabilitated;
- in *managerial* terms it has made PA management more feasible (see Chapters 8–10) and has begun to introduce the idea into conservation bureaucracies that they may need a variety of strategies depending on goals and contexts.

Policy should continue to experiment and elaborate on community conservation and integrate conservation more effectively into the wider economy and broader processes of governance. There is a need, however, to clarify the goals of community conservation initiatives so that they are recognized as a means of developing institutions that can manage the trade-off between the conservation of species and habitats (against a context of species and habitat loss) and permitting natural resource access and use by rural Africans to improve their livelihoods. In some situations, especially those with tourist or safari-hunting potential, a 'win–win' solution may be feasible but in many others conservation will mean the negotiation of 'least worst' scenarios for environmental change. Meeting the basic needs and rising aspirations of Africa's growing population will entail significant modifications to most environments, as has been the case on all other continents. Governments, organizations and individuals in the West who seek pro-conservation processes of environmental change in protected and unprotected areas suited to agriculture, cattle-raising or timber extraction will need to increase their capacity to transfer revenues from the West to Africa to subsidize land uses that are economically sub-optimal from a livelihoods perspective.

Towards better practice

'Best practice' in community conservation is not so much about transferring 'good' experiences from one programme to another. Rather, it is about strengthening the capacities of conservation agencies, communities and programme managers to experiment, learn and take effective decisions within the constraints of the contexts in which they work. Indeed, if there is a clear practical lesson from our research it is for the need to avoid seeing the organization of community conservation in terms of a 'project model', especially during the early phases of implementation. The experience in Namibia, Uganda, Tanzania and Zimbabwe indicates that progress in community-oriented approaches is through an experimental process that responds to local contexts and contingencies. Ideas about adaptive management (Holling 1978) and process projects (Rondinelli 1993; Bond and Hulme 1999), based on organic rather than mechanical metaphors, are the ones that managers need to take as their guides. Agi Kiss, Environmental Adviser for East Africa to the World Bank, is highly critical of standard project approaches: 'CBC [community-based conservation] is generally not working because it is being pursued primarily through projects, and the project model is the wrong mechanism for achieving biodiversity conservation' (Kiss 1999: 2).

There are a number of key decisions that usually need to be taken early on in a community-based approach that have profound implications for later stages. These decisions need considerable attention, even though it is hard to predict how they will affect future performance. The most significant relate to the delimitation of the 'community'; the selection of the agency or institution within the community that will take on management responsibilities; and the authorities that will be delegated to the community. Managers should anticipate that the delimitation of a community will commonly generate contestation as local residents (and others) seek to ensure that they are included within the unit and as local powerholders try to make sure that their influence is not eroded. While the main focus of both action and research on institutions has been 'the community', our research findings concur with Agrawal and Gibson's (1999) that the focus should be on the linkages between different organizations and the means by which checks and balances can be introduced so that no organization has unchecked authority. Effective community conservation is not simply about conservation agency–community links, but about a network of public, community and private institutions. Monitoring experimental initiatives and seeking to influence the behaviour of other stakeholders are often far more important to goal achievement than tightly controlling activities according to a plan.[12]

The selection of the management authority within the community is also likely to generate competition, except in cases when there is no choice. At times managers may have some discretion about this matter, but at other times politicians will take the decision. A key issue concerns the relative advantages and disadvantages of selecting an existing community institution (such as the 'traditional authority'), a unit of local administration or creating a new unit. In Zambia, ADMADE has opted for the traditional authority. This has facilitated rapid implementation and reduced the costs of institutional development. However, critics of the programme describe it as 'chief-based conservation' (a parody of community-based conservation) and argue that the benefits of wildlife utilization are largely captured by the rural elite. In Uganda, parish resource management committees (PRMCs) and park management advisory committees (PMACs) have worked well for the Uganda Wildlife Authority – leaving most authority in the hands of wardens – but have produced a very passive form of community involvement. CAMPFIRE was based on a 'strategic compromise' (Murphree 1997a; Jones and Murphree, Chapter 4, this volume) that gave authority to the rural district councils. This worked well initially but has now become a major constraint for the programme. The 'rule of thumb' that many now advise is that the level at which benefits accrue should be the level at which management occurs and that tenure over natural resources should be delegated to the lowest level of social scale possible.[13] Devolution needs to focus on creating 'nested sets' of institutions – at different levels of scale and sometimes involving federations of local organizations – rather than an all-powerful authority (as occurred with the RDCs in Zimbabwe).

While many analysts recommend the adoption of the deepest level of community participation that is possible (see Pimbert and Pretty 1994 for a discussion), experienced managers and detailed analyses of rural development (Uphoff 1986) caution that local institutions have to develop their managerial capacities and so it is best to plan for a sequenced build-up of responsibilities in line with the development of their capacity.

The final observation in this section concerns the importance of ensuring that the managers of community-based approaches and community conservation wardens (and their line managers) are part of a network that encourages them to exchange ideas and experiences and reflect on their practice. This can help to make them pursue adaptive management strategies. While such activities, especially attending seminars, can become a time management problem for those involved in community conservation, regular opportunities to informally talk things through with peers is important in a field where opportunities to routinize decisions are often limited and innovation is so important.

The missing link

The move to community-based approaches has led to the forging of new relationships between rural Africans and a variety of different agencies. The main focus of programme attention has been on developing community linkages with the public and non-profit sectors, however, and linkages with the private sector have been relatively neglected, except in some parts of southern Africa. This is not surprising, given that most of the proponents of community conservation are public servants, work for NGOs or are academics and researchers. It is, though, a weakness in many programmes as the 'high value-added' activities associated with conservation (tourism and safari-hunting) are fields in which local communities have a considerable comparative disadvantage. Such enterprises require international contacts, reliable access to e-mail, fax and telephone, a capacity to handle foreign-exchange transactions, equipment (cars, refrigerators, generators and air-conditioners), staff fluent in English and the social skills associated with providing services to wealthy Europeans and Americans. Such concentrations of skills and capacities reside largely in the formal private sector at national and international levels. Well-intentioned attempts by public servants and NGOs to assist villagers to provide services on a direct basis to tourists have often foundered (as with the community camping site at Mgahinga Gorilla National Park in Uganda and the community rondavels at Gatche Gatche in Zimbabwe). For safari-hunting direct provision is not usually feasible as hunts must be run by qualified and registered professional hunters. There is also much anecdotal evidence that a significant proportion of safari hunters hold right-wing views that shade into racism and that they prefer to be guided by 'white hunters' rather than black Africans.

Given this situation, the economic arguments for community conservation indicate that there is a need for community–business partnerships and, if communities are to see a significant return on conservation as a land use, for such partnerships to reward communities with a significant share of the value added. The Kunene and Mahenye case studies (Chapters 11 and 12, this volume) provide examples of such partnerships but such experiences are relatively rare. Not uncommonly, private business seeks to pay very low rates for access to community wildlife resources (for an example see Southgate and Hulme 1996 on a Kenyan tour operator), and to concentrate payments in the hands of village headmen (who, in effect, become rentiers of the community's resources) and sometimes 'cheat' villagers in both blatant and sophisticated ways.[14] To improve the 'share' that communities receive from activities managed by private businesses requires action on at least three fronts. One is developing community capacity to negotiate 'better deals' with the private sector and to regulate them more effectively (WWF in Zimbabwe has worked extensively in this field) and/or to encourage NGOs or private businesses to offer advisory services to communities (Coopers and Lybrand in Zimbabwe provide such services on a fee-paid basis to some CAMPFIRE communities). The second is to foster a more socially responsible private sector by 'educating' private operators and by encouraging self-regulation.[15] This can be done on the grounds that it is 'right' (a moral argument) and also that it is profitable as it will allow businesses and communities to reach long-term agreements that benefit both parties (a 'bottom line' argument). Further work in this area is crucial to the development of community-based conservation as, if the bulk of rewards generated by pro-conservation practices do not reach villagers, other land uses (agriculture, grazing and 'poaching') will be preferred. The third front is to develop wildlife regimes that give communities legal status as the proprietors of wildlife and its habitats. As proprietors local people are in a much stronger position to negotiate with the private sector (see Jones, Chapter 11, this volume).

Conclusion

The move to more community-oriented approaches to conservation in Africa has taken many different forms. As this chapter has argued, judgements about whether their performance has matched their promise depend on the perspective and time scale that are taken and the criteria that are set. Community conservation has not proved the panacea that many had hoped for and short-term technical analyses seeking to measure whether 'conservation' and 'development' have both improved are likely to lead to negative conclusions and 'disenchantment' with the strategy. However, re-inventing conservation in Africa – for that is the task in hand – was never going to be a quick job that could be easily accomplished.

If a longer-term perspective is adopted then the evidence from our studies points to the conclusion that community conservation has made a useful contribution to pushing forward knowledege about more effective institutional frameworks for conservation. It has not displaced protectionist approaches, rather it extends the range of strategies that conservation managers can pursue. In some contexts it may represent the optimal approach, while in others it may best serve as an adjunct to law enforcement. For certain conservation goals, for example the conservation of a small habitat containing rare species and surrounded by intensive agriculture, it may be inappropriate, and well-functioning law enforcement may be the sole strategy.

In the future the institutional focus must move beyond the community to explore ways in which networks of institutions – conservation bureaucracies, local author-ities, community organizations, federations, NGOs and private businesses – can evolve that can negotiate the needs of different stakeholders, provide checks and balances on each other's activities and performance and provide support services. Our research points to the urgent need to improve community–private sector linkages.

A conservation that can protect Africa's unique species and habitats; that can reduce the costs it imposes on, and increase the benefits it provides to, rural people; and that can make conservation less socially illegitimate than it presently is for the citizens of African countries, is many decades away. The community conservation initiatives that we have described and analysed here may have made only small contributions to conservation and development goals in concrete terms. They have created, however, a knowledge base from which a more effective institutional framework for conservation can evolve. We urge those engaged with conservation in Africa to take a long-term view and to continue with this experiment.

Notes

[1] In a smaller number of examples this is attempted by having public distributions of equally sized cash payments to each household.

[2] Patel's (1998) critique of CAMPFIRE criticizes USAID and other donors for creating an air of local origins and sustainability around the programme. Many in Zimbabwe would argue that she does not understand the history of CAMPFIRE and that her analysis arises more from inter-agency polemics than from a grasp of its evolution.

[3] This is a behaviour that sometimes precedes donor policy change. The classic example is of integrated rural development projects (IRDPs). USAID and the World Bank moved heavily into monitoring and evalu-ating these two or three years prior to their rejection of the IRDP strategy (Hulme and Limcaoco 1991).

[4]The closest that we have come to this is an analysis being undertaken of aerial wildlife counts in Kenya over 17 years. These reveal a statistically significant relationship between changes in wildlife population and the KWS pilot wildlife utilization programme. In the two districts where this has operated, wildlife numbers have been steady or marginally increasing. In all other districts (all of which are not part of the pilot programme) wildlife numbers have decreased (pers. comm., E Barrow).

[5]Against such a background it would be possible to run a conservation programme that 'saves' a species but could be judged to have degraded the environment as that species would have become extinct under 'natural' processes!

[6]Such questions and related forms of analysis are becoming increasingly important in Europe.

[7]Several groups, including Tourism Concern and Voluntary Services Overseas (VSO), are working on the issue of how to change the preferences of Western tourists visiting the 'third world'.

[8]These include debates about whether poverty is an absolute or relative concept, whether it is a condition or a social process and whether it can be assessed in terms of income or consumption or more holistically. See Maxwell (1999) for a concise review.

[9]A comprehensive approach would require large-scale baseline and follow-up poverty surveys, analysis to factor out what changes are attributable to variables other than community conservation and, probably, some very detailed ethnographic work.

[10]In addition, the practices associated with donor projects (four-wheel-drive vehicles, high levels of travel allowance, transport-intensive procedures) undermine prospects of financial sustainability (see the Ugandan examples).

[11]Brandon et al. (1998: 417) writes of the 'unrealistic, externally imposed missions' that are associated with external support for the conservation of protected areas.

[12]At the time of finalizing the manuscript we see that the Michael Wells et al. (1999) review of ICDPs in Indonesia has reached very similar conclusions. The processes by which ICDPs are designed and implemented are as much a cause of underperformance as the content of ICDPs. 'Conventional donor agency project cycles, with their heavy emphasis on planning at the expense of implementation, are proving incompatible with ICDPs... standard blueprint design approaches need to be replaced with alternatives that are more geared toward problem identification and solving through adaptive management' (ibid. 6).

[13]As discussed in Barrow and Murphree (Chapter 3, this volume) and as illustrated in the case study chapters, tenure over land and resources is central to the long-term prospects of community conservation initiatives. Reforming tenure policies is a long-term goal in most countries and while programme planners and managers should seek to influence policy, for extended periods they must expect to have to accommodate community conservation activities to the pre-existing legal framework.

[14]Examples of the blatant are safari hunting operators who do not transfer to communities their share of fees. More subtle are operators, such as one reported in Zimbabwe, who took out hunting leases on adjacent blocks where one block is attractive (flat and easily accessible flood plain) and another is not (rocky, scarp faces). Leasing the latter block is cheap, but the operator then lumps together the hunting quotas for both blocks and does all the hunting on the flood plain. Proving that this is happening is very difficult for villagers!

[15]In Europe and North America there has been rapidly growing interest by private businesses in 'social responsibility' and 'ethical trading' with partners.

Bibliography

Abrahamson, H (1997) *Seizing the Opportunity: Power and Powerlessness in a Changing World Order: the Case of Mozambique*, Zed Books, London and New York

Abrahamson, H and Nilsson, A (1995) *Mozambique the Troubled Transition: From Socialist Construction to Free Market Capitalism*, Zed Books, London and New York

Adams, J S and McShane, T O (1992) *The Myth of Wild Africa: Conservation Without Illusion*, Norton, New York

Adams, W M (1990) *Green Development: Environment and Sustainability in the Third World*, Routledge, London

Adams, W M (1996a) 'Creative Conservation, Landscapes and Loss', *Landscape Research* 21(3), 265–76

Adams, W M (1996b) *Future Nature*, Earthscan, London

Adams, W M (1997) 'Rationalisation and Conservation: Ecology and the Management of Nature in the United Kingdom', *Transactions of the Institute of British Geographers* NS 22, 277–91

Adams, W M and Infield, M (1998) *Community Conservation at Mgahinga Gorilla National Park, Uganda*, Community Conservation in Africa Working Papers No 10, IDPM, University of Manchester

Adams, W M and Thomas, D H L (1993) 'Mainstream Sustainable Development: the Challenge of Putting Theory into Practice', *Journal of International Development* 5(6), 591–604

Adams, W M and Thomas, D H L (1996) 'Conservation and Sustainable Resource Use in the Hadejia-Jama'are Valley, Nigeria', *Oryx* 30, 131–42

Africa Resources Trust (1998) 'Report on a Workshop on Community Tourism in Southern Africa', Windhoek, Namibia. Mimeo, ART, Harare

African Wildlife Foundation (1990) *Lake Mburo National Park: Park Support and Community Conservation* (a Proposal submitted to SIDA), AWF, Nairobi

African Wildlife Foundation (1992) *Strategic Action Plan for the TANAPA Community Conservation Service,* AWF, Nairobi

African Wildlife Foundation (1993) *Project Proposal: Community Conservation Around Tanzanian Wildlife Areas: Tarangire National Park Proposal,* AWF, Nairobi

African Wildlife Foundation (1994) *Protected Areas: Neighbours as Partners. Community Conservation around Tsavo West National Park,* Tsavo West Community Conservation Project Phase 2 Final Report, AWF, Nairobi

African Wildlife Foundation (1997) African Wildlife Foundation Community Conservation Service Centre, Arusha, *Bimonthly Report*, AWF, Nairobi

African Wildlife Foundation/TANAPA (1992a) *African Wildlife Foundation Community Conservation "Neighbours as Partners Programme" Knowledge, Attitudes and Practices Assessment, Tarangire National Park Survey*, AWF, Nairobi

African Wildlife Foundation/TANAPA (1992b) Tanzania National Parks Community Conservation Service, *Knowledge, Attitudes and Practices Assessment,* AWF, Nairobi

Agrawal, A (1997) *Community in Conservation: Beyond Enchantment and Disenchantment,* Conservation and Development Forum Discussion Paper, Conservation and Development Forum, University of Florida, Gainsville, FL

Agrawal, A and Gibson, C C (1999) 'Enchantment and Disenchantment: the Role of Community in Natural Resource Conservation', *World Development* 27(4), 629–50

Ahmed, M (1998) 'Urban and Peri-urban Land Tenure in Southern Lusophone Africa: Lessons from Post Socialist Countries' Experiences', *Proceedings of the International Conference on Land Tenure in the Developing World with a Focus on Southern Africa,* University of Cape Town, Cape Town, 10–20

Alchian, A A (1987) *Property Rights: The New Palgrave Dictionary of Economics,* Macmillan, London, 1031–4

Alexander, J (1997) 'The Local State in Post War Mozambique: Political Practice and Ideas about Authority', *Africa* 67(1), 32–51

Alexander, J and McGregor, J (1996) '"Our sons didn't die for animals." Attitudes to Wildlife and the Politics of Development: Campfire in the Nkayi and Lupane Districts', International Conference on the Historical Dimensions of Democracy and Human Rights in Zimbabwe, Harare

Anderson, D and Grove, R (eds) (1987) *Conservation in Africa: People, Policies and Practice,* Cambridge University Press, Cambridge

Anstey, S G and Chonguica, E W (1997) 'A Review of Community Natural Resource Management Initiatives in Mozambique', unpublished report to Southern African Sustainable Use Specialist Group/IIED Evaluating Eden Programme, mimeo, Maputo

Ashley, C (1995) *Tourism, Communities and the Potential Impacts on Local Incomes and Conservation,* Research Discussion Paper No 10, Directorate of Environmental Affairs, Windhoek, Namibia

Ashley, C and Barnes, J (1996) *Wildlife Use for Economic Gain: the Potential for Wildlife to Contribute to Development in Namibia,* Research Discussion Paper No 12, Directorate of Environmental Affairs, Windhoek, Namibia

Baldus, R D (1991) *Community Wildlife Management Around the Selous Game Reserve,* Wildlife Division and Selous Conservation Project, Dar-es-Salaam

Barber, C V, Afiff, S A and Purnomo, A (1996) *Tiger by the Tail? Reorienting Biodiversity Conservation and Development in Indonesia,* World Resources Institute, Washington DC

Barker, J (1989) *Rural Communities under Stress: Peasant Farmers and the State in Africa,* Cambridge University Press, Cambridge

Barnes, J and de Jager, J (1996) *Economic and Financial Incentives for Wildlife Use on Private Land in Namibia and the Implications for Policy,* Research Discussion Paper No 8, Directorate of Environmental Affairs, Windhoek, Namibia

Barrett, C S and Arcese, P (1995) 'Are Integrated Conservation-Development Projects (ICDPs) Sustainable? On the Conservation of Large Mammals in Sub-Saharan Africa', *World Development* 23(7), 1073–84

Barrow, E G C (1995) 'Community Conservation Approaches to Conservation in East Africa: An Overview of Experiences to Date', *Proceedings of a Participatory*

Wildlife Management Workshop, Ministry of Natural Resources Development and Environmental Protection, Addis Ababa, Ethiopia

Barrow, E G C (1996a) 'Partnerships and Empowerment – Community Conservation Approaches and Experience from East Africa', *Rural Extension Bulletin* No 10, Reading University, 5–13

Barrow, E G C (1996b) *Community Conservation Approaches and Experiences from East Africa,* Community Conservation Discussion Papers No 4, African Wildlife Foundation, Nairobi

Barrow, E G C (1997) 'Framework for Community Conservation', mimeo, African Wildlife Foundation, Nairobi

Barrow, E G C and Infield, M (1997) 'Community Conservation in Uganda: a Review', mimeo, African Wildlife Foundation, Nairobi

Barrow, E G C, Bergin, P, Infield, M and Lembuya, P (1995a) 'Community Conservation Lessons from Benefit Sharing in East Africa', in J A Bissonette and P R Krausman (eds) *Integrating People and Wildlife for a Sustainable Future,* Bethesda Wildlife Society, 21–6

Barrow, E G C, Bergin, P, Infield, M and Lembuya, P (1995b) 'The People's Voice: Partnership and Community Conservation', in J A Bissonette and P R Krausman (eds) *Integrating People and Wildlife for a Sustainable Future,* Bethesda Wildlife Society, 225–59

Barrow, E G C, Kangwana, K and Berger, D (1995c) 'The Role of the African Wildlife Foundation in the Evolution of Community Conservation Practise and Policy in Kenya', in *Environmental Policy Formulation in Kenya: Private Sector/NGO Roles,* Proceedings of a Workshop in Washington DC, African Centre for Technology Studies, Nairobi

Barrow, E G C, Kangwana, K and Berger, D (1996) *The Role of the African Wildlife Foundation in the Evolution of Community Conservation Practice and Policy in Kenya,* Community Conservation Discussion Paper No 10, African Wildlife Foundation, Nairobi

Barrow, E G C, Gichohi, H and Infield, M (1998) *A Review of Community Conservation in East Africa,* Institute for Development Policy and Management, University of Manchester, and IIED, London

Bataamba, A M (1994) *The Lake Mburo National Park Management Plan 1994–1998,* Ugandan National Parks, Kampala

Bayart, J F, Ellis, S and Hibou, B (1999) *The Criminalization of the State in Africa,* James Currey, Oxford

Bell, R H V (1987) 'Conservation with a Human Face: Conflict and Reconciliation in African Land Use Planning', in D Anderson and R Grove (eds) *Conservation in Africa: People, Policies and Practice,* Cambridge University Press, Cambridge

Bell, R H V and McShane-Caluzi, E (eds) (1985) *Conservation and Wildlife Management in Africa,* Proceedings of a Workshop held at Kasungu National Park, Malawi, October 1984, US Peace Corps, Lilongwe

Bensted-Smith, R (1992) *Let the Money Go Where the Wildlife Goes,* Kenya Wildlife Service Public Briefing Document on Revenue Sharing, KWS, Nairobi

Bensted-Smith, R and Leaver, B (1996) *Report of Evaluation of Ngorongoro Conservation and Development Project Phase II: Management Plan Development,* IUCN, The World Conservation Union, Oxford

Berger, D O (1993) *Wildlife Extension: Participatory Conservation by the Maasai of Kenya*, ACTS, Nairobi

Berger, J (ed) (1988) *People, Parks and Wildlife: Guideline for Public Participation in Wildlife Conservation: Case Studies in Kenya*, UNEP and Wildlife Fund Trustees, Nairobi

Berger, J (1989) 'Wildlife Extension: a Participatory Approach to Conservation', PhD Dissertation, University of California, Berkeley

Bergin, P (1995a) *Community Based Conservation in Tanzania*, Department of Wildlife with AWF and WWF, Dar-es-Salaam, Tanzania

Bergin, P (1995b) 'Conservation and Development: the Institutionalization of Community Conservation in Tanzania National Parks', PhD Thesis, University of East Anglia, Norwich

Bergin, P and Dembe, E (1996) 'Parks and People in Tanzania: an Overview of the Tanzania National Parks Community Conservation Service', in *Participatory Wildlife Management, Rural Extension Bulletin* No 10, 14–18

Bergin, P and Lyamuya, V (1996) *Rehabilitation of Kagera Game Reserves Project: Appraisal of Bill of Quantities for Community Based Conservation Program*, report to CARE, Dar es Salaam, Tanzania

Berkes, F (ed) (1989) *Common Property Resources: Ecology and Community-Based Sustainable Development*, Belhaven Press, London

Blaikie, P and Brookfield, H (1987) *Land Degradation and Society*, Methuen, London

Blowers, J (1984) 'National Parks for Developing Countries', in A McNeely and K R Miller (eds) *National Parks, Conservation and Development: the Role of Protected Areas in Sustaining Society*, Smithsonian Institute Press, Washington DC, 722–7

Blunt, P and Jones, M L (1992) *Managing Organisations in Africa*, 2 Volumes, Walter de Gruyter, Berlin

Boardman, R (1981) *International Organisations and the Conservation of Nature*, Indiana University Press, Bloomington, IN

Bojö, J (1996) *The Economics of Wildlife: Case Studies from Ghana, Kenya, Namibia and Zimbabwe*, AFTES Working Paper, World Bank, Washington DC

Bond, I (1993) 'The Economics of Wildlife and Land Use in Zimbabwe: an Examination of Current Knowledge and Issues', WWF Multispecies Animal Production Systems Project Paper No 36, WWF, Harare

Bond, I (1994) 'The Importance of Sport-Hunted African Elephants to CAMPFIRE in Zimbabwe', *Traffic Bulletin* 14, 117–19

Bond I (1997a) 'Tourism and Sport Hunting in Zimbabwe: a Summary of Current Status, Potential and Constraints', in D H M Cumming and T J P Lynam (eds) *Land Use Changes, Wildlife Conservation and Utilisation, and the Sustainability of Agro-Ecosystems in the Zambezi Valley, Final Technical Report*, Volume Two, WWF Programme Office, Harare

Bond, I (1997b) 'An Assessment of the Financial Benefits to Households from CAMPFIRE: the Wildlife Benefit-Cost Ratio', *CAMPFIRE News* 15, May, CAMPFIRE Association, Harare

Bond, I (1998) 'The Financial Performance of Three Non-Lease Tourism Projects: Money and Markets', *CAMPFIRE News* 17, CAMPFIRE Association, Harare

Bond, I (1999) CAMPFIRE as a Vehicle for Sustainable Rural Development in the Semi-Arid Communal Lands of Zimbabwe: Incentives for Institutional Change,

PhD thesis, Department of Agricultural Economics and Extension, Faculty of Agriculture, University of Zimbabwe, Harare

Bond, R (1997) *Operationalizing Process: the Experience of the First Decade of the Moneragala IRDP in Sri Lanka*, IDPM Discussion Paper 50, Institute for Development Policy and Management, University of Manchester

Bond, R and Hulme, D (1999) 'Process Approaches to Development: Theory and Sri Lankan Practice', *World Development* 27(8), 1339–58

Bonner, R (1985) *At the Hand of Man: Peril and Hope for Africa's Wildlife*, Knopf, New York

Booth, V R (1991) *An Ecological Resource Survey of Mahenye Ward, Ndowoyo Communal Land, Chipinge District*, WWF Multispecies Animal Production Systems Project Paper No 20, WWF, Harare

Borner, M (1985) 'The Increasing Isolation of Tarangire National Park', *Oryx* 19, 80–8

Borrini-Feyerbend, G (1996) 'Collaborative Management of Protected Areas: Tailoring the Approach to the Context', *Issues in Social Policy*, IUCN, Gland, Switzerland

Boshe, J (1996) *Models of Wildlife Management: Tanzania, African Wildlife Policy Consultation, Final Report of the Consultation*, Overseas Development Administration, London, 73–94

Botkin, D (1990) *Discordant Harmony*, Oxford University Press, Oxford

Bourdillon, M F C (1987) *The Shona Peoples*, Mambo Press, Gweru, Zimbabwe

Brandon, K, Redford, K H and Sanderson, S E (1998) *Parks in Peril: People, Politics and Protected Areas*, Island Press, Washington DC

Brockington, D and Homewood, K (1996) 'Debates Concerning Mkomazi Game Reserve, Tanzania', in M Leach and R Mearns (eds) *The Lie of the Land: Challenging Received Wisdom on the African Environment*, James Currey, London, 91–104

Bromley, D W (1994) 'Economic Dimensions of Community-Based Conservation', in D Western and R M Wright (eds) *Natural Connections, Perspectives in Community Based Conservation*, Island Press, Washington DC, 428–47

Bromley, D W and Cernea, M M (1989) *The Management of Common Property Natural Resources: Some Conceptual and Operational Fallacies*, World Bank Discussion Papers No 57, The World Bank, Washington DC

Brown, C J (1991) 'Socio-ecological Survey of Parts of East Caprivi – Interim Report', Internal report, Ministry of Wildlife, Conservation and Tourism, Windhoek

Brown, C J (1996) 'The Outlook for the Future', in: *Namibia Environment, Vol.1*, Directorate of Environmental Affairs, Windhoek

Brown, C J and Jones, B T B (eds) (1994) 'Results of a socio-ecological survey of the West Caprivi Strip, Namibia: A Strategic Community-based Environment and Development Plan', Directorate of Environmental Affairs, Windhoek

Brown, G and Henry, W (1989) *The Economic Value of Elephants*, London Environmental Economics Centre Discussion Paper, London

Brown, L D and Ashman, D (1996) 'Participation, Social Capital and Inter-Sectoral Problem Solving: African and Asian Cases', *World Development* 24(9), 1467–79

Brown, M and Wyckoff-Baird, B (1992) *Designing Integrated Conservation and Development Projects*, Biodiversity Support Program, Washington DC

Bruce, J W (1990) *Legal Issues in Land Use and Resettlement*, background paper for the Agriculture Division, Southern Africa Department of the World Bank, Harare

Bruce, J W (1998) 'Learning from the Comparative Experience with Agrarian Land Reform', *Proceedings of the International Conference on Land Tenure in the Developing World with a Focus on Southern Africa*, University of Cape Town, Cape Town, 39–48

Buckland, S T, Anderson, D R, Burnham, K P and Laake, J L (1993) *Distance Sampling: Estimating Abundance of Biological Populations*, Chapman and Hall, London

Budiansky, S (1995) *Nature's Keepers: the New Science of Nature Management*, Phoenix Publishing, New York

Busulwa, H (1992) *Lake Mburo Fisheries Management Study*, report to Uganda National Parks, Kampala

Butynski, T M and Kalina, J (1993) 'Three New Mountain Parks for Uganda', *Oryx* 27(4), 214–24

Caldecott, J (1996) *Designing Conservation Projects*, Cambridge University Press, Cambridge

Campbell, K L I (1988) *Serengeti Ecological Monitoring Programme: Programme Report*, March, Serengeti Wildlife Research Centre, Arusha, Tanzania

Campbell, L M (1997) International Conservation and Sustainable Development: the Conservation of Marine Turtles in Costa Rica, PhD Thesis, University of Cambridge, Cambridge

CAMPFIRE News (1998) 'Further Devolution is Needed', CAMPFIRE News 17, CAMPFIRE Association, Harare

CARE International (1997) *EIA Study of the Proposed Upgrading of the Kabiranyuma Gravity Flow Water Scheme in Mgahinga Gorilla National Park*, CARE International in Uganda, Kampala

Carley, M and Christie, I (1997) *Managing Sustainable Development*, Earthscan Publications, London

Carney, D (ed) (1998) *Sustainable Rural Livelihoods*, Department for International Development, London

Carpenter, S and Kennedy, W J D (1985) 'Managing Environmental Conflict by Applying Common Sense', *Negotiation Journal* 1(2), 62–74

Carswell, G (1997) African Farmers in Colonial Kigezi, Uganda, 1930–1962: Opportunity, Constraint and Sustainability, PhD dissertation, University of London

Caughley, G (1977) *Analysis of Vertebrate Populations*, Wiley-Interscience, New York

Cernea, M (ed) (1991) *Putting People First*, Oxford University Press, Oxford

Chambers, R (1983) *Rural Development: Putting the Last First*, Longman, London

Chambers, R (1993) *Challenging the Professions: Frontiers for Rural Development*, Intermediate Technology Publications, London

Chambers, R, Pacey, A and Thrupp, L A (eds) (1989) *Farmer First: Farmer Innovation and Agricultural Research*, Intermediate Technology Publications, London

Cheater, A P (1989) 'The Ideology of "Communal" Land Tenure in Zimbabwe: Mythogenesis Enacted', *Africa* 60(2), 188–206

Cheater, A P (1994) Problems of Scaling in Rural Technology and Development: the Role of Institutions and Technology in Resource Management, University of Zimbabwe, Harare

Child, B A (1988) The Role of Wildlife Utilisation in the Sustainable Development of Semi-Arid Rangelands in Zimbabwe, DPhil Thesis, Oxford University, Oxford

Child, B A (1995a) *A Summary of the Marketing of Trophy Quotas in CAMPFIRE Areas 1990 -1993*, CAMPFIRE Coordination Unit, Department of National Parks and Wildlife Management, Harare

Child, B A (1995b) *Guidelines for Managing Communal Lands Wildlife Revenue in Accordance with Policy for Wildlife, Zimbabwe*, CAMPFIRE Coordination Unit, Department of National Parks and Wildlife Management, Harare

Child, B A (1996) 'Conservation Beyond Yellowstone: an Economic Framework for Wildlife Conservation', *African Wildlife Policy Consultation*, Overseas Development Administration, London

Child, G F T (1995) *Wildlife and People: the Zimbabwean Success. How the Conflict Between Animals and People Became Progress for Both*, WISDOM Foundation, Harare and New York

Chipinge Rural District Council (1986–1994) *Files on CAMPFIRE; Mahenye Ward; Council Minutes at Chipinge RDC*, Chipinge, Zimbabwe

Chipinge Rural District Council (1996) *Memorandum of a Lease Agreement for Communal Land for Trading or Other Purposes Made and Entered into and Between Chipinge Rural District Council and Zimbabwe Sun Limited*, in Chipinge RDC files, Chipinge, Zimbabwe

Chiwewe, W (1994) 'Address to Gokwe North Rural District Council (13–06–94)', *Minutes of a Special Full Council Meeting*, Nembudziya, Zimbabwe

Coleman, J (1990) *Foundations of Social Theory*, Belknap Press, Cambridge

Collinson, R (1985) 'Selecting Wildlife Census Techniques', *Monograph* 6, Institute of Natural Resources, University of Natal

Cooke, A and Hamid, A S (1998) 'Misali Island Conservation Area, Pemba: an Analysis of Activities and Lessons Learnt', paper presented to Workshop on Experiences in Local and Community Integrated Coastal Zone Management Projects: Lessons to Date, Zanzibar, 4–6 March, mimeo at African Wildlife Foundation, Nairobi

Cooksey, B (1992) 'Who's Poor in Tanzania? A Review of Recent Poverty Research', *Bagachwa*, 57–90

Corbett, A and Daniels, C (1996) 'Legislation and Policy Affecting Community-based Natural Resource Management in Namibia', Social Science Division, University of Namibia, Windhoek

Cousins, B (1998) 'How do Rights Become Real? Formal and Informal Institutions in South Africa's Tenure Reform Program', *Proceedings of the International Conference on Land Tenure in the Developing World with Focus on Southern Africa*, University of Cape Town, Cape Town, 88–100

Coward, E W (1979) 'Principles of Social Organisation in an Indigenous Irrigation System', *Human Organization* 38(1), 28–36

Cumming, D H M (1990) *Wildlife Products and the Marketplace: A View from Southern Africa*, WWF Multispecies Project, Harare

Cumming, D H M (1989) 'Commercial and Safari Hunting in Zimbabwe', in R J Hudson, K R Drew and L M Baskin (eds) *Wildlife Production Systems: Economic Utilisation of Wild Ungulates*, Cambridge University Press, Cambridge

Cumming, D H M (1983) 'The Decision-Making Framework with Regard to the Culling of Large Mammals in Zimbabwe', in R N Owen-Smith (ed) *Management of Large Mammals in African Conservation Areas*, Haum, Pretoria

Cumming D H M and Lynam, T J P (1997) *Landuse Changes, Wildlife Conservation and Utilisation and the Sustainability of Agro-Ecosystesms in the Zambezi Valley, Final Technical Report,* volume 1, WWF, Harare

Cunningham, A B (1996) *People, Park and Plant Use: Recommendations for Multiple-Use Zones and Development Alternatives Around Bwindi Impenetrable National Park, Uganda,* People and Plants Working Paper No 4, UNESCO, Paris

Cunningham, A B, Wild, R, Mutebi, J and Tsekeli, A (1993) *People and Wild Plant Use: Mgahinga Gorilla National Park,* CARE-International, Kampala, Uganda

Cutshall, C R (1989) *Masoka/Kanyurira Ward: a Socio-Economic Baseline Survey of Community Households,* Center for Applied Social Sciences, University of Zimbabwe, Harare

Da Cunha, F J (1998) *Aspectos Juridico-Legais da Participaçao das Communidades na Gestao dos Recursos Naturais,* IUCN Mozambique Publication, Maputo

Dassmann, D and Mossman, A (1960) 'The Utilisation of Game Mammals on a Rhodesian Ranch', paper presented at the annual meeting of the Wildlife Society, California Section, Davis, California

Davies, R (1993) Cost Benefit Analysis of Pilansberg National Park, MS thesis, Graduate School of Business Leadership, University of South Africa

De La Harpe, D A (1994) *The Lowland Conservancies: New Opportunities for Productive and Sustainable Land Use,* Price-Waterhouse, Harare

Dembe, E and Bergin, P (1996) *Defining the 'Conservation' in Community Conservation: Strategic Planning in Tanzania National Parks,* Community Conservation Discussion Paper No 5, African Wildlife Foundation, Nairobi

Deodatus, F (1996) 'Wildlife Damage in Rural Areas', paper presented at Workshop on Costs and Benefits of Wildlife in Africa, Lewa Downs, Kenya

Department of Social Welfare (1994) *A Statistical Overview of the Department of Social Welfare Drought Relief Operations 1982–1993,* Drought Relief Programme, Department of Social Welfare, Ministry of Public Service, Labour and Social Welfare, Government of Zimbabwe

Derman, B W (1990) *The Unsettling of the Zambezi Valley: an Examination of the Mid-Zambezi Rural Development Project,* CASS Working Paper, University of Zimbabwe, Harare

Derman, B W (1997) *Changing Land-Use in the Eastern Zambezi Valley: Socio-Economic Considerations,* Report submitted to World Wide Fund for Nature and the Center for Applied Social Sciences, University of Zimbabwe, Harare

De Valk, P and Wekwete, K H (1990) 'Challenges for Local Government in Zimbabwe', in P De Valk and K H Wekwete (eds) *Decentralising for Participatory Planning: Comparing the Experiences of Zimbabwe and Other Anglophone Countries in East and Southern Africa,* Avebury, Aldershot

Dewdney, R (1996) 'Policy factors and desertification – analysis and proposals', Namibian Programme to Combat Desertification Steering Committee, Windhoek

DICE (1997) *Tourism, Conservation and Development, Volume IV, The South-East Louveld, Zimbabwe,* Final Report to the Department for International Development, by the Durrell Institute of Conservation and Ecology (DICE) and the Institute of Mathematics and Statistics (IMS) of the University of Kent

DNFFB (1997) *Forestry and Wildlife Policy and Strategies,* Ministry of Agriculture and Fisheries, Maputo

DNFFB (1998) 'Forestry and Wildlife Component: Agriculture Programme (PROAGRI) of Ministry of Agriculture and Fisheries', unpublished MAP report, Maputo

DNFFB/GEF (1996) *Mozambique Transfrontier Conservation Areas Pilot and Institutional Strengthening Project,* Project Document DNFFB/World Bank/GEF, Maputo

Dorobo Tours and Safaris (1997a) *Guidelines for Facilitating Village Based Planning and Management of Land Resources,* Dorobo Tours and Safaris, Arusha

Dorobo Tours and Safaris (1997b) *Potential Model for Community-Based Conservation Among Pastoral Communities Adjacent to Protected Areas in Northern Tanzania,* Dorobo Tours and Safaris, Arusha

Dorobo Tours and Safaris (1997c) *Community Centered Conservation: a Potential Model for Pastoral Communities Adjacent to Protected Areas in Northern Tanzania,* Dorobo Tours and Safaris, Arusha

Douglas-Hamilton, I and Associates (1988) *Identification Study for the Conservation and Sustainable Use of the Natural Resources in the Kenyan Portion of the Mara-Serengeti Ecosystem,* report prepared for the European Development Fund of the European Economic Community, Nairobi

Douglas-Hamilton, I and Douglas-Hamilton, O (1992) *Battle for the Elephants,* Doubleday, New York

Drinkwater, M (1991) *The State and Agrarian Change in Zimbabwe's Communal Areas,* Macmillan Publishing, London

Durbin, J, Jones, B T B and Murphree, W M (1997) *Namibian Community-Based Natural Resource Management Programme,* WWF NA 0004, Namibia, Project Evaluation, World Wide Fund for Nature, Gland, Switzerland

Dutton, T F and Dutton, E A R (1973) *Reconhecimento Preliminar das Montanhas de Chimanimani e Zonas Adjacentes com Vista a Criacao Duma Area de Conservacao,* Ministry of Agriculture and Fisheries, Maputo

Dzingirai, V (1994) *Politics and Ideology in Human Settlement: Getting Settled in the Sokomena Area of Chief Dobola,* CASS Working Paper, University of Zimbabwe, Harare

Earthy, E D (1933) *Valenge Women,* Frank Cass, London

EC and TANAPA (1997) *Analysis of Migratory Movement of Large Mammals and Their Interaction with Human Activities in the Tarangire Area in Tanzania as a Contribution to a Conservation and Sustainable Development Strategy,* Tarangire Conservation Project, Final Report, a joint project of the European Commission, Tanzania National Parks, University of Milan and Europe Conservation, Arusha

The Economist (1999) 'A Hard-Edged Attitude to Wildlife Conservation', *The Economist,* 12 June, 121–2

Eilerts, G (1994) *An Assessment of Vulnerability in Zimbabwe's Communal Lands,* USAID Famine Early Warning System (FEWS) Zimbabwe, Project Office, Harare

Eilerts, G and Vhurumuku, E (1997) *Zimbabwe Food Security and Vulnerability Assessment 1996/97,* USAID Famine Early Warning System (FEWS), Zimbabwe, Project Office, Harare

Eltringham, S K and Malpas, R C (1992) *The Conservation Status of Uganda's Game and Forest Reserves in 1982 and 1983*, Uganda Institute of Ecology, Kampala

Emerton, L (1992) *Socio-Economic Findings on Utilisation of Kakamega Forest*, KIFCON/Forest Department, Ministry of Environment and Natural Resources, Nairobi

Emerton, L (1996) *Maasai Livelihoods, Forest Use and Conservation in Oldonyo Orok, Kenya*, Applied Conservation Economics Discussion Paper No. 2, African Wildlife Foundation, Nairobi

Emerton, L (1997a) *The Economics of Tourism and Wildlife Conservation in Africa*, Applied Conservation Economics Discussion Paper No. 4, African Wildlife Foundation, Nairobi

Emerton, L (1997b) *An Economic Assessment of Mount Kenya Forest*, report prepared by African Wildlife Foundation for EU Project 7 ACP KA 009, Nairobi

Emerton, L (1997c) *Summary of the Local Economic Value of Forests in Central, Copperbelt and Luapula Provinces of Zambia*, Provincial Forestry Action Plan Publication, Ndola, Zambia

Emerton, L (1998) *The Economics of Community Conservation at Lake Mburo National Park, Uganda*, Community Conservation in Africa Working Papers No 6, IDPM, University of Manchester, Manchester

Emerton, L and Mogaka, H (1996) 'Participatory Environmental Valuation: Subsistence Forest Use Around the Aberdares, Kenya', *Participatory Learning and Action Notes* 26, International Institute for Environment and Development, London, 6–10

Engelbrecht, W and van der Walt, P (1993) 'Notes on the Economic Use of Kruger National Park', *Koedoe* 35(2), 113–19

Esman, M J and Uphoff, N (1984) *Local Organizations: Intermediaries in Rural Development*, Cornell University Press, Ithaca, NY

Etzioni, A (1993) *The Spirit of Community*, Fontana, New York

Evans, D (1992) *A History of Nature Conservation in Great Britain*, Routledge, London

EXA (1992) *Zimbabwe Tourism Development Programme: Regional Market Analysis*, prepared by David Kaufman on behalf of Exa International, Paris, France

FAO (1988) *An Interim Report on the State of Forest Resources in Developing Countries*, FAO, Rome

Farquharson, L (1993) Commercial Wildlife Utilization in Zimbabwe: Are Commercial Farms the Appropriate Model for CAMPFIRE?, unpublished dissertation, McGill University, Montreal

Feldmann, F (1994) 'Community Environmental Action: The National Policy Context', in D Western and R M Wright (eds) *Natural Connections: Perspectives on Community-based Conservation,* Island Press, Washington DC, 393–402

Fisher, R J (1995) *Collaborative Management of Forests for Conservation and Development,* IUCN, Gland, Switzerland

Fitter, R S R and Scott, P (1978) *The Penitent Butchers*, Collins, London

Food and Agriculture Organization (1997) *Annotated Discussion Draft of the Proposed National Parks Act*, FAO, Rome

Forum (1993) 'Science and Sustainability', *Ecological Applications* 3, 545–89

Fotso, R C (1996) 'Two Models for Bio-diversity Conservation and Community Development Integrated Projects in Cameroon', paper presented to Pan African Symposium on Sustainable Use of Natural Resources and Community

Participation, Harare, June, mimeo at CASS Library, University of Zimbabwe, Harare

Fraser Stewart, J W (1992) *Integrating Local Communities with Protected Area and Wildlife Management in Uganda*, Field Document No 6 for FAO Project DP: FO UGA/86/010 for Ministry of Tourism, Wildlife and Antiquities, Kampala

Gavron, J (1993) *The Last Elephant: an African Quest*, Harper Collins, London

GEF (1992) *Guidelines for Monitoring and Evaluation of Biodiversity Projects*, World Bank, Washington DC

Gibson, C C and Marks, S A (1995) 'Transforming Rural Hunters into Conservationists: an Assessment of Community-Based Wildlife Management Programs in Africa', *World Development* 23(6), 941–58

Gichohi, H (1996) 'Functional Relationships Between Parks and Agricultural Areas', paper presented at Workshop on Costs and Benefits of Wildlife in Africa, Lewa Downs, Kenya

Gittinger, J P (1972) *Economic Analysis of Agricultural Projects*, Johns Hopkins University Press, Baltimore for World Bank

Goodman, P S (1996) 'Large Mammal Wet Season Census and Trend Monitoring Proposals for the West Caprivi', unpublished Report to Ministry of Environment and Tourism, Windhoek

Goodwin, P P (1997) Expectations, Trust and Defining the Countryside: Understandings and Experience of Local Participation in Conservation, PhD thesis, University of London

Gordon D L (1993) From Marginalisation to Center Stage? A Communities Perspective on Zimbabwe's CAMPFIRE Programme, MS paper, York University, North York, Ontario, Canada

Graham, A (1973) *The Gardeners of Eden*, Allen and Unwin, Hemel Hempstead, UK

Grainger, A (1993) 'Rates of Deforestation in the Humid Tropics: Estimates and Measurements', *The Geographical Journal* 159, 33–44

Grainger, A (1996) 'Forest Environments', in W M Adams, A S Goudie and A R Orme (eds) *The Physical Geography of Africa*, Oxford University Press, Oxford, 173–95

Green, M J (1995) *A Framework for Planning Uganda's Protected Area System*, MIENR, Kampala

Grindle, M and Thomas, J W (1991) *Public Choices and Policy Change*, Johns Hopkins University Press, Baltimore

GRN (1996a) 'Nature Conservation Amendment Act, 1996', Government Gazette No. 1333, Government of the Republic of Namibia, Windhoek

GRN (1996b) 'Amendment of Regulations Relating to Nature Conservation', Government Gazette No. 1446, Government of the Republic of Namibia, Windhoek

GRN (1997) 'Republic of Namibia, National Land Policy "White Paper" ', Government of the Republic of Namibia, Windhoek

Groombridge, B (ed) (1992) *Global Biodiversity – Status of the Earth's Living Resources*, a report compiled by the World Conservation Monitoring Centre, Chapman and Hall, London

Grootenhuis, J (1996) 'Wildlife, Livestock and Animal Disease Reservoirs', paper presented at Workshop on Costs and Benefits of Wildlife in Africa, Lewa Downs, Kenya

Grzimek, B (1960) *Serengeti Shall Not Die,* Hamish Hamilton, London

Guard, M (1993) *The Potential of Papyrus (Cyperus Papyrus) Sustainable Utilization by Local Communities Around Lake Mburo National Park,* Uganda National Parks, Kampala

Guggisberg, G A W (1966) *SOS Rhino,* Andre Deutsch, London

Halderman, J M (1995) 'Draft Report – Pastoralism as Practiced in Monduli District, Environmental Problems', mimeo at Kenya Wildlife Service, Nairobi

Hamilton, C A (1984) *Deforestation in Uganda,* Oxford University Press, Nairobi

Hammett, J (1998) 'Mgahinga Gorilla National Park Management Plan Revision 1998–2000', mimeo at UWA, Kampala

Hanlon, J (1996) *Peace Without Profit: How the IMF Blocks Rebuilding in Mozambique,* James Currey, London

Hanna, S, Folke, C and Mäler, K G (1995) 'Property Rights and Environmental Resources', in S Hanna and M Munasinghe (eds) *Property Rights and the Environment: Social and Ecological Issues,* The Beijer International Institute of Ecological Economics and the World Bank, Washington DC

Hanna, S, Folke, C and Mäler, K G (1996) (eds) *Rights to Nature: Ecological, Economic, Cultural and Political Principles of Institutions for the Environment,* Island Press, Washington DC

Hannah, L (1992) *African People, African Parks,* Conservation International, Washington DC

Harcourt, C S and Collins, N M (1992) *Uganda: the Conservation Atlas of Tropical Forests: Africa,* Macmillan, London, 262–9

Harper, F A (1974) 'Property in its Primary Form', in S L Blumenfeld (ed) *Property in a Human Society,* Open Court, La Salle, USA

Hartley, D (1997) *Community Wildlife Management: a Review of the ODA's Experience in Tanzania,* Report to the Overseas Development Administration, London

Hartwick, J M and Olewiler, N D (1986) *The Economics of Natural Resource Use,* Harper and Row, New York

Hasler, R (1994) *Political Ecologies of Scale and the Multi-Tiered Co-Management of Zimbabwean Wildlife Resources under CAMPFIRE,* Center for Applied Social Sciences, University of Zimbabwe, Occasional Paper, University of Zimbabwe

Hatton, J C (ed) (1995) *Status Quo Assessment of the Chimanimani Transfrontier Conservation Area,* IUCN Report to DNFFB, Maputo

Hays, S P (1959) *Conservation and the Gospel of Efficiency: the Progressive Conservation Movement 1890–1920,* Harvard University Press, Cambridge, MA

Heath, R (1992) 'Wildlife-Based Tourism in Zimbabwe: an Outline of its Development and Future Policy Options', *Geographical Journal of Zimbabwe* 23, 59–78

Hilborn, R and Ludwig, D (1993) 'The Limits of Applied Ecological Research', *Ecological Applications* 3, 550–2

Hill, K A (1996) 'Zimbabwe's Wildlife Utilization Programs: Grassroots Democracy or an Extension of State Power?', *African Studies Review,* 39(1), April, 103–23

Hinchley, D and Turyomurugyendo, L (1998) *Review of Collaborative Management Arrangements for Mt Elgon National Park,* IUCN Discussion Paper, Nairobi

Hirschman, A O (1963) *Journeys Towards Progress,* Twentieth Century Fund, New York

Hirschman, A O (1968) *Development Projects Observed*, Brookings Institution, Washington DC

Hirst, P (1994) *Associative Democracy: New Forms of Economic and Social Governance*, Polity Press, Cambridge

Hlatshwayo, B (1992) *Demarcation of Centre-Local Fiscal Relations and Financial Viability of Rural Local Authorities: a Critical Analysis*, Friedrich Ebert Stiftung, Harare, Zimbabwe

Hoare, R E (1997) The Effects of Interaction with Humans on Elephant Populations of the Sebungwe Region, Zimbabwe, PhD thesis, Department of Biological Sciences, Faculty of Science, University of Zimbabwe, Harare

Hoben, A (1995) 'Paradigms and Politics: the Cultural Construction of Environmental Policy in Ethiopia', *World Development* 23, 1007–21

Hoben, A (1996) 'The Cultural Construction of Environmental Policy: Paradigms and Politics in Ethiopia', in M Leach and R Mearns (eds) *The Lie of the Land: Challenging Received Wisdom in the African Environment*, Heinemann, Portsmouth, NH and James Currey, London, 186–208

Hoefsloot, H (1997) *Collaborative Management on Mount Elgon: an Account of First Experiences*, IUCN Eastern Africa Programme, Issues in Conservation, Nairobi

Holling, C S (ed) (1978) *Adaptive Environmental Assessment and Management*, John Wiley and Sons, New York

Holling, C S (1993) 'Investing in Research for Sustainability', *Ecological Applications* 3(4), 552–5

Holling, C S and Meffe, G K (1996) 'Command and Control and the Pathology of Natural Resource Management', *Conservation Biology* 10(2), April, 329–37

Holling, C S, Berkes, F and Folke, C (1997) 'Science, Sustainability and Resource Management', in F Berles and C Folke (eds) *Linking Social and Ecological Systems: Institutional Learning for Resilience*, Cambridge University Press, Cambridge

Homewood, K M and Rodgers, W A (1991) *Maasailand Ecology: Pastoral Development and Wildlife Conservation in Ngorongoro, Tanzania*, Cambridge University Press, Cambridge

Hove, S (1995) 'Participant Experiences in Project Design and Implementation: Nyaminyami Rural District Council', paper presented to the Africa Regional Environmental Assessment Training Course, Kadoma Ranch Motel, Kadoma, Zimbabwe

Howard, P (1995) The Economics of Protected Areas in Uganda: Costs, Benefits and Policy Issues, MSc Dissertation, University of Edinburgh

Hughes, D M (1995) Community Based Forest Management in the Lucite Valley: People and Policies of a Proposed Mozambique–Zimbabwe Transfrontier Conservation Area, PhD thesis, University of California, Berkeley

Hulme, D (1997a) *A Framework for the Study of Community Conservation in Africa,* Community Conservation in Africa Working Paper No 1, IDPM, University of Manchester

Hulme, D (1997b) *Community Conservation in Practice: a Case Study of Lake Mburo National Park, Uganda,* Community Conservation in Africa Working Paper No 3, IDPM, University of Manchester

Hulme, D and Limcaoco, J A A (1991) 'Integrated Rural Development Projects in the Philippines: from Blueprint to Process?', *Project Appraisal* 6(4), 374–90

Hulme, D and Murphree, M (1999) 'Communities, Wildlife and the "New Conservation" in Africa', *Journal of International Development* 11(2), 277–86

Hulme, D and Turner, M M (1990) *Sociology and Development: Theories, Policies and Practices*, Harvester-Wheatsheaf, London

Hutton, C (1973) *Reluctant Farmers? A Study of Uunemployment and Planned Rural Development in Uganda*, East African Publishing House, Nairobi

Ibo, J and Leonard, E (1996) 'The Structure, Substance, Theory and Practise of Participatory Forest Management in Cote d'Ivoire', paper presented to Pan African Symposium on Sustainable Use of Natural Resources and Community Participation, Harare

IIED (1994) *Whose Eden? An Overview of Community Approaches to Wildlife Management*, International Institute for Environment and Development, London

Iliffe, J (1987) *The African Poor: a History*, Cambridge University Press, Cambridge

Infield, M (1987) 'Attitudes of a Rural Community towards Conservation and a Local Conservation Area in Natal, South Africa', *Biological Conservation* 45, 21–46

Infield, M (1989) The Importance of Hunting in the Conservation of Large Mammals: a Case Study in Korup National Park, Cameroon, Fifth Theriological Congress, Centre for International Agricultural Development, Rome

IRDNC (1996) 'Namibia: WWFNA0004 Technical Report to BMZ', Integrated Rural Development and Nature Conservation, Windhoek

IRDNC (1997) 'Community-based Natural Resource Management in Caprivi. A 21-month Grant', Proposal to the LIFE Project. Integrated Rural Development and Nature Conservation, Windhoek

Ite, U E (1996) 'Community Perceptions of the Cross River National Park, Nigeria', *Environmental Conservation* 23(4), 351–7

Ite, U E (1997) 'Small Farmers and Forest Loss in the Cross River National Park, Nigeria', *The Geographical Journal* 163(1), 47–56

IUCN (1980) *World Conservation Strategy*, IUCN, Washington DC

IUCN (1984) 'Categories, Objectives and Criteria for Protected Areas', in J A McNeely and K R Miller (eds) *National Parks, Conservation and Development*, Smithsonian Institution Press, Washington DC, 47–53

IUCN (1986) *Towards a Regional Conservation Strategy for Serengeti,* report of a Workshop held at Serengeti Wildlife Research Centre, 2–4 December 1985, IUCN Regional Office for East Africa, Nairobi

IUCN (1990) *United Nations List of National Parks and Protected Areas*, IUCN, Gland, Switzerland and Cambridge, UK

IUCN (1992) *Protected Areas of the World: a Review of National Systems*, Volume 3, IUCN, Gland, Switzerland and Cambridge, UK

IUCN (1996) 'Forest Cover and Forest Reserves in Kenya: Policy and Practice', *Issues in Conservation* 24, IUCN, Eastern Africa Programme, Nairobi

IUCN (1997) *NRMP II Annual Planning Workshop*, Standard Chartered Club, November 1996, IUCN Regional Office for Southern Africa and the CAMPFIRE Association, Harare

Jacobsohn, M (1990) *Himba. Nomads of Namibia*, Sturik Publishers, Cape Town

Johnston, B F and Clark, W C (1982) *Redesigning Rural Development*, Johns Hopkins University Press, Baltimore

Jolly, G M (1969) 'Sampling Methods for Aerial Censuses of Wildlife Populations', *East African Agriculture and Forestry Journal*, Special Issue, 46–9

Jones, B T B (1997) *Community Based Natural Resource Management in Botswana and Namibia – an Inventory and Preliminary Analysis of Progress*, Review for IIED Study of Evaluating Eden, London, IIED

Junod, H A (1927) *The Life of a South African Tribe*, 2 volumes, Macmillan, London

Kamugisha, J R (1993) *Management of Natural Resources and Environment in Uganda: Policy and Legislation Landmarks, 1890–1990*, Regional Soil Conservation Unit, SIDA, Nairobi

Kamugisha, J R and Stahl, M (1993) *Parks and People: Pastoralists and Wildlife*, Regional Soil Conservation Unit, SIDA, Nairobi

Kangwana, K (1993) Conflict and Conservation: Elephants and Maasai in Amboseli, Kenya, PhD dissertation, University of Cambridge, Cambridge

Kangwana, K (1998) 'Lake Mburo National Park, Uganda: a Case Study of the Conservation Achievements of Community Conservation', mimeo, IDPM, University of Manchester and AWF, Nairobi

Kapungwe, E (1996) *Management and Utilisation of Wildlife Resources in Forestry Areas of Central, Copperbelt and Luapula Provinces, Zambia*, Publication No 4, Provincial Forestry Action Programme, Ndola, Zambia

Kasoma, P M B and Kamugisha, J R (1993) *Livestock in LMNP*, GAF Consult for LMNPCC and USAID, Kampala

Kaufmann, B (1992) *Development of Wildlife Tourism in Zimbabwe, Wildlife Management and Environmental Conservation Project*, Policy Review Workshop Outputs, Volume 7, Price Waterhouse, Harare

Kazoora, C and Victurine, R (1997) *The Economics of Community Conservation and Enterprise Development*, report to African Wildlife Foundation, Nairobi

Kemf, E (ed) (1993) *The Law of the Mother: Protecting Indigenous Peoples in Protected Areas*, Sierra Club Books, San Francisco

Kenya, Republic of (1975) *Statement on Future Wildlife Management Policy in Kenya*, Government Printer, Nairobi

Kenya, Republic of (1976) *The Wildlife (Conservation and Management) Act CAP. 376, Laws of Kenya*, Government Printer, Nairobi

Kenya, Republic of (1989) *The Wildlife (Conservation and Management) (Amendment) Bill, Kenya Gazette Supplement*, Special Issue No 83 (Bill No 15), Nairobi, Government Printers, 1361–76

Kenya Wildlife Service and Forestry Department in the Ministry of Environment and Natural Resources (1991) *Memorandum of Understanding for the Joint Management of Selected Forests*, KWS and Forestry Department, Nairobi

Kingdon, E (1990) 'Caught Between Two Worlds: Moral Problems Relating to Conservation in South-West Uganda', *International Journal of Moral and Social Studies* 5(3), 235–49

Kipuri, N and Ole Nangoro, B (1996) *Evaluation Report for TANAPA's CCS Programme*, submitted to the Royal Netherlands Embassy, Dar es Salaam

Kiss, A (ed) (1990) *Living with Wildlife: Wildlife Resource Management with Local Participation in Africa*, World Bank, Washington DC

Kiss, A (1999) 'Making Community-Based Conservation Work', paper presented to the Society for Conservation Biology Annual General Meeting at College Park, Maryland, 18 June 1999, mimeo at IDPM, University of Manchester

Kitching, G (1982) *Development and Underdevelopment in Historical Perspective*, Methuen, London

Kjekshus, H (1996) *Ecology Control and Economic Development in East African History*, 2nd edn, James Currey, London

Kolko, G (1997) *Vietnam: Anatomy of a Peace*, Routledge, London

Korten, D (1980) 'Community Organization and Rural Development: a Learning Process Approach', *Public Administration Review* 40(5), 480–511

Kramer, R, van Schaik, C and Johnson, J (1997) *Last Stand: Protected Areas and the Defense of Tropical Diversity*, Oxford University Press, Oxford

Krishke, H, Lyamuya, V and Ndunguru, I F (1995) *The Development of Community Based Conservation around Selous Game Reserve*, Department of Wildlife, with AWF and WWF, Dar-es-Salaam, Tanzania

KWS (1990a) *A Policy Framework and Development Programme 1991–1996*, KWS, Nairobi, Kenya

KWS (1990b) *A Policy Framework and Development Programme 1991–1996*, Annex 6, *Community Conservation and Wildlife Management Outside Parks and Reserves*, KWS, Nairobi

KWS (1994) *Guidelines for Revenue Sharing and the Wildlife for Development Fund (WDF) Operational Summary*, KWS, Nairobi

KWS (1997) *Wildlife Associations, Partnership News: a Newsletter of the Partnership Department of the Kenya Wildlife Service*, KWS, Nairobi

Lado, C (1992) 'Problems of Wildlife Management and Land Use in Kenya', *Land Use Policy* 9, 169–84

Lake Naivasha Riparian Owners Association (1996) *Lake Naivasha Management Plan*, Lake Naivasha Riparian Owners Association, Naivasha, Kenya

Lamprey, R H and Michelmore, F (1996) *The Wildlife in Protected Areas of Uganda: Preliminary Aerial Survey Results and their Assessment plus Initial Recommendations*, EC Wildlife Support Project Report for Ministry of Tourism, Wildlife and Antiquities, Kampala

Lane, C (1996) *Ngorongoro Voices: Indigenous Residents of the Ngorongoro Conservation Areas in Tanzania Give Their Views on the Proposed General Management Plan*, Forest Trees and People Programme Working Paper 29, Uppsala

Larkin, P (1977) 'An Epitaph for Maximum Sustained Yield', *Transactions of the American Fisheries Society* 106, 1–11

Leach, M and Mearns, R (1996) *The Lie of the Land: Challenging Received Wisdom on the African Environment*, Heinemann, Portsmouth, NH and James Currey, London

Leach, M, Mearns, R and Scoones, I (1997) 'Community-Based Sustainable Development: Consensus or Conflict?', *IDS Bulletin* 28(4), 1–14

Leader-Williams, N (1996) 'Wildlife Utilisation in Tanzania', paper presented at Workshop on Costs and Benefits of Wildlife in Africa, Lewa Downs, Kenya

Leader-Williams, N, Albon, S D and Berry, P S M (1990a) 'Illegal Exploitation of Black Rhinoceros and Elephant Populations: Patterns of Decline, Law Enforcement and Patrol Effort in Luangwa Valley, Zambia', *Journal of Applied Ecology* 27, 1055–87

Leader-Williams, N, Harrison, J and Green, M J B (1990b) 'Designing Protected Areas to Conserve Natural Resources', *Scientific Progress Oxford* 74, 189–204

Leader-Willams, N, Kayera, J A and Overton, G L (eds) (1995) *Community Based Conservation in Tanzania*, Workshop, Dar-es-Salaam, Planning and Assessment for Wildlife Management Project, Department of Wildlife, Tanzania

Lee, K N (1993) *Compass and Gyroscope: Integrating Science and Politics for the Environment,* Island Press, Washington DC

Lele, S and Norgaard, R B (1996) 'Sustainability and the Scientist's Burden', *Conservation Biology* 10(2), April, 354–65

Lerner, D (1962) *The Passing of Traditional Society: Modernising the Middle East,* The Free Press, Glencoe, IL

Lewis, D, Kaweche, G B and Mwenya, A (1990) 'Wildlife Conservation Areas Outside Protected Areas: Lessons from and Experiment in Zambia', *Conservation Biology* 4, 171–80

Lewis, D M (1995) 'Importance of GIS to Community-Based Management of Wildlife: Lessons from Zambia', *Ecological Applications* 5, 861–71

Lindblom, C (1979) 'Still Muddling, Not Yet Through', *Public Administration Review* 39(6), 517–26

Lindsay, W K (1987) 'Integrating Parks and Pastoralists: Some Lessons from Amboseli', in D M Anderson and R H Grove (eds) *Conservation in Africa,* Cambridge University Press, Cambridge, 149–67

Little, P D (1994) 'The Link Between Local Participation and Improved Conservation', in D Western and M Wright (eds) *Natural Connections: Perspectives in Community-Based Conservation,* Island Press, Washington, DC, 347–72

Low, A (1986) *Agricultural Development in Southern Africa: Farm-Household Economics and the Food Crisis,* James Currey, London

Lubanga, M (1991) *The Use of Indigenous Plants by Forest Dwellers: Findings from a Sample Community in the SW Mau,* KIFCON/Forest Department, Ministry of Environment and Natural Resources, Nairobi

Ludwig, D (1993) 'Environmental Sustainability: Magic, Science, and Religion in Natural Resource Management', *Ecological Applications* 3, 555–8

Ludwig, D, Hilborn, R and Walters, C (1993) 'Uncertainity, Resource Exploitation and Conservation: Lessons from History', *Science* 260, 17–36

MacKenzie, J M (1987) 'Chivalry, Social Darwinism and Ritualised Killing: the Hunting Ethos in Central Africa up to 1914', in D M Anderson and R Grove (eds) *Conservation in Africa,* Cambridge University Press, Cambridge, 41–62

MacKenzie, J M (1989) *The Empire of Nature: Hunting, Conservation and British Imperialism,* University of Manchester Press, Manchester

Mackie, C (1993) 'Participatory Wildlife Census Techniqiues: a Preliminary Attempt in North Gokwe', unpublished report, WWF Multispecies Project, Harare

Mackinnon, J, Mackinnon, K, Child, G and Thorsell, J (1986) 'Local People and Protected Areas', in McKinnon, J. et al. (eds) *Managing Protected Areas in the Tropics,* IUCN, Gland, Switzerland

Macnab, J (1983) 'Wildlife Management as Scientific Experimentation', *Wildlife Society Bulletin* 11, 397–401

Madzudzo, E (1997) 'Power and Empowerment in Community Based Natural Resource Management', *Conference of the Association of Social Anthropologists,* Harare

Maine, H (1905) *Ancient Law,* Murray, London

Marks, S A (1994) 'Local Hunters and Wildlife Surveys: a Design to Enhance Participation', *African Journal of Ecology* 32, 233–54

Marquardt, M, Infield, M and Namara, A (1994) *Socio-Economic Survey of Communities in the Buffer Zone of Lake Mburo National Park. Access to Lands and other Natural Resources,* Uganda National Parks, Kampala

Martin, R B (1986) *Communal Areas Management Program for Indigenous Resources (CAMPFIRE)*, Government of Zimbabwe, Department of National Parks and Wildlife Management, Branch of Terrestrial Ecology, Harare

Mascarenhas, A (1994) 'Environmental Issues and Poverty Alleviation in Tanzania', *Bagachwa*, 123–70

Mason, P M (1995) Wildlife Conservation in the Long Term – Uganda as a Case Study, MPhil dissertation, Oxford University

Matowanyika, J Z Z (1989) 'Cast Out of Eden: Peasants Versus Wildlife Policy in Savanna Africa', *Alternatives* 16(1)

Matowanyika, J Z Z, Garibaldi, V and Musimwa, E (eds) (1995) *Indigenous Knowledge Systems and Natural Resource Management in Southern Africa*, report of the Southern Africa Regional Workshop, Zimbabwe, 20–22 April 1994, IUCN-ROSA, Harare

Maxwell, S (1999) 'The Meaning and Measurement of Poverty', *ODI Poverty Briefing*, Overseas Development Institute, London

McLain, R and Jones, E (1997) *Challenging 'Community' Definitions in Sustainable Natural Resource Management: The case of wild mushroom harvesting in the U.S.A.,* – (Gatekeeper Series, 68). IIED, London

McNeely, J A (1984) 'Introduction: Protected Areas are Adapting to New Realities', in J A McNeely and K R Miller (eds) *National Parks, Conservation and Development: the Role of Protected Areas in Sustaining Societies*, Smithsonian Institution Press, Washington DC

McNeely, J A (1989) 'Protected Areas and Human Ecology: How National Parks can Contribute to Sustaining Societies of the Twenty-first Century', in D Western and M C Pearl (eds) *Conservation for the Twenty-First Century*, Oxford University Press, New York

McNeely, J A (1993) 'Economic Incentives for Conserving Biodiversity: Lessons for Africa', *Ambio* 22, 144–50

McNeely, J A and Miller, K R (eds) (1984) *National Parks, Conservation and Development: the Role of Protected Areas in Sustaining Society*, Smithsonian Institute Press, Washington DC

MET (1995) *Wildlife Management, Utilisation and Tourism in Communal Areas*, Policy Document, Ministry of Environment and Tourism, Windhoek

MET (1994a) *Conservation of Biotic Diversity and Habitat Protection*, Policy Document, Ministry of Environment and Tourism, Windhoek

MET (1994b) *Land-use Planning: Towards Sustainable Development*, Policy Document, Ministry of Environment and Tourism, Windhoek

Metcalfe, S (1992) 'Planning for Wildlife in an African Savanna: a Strategy Based on the Zimbabwean Experience: Emphasizing Communities and Parks', paper presented to the IVth World Congress of National Parks and Protected Areas, Zimbabwe Trust, Harare

Metcalfe, S (1994) 'The Zimbabwe Communal Areas Management Programme for Indigenous Resources (CAMPFIRE)', in D Western and R M Wright (eds) *Natural Connections: Perspectives in Community-Based Conservation*, Island Press, Washington DC, 161–92

Metcalfe, S and Kamugisha-Ruhombe, J (1993) *Project Evaluation: Lake Mburo Community Conservation Project*, UNP, Kampala and AWF, Nairobi

Middleton, N (1994) *Kalishnikovs and Zombie Cucumbers: Travels in Mozambique,* Phoenix, London

Midgley, J (1986) *Community Participation, Social Development and the State,* Methuen, London

Ministry of Social Welfare (1994) 'Report on Drought Relief Programmes', mimeo at Ministry of Social Welfare, Harare

Ministry of Tourism, Wildlife and Antiquities (1996) *Outputs of the Taskforce on Collaborative Management for the Uganda Wildlife Authority,* IUCN, Kampala

Mitchell, C R (1991) *Classifying Conflicts: Asymmetry and Resolution. Resolving Regional Conflict: International Perspectives,* Sage Publications, New York

Mkandawire, T (1998) *The Social Sciences in Africa: Breaking Local Barriers and Negotiating International Presence,* Occasional Paper No 19, International Development Studies, Roskilde University, 92–119

Modise, S (1996) 'Models of Wildlife Management: the Botswana Experience', *African Wildlife Policy Consultation,* Overseas Development Administration, London

Mogaka, H (1991) *Report on a Study of Hunting in Arabuko Sokoke Forest Reserve,* Kenya Indigenous Forest Conservation Project, Overseas Development Administration, London and Kenya Forest Department, Nairobi

Monday, G (1991) Interaction between Domestic and Wild Animals, MSc thesis, Makerere University, Kampala

Monday, G (1993) *Lake Mburo National Park Habitat Project Report,* Uganda National Parks, Kampala

Moore, A (1990) 'National Parks and Wildlife Management Tourism Statistical Report for 1990', mimeo, DNPWLM, Harare

Moore, D S (1996) *A River Runs Through It. Environmental History and the Politics of Community in Zimbabwe's Eastern Highlands,* Centre for Applied Social Sciences (CASS), University of Zimbabwe, Harare

Moore, M (1993) 'Good Government? Introduction', *IDS Bulletin* 24(1), 1–6

Moris, J (1987) 'Irrigation as a Privileged Solution in African Development', *Development Policy Review* 5, 99–123

Moyo, S K (1998) 'Speech' by S K Moyo, Minister of Mines, Environment and Tourism, reproduced in *CAMPFIRE News* 17, March, 2

MTWA (1996a) *A Survey of the Wildlife Protected Areas of Uganda. Phase I: September 1995 – January 1996,* Ministry of Tourism Wildlife and Antiquities, Kampala, Uganda

MTWA (1996b) *A Survey of the Wildlife Protected Areas of Uganda. Phase II: April – June 1996,* Ministry of Tourism Wildlife and Antiquities, Kampala, Uganda

Muhweezi, A (1994) 'Interim Management Plan for Lake Mburo National Park 1994–1998', mimeo at Uganda Wildlife Authority, Kampala

Muir, K, Bojö, J and Cunliffe, R (1996) 'Economic Policy, Wildlife and Land Use in Zimbabwe', in J Bojö (ed) *The Economics of Wildlife: Case Studies from Ghana, Kenya, Namibia and Zimbabwe,* World Bank, Washington DC

Mukamuri, B B (1995) 'Local Environmental Conservation Strategies: Karanga Religion, Politics and Environmental Control, *Environment and History* 1, 297–311

Mundy, V S (1995) *The Urban Poverty Datum Line in Zimbabwe,* The Catholic Commission for Justice and Peace in Zimbabwe, Harare

Murindagomo, F (1997) Cattle, Wildlife Comparative Advantage in Semi Arid Communal Lands and Implications for Agro-Pastoral Options, Institutions and Government Policy: a Case Study in the Sebungwe Region, Zimbabwe, DPhil thesis, Department of Agricultural Economics, University of Zimbabwe, Harare

Murombedzi, J C (1992) *Decentralization or Recentralization? Implementing CAMPFIRE in the Omay Communal Lands of the Nyaminyami District*, CASS Working Paper, University of Zimbabwe, Center for Applied Social Sciences, Harare

Murombedzi, J C (1994) The Dynamics of Conflict in Environmental Management Policy in the Context of the Communal Areas Management Programme for Indigenous Resources, DPhil dissertation, University of Zimbabwe, Center for Applied Social Sciences, Harare

Murombedzi, J C (1995) 'Zimbabwe's CAMPFIRE Programme: Using Natural Resources for Rural Development', mimeo, University of Zimbabwe, Centre for Applied Social Sciences, Harare

Murombedzi, J C (1997) *Community Wildlife Management in Southern Africa: Malawi, Zambia and Zimbabwe*, paper prepared for IIED study on 'Evaluating Eden', IIED, London

Murphree, M W (1991) 'Communities as Institutions for Resource Management', paper presented to the National Conference on Environment and Development, Maputo, October. Also published as *CASS Occasional Paper Series* NRM, Centre for Applied Social Sciences, University of Zimbabwe, Harare

Murphree, M W (1993) 'Decentralizing the Proprietorship of Wildlife Resources in Zimbabwe's Communal Lands', in D Lewis and N Carter (eds) *Voices from Africa: Local Perspectives on Conservation,* WWF, Washington DC

Murphree, M W (1994a) 'The Role of Institutions in Community-Based Conservation', in D Western and R M Wright (eds) *Natural Connections. Perspectives in Community-based Conservation,* Island Press, Washington DC, 403–27

Murphree, M W (1994b) 'The Evolution of Zimbabwe's Community-based Wildlife Use and Management Programme', mimeo, Community Conservation Workshop, Tanzania, 8–11 February, AWF, Arusha, Tanzania

Murphree, M W (1995) 'Optimal Principles and Pragmatic Strategies: Creating an Enabling Politico-Legal Environment for Community Based Natural Resource Management (CBNRM)', in L Rihoy (ed) *The Commons Without the Tragedy? Strategies for Community Based Natural Resources Management in Southern Africa,* SADC Wildlife Technical Co-operation Unit and USAID Regional NRMP, Harare, 47–52

Murphree, M W (1996) 'Approaches to Community Participation', *African Policy Wildlife Policy Consultation,* Final Report of the Consultation, Overseas Development Administration, London, 153–88

Murphree, M (1997a) *Congruent Objectives, Competing Interests and Strategic Compromise: Concepts and Process in the Evolution of Zimbabwe's CAMPFIRE Programme*, Community Conservation in Africa Working Paper No 2, IDPM, University of Manchester

Murphree, M W (1997b) 'Articulating Voices from the Commons, Interpretation, Translation, and Facilitation: Roles and Modes for Common Property Scholarship', *Society and Natural Resources* 10, 415–21

Murphree, M J and Nyika, E (1998) *Investigation into the Performance of Non-lease Tourism Projects in the Communal Lands of Zimbabwe,* four volumes, ISCS IRT/Speciss Consulting Services on behalf of WWF, Harare

Murphree, M W and Cumming, D H M (1993) 'Savanna Land Use: Policy and Practice in Zimbabwe', in M D Young and O T Solbrig (eds) *The World's Savannas. Economic Driving Forces, Ecological Constraints and Policy Options for Sustainable Land Use,* UNESCO and Parthenon Publishing Group, Paris, 139–78

Mwamadzingo, M (1992) 'Conservation of Wildlife Resources in Kenya', annex to *The Costs, Benefits and Unmet Needs of Biological Diversity Conservation in Kenya,* National Biodiversity Unit, National Museums of Kenya, Nairobi

Mwangi, S (1995) An Economic Assessment of Group Ranching in the Dispersal Areas of the Maasai Mara National Reserve, Kenya, MPhil thesis, Moi University, Eldoret, Kenya

Mwau, G (1996) *Wildlife Utilisation Study: Report No 2, Economic Analysis,* Kenya Wildlife Service and African Wildlife Foundation, Nairobi

Mwenya, A N (1990) *ADMADE: Policy, Background and Future: National Parks and Wildlife Services New Administrative Management Design for Game Management Areas,* Dept of National Parks and Wildlife, Lusaka

Nabane, N (1997) 'Gender Dimensions in the Communal Areas Management Programme for Indigenous Resources: A Zambezi Valley Community Case Study', Unpubl. M. Phil. thesis, Centre for Applied Social Sciences (CASS), University of Zimbabwe, Harare

NACOBTA (1995) 'Institutional Support to the Namibia Community–Based Tourism Association (NACOBTA)', Project proposal to the LIFE Programme, Namibia Community-based Tourism Association, Windhoek

Namara, A and Infield, M (1998) *The Influence of a Community Conservation Programme on Farmers and Pastoralist Communities: Lake Mburo National Park, Uganda,* Uganda Wildlife Authority, Kampala

Nash, R (1973) *Wilderness and the American Mind,* Yale University Press, New Haven, CT

Ncube, W (1996) 'Land Tenure Issues in Zimbabwe', paper presented at the National Workshop on Environmental Law Reforms in Zimbabwe, The Way Forward, 28–29 March, Ministry of Environment and Tourism, Harare

Negrao, J (1998) 'Land Reform and Strategies for Sustainable Rural Livelihoods in Mozambique', unpublished report to ZERO, Harare

Neumann, R P (1992a) The Social Origins of Natural Resource Conflict in Arusha National Park, Tanzania, PhD thesis, University of California, Berkeley

Neumann, R P (1992b) 'Political Ecology of Wildlife Conservation in the Mount Meru Area of Northeastern Tanzania', *Land Degradation and Rehabilitation* 3, 85–98

Neumann, R P (1996) 'Dukes, Earls and Ersatz Edens: Aristocratic Nature Preservationists in Colonial Africa', *Environment and Planning D: Society and Space* 14, 79–98

Neumann, R P (1997) 'Primitive Ideas: Protected Area Buffer Zones and the Politics of Land in Africa', *Development and Change* 28, 559–82

Newitt, M (1995) *A History of Mozambique,* Hurst and Company, London

Newmark, W D (ed) (1991) *The Conservation of Mount Kilimanjaro,* IUCN, Gland, Switzerland

Newmark, W D, Leonard, N L, Sariko, H I and Gamassa, D M (1993) 'Conservation Attitudes of Local People Living Adjacent to Five Protected Areas in Tanzania', *Biological Conservation* 63, 177–83

Newmark, W D, Manyanza, D N, Gamassa, D M and Sariko, H I (1994) 'The Conflict Between Wildlife and Local People Living Adjacent to Protected Areas in Tanzania: Human Density as a Predictor', *Conservation Biology* 8, 249–55

Ngorongoro Conservation Area Authority (1995) *Ngorongoro, Conservation Area General Management Plan*, Ngorongoro, Conservation Area Authority, Arusha

North, D C (1990) *Institutions, Institutional Change and Economic Performance*, Series on Political Economy of Decisions, Cambridge University Press, Cambridge, MA

Norton, B C (1991) *Towards Unity Among Environmentalists*, Oxford University Press, Oxford

Norton-Griffiths, M (1978) 'Counting Animals', in J J R Grimsdell (ed) *Handbooks on Techniques Currently Used in African Wildlife Ecology* No1, African Wildlife Leadership Foundation, Nairobi

Norton-Griffiths, M (1995) *Property Rights and the Marginal Wildebeest: an Economic Analysis of Wildlife Conservation Options in Kenya*, Centre for Social and Economic Research on the Global Environment, University College, London

Norton-Griffiths, M (1996) 'Why Kenyan Conservation is Failing', *Swara* November 1996–February 1997, 6–8

Norton-Griffiths, M and Southey, C (1995) 'The Opportunity Costs of Biodiversity Conservation in Kenya', *Ecological Economics* 12, 125–39

Noss, A J (1997) 'Challenges to Nature Conservation with Community Development in Central African Forests', *Oryx* 31, 180–8

Nott, C, Owen-Smith, G and Jacobsohn, M (1993) 'Report on the 1993 Hunting Season, Sesfontein District and Bergsig Area', Integrated Rural Development and Nature Conservation, Windhoek

Nurse, M and Kabamba, J (1998) *Defining Institutions for Collaborative Mangrove Management: a Case Study from Tanga, Tanzania*, Workshop on Participatory Resource Management in Developing Countries, Mansfield College, Oxford

Nyamweru, C (1996) 'Sacred Groves Threatened by Development', *Cultural Survival Quarterly*, Fall, 19–21

Nyerere, J (1973) *Freedom and Development: a Selection from Writings and Speeches*, Oxford University Press, Dar es Salaam

Oakley, P (1991) *Projects with People*, Blackwells, Cambridge

Oates, J F (1995) 'The Dangers of Conservation by Rural Development: a Case Study from the Forests of Nigeria', *Oryx* 29, 115–22

Odendaal, N (1995) 'Community Hunting in the Kunene Region', Polytechnic of Namibia, Windhoek

Ogwang, D O and DeGeorge, P A (1992) *Community Participation in Interactive Park Planning and the Privatisation Process in Uganda's National Parks*, USAID and Uganda National Parks, Kampala

Okoth-Owiro, P (1988) 'Land Tenure and Land Use Legislation Issues in Agroforestry Development', in D B Thomas, E K Biamah, A M Kilewe, L Lundgren and B Mochoge (eds) *Soil Conservation in Kenya, Proceedings of the Third International Workshop, 16–19 September*, Dept Agricultural Engineering, University of Nairobi, Nairobi

Oliver, P (1994) 'Extending the Northern Circuit "Ecotourism in Tanzania"', mimeo at TANAPA headquarters, Arusha

Oliver, P (nd) 'Ecotourism Outside Tarangire National Park in Northern Tanzania', Draft Report, mimeo at TANAPA headquarters, Arusha

Oliver's Camp Safaris (1994) *Oliver's Camp and Community Conservation*, Tanzanian Community Conservation Workshop, TANAPA, Arusha

Olivier, R C (1990) *The Queeen Elizabeth National Park Management Plan*, Uganda National Parks, Kampala

Olivier, R C (1992) 'Aerial Total Counts in Uganda', unpublished report, Uganda National Parks, Kampala

Omondi, R (1994) Wildlife–Human Conflict in Kenya, DPhil thesis, McGill University, Montreal

ORAM (1997) *Identificacao das Communidades Chave*, Outobro-Decembro 1997, Quarterly Report of ORAM Manica

Ostrom, E (1990) *Governing the Commons: the Evolution of Institutions for Collective Action*, Cambridge University Press, Cambridge

Ostrom, E (1998) 'How Communities Beat the Tragedy of the Commons', keynote presentation to an International Workshop on Community Based Natural Resource Management, Washington DC, mimeo at CASS Library, University of Zimbabwe, Harare

Ouko, E and Marekia, N (1996) 'Land Tenure and Wildlife Management', in C Juma and J Ojwang (eds) *In Land We Trust*, Initiatives Publishers, Nairobi

Owen, R and Maponga, O (1996) *Mining Revenues: Who Gets What? A Comparison of Mining Revenue Distribution Between Central Government and Rural District Councils*, a study commissioned by the Association of Rural District Councils and the Friedrich Ebert Foundation, Harare

Owen-Smith, G and Jacobsohn, M (1991) 'Pastoralism in Arid and Semi-Arid North-West Namibia', paper presented at the Nordic Man and Biosphere Meeting, mimeo at CASS Library University of Zimbabwe, Harare

OXFAM (1996) *Natural Forest Management and Conservation Project, Uganda: a Profile of European Aid*, OXFAM, Oxford

Parker, I S C (1984) 'Perspectives in Wildlife Cropping or Culling', in R H V Bell and E McShane Caluzi (eds) *Conservation and Wildlife Management in Africa*, US Peace Corps, Washington DC, 238–9

Parker, I S C and Graham, A D (1964) 'The Ecological and Economic Basis for Game Ranching in Africa', in E Duffey and A S Watt (eds) *The Scientific Management of Animal and Plant Communities for Conservation*, Blackwell Scientific, Oxford, 393–404

Parker, I S C and Graham, A D (1989) 'Elephant Decline (Part I): Downwards Trends in African Elephant Distribution and Numbers', *International Journal of Environmental Studies* 34, 287–305

Parker, I (1993) 'Natural Justice, Ownership and the CAMPFIRE Programme', unpublished essay at the CASS Library, University of Zimbabwe, Harare

Parkipuny, M S (1989) *Pastoralism, Conservation and Development in the Greater Serengeti Region,* Ngorongoro Conservation and Development Project Occasional Paper No 1, IUCN Eastern Africa Regional Office, Nairobi

Parsons, T and Shils, E (1962) *Toward a General Theory of Action*, Harper, New York

Patel, H (1998) *Sustainable Utilization and African Wildlife Policy: Rhetoric or Reality?*, Indigenous Environmental Policy Centre, Cambridge MA

PDS (1997) A *Socio-Economic Survey of Communities Bordering the Shimba Hills National and Forest Reserves*, report prepared for GTZ/Forest Department Integrated Natural Resources and Conservation Project, Nairobi

Pearce, D (1996) 'An Economic Overview of Wildlife and Alternative Land Uses', *African Wildlife Policy Consultation*, Overseas Development Administration, London

Peluso, N L (1993) 'Coercing Conservation? The Politics of State Resource Control', *Global Environmental Change*, June, 199–217

Perkin, S L and Mshanga, P J (1992) 'Ngorongoro: Striking a Balance Between Conservation and Development', in J Thorsell and J Sawyer (eds) *World Heritage Twenty Years Later*, IUCN and UNESCO, Gland, 157–65

Peterson, J H (1991a) *CAMPFIRE: a Zimbabwean Approach to Sustainable Development and Community Empowerment Through Wildlife Utilisation*, Center for Applied Social Sciences, University of Zimbabwe, Harare

Peterson, J H (1991b) *A Proto-CAMPFIRE Initiative in Mahenye Ward, Chipinge District: Development of a Wildlife Programme in Response to Community Needs*, Centre for Applied Social Sciences, University of Zimbabwe, Harare

Phimister, I (1986) 'Discourse and the Discipline of Historical Context: Conservationism and Ideas about Development in Southern Rhodesia', *Journal of Southern Africa Studies* 12, 264–75

Pimbert, M P and Pretty, J N (1994) 'Participation, People and the Management of National Parks and Protected Areas: Past Failures and Future Promise', United Nations Research Institute for Social Development, IIED and WWF, London, mimeo

Pomeroy, D (1991) *Conservation and the Community: Proceedings of the Third Conservation Forum*, Uganda Conservation Forum, Mount Elgon Hotel, Mbale, Makerere University Biological Field Station

Pratt, D J and Gwynne, M D (eds) (1977) *Range Management and Ecology in East Africa*, Hodder and Stoughton, London

Price Waterhouse (1994) *The Lowveld Conservancies: New Opportunities for Productive and Sustainable Land-Use, Savé Valley, Bubianna and Chiredzi River Conservancies*, Price Waterhouse, Harare

Putnam, R (1993) *Making Democracy Work*, Princeton University Press, Princeton, NJ

Ranger, T O (1985) *Peasant Consciousness and Guerrilla War in Zimbabwe*, James Currey, London

Ranger, T O (1988) *The Communal Areas of Zimbabwe*, Land in Agrarian Systems Symposium, University of Illinois, Urbana–Champaign

Ratter, A (1997) *Participatory Evaluation: Community Conservation for Uganda*, Community Conservation for Uganda Wildlife Authority Project, Kampala

Redfield, R (1947) 'The Folk Society', *American Journal of Sociology* 52, 293–308

Redford, K H and Mansour, J A (eds) (1996) *Traditional Peoples and Biodiversity Conservation in Large Tropical Landscapes*, America Verde Publications, The Nature Conservancy, Arlington, VA

Repetto, R and Gillis, M (eds) (1988) *Public Policies and the Misuse of Forest Resources*, Cambridge University Press, Cambridge

Reynolds, N (1991) *A Structural Adjustment Programme for the Communal Areas*, Southern African Foundation for Economic Research (SAFER), Harare, Zimbabwe

Ribot, J C (1995) 'From Exclusion to Participation: Turning Senegal's Forestry Policy Around?', *World Development* 23, 1587–99

Richards, P (1985) *Indigenous Agricultural Development*, Longman, London

Rihoy, E (ed) (1995) *The Commons Without the Tragedy? Strategies for Community-Based Natural Resoruces Management in Southern Africa*, USAID, Lilongwe, Malawi

Robinson, M (1993) 'Governance, Democracy and Conditionality: NGOs and the New Policy Agenda', in A Clayton (ed) *Governance Democracy and Conditionality: What Role for NGOs?*, INTRAC, Oxford

Rodwell, T C, Tagg, J and Grobler, M (1995) *Wildlife Resources in the Caprivi, Namibia: The Results of an Aerial Census in 1994 and Comparisons with Past Surveys*, Research Discussion Paper No. 9, Directorate of Environmental Affairs, Windhoek

Roe, E (1991) 'Development Narratives, or Making the Best of Blueprint Development', *World Development* 19, 287–300

Roe, E (1995) 'Except-Africa: Postscript to a Special Section on Development Narratives', *World Development* 23, 1065–9

Rondinelli, D A (1983 and 1993) *Development Projects as Policy Experiments*, Routledge, London

Rukuni, M (1994) *Report of the Commission of Inquiry into Appropriate Agricultural Land Tenure Systems*, three volumes, Government of Zimbabwe, Harare

Runte, A (1979) *National Parks: the American Experience*, University of Nebraska Press, Lincoln, NE

SASUSG (1997) *Evaluating Eden Phase One, Southern Africa Synthesis Report*, a review of Community Wildlife Management in Southern Africa by the Southern African Sustainable Use Specialist Group (Fourth Draft), IUCN-ROSA, Harare

Schaffer, B (1984) 'Towards Responsibility: Public Policy in Concept and Practice' in E J Clay and B Schaffer (eds) *Room for Manoueuvre: Exploring Public Policy in Agriculture and Rural Development*, Heinemann, London, 142–90

Schoepf, B G (1984) 'Man and the Biosphere in Zaire', in J Barker (ed) *The Politics of Agriculture in Tropical Africa*, Sage, Beverley Hills, 269–90

Schumacher, E F (1973) *Small is Beautiful: Economics as if People Mattered*, Blond and Briggs, London

Scoones, I and Wilson, K (1989) 'Households, Lineage Groups and Ecological Dynamics: Issues for Livestock Development', in B Cousins (ed) *People, Land and Livestock, Proceedings of a Workshop on the Socio-Economic Dimensions of Livestock Production in Zimbabwe's Communal Lands,* GTZ and Center for Applied Social Sciences, University of Zimbabwe, Harare

Scott, J C (1998) *Seeing Like a State*, Yale University Press, New Haven, CT

Scott, P (1993) *Traditional Medicine as a Tool in the Conservation of LMNP*, report to Uganda National Parks, Kampala

Scott, P (1994a) *Assessment of Natural Resource Use by Communities from Mount Elgon National Park*, IUCN, Kampala

Scott, P (1994b) *Bamboo: Potential for Utilisation by the Communities Surrounding Mount Elgon National Park*, IUCN, Kampala

Scott, P (1996a) *Collaborative Management in Rwenzori Mountains National Park*, IUCN, Kampala

Scott, P (1996b) *Outputs of the Taskforce on Collaborative Management for the Uganda Wildlife Authority*, Ministry of Tourism, Wildlife and Antiquities, Kampala

Serengeti Ecological Monitoring Programme (1987) 'Environmental Monitoring in the Serengeti and Ngorongoro Regions of Tanzania', *Quarterly Report*, June 1987, Serengeti Wildlife Research Centre, Arusha

Serodio, K (ed) (1998) 'The Bushmeat Trade in Mozambique', unpublished report to TRAFFIC TESA Office, IUCN Mozambique, Maputo

Sharpe, B (1998) 'First the Forest...: Conservation, "Community" and "Participation" in South-West Cameroon', *Africa* 68(1), 25–45

Sheail, J (1976) *Nature in Trust: the History of Nature Conservation in Britain*, Blackie, Glasgow

Shore, C (1993) 'Community', in W Outhwaite and T Bottomore (eds) *The Blackwell Dictionary of Twentieth Century Social Thought*, Blackwell, Oxford

Siachoono, S (1995) 'Contingent Valuation as an Additional Tool for Evaluating Wildlife Utilisation Management in Zambia: Mumbwa Game Management Area', *Ambio* 24(4), 246–9

Sithole, B (1997) *The Institutional Framework for Management and Use of Natural Resources in Communal Areas in Zimbabwe: Village Cases of Access to and Use of Dambos from Mutoko and Chiduku*, CASS report, University of Zimbabwe, Harare

Sjoberg, G (1964) 'Community', in J Gould and W L Kolb (eds) *A Dictionary of the Social Sciences*, The Free Press, Glencoe, IL 114–15

Snelson, D and Wilson, A (1994) *Lake Mburo National Park Guidebook*, AWF, Nairobi and UWA, Kampala

Southgate, C (1998) From Cooperation to Conflict: the Decline of the Commons in Kenya's Maasailand, PhD thesis, University of Manchester

Southgate, C and Hulme, D (1996) *Land, Water and Local Governance in a Kenyan Wetland in Dryland: the Kimana Group Ranch and Its Environs,* Rural Resources, Rural Livelihoods Working Paper No 4, IDPM, University of Manchester

Southgate, C and Hulme, D (2000) 'Uncommon Property: the Scramble for Wetland in Southern Kenya', in P Woodhouse, H Bernstein and D Hulme, *African Enclosures? The Social Dynamics of Wetlands in Drylands,* James Currey, Oxford

Steiner, A and Rihoy, E (1995) 'The Commons Without the Tragedy? Strategies for Community Based Natural Resources Management in Southern Africa: a Review of Lessons and Experiences from Natural Resources Management Programmes in Botswana, Namibia, Zambia and Zimbabwe', in E. Rihoy (ed) *The Commons Without the Tragedy? Strategies for Community Based Natural Resources Management in Southern Africa, Proceedings of the Regional Natural Resources Management Programme Annual Conference,* SADC Wildlife Technical Coordination Unit, Lilongwe, Malawi

Stockil, C (1987) 'Ngwachumene Island: the Mahenye Project', *The Hartebeest* (Magazine of the Lowveld Natural History Society) 19, 7–11

Stocking, M and Perkin, S (1992) 'Conservation-with-Development: an Application of the Concept in the Usambara Mountains, Tanzania', *Transactions of the Institute of British Geographers* NS 17, 337–49

Stotz, D F, Fitzpatrick, J W, Parker III, T A and Moskovits, D K (1996) *Neotropical Birds: Ecology and Conservation*, University of Chicago Press, Chicago

Struhsaker, T T (1997) *Ecology of an African Rain Forest*, University Press of Florida, Gainseville, FL

Sullivan, S (1999) 'Folk and Formal, Local and National: Damara Kowledge and Community-Based Conservation in Southern Kunene', Namibia, mimeo at School of Oriental and African Studies, University of London

Sullivan, S (2000) 'Gender, Ethnographic Myths and Community-based Conservation in a Former Namibian "Homeland"', in D Hodgson (ed) *Rethinking Pastoralism in Africa: Gender, Culture and the Myth of the Patriarchal Pastoralist,* James Currey, Oxford

Sutherland, A, Martin, A and Salmon, J (1998) 'Recent Experiences with Participatory Technology Development in Africa: Practitioners' Review', *Natural Resource Perspectives* 25, ODI, London

Swanson, T M and Barbier, E B (eds) (1992) *Economics for the Wilds: Wildlife, Wildlands, Diversity and Development*, Earthscan, London

Tagg, J (1996) 'Communities and Government Jointly Managing Wildlife in Namibia: Information Systems (GIS) as a Monitoring and Communication Tool', unpublished Report, Ministry of Environment and Tourism, Windhoek

TANAPA (1992) *Tanzania National Parks Community Survey: Agenda for Teachers for Orientation*, TANAPA, Arusha

TANAPA (1994a) *Integrating Conservation and Development, a Cabinet Paper on Responsible Benefit Sharing Mechanisms for National Parks*, TANAPA, Arusha

TANAPA (1994b) *Tarangire National Park – CCS Strategic Action Plan*, proceedings of a Workshop held 8–9 September, at Tarangire National Park, TANAPA, Arusha

TANAPA (1994c) *National Policies for National Parks*, TANAPA, Arusha

TANAPA (1995) *SCIP Project Proposal Form*, TANAPA, Arusha

TANAPA (1996) *Suggested Guidelines on the Administration of TANAPA Support for Community Initiated Projects (SCIP) Funds,* submitted by the Community Conservation Coordination Committee, TANAPA, Arusha

TANAPA (1997a) Tanzania National Parks Department of Extension 'Job Description of Community Conservation Wardens', mimeo at TANAPA, Arusha

TANAPA (1997b) *Tanzania National Parks Five Years CCS Report*, Community Conservation Service, TANAPA, Arusha

TANAPA (nd) Tanzania National Parks Management Policy *Extension and Benefit Sharing Policy*, TANAPA, Arusha

TANAPA and AWF (1989) *Extension and Community Relations Work in Tanzania National Parks*, Proceedings of Workshop at Lake Manyara NP, TANAPA, Arusha

Tanzania, Government of (1975) *Villages and Ujamaa Villages (Registration, Designation and Administration) Act, No. 21 of 1975, CAP 588*, Government Printer, Dar-es-Salaam

Tanzania National Parks and Serengeti Ecological Monitoring Programme (1988) *Land Use Conflict in the Tarangire-Simanjiro area, Land Use Report and Action Proposal*, a report to the National Land Use Commission and Regional Development Director, Arusha Region

Tanzania National Parks, Community Conservation Service (1994) *Tarangire National Park CCS Strategic Action Plan*, Proceedings of Workshop held in Tarangire, Arusha, Tanzania National Parks

Tanzania, United Republic of (1998) *The Wildlife Policy of Tanzania*, Ministry of Natural Resources and Tourism, Dar-es-Salaam

Taylor, G and Johannson, L (1996) 'Our Voices, Our Words and Our Pictures: Plans, Truths and Videotapes from Ngorongoro Conservation Area', *Forests, Trees and People* 30, 28–39

Taylor, R D (1999) 'An Analysis of Twelve Wildlife-Producing Districts in the CAMPFIRE Programme', mimeo at WWF, Harare

Taylor, R D (1990) 'Zimbabwe', in C W Allin (ed) *International Handbook of National Parks and Nature Reserves*, Greenwood, CT

Taylor, R D (1994) 'Wildlife Management and Utilisation in a Zimbabwean Communal Land: a Preliminary Evaluation in Nyaminyami District, Kariba', in W van Hoven, H Ebedes and A Conroy (eds) *Wildlife Ranching: a Celebration of Diversity*, Promedia, Pretoria

Taylor, R D (1998) 'Wilderness and the CAMPFIRE Programme: The Value of Wildlands and Wildlife to Local Communities in Zimbabwe', paper presented at the *Wilderness Symposium, Waterberg Plateau Park, Namibia, 24–27 June 1996*, IUCN, Gland, Switzerland and Cambridge, UK

Taylor, R D and Mackie, C (1997) 'Aerial Census Results for Elephant and Buffalo in Selected CAMPFIRE Areas', *CAMPFIRE Association Publication Series* 4, 4–11

Thompson, D M (1997) *Integrating Conservation and Development, Multiple Land-Use: the Experience of the Ngorongoro Conservation Area, Tanzania*, IUCN, Gland, Switzerland and Cambridge, UK

Thornton, A and Currey, D (1991) *To Save an Elephant*, Doubleday, New York

Thresher, P (1992) 'Rural Income from Wildlife: a Practical African Model', paper presented at African Forestry and Wildlife Commission, 10th Session, Kigali, mimeo at AWF, Nairobi

Tinley, K L (1990) *Assessment of Biodiversity Importance in Mozambique*, report to DNFFB/FAO, Maputo

Tonnies, F (1963) *Community and Society*, translated by C P Loomis, Harper, New York

Tordoff, W (1994) 'Decentralisation: Comparative Experiences in Commonwealth Africa', *Journal of Modern African Studies* 32(4), 412–32

Toye, J (1993) *Dilemmas of Development*, 2nd edn, Basil Blackwell, Oxford

TRAFFIC (1999) *Documenting the Trade in Bushmeat in Eastern and Southern Africa*, Report by TRAFFIC – TESA Office, Malawi

Turnbull, C M (1972) *The Mountain People*, Simon and Schuster, New York

Turner, M and Hulme, D (1997) *Governance, Administration and Development: Making the State Work*, Macmillan, London

Turner, S (1996) *Conservancies in Namibia: a Model for Successful Common Property Resource Management?*, Social Sciences Division, Multi-disciplinary Research Centre, University of Namibia, Windhoek

Turton, D (1987) 'The Mursi and National Park Development in the Lower Omo Valley', in D M Anderson and R H Grove (eds) *Conservation in Africa: People, Policies and Practice*, Cambridge University Press, Cambridge, 169–86

Turyaho, M and Infield, M (1996) 'Uganda: From Conflict to Partnership – the Work of the Lake Mburo Community Conservation Project with Pastoralists, Fisherman and Farmers', *Rural Extension Bulletin* 10, Reading University, 42–5

TWCM (1990) *Tanzania Wildlife Conservation Monitoring, Wildlife Census, Tarangire* (TWCM is a joint project between Serengeti Wildlife Research Institute, the Wildlife Division, Tanzania National Parks, Ngorongoro Conservation Area Authority and Frankfurt Zoological Society), TANAPA, Arusha

TWCM (1994) *Tanzania Wildlife Conservation Monitoring, Aerial Wildlife Census of Tarangire National Park – Wet and Dry Seasons*, TANAPA, Arusha

TWCM (1995) *Tanzania Wildlife Conservation Monitoring, Total Count of Buffalo and Elephant in the Tarangire Ecosystem*, TANAPA, Arusha

Uganda, Government of (1992) *The 1991 Population and Housing Census*, Statistics Department, Ministry of Finance and Economic Planning, Entebbe

Uganda, Government of (1995) *Uganda Wildlife Policy*, Wildlife and Antiquities Ministry of Tourism, UWA, Kampala

Uganda, Government of (1996a) *National Environmental Statute*, Government Printers, Entebbe

Uganda, Government of (1996b) *Uganda Wildlife Statute*, Government Printers, Entebbe

Uganda, Government of (1996c) *Statute No 14: Uganda Wildlife Statute*, Statutes Supplement No 8, Government Printers, Kampala

Uganda National Parks (1994) *First Revenue-Sharing Workshop Report*, Uganda National Parks, Kampala

Uganda National Parks (1996) *Mgahinga Gorilla National Park Management Plan 1996–2000*, Uganda National Parks, Kampala

Uganda National Parks Restructuring Committeee (1997) *Recommended UWA Staffing Levels*, Ministry of Tourism, Wildlife and Antiquities, Kampala

Ugandan Wildlife Authority (1997) *Report of the Collaborative Management Taskforce*, UWA, Kampala

UNDP (1994) *Human Development Report 1994*, Oxford University Press, Oxford

United Nations (UN) (1992) *Agenda 21: the United Nations Plan of Action from Rio*, United Nations, New York

University of Bayreuth (1997) *Sustainability of Competing Land Use Systems in the Semi-Arid Regions in Northern Tanzania*, Proceedings of a Workshop held in Arusha, 9 April, mimeo at AWF, Nairobi

Uphoff, N (1986) *Local Institutional Development*, Kumarian Press, West Hartford, CT

Uphoff, N (1992) *Learning from Gal Oya: Possibilities for Participatory Development and Post-Newtonian Social Science*, Cornell University Press, New York

USAID (1995) 'Natural Resource Management Project Namibian Component: 690–0251.73 *Living in a Finite Environment*', Project Paper Supplement (Amended), United States Agency for International Development (USAID), Windhoek

UWA (1997) *Community Involvement in Natural Resource Management in Nepal,* Study Tour Report to Nepal 26/7/97 to 6/8/97, UWA, IUCN, AWF, CARE, Kampala

Van Schaik, C P and Kramer, R A (1997) 'Towards a New Protection Paradigm', in R Kramer, C van Schaik and J Johnson (eds) *Last Stand: Protected Areas and the Defense of Tropical Biodiversity*, Oxford University Press, Oxford, 212–30

Veldman, M (1993) *Fantasy, the Bomb and the Greening of Britain: Romantic Protest 1945–1980*, Cambridge University Press, Cambridge

Venter, A K and Breen, C M (1996) 'Partnership Forum Framework: a Conceptual Framework for the Development of Integrated Conservation and Development Programmes', paper presented to Pan African Symposium on Sustainable Use of Natural Resources and Community Participation, June, mimeo at CASS Library, University of Zimbabwe, Harare

Vines, A (1996) *Renamo: From Terrorism to Democracy in Mozambique*, James Currey, London

Vorhies, F (1996) *Making Community Conservation Economically Attractive*, Community Conservation Discussion Paper No 9, AWF, Nairobi

Wainwright, C and Wehrmeyer, W (1998) 'Success in Integrating Conservation and Development?: a Study from Zambia', *World Development* 26, 933–44

Wass, P (ed) (1995) *Kenya's Indigenous Forests – Status, Management and Conservation*, IUCN Forest Conservation Programme, Gland, Switzerland and Cambridge, UK

WCMC (1996) *Assessing Biodiversity Status and Sustainability*, World Conservation Monitoring Centre, Cambridge

Wells, M (1994) 'A Profile and Interim Assessment of the Annapurna Conservation Area Project, Nepal', in D Western and R M Wright (eds) *Natural Connections in Community Based Conservation*, Island Press, Washington DC, 261–81

Wells, M P (1995) 'Biodiversity Conservation and Local Development Aspirations: New Priorities for the 1990s' in C A Perrings et al. (eds) *Biodiversity Conservation*, Kluwer Academic Publishers, The Hague, Netherlands, 319–33

Wells, M (1996a) 'The Economic and Social Role of Protected Areas in the New South Africa', paper presented at Economic Policies and the Environment in South Africa Workshop, Johannesburg, mimeo at CASS Library, University of Zimbabwe, Harare

Wells, M (1996b) 'The Role of Economics in Critical African Wildlife Policy Debates', *African Wildlife Policy Consultation*, Overseas Development Administration, London

Wells, M, Brandon, K and Hannah, L (1992) *People and Parks: Linking Protected Areas with Local Communities*, World Bank, Washington DC

Wells, M, Guggenheim, S, Khan, A, Wardojo, W and Jepson, P (1999) *Investing in Biodiversity: a Review of Indonesia's Integrated Conservation and Development Projects*, World Bank, Washington DC

Werikhe, S E (1991) An Ecological Survey of the Gorilla Game Reserve (GGR), South-West Uganda, MSc thesis, Makerere University

Werikhe, S E (not dated) *Socio-demographic Survey of the Encroached Area of the Proposed Mgahinga Gorilla National Park in South-West Uganda*, CARE-International, Uganda with the Impenetrable Forest Conservation Project of World Wildlife Fund, USA

West, P C and Brechin, S R (1991) *Resident Peoples and National Parks: Social Dilemmas and Strategies in International Conservation*, University of Tucson, Tucson, AZ

Western, D (1982) 'Amboseli National Park: Enlisting Landowners to Conserve Migratory Wildlife', *Ambio* 11(5), 302–8

Western, D (1989) 'Why Manage Nature?', in D Western and M C Pearl (eds) *Conservation for the Twenty-First Century*, Oxford University Press, New York

Western, D and Thresher, P (1973) *Development Plans for Amboseli*, International Bank for Reconstruction and Development, Washington DC

Western, D and Wright, R M (eds) (1994a) *Natural Connections: Perspectives on Community-based Conservation*, Island Press, Washington DC

Western, D and Wright, R M (1994b) 'The Background to Community-Based Conservation', in D Western and R M Wright (eds) *Natural Connections: Perspectives on Community-based Conservation*, Washington, Island Press, 1–14

Wild, R G and Mutebi, J (1996) *Conservation Through Community Use of Plant Resources: Establishing Collaborative Management at Bwindi Impenetrable and Mgahinga Gorilla National Parks, Uganda*, People and Plants Working Paper No 5, UNESCO, Paris

Wild, R G and Mutebi, J (1997) 'Bwindi Impenetrable Forest Uganda: Conservation Through Collaborative Management', *Nature and Resources* 33(3/4), 33–51

Wildlife Division, Tanzania (1994) *Community Based Conservation in Tanzania*, Proceedings of a Workshop, Ministry of Natural Resources, Dar es Salaam

Wildlife Sector Review Task Force (1995) *A Review of the Wildlife Sector in Tanzania, Volume 1: Assessment of the Current Situation*, Ministry of Tourism, Natural Resources and Environment, Dar-es-Salaam

Willis, J (1996) 'The Northern Kayas of the Mijikenda: a Gazetteer, and an Historical Reassessment', *Azania* 31, 75–98

Willock, C (1964) *The Enormous Zoo: a Profile of the Uganda National Parks*, Longman, London

Wilson, E O (1989) 'Threats to Biodiversity', *Scientific American* 261, 108–16

Wilson, K (1997) 'Of Diffusion and Context: the Bubbling Up of Community Based Conservation in Mozambique', unpublished paper to the Representing Communities Conference, Helen Lodge, GA

Wily, L (1995) *Collaborative Forest Management, Villagers and Government: the Case of Mgori Forest, Tanzania*, Forest, Trees and People Working Paper, 44, FAO, Foresty Policy and Planning Division, Rome

Wily, L (1997) *New Land and the Poor: Implications for the Draft Uganda Land Bill with Comparative reference to the Tanzania Bill for the Land Act*, Land Tenure Seminar, Economic Policy Research Centre in Collaboration with the Ministry of Lands, Housing and Planning, Kampala

Wily, L and Othmar, H (1995) 'Good News from Tanzania: Village Forest Reserves in the Making – the Story of Duru-Haitemba', *Forest Trees and People Newsletter* 29, 28–37

Wirth, L (1938) 'Urbanism as a Way of Life', *American Journal of Sociology* 44, 1–24

Wood, J B (1991) 'CAMPFIRE: the Legal Issues', unpublished report for the Department of National Parks and Wildlife Management, Harare

Woodhouse, P, Bernstein, H and Hulme, D (2000) *African Enclosures? The Social Dynamics of Wetlands in Drylands,* James Currey, Oxford

World Bank (1991) *Zimbabwe Agriculture Sector Memorandum: Volume II: Main Report*, Southern Africa Department, Agriculture Operations Division, World Bank, Washington DC

World Bank (1992) *World Development Report 1992*, Oxford University Press, Oxford and New York

World Commission on the Environment and Development (WCED) (1987) *Our Common Future*, Oxford University Press, Oxford

World Conservation Monitoring Centre (1992) *Global Biodiversity: Status of the Earth's Living Resources*, Chapman and Hall, London

World Conservation Union, East Africa Regional Office (1996) *Forest Cover and Forest Reserves in Kenya: Policy and Practise*, IUCN East Africa Regional Office, Issues in Conservation, 24, Nairobi

Worster, D (1985) *Rivers of Empire: Water, Aridity and the Growth of the American West*, Oxford University Press, New York

Wright, A (1972) *Valley of the Ironwoods*, Cape and Transvaal Printers, Cape Town

Wright, R M (1993) 'Conservation and Development: Donor's Dilemma', in Lewis and Carter, 183–92

Wright, S and Nelson, S (1995) *Power and Participatory Development: Theory and Practice*, IT Books, London

WWF (1995) *Namibian Community-Based Natural Resource Management Programme*, World Wide Fund for Nature, Gland, Switzerland

WWF (1997) *Measuring the Conservation Impact of ICDPs, Final Report*, Workshop IV of the ICDP Review, World Wide Fund for Nature, Gland, Switzerland

Yaron, G, Healy, T and Tapscott, C (1996) 'The Economics of Living with Wildlife in Namibia', in J Bojö (ed) *The Economics of Wildlife: Case Studies from Ghana, Kenya, Namibia and Zimbabwe*, World Bank, Washington DC

Zimbabwe, Government of (1975) *Parks and Wildlife Act (Amended 1982)*, Government of Zimbabwe, Government Printer, Harare

Zimbabwe, Government of (1989) 'Policy for Wild Life', Department of National Parks and Wild Life Management, Harare

Zimbabwe, Government of (1991) *Statutory Instruments SI 12/1991 and SI 61/1991*, Government Printers, Harare

Zimbabwe, Government of (1998) 'Revised Guidelines for CAMPFIRE', SI 38/98, Government of Zimbabwe, Government Printers, Harare

Zimbabwe Trust (1990–1998) *Files of the Zimbabwe Trust*, South East Lowveld Regional Office, Chipinge

Index

access 4, 27, 29, 31, 33, 56, 57, 61, 66,
    73n13, 107, 113, 118, 128, 132, 252, 253,
    267, 268, 281, 282
accountability 53, 152, 168, 169, 277, 284
accumulation 7, 50, 112, 252, 254, 255
adjustment, structural 60, 61, 75
administration 11, 40, 49, 75–9 *passim*, 191,
    197, 199, 200
African Special Project 11–12
agriculture 1, 7, 12, 25, 34, 41, 43, 60, 94,
    106, 109, 127, 133–4, 149, 153, 203,
    216, 218–22 *passim*, 228, 235, 241, 245,
    248–55 *passim*, 263, 293, 295;
    commercial 39, 41–2, 44, 46, 52, 56, 60,
    230
aid 5, 6, 17–20 *passim*, 25, 48, 54, 61, 62,
    70–1, 75, 79–82 *passim*, 95, 126, 145,
    228, 283–5, 388–92 *passim*
Amajambere Iwacu Campground 138, 145
Amboseli NP 11, 13, 61, 62, 67, 212, 214,
    222, 259
Amin, Idi 109
anthropocentrism 14–15
Angola 19, 79, 162
Arusha NP 61, 90, 94, 101, 103
authority 30, 31, 34, 36, 38, 47, 56, 190,
    236; appropriate 42, 47–9 *passim*, 58n19,
    184, 193, 228–31 *passim*, 236, 240, 242,
    244, 246, 252, 268, 273, 278
AWF 2, 13, 61, 65, 69, 89, 90, 92, 93, 112,
    151–3 *passim*, 159, 260, 284

bamboo 134, 136–8 *passim*, 142, 143, 145
Bazaruto Archipelago project 81, 86
bed–night levies 165, 172, 175
benefits 6, 20, 32–4, 50–5 *passim*, 66, 72, 85,
    90, 102–3, 113–22, 127, 140–8, 152–9
    passim, 164, 167, 175, 183, 187–8,
    208–16, 223–7 *passim*, 233–4, 239, 241,
    244–57 *passim*, 281–2, 288–9, 292;
    sharing 6, 33, 67, 91, 92, 102, 105, 151,

156–9 *passim*, 208, 212–16, 220, 224–6
    passim, 246, 257, 266, 269, 289
biocentrism, 14, 15, 29
biodiversity 1, 2, 4, 7, 16, 25, 29, 60, 61, 72,
    78, 127, 145, 197, 199, 200, 256–61
    passim, 266, 281, 286, 293; Convention
    on 131
biology 17–18, 25, 31, 44, 258–61 *passim*,
    264, 266
Blanchard Enterprises 84, 87
Botswana 166, 211, 222; Chobe project 225
bribes 68, 80, 120, 284
buffalo 49, 121, 124, 139, 154, 155, 159,
    181, 270, 271, 275
buffer zones 18, 213, 257
Brundtland Report 15, 16
bureaucracies 2, 17, 23, 25, 31, 60, 88–105
    passim, 127, 183, 191, 281–3, 290–2
    passim, 296
Burundi 132
Bwindi Forest Reserve 66, 68, 69;
    Impenetrable NP 73n13, 139, 141, 144,
    147n9, 283; Trust 139, 144

Cameroon 282, 289
CAMPFIRE programme 6–7, 18, 23, 43,
    45–53 *passim*, 55, 58n19, 81, 88, 166,
    177, 178, 181–7 *passim*, 190, 214,
    227–55, 268–72, 283, 285, 287, 289, 291,
    292, 294, 295; Agency 45; Association 48,
    51, 275, 277; Guidelines 232, 236, 242,
    268, 271, 272, 283
capacity building 84, 86, 88, 165, 173
Caprivi 164, 218
CARE 13, 65, 68, 138–45 *passim*, 285
cattle 49–50, 120, 124, 155, 159, 162, 228,
    235, 254, 264; 'corridor' 127
censuses 270–1, 273–5 *passim*, 278
Chande, Baldeu 83
Chauke, Phineas 183–4
Chimanimani Mountains 2, 6, 87, 196–207